THE SELJUQS

THE SELJUQS

POLITICS, SOCIETY AND CULTURE

✦ ✦ ✦

EDITED BY
CHRISTIAN LANGE AND SONGÜL MECIT

EDINBURGH
University Press

First published in 2011 by
Edinburgh University Press Ltd
22 George Square, Edinburgh EH8 9LF
www.euppublishing.com

This paperback edition 2012

Typeset in JaghbUni by
Servis Filmsetting Ltd, Stockport Cheshire

A CIP record for this book is available from the British Library

ISBN 978 0 7486 3994 6 (hardback)
ISBN 978 0 7486 6857 1 (paperback)

CONTENTS

List of figures vii
Acknowledgements ix
List of abbreviations x

INTRODUCTION 1

PART I. POLITICS

1. THE ORIGINS OF THE SELJUQS 13
C. Edmund Bosworth, University of Manchester

2. ASPECTS OF THE COURT OF THE GREAT SELJUQS 22
Carole Hillenbrand, University of Edinburgh

3. 'SOVEREIGN AND PIOUS': THE RELIGIOUS LIFE OF THE GREAT SELJUQ SULTANS 39
D. G. Tor, University of Notre Dame

4. KINGSHIP AND IDEOLOGY UNDER THE RUM SELJUQS 63
Songül Mecit, University of Edinburgh

5. SELJUQ LEGITIMACY IN ISLAMIC HISTORY 79
A. C. S. Peacock, British Institute at Ankara

PART II. SOCIETY

6. ARSLĀN ARGHŪN – NOMADIC REVIVAL? 99
Jürgen Paul, University of Halle

7. CONTROLLING AND DEVELOPING BAGHDAD: CALIPHS, SULTANS AND THE BALANCE OF POWER IN THE ABBASID CAPITAL (MID-5TH/11TH TO LATE 6TH/12TH CENTURIES) 117
Vanessa Van Renterghem, Institut National des Langues et Civilisations Orientales, Paris

8. THE SELJUQS AND THE PUBLIC SPHERE IN THE PERIOD OF SUNNI REVIVALISM: THE VIEW FROM BAGHDAD 139
Daphna Ephrat, The Open University of Israel

9. CHANGES IN THE OFFICE OF *ḤISBA* UNDER THE SELJUQS 157
Christian Lange, Utrecht University

10. AN EMBLEMATIC FAMILY OF SELJUQ IRAN: THE KHUJANDĪS OF ISFAHAN 182
David Durand-Guédy, University of Halle

PART III. CULTURE

11. SHIʿI JURISPRUDENCE DURING THE SELJUQ PERIOD: REBELLION AND PUBLIC ORDER IN AN ILLEGITIMATE STATE 205
Robert Gleave, University of Exeter

12. IN DEFENCE OF SUNNISM: AL-GHAZĀLĪ AND THE SELJUQS 228
Massimo Campanini, L'università degli studi di Napoli 'L'Orientale'

13. ARABIC AND PERSIAN INTERTEXTUALITY IN THE SELJUQ PERIOD: ḤAMĪDĪ'S *MAQĀMĀT* AS A CASE STUDY 240
Vahid Behmardi, Lebanese American University

14. CITY BUILDING IN SELJUQ RUM 256
Scott Redford, Georgetown University

15. THE SELJUQ MONUMENTS OF TURKMENISTAN 277
Robert Hillenbrand, University of Edinburgh

Index 309

FIGURES

CHAPTER 2

2.1 FRONTISPIECE OF THE KITĀB AL-DIRYĀQ OF PSEUDO-GALEN, C. 648/1250 26
2.2 AL-JAZARĪ *NAWBA* SCENE, KITĀB FĪ MAᶜRIFAT AL-ḤIYAL AL-HANDASIYYA, IRAQ, 602/1206 29
2.3 ILLUSTRATION FROM VARQA VA-GULSHĀH BY ᶜAYYŪQĪ, C. 648/1250 32

CHAPTER 14

PHOTOGRAPHS BY TUFAN KARASU
14.1 MAP OF ANATOLIA IN THE EARLY 7TH/13TH CENTURY 258
14.2 SINOP CITADEL, 612/1215, PERSIAN POETIC INSCRIPTION 262
14.3 SINOP CITADEL, 612/1215, INSCRIPTION OF EMIRS AND NOTABLES OF AMASYA 264
14.4 SINOP CITADEL, 612/1215, INSCRIPTION OF SULTAN ᶜIZZ AL-DĪN KAY KĀWŪS 265
14.5 ANTALYA CITADEL, ELEVATION OF WALLS AND TOWERS 267
14.6 CARVED PROFILE BUST ABOVE ENTRANCE TO THE KIZIL KULE, ALANYA 272

CHAPTER 15

IMAGES ALL DRAWN FROM G. HERRMANN, H. COFFEY, S. LAIDLAW AND K. KURBANSAKHATOV, *THE MONUMENTS OF MERV. A SCANNED ARCHIVE OF PHOTOGRAPHS AND PLANS* (LONDON, 2002)

15.1 MAUSOLEUM OF MUḤAMMAD B. ZAYD, MERV, FAÇADE 279
15.2 KIZ BIBI MAUSOLEUM, MERV, SQUINCH ZONE 282
15.3 GREATER KIZ QALᶜA, MERV, EXTERIOR FROM SOUTH-EAST 283
15.4 LESSER KIZ QALᶜA, MERV, MULTIPLE RECESSED ARCHES 284
15.5 MAUSOLEUM OF IMAM BĀḤIR, SQUINCH ZONE 285
15.6 LESSER KIZ QALᶜA, MERV, UPPER STOREY 286
15.7 MAUSOLEUM OF KHUDĀY NAẒAR AWLIYĀᵓ, EXTERIOR 287
15.8 MOSQUE OF TALKHATĀN BĀBĀ, INTERIOR 289
15.9 MAUSOLEUM OF ᶜABDALLĀH B. BURAYDA, VAKĪL BĀZĀR, STUCCOWORK 291
15.10 MAUSOLEUM OF MUḤAMMAD B. ZAYD, MERV, INSCRIPTION 292
15.11 MAUSOLEUM OF ᶜABDALLĀH B. BURAYDA, VAKĪL BĀZĀR, INSCRIPTION 292
15.12 MAUSOLEUM OF SULTAN SANJAR, MERV, GALLERY, INSCRIPTION 293
15.13 MOSQUE OF TALKHATĀN BĀBĀ, ROW OF BLIND ARCHES 295
15.14 PALACE OF SHĀHRIYĀR ARG, MERV, PATTERNED BRICKWORK 296
15.15 MOSQUE OF TALKHATĀN BĀBĀ, MAIN FAÇADE 297
15.16 MAUSOLEUM OF SULTAN SANJAR, MERV, AERIAL VIEW 297
15.17 MAUSOLEUM OF SULTAN SANJAR, MERV, EXTERIOR 299
15.18 MAUSOLEUM OF SULTAN SANJAR, MERV, WEST FAÇADE 300
15.19 MAUSOLEUM OF SULTAN SANJAR, MERV, INTERIOR, ZONE OF TRANSITION 301
15.20 MAUSOLEUM OF SULTAN SANJAR, MERV, INTERIOR, RIBS OF DOME 302

ACKNOWLEDGEMENTS

It is a pleasure to acknowledge the institutions and individuals who helped this volume to see the light of day. We are grateful to those who facilitated the conference from which the great majority of the contributions in this volume are derived ('The Seljuqs: Islam revitalized?', Edinburgh, 14–15 September 2008). We would like to thank in particular the Iran Heritage Foundation, the Royal Academy of Edinburgh, and the Binks Trust, who all supported this event generously. Edinburgh University's Islamic and Middle Eastern Studies (IMES), under the auspices of Carole Hillenbrand, as well as the School of Divinity/ New College graciously agreed to host the conference in their splendid buildings. At IMES, Rhona Cullen and Sophie Lowry provided the usual reliable administrative support.

The comments and suggestions of the two anonymous reviewers of the book proposal were gratefully received and incorporated into the volume. Nicola Ramsey, James Dale and Eddie Clark at Edinburgh University Press accompanied the volume since its conception, offering a wealth of good advice and support. Robert Hillenbrand kindly helped us locate a suitable image for the front cover of the book. Finally, we would like to thank our copy-editor, Suzanne Dalgleish, and our indexer, Howard Cooke, for their expert work.

The editors
Utrecht/Edinburgh, March 2011

ABBREVIATIONS

AI	*Annales Islamologiques*
BSOAS	*Bulletin of the School of Oriental and African Studies*
CHI5	*The Cambridge History of Iran,* vol. 5, *The Saljuq and Mongol Periods*, ed. J. A. Boyle (Cambridge, 1968)
EI2	*The Encyclopaedia of Islam: New Edition*, ed. H. A. R. Gibb *et al.* (Leiden, 1954–2004)
EIr	*Encyclopaedia Iranica*, ed. E. Yarshater (London/Boston, 1982–)
IJMES	*International Journal of Middle East Studies*
JRAS	*Journal of the Royal Asiatic Society*
RSO	*Rivista degli Studi Orientali*
SI	*Studia Islamica*
WZKM	*Wiener Zeitschrift für die Kunde des Morgenlandes*
ZDMG	*Zeitschrift der Deutschen Morgenländischen Gesellschaft*

INTRODUCTION

The Seljuqs, who ruled over the lands of Persia and large swaths of the Islamic world in the 5th–7th/11th–13th centuries, have been the object of continued interest by historians of Islam.[1] However, despite the many important developments and innovations traceable to the Seljuq period, such as the institutionalisation of sultanic authority vis-à-vis the caliph, the introduction of the atabegate, the restructuring of the system of fiefs, the establishment of institutions of higher learning and the concomitant consolidation of the Sunni legal schools, the proliferation of translocal Sufi networks organised in lodges, and significant advances in art and architecture due to Seljuq patronage, the Seljuqs remain one of the understudied Muslim dynasties. Nor have the long-term ramifications of the Seljuq coming to power, their formative influence on later socio-political orders and their reception history among them received adequate scholarly attention. Not only did a branch of the Seljuq family take over formerly Byzantine and Armenian territories in Anatolia, founding the Rum Seljuq sultanate (c. 483–707/1081–1307) within roughly the same geographical boundaries as the modern Republic of Turkey. Indeed, the Seljuqs can be credited with entertaining structures of political, social and cultural organisation that long outlasted them. The Seljuqs thus acted as switchmen who, while not in each instance setting new developments in motion, irreversibly changed the course of Islamic history. This volume aims to contribute to the growing interest in this pivotal dynasty.

The words of Claude Cahen, written in 1962, that 'the Seljuqs, in spite of several useful partial studies, still await the comprehensive historian whom their role in Muslim history would seem to deserve',[2] still ring true today, even if significant progress has been made. Already in Cahen's days, important studies especially of the Great Seljuqs of Persia and Iraq had appeared, not least from

Cahen's own pen.[3] Ann K. S. Lambton's numerous articles and books dealing with the administrative organisation of the Seljuq empire went a long way in answering Cahen's call,[4] and her chapter in the fifth volume of the *Cambridge History of Iran* (1968), together with C. Edmund Bosworth's detailed account in the same volume of the major political and dynastic events of the Seljuq period, remain perhaps the closest one gets to a 'comprehensive' history of the Seljuqs.[5] A few years after this groundbreaking collaborative effort, Carla Klausner published her study of the Seljuq vizierate.[6] Though Klausner's approach was limited to one particular institution of the Seljuq administration, that of the vizierate, her work showcased the level of detail and nuance to which research on the Seljuqs and the networks that buttressed their power could henceforth aspire.

In the same year as Klausner's work appeared, George Makdisi first formulated his well-known reassessment of the so-called Sunni revival of the 5th/11th century. Makdisi suggested that the return to dominance of Sunnism began some fifty years before the arrival of the Seljuqs and was due more to the rise of a class of Sunni 'traditionalists' (especially in Baghdad) than to any state-sponsored patronage of Sunnism by the likes of the vizier Niẓām al-Mulk and the early Seljuq sultans.[7] This revisionist view of the Seljuqs provoked several critical rejoinders and reformulations,[8] even though on the whole his challenge, at least initially, did not find the echo that one could have expected or wished for. Some contributions in this volume engage with Makdisi's theory directly, while it also serves as background to a number of others. The focus on the Seljuqs' relationship with Sunnism, however, should not detract, as it arguably has done at times, from other aspects of their rule. Consequently, this volume seeks to broaden the discussion in a variety of ways.

Since the turn of the century, the Seljuqs have had their own kind of revival, and Seljuq studies have picked up pace. Daphna Ephrat's study of the networks of *ᶜulamāᵓ* in 5th/11th-century Baghdad[9] and Omid Safi's dismantling of the 'Great Seljuq Myth' (according to which they were the champions of Sunnism)[10] have thrown new light particularly on the Seljuqs' relationship with the religious sphere, their 'politics of knowledge', to use Safi's phrase; here, one should also draw attention to the veritable flurry of publications devoted to that most celebrated of all Seljuq-time intellectuals, al-Ghazālī (d. 505/1111).[11] As for studies that emphasise dynastic aspects and questions of political history and organisation, a volume edited by C. E. Bosworth has brought together a series of articles on the Central Asian background of the Seljuqs,[12] A. C. S. Peacock has revisited the beginnings of Seljuq rule,[13] Christian Lange has analysed the economy of state violence under the Great Seljuqs,[14] and David Durand-Guédy has produced a study of the eastern half of the Seljuq empire, focusing on the urban elites of Isfahan.[15] As if to cap this decade of renewed activity, in addition to Osman Aziz Basan's recent survey work[16] two 'comprehensive' histories of the Seljuqs, by D. G. Tor and A. C. S. Peacock, are in preparation for publication with the University Presses at Cambridge and Edinburgh.[17] In comparison with the Great Seljuqs of Persia and Iraq, the Rum Seljuqs have received less attention,[18] but here also, the tide may be turning, as is suggested by the articles collected by Gary Leiser in a volume published in 2005,[19] Carole Hillenbrand's in-depth study of the battle of Manzikert and its reception history (2007),[20] and a number of other recent contributions.[21]

In other words, this volume goes to press at an auspicious moment in the history of Seljuq studies. The papers collected here build on, and indeed presuppose, the earlier work of historians like Barthold, Cahen, Lambton, Bosworth, Hodgson,[22] Agadzhanov[23] and Makdisi, but they do so in the context of a renewed critical interest in the Seljuq period, an interest which has already produced some thought-provoking studies in the recent past, as indicated in the preceding paragraph. Almost all of the chapters in this volume are based on papers given at a symposium organised by the editors and titled 'The Seljuqs: Islam revitalized?' (Edinburgh, 14–15 September 2008). Several factors motivated this symposium. The organisers felt that, while Seljuq history had tended to be examined through the lens of traditional scholarly concerns, such as political and military history, a great number of other questions deserved to be pursued: issues of ideology and mentality, the competing definitions of authority, the visual and ritual expressions of political power, the development of legal theory and practice vis-à-vis the state, the organisation of space, and the relationship between nomads and the settled peoples, to name just a few.

Seljuq scholars face a number of specific challenges. Not only did a number of intellectual traditions peak in the Seljuq period, but a massive reorganisation occurred on the political, social and economic levels. This makes synthetic judgements about Seljuq history and social organisation extremely difficult. To compound this challenge, scholars of the Seljuq period must usually deal with no less than three major Oriental languages (Arabic, Persian, Turkish), as well as a spate of other primary and secondary languages. This is a problem which is reflected, inter alia, in the fact that a uniform system of transliteration of terms and names relating to the Seljuqs is hitherto unavailable in any of the major Western research languages – hence no attempt at uniformity of transliteration has been undertaken in this volume, albeit consistency within each article is preserved.[24] Research about the Seljuq period has, broadly speaking, tended to be rather specialised. Intellectual, political, social and material historians of the Seljuq period have all too often worked intensively in their own fields to the detriment of inter-disciplinarity. Contributors in this volume reflect on a wide range of challenges presented by Seljuq history, as outlined above. The examples they discuss are taken from all of Seljuq history, ranging from the 4th to the 7th/10th to the 13th century and beyond, that is, from the early history of the Seljuq family and the Great Seljuq dynasty ruling over Persia, Iraq and Syria to the main sub-branch, the Rum Seljuqs ruling over Byzantine Anatolia (Arabic Rum), and on to the 'survival' of the Seljuqs in the memory of later dynasties and historians. The various contributions in this volume also cover a representative geographical spectrum, from Central Asia and Persia to Iraq, Syria and Anatolia.

In sum, this volume seeks to map out a broad panoply of topics. Inevitably, such a kaleidoscope of approaches can never be complete. For instance, although the urban economy of the Seljuq domain is touched upon in a number of chapters, other aspects of economic history (such as the system of *iqṭā*^{c}, the network of trade routes and caravanserais, or the legal developments in the economic sphere) would have deserved more extensive discussion. The history of Seljuq art could have likewise been given more room, as could have questions about the religious and sectarian developments in the Seljuq period, or about the relations between the Rum Seljuqs and the Great Seljuq empire, to mention only some of the possible directions which future work will hopefully address.

Part one of this volume is devoted to questions of the Central Asian origins of the Seljuqs, their transformation from one of the leading families in a tribal confederation of nomads into a Muslim dynasty, and their concepts of political legitimisation. C. Edmund Bosworth's 'The origins of the Seljuqs' examines the information given by Byzantine chronicles, Chinese royal annals, the Old Türk and Uyghur inscriptions, and especially, by medieval geographers and Arab travellers about the Turkish tribe of Oghuz, from whose midst the Seljuqs arose. Carole Hillenbrand's 'Aspects of the court of the Great Seljuqs' offers a look through the magnifying glass at three characteristic elements of the Great Seljuq court: the *nawba* (drum beating) ceremony, the sultan's habitus of surrounding himself with learned *littérateur*s doubling as boon companions, and the royal hunt. All three of these phenomena served to connect the Seljuqs to their illustrious predecessor dynasties of Central Asian, Persian and Near Eastern stock, and thus to symbolise their power; echoes of all three can be found in the court protocol of later dynasties as well, as some of the other contributions in the volume demonstrate. In '"Sovereign and pious": the religious life of the Great Seljuq sultans', D. G. Tor takes the question of Seljuq self-understanding and self-representation into the religious sphere, by tracing the spiritual biographies of a number of the Great Seljuq sultans. This leads to a re-examination of Makdisi's view of the Sunni revival and questions the perception that piety and commitment to Sunnism was a mere public relations ploy for them. Songül Mecit's 'Kingship and ideology under the Rum Seljuqs' is an analysis of Rum Seljuq inscriptions that sheds light on the development of kingship ideology formulated by the Rum Seljuq sultans to legitimise their rule. Mecit traces the gradual development away from, and elaborating upon, the 'Great Seljuq model', in the official formulation of political legitimacy from the time of Kılıç Arslan II (r. 551–88/1156–92) to that of his grandson Kay Qubādh I (r. 616–34/1220–37). This theme of the spread of Seljuq models of government and political legitimisation is picked up in A. C. S. Peacock's contribution, which concludes the first part of the volume. In his 'Seljuq legitimacy in Islamic history', Peacock investigates instances in which a Seljuq genealogy, whether real or faked, served to legitimise the power of later Islamic elites, from the Atabegs to the Ottomans and including a spate of other minor dynasties and political movements. While highlighting 'the astonishing longevity of the political potency of the Seljuq name', Peacock also warns against drawing generalising conclusions from this heritage – such as, for example, that the Seljuqs were an in all respects uniquely formative dynasty – too quickly.

Contributors to the second part of this volume discuss aspects of the social and economic history of the Seljuqs: the various relationships between the Seljuq rulers, their slave soldiers (*mamlūks*) and nomadic Turkmen followers, the urban *ᶜulamāᵓ*, the merchant and trading classes, and the urban populace at large. Jürgen Paul's 'Arslān Arghūn – nomadic revival?' is a case study dedicated to one of the brothers of Sultan Malikshāh (d. 485/1092), Arslān Arghūn, who in the four years after Malikshāh's death sought to establish regional power in Khurasan, based, as it appears, on the support of Turkmen nomads of the Balkh region. Paul pinpoints Arslān Arghūn's (deliberate?) strategy of demolishing the walls of important Khurasanian cities in order to determine whether his ultimately unsuccessful bid for power can be regarded as an attempt at re-nomadisation, foreshadowing the events that would eventually lead to the demise of Seljuq power some sixty years later. Vanessa Van Renterghem's 'Controlling and developing Baghdad: caliphs, sultans, and the balance of power in the Abbasid capital' is a discussion of the relationship between the Great Seljuq sultans on the one hand and, on the other hand, the Abbasid capital Baghdad and its religious elites. Van Renterghem lays open the profound social changes that Baghdad underwent under the Seljuqs; she also emphasises the complex heritage created by the amalgamation of Turkish and Perso-Islamic traditions under the Seljuqs, which brought Baghdad and the western parts of their empire into ever closer exchange with the Iranian east. Like Van Renterghem's (and Tor's) study, Daphna Ephrat's 'The Seljuqs and the public sphere in the period of Sunni revivalism' revisits the question of the so-called Sunni revival under the Seljuqs. The focus of Ephrat's analysis is the relationship between the official and public spheres; this leads her to propose that the mainstream Sunni camp emerged out of internal dynamics independently of the official sphere and was little affected by Seljuq policies. Sharing with Ephrat an interest in the history of space under the Seljuqs, Christian Lange, in 'Changes in the office of *ḥisba* under the Seljuqs', investigates changes in conceptions of the public and the private spheres in the Seljuq period, as viewed through *ḥisba*, the office of the market inspector (*muḥtasib*). Basing his analysis on *ḥisba* manuals as well as chancery documents of investiture for the *muḥtasib* from the Buyid, Seljuq and Ayyubid periods, Lange argues that under the Seljuqs the office of *muḥtasib* became increasingly involved in the administration of punishment, as the repressive state apparatus in general became more interventionist. In conclusion to this second part of the volume, David Durand-Guédy, in 'An emblematic family of Seljuq Iran: the Khujandīs of Isfahan', shifts the focus back to the eastern part of the Seljuq empire. He proposes to see the fortunes of the Khujandīs, a powerful family brought from Khurasan to Isfahan by the early Seljuqs, as emblematic of the broader social and urban developments in the 5th/11th and 6th/12th centuries.

The third part of this volume tackles developments in religious thought, jurisprudence, belles-lettres and architecture in the Seljuq period. In his contribution, Robert Gleave examines 'Shiᶜi jurisprudence during the Seljuq period: rebellion and public order in an illegitimate state' by surveying works of Shiᶜi jurisprudence written under Seljuq rule. Gleave concludes, through the study of selected legal doctrines, that the productivity of Shiᶜi jurists, though reduced, was not at all extinguished under the Sunni Seljuqs, but rather showed considerable originality. Massimo Campanini's 'In defence of Sunnism: al-Ghazālī and the Seljuqs' is a succinct discussion of al-Ghazālī's political thought in the context of the Seljuq sultanate and the late-Abbasid caliphate. Campanini suggests that al-Ghazālī, while not an 'official thinker' of the Seljuqs, regarded their rule as a necessary means to defend Sunni Islam. Vahid Behmardi's 'Arabic and Persian intertextuality in the Seljuq period: Ḥamīdī's *Maqāmāt* as a case study' takes a look at the complex relations between Arabic and Persian belles-lettres under the Seljuqs, particularly in the eastern part of the empire. Behmardi analyses the process of imitation and innovation that links the famous *maqāmāt* of al-Hamadhānī and al-Ḥarīri to Ḥamīdī's less well-known Persian contribution to the *maqāmāt* genre. Scott Redford discusses 'City building in Seljuq Rum' by studying epigraphic and architectural evidence from the years 612–23/1215–26. He traces the movement toward centralisation of government in this period of prosperity, which followed the Fourth Crusade of 1202–4 and saw the consolidation of the Rum Seljuq state apparatus. His observations about the hierarchisation of the military and non-military elite of the Rum Seljuq state point to intriguing continuities and differences from the Great Seljuq model. Finally, Robert Hillenbrand directs our gaze to the Seljuq architectural heritage in Turkmenistan. He poses the question whether this most north-western of all Seljuq domains, especially in the period of its flourishing as the power base of Sultan Sanjar (r. 490–552/1097–1157), developed its own local school of architecture. As Hillenbrand points out, the Iron Curtain had hampered scholarly research on the mutual relationships between Seljuq Iran and its northern Seljuq neighbour Turkmenistan; it is only in the last decade that the polycentric understanding of Seljuq history and culture has developed in such a way as to include the Seljuq Central Asian territories. Hillenbrand's study pushes the boundaries, both physical and intellectual, of Seljuq studies, and is therefore a fitting conclusion to this volume.

Debates about the Seljuq achievement, their overall importance in the formation of late-medieval Islamic civilisation, are likely to continue for some time to come – as the reader will notice, there are differences of opinion even among the various contributors to this volume. However, it is the editors' hope that this volume can serve to focus at least some of the strands of this ongoing conversation as it takes place simultaneously across a number of academic fields of inquiry within the broader discipline of Islamic and Middle Eastern Studies. The studies presented here have been brought together to showcase the current state-of-the-art in Seljuq studies, and to stimulate the growing interest in the Seljuqs. It is in this spirit that this volume is offered to the reader.

The editors
Utrecht/Edinburgh, January 2011

NOTES

1. The bibliography for studies of the Seljuq period is immense, and no attempt at comprehensiveness has been made here. In this introduction, next to recent publications since the turn of the century, only some of the outstanding 20th-century works are listed, although other important contributions would have deserved to be mentioned. Extensive bibliographies can be found in C. Edmund Bosworth, 'The political and dynastic history of the Iranian world (AD 1000–1217)', in *CHI5*, pp. 683–9; Gary Leiser, *A History of the Seljuks: İbrahim Kafesoğlu's Interpretation and the Resulting Controversy* (Carbondale, IL, 1988), pp. 190–6; and in *EI2*, s.v. 'Saldjūḳids' (C. E. Bosworth).
2. Claude Cahen, 'The historiography of the Seljuq period', in *Historians of the Middle East*, eds B. Lewis and P. M. Holt (London, 1962), p. 59.
3. Claude Cahen, 'The Turkish invasion: the Selchükids', in *A History of the Crusades*, vol. I: *The First Hundred Years*, ed. K. M. Setton (2nd edn, Madison, WI, 1969–89), pp. 135–76; Claude Cahen, s.v.v., 'Ghuzz', 'Alp Arslān', *EI2*, and other articles and chapters, in particular on the Rum Seljuqs (cf. note 18, below). Other foundational studies include Wilhelm [Vasily Vladimirovich] Barthold, *Turkestan v epokhu mongolskogo nashestviia* (1898–1900), trans. and ed. W. Barthold, H. A. R. Gibb, T. Minorsky and C. E. Bosworth,

Turkestan down to the Mongol Invasion (4th edn, London, 1977); M. F. Sanaullah, *The Decline of the Saljūqid Empire* (Calcutta, 1938).

4. A. K. S. Lambton, *Contributions to the Study of Seljuq Institutions* (PhD London, 1939), and the many articles and chapters that spawned from it: 'The administration of Sanjar's empire as illustrated in the '*ᶜAtabat al-Kataba*', *BSOAS* 20 (1957), pp. 367–88; 'Aspects of Saljūq-Ghuzz settlement in Persia', in *Islamic Civilisation 950–1150*, ed. D. S. Richards (Oxford, 1973), pp. 105–25; 'Changing concepts of justice and injustice from the 5th/11th century to the 8th/14th century in Persia: the Saljuq Empire and the Ilkhanate', *SI* 68 (1988), pp. 27–60.
5. Lambton, 'The internal structure of the Seljuq Empire', in *CHI5*, pp. 203–83; Bosworth, 'The political and dynastic history', pp. 1–202. Many other articles by C. E. Bosworth also touch on aspects of Seljuq history. See in particular his 'Barbarian incursions: the coming of the Turks into the Islamic World', in *Islamic Civilization 950–1150: Papers on Islamic History*, ed. D. S. Richards (Oxford, 1973), pp. 1–16, and his many contributions to *EI2*, e.g. s.v. 'Saldjūḳids' and passim.
6. Carla Klausner, *The Seljuq Vezirate: a Study of Civil Administration 1055–1194* (Cambridge, MA, 1973).
7. George Makdisi, 'The Sunni revival', in *Islamic Civilisation 950–1150*, ed. D. S. Richards (Oxford, 1973), pp. 155–68. (Republished in George Makdisi, *History and Politics in Eleventh-Century Baghdad* (Aldershot, 1991), VI.) See also the same author's 'The marriage of Tughril Beg', *IJMES* 1, 3 (1970), pp. 259–75.
8. See, for example, Richard Bulliet, *Islam: the View from the Edge* (New York, 1994), ch. 9.
9. Daphna Ephrat, *A Learned Society in a Period of Transition: the Sunni* ᶜUlamaʾ *of Eleventh-Century Baghdad* (Albany, 2000). A wider angle on the entire urban elite in Seljuq Baghdad is offered by Vanessa Van Renterghem, 'Les élites baghdadiennes' (PhD Paris-Sorbonne, 2004).
10. Omid Safi, *The Politics of Knowledge in Premodern Islam: Negotiating Ideology and Religious Inquiry* (Chapel Hill, NC, 2006).
11. Timothy Gianotti, *Al-Ghazālī's Unspeakable Doctrine of the Soul: Unveiling the Esoteric Psychology and Eschatology of the* Iḥyāʾ (Leiden, 2001); Ebrahim Moosa, *Ghazali and the Poetics of Imagination* (Chapel Hill, NC, 2005); Martin Whittingham, *Al-Ghazālī and the Qurʾān: One Word, Many Meanings* (London, 2007); Eric Ormsby, *Ghazali: the Revival of Islam* (Oxford, 2008); Frank Griffel, *Al-Ghazālī's Philosophical Theology* (Oxford, 2009). Earlier studies that explore al-Ghazālī's thought in the context of Seljuq rule include, notably, Mustapha Hogga, *Orthodoxie, subversion et réforme en Islam: Ġazālī et les seljūqides* (Paris, 1993); W. Montgomery Watt, *Muslim Intellectual: a Study of al-Ghazali* (Edinburgh, 1963).
12. C. Edmund Bosworth (ed.), *The Turks in the Early Islamic World* (Burlington, VT, 2007).
13. A. C. S. Peacock, *Early Seljūq History: a New Interpretation* (London, 2010).
14. Christian Lange, *Justice, Punishment and the Medieval Muslim Imagination* (Cambridge, 2008).
15. David Durand-Guédy, *Iranian Elites and Turkish Rulers: a History of Iṣfahān in the Saljūq Period* (London, 2010).
16. Osman Aziz Basan, *The Great Seljuqs: a History* (London, 2010). Add to this the study by G. E. Tetley, *The Ghaznavid and Seljuk Turks: Poetry as a Source for Iranian History* (London-New York, 2009).
17. D. G. Tor, *The Great Saljuqs and the Formation of Islamic Civilization: a Thematic*

History (forthcoming in *Cambridge Studies in Islamic Civilization*); A. C. S. Peacock, *The Great Seljuq Empire* (forthcoming in *The Edinburgh History of the Islamic Empires*).

18. The standard works here are Speros Vryonis, *The Decline of Medieval Hellenism in Asia Minor and the Process of Islamization from the Eleventh through the Fifteenth Century* (Berkeley, CA, 1971); Osman Turan, *Selçuklar zamanında Türkiye: Siyâsi tarih Alp Arslan'dan Osman Gazi'ye 1071-1318* (Istanbul, 1971); Claude Cahen, *La Turquie pré-ottomane* (Istanbul, 1988).
19. Gary Leiser (ed.), *Les Seljukides d'Anatolie*, special issue of *Mésogeios Méditerranée* 25–6 (2005).
20. Carole Hillenbrand, *Turkish Myth and Muslim Symbol: the Battle of Manzikert* (Edinburgh, 2007).
21. In recent years, A. C. S. Peacock has published a series of articles touching on aspects of the history of Seljuq Rum. See now also Songül Mecit, 'The Rum Seljuqs (473–641/1081–1243): Ideology, Mentality and Self-Image' (PhD Edinburgh, 2010). Sara Nur Yildiz is preparing a monograph entitled *The Seljuq Empire of Anatolia* for *The Edinburgh History of the Islamic Empires.*
22. Marshall G. S. Hodgson, *The Venture of Islam*, 3 vols (Chicago, IL, 1974), particularly vol. 2.
23. Sergei G. Agadzhanov, *Seldzukidy i Turkmenija v XI–XII vv.* (Ashkhabad, 1973), German trans. R. Schletzer, *Selǧukīden und Turkmenien im 11.-12. Jahrhundert* (*Turkmenenforschung Bd. 9*), (Hamburg, 1986); Sergei G. Agadzhanov, *Gosudarstvo seldzhukidov i Sredniaia Aziia v XI-XII vv.* (Moscow, 1991), German trans. R. Schletzer, *Der Staat der Seldschukiden und Mittelasien im 11. und 12. Jahrhundert* (*Turkmenenforschung Bd. 17*), (Berlin, 1994).
24. Transliteration in this volume generally follows the *IJMES* conventions; but depending on whether the Arabic, Persian or Turkish (Ottoman) view on the Seljuqs is emphasised, transliterated names (e.g. Ṭoghrïl/Ṭughril) can appear in a variety of forms – no one way of dealing with this issue has been imposed on contributors, who all have their own preferences. However, anglicised Islamicate terms (sultan, vizier, Sunni, etc.) as well as common names of dynasties (Abbasids, Buyids, etc.), cities (Baghdad, Isfahan, etc.) and toponyms (Khurasan, Quhistan, etc.) – but not proper names of individuals – are generally given without diacritical marks.

PART I

. . .

POLITICS

CHAPTER

1

THE ORIGINS OF THE SELJUQS

C. Edmund Bosworth

The farthest back that we can trace Seljuq origins is to the Turkish tribe of the Oghuz, but beyond the opening years of the 10th century we are in the realm of conjecture and inference. In the later 6th century, Byzantine envoys visited the Qaghans of the Western Türkü, the T'u-chüeh of the Chinese annals, Ishtemi and his son Tardu, in their summer pasture lands in the Tien Shan mountains, with the aim of concerting an alliance against the common enemy, Sasanid Persia, but the accounts of the Byzantine historians regrettably give us no information about the component units of the Qaghans' confederation.[1] In fact, the Oghuz do not appear specifically as the Ouzoi in Byzantine sources such as Constantine Porphyrogenitus and others until the 10th century.[2]

The actual name Oghuz corresponds to that of the Oghur in Western Turkic of the LIR variety (this being opposed to the more widespread and better-attested ŠAZ variety, what Golden calls 'Common Turkic'), now known to us only from fragments of the Turkic language of the Bulghars on the middle Volga in early Islamic times and from modern Chuvash, whose speakers are located to the west of the confluence of the Volga and Kama rivers.[3] The Oghur mentioned in Byzantine Greek sources, like the historian Priscus, as *Ogouroi and *Onogouroi go back to events of the 5th century and information on the Hunnic invasions of Europe from Inner Asia at that time. These tribal groups (with whom the Sarogour, perhaps 'White Oghur', are mentioned) sent embassies to the Emperors in Constantinople and were probably part of the Western Türkü/T'u-chüeh confederation.[4]

The Oghuz so-called only appear in this form of the Eastern Turkic ŠAZ- languages in the 8th century, with the Orkhon and other Old Turkic and then Uyghur inscriptions of Mongolia and adjacent parts of Siberia. Golden, again, derives the name from a Turkic root **ogh/uq* denoting kinship, hence meaning something like a clan or tribal grouping. The term is often found qualified by a numeral, showing the component parts of such groupings, like the Üch Oghuz 'Three Oghuz', Sekiz Oghuz 'Eight Oghuz' and, most frequently found, the Toquz Oghuz 'Nine Oghuz'.[5] The Chinese annals and the Old Turkic inscriptions most frequently refer to the latter, but there is much confusion here. Sharaf al-Zamān Ṭāhir Marvazī, writing at Seljuq courts in Khurasan during the last years of the 11th century and opening decades of the 12th century, was concerned to explain the Oghuz origins of his Seljuq masters. He calls the Ghuzz/Oghuz a great tribe of the Turks which comprised twelve subdivisions, one of which was called the Toghuzghuz, with a ruler called Toghuz-Khāqān who headed powerful armies and had territories on the fringes of Khwarazm and Transoxania. Marvazī's information seems thus to relate to earlier Samanid times, locating these Turks in the steppes to the north of the Aral Sea and the lower reaches of the Syr Darya.[6]

It is the period of about a century and a half, between the mention of the Toquz Oghuz in the Old Turkic inscriptions and the presence of Oghuz nomads on the northern fringes of the Khwarazmian kingdom and the Samanid amirate in the early 10th century, which is most obscure. We cannot be sure of any linkage between the Toguz Oghuz of the 8th century and the later Oghuz. Pritsak conjectured that, at the time of the events of 744, when the older Turkic ruling house was replaced by the Uyghur one, the head of the Qarluq tribal group was raised to the post of 'Left-Hand Yabghu', just below the supreme Qaghan, and the Oghuz to the slightly inferior post of 'Right-Hand Yabghu'.[7] Certainly, the title Yabghu (which in Orkhon Turkish times was one of rank, not birth, coming immediately after the Qaghan and before the Shadh) is attributed by the Samanid official Abū ᶜAbdallāh Khwārazmī (wrote soon after 366/977) both to the Qarluq and the Oghuz in the form *Jabbūya*.[8] However, there is mention of a migration of Oghuz from the eastern end of the Eurasian steppes by Ibn al-Athīr, under the year 548/1153–4 and his account of Sultan Sanjar's involvement with the Ghuzz of Khurasan, which may represent an earlier Khurasanian historical tradition, perhaps that of Sallāmī in his *History of the Governors of Khurasan* or a parallel source.[9] In this report, the Oghuz are said to have migrated from the farthest frontier regions of the land of the Turks to Transoxania during the caliphate of al-Mahdī (158–69/775–85), to have become Muslims, but then to have aided the pseudo-prophet al-Muqannaᶜ against the caliphal authorities, nevertheless finally betraying him 'as is their wont regarding every ruling power they find themselves within'. This Far Eastern origin of these Turks would accordingly be in the region of Mongolia and was perhaps connected with the Toquz Oghuz, who, according to the *Ḥudūd al-ᶜālam* (compiled in 372–3/982–3), were still essentially centred on lands to the east of the Tien Shan adjoining China and

Tibet, that is, the heartlands of the Uyghur Khanate which had succeeded to the older Türkü one and which from 225/840 onwards occupied these lands of what eventually became known as Eastern Turkestan and, nearly a thousand years later, became the Chinese province of Sinkiang.[10]

Within the western steppes of Inner Eurasia the Oghuz disputed possession of the steppe lands stretching from the Irtysh river in the east, along the northern fringes of Khwarazmia and Transoxania to the lower and middle Volga, with another Turkic people, the Pechenegs, perhaps securing aid against these last from the Khazars of the lower Volga and Kuban steppes; a memory of these protracted struggles is preserved in later Oghuz tribal tradition, the *Oghuz-nāma*.[11] By the later 9th century, however, the Oghuz were victorious and pushed the Pechenegs westwards into the Pontic steppes north of the Black Sea, where they displaced the Hungarians and set the latter off on their migration across the Carpathians into the Danube-Tisza basin.[12]

Hence when in 309–10/921–2 the caliphal envoy Ahmad b. Faḍlān made his celebrated journey to the Yiltawar/Ilteber, king of the Bulghars, he first traversed essentially lands controlled by the Oghuz once he left Muslim territory. He came from Baghdad to the Samanid capital Bukhara and thence sailed down the Oxus, wintering in the Khwarazmian city of Gurganj, one of the jumping-off places for trade caravans into the steppes (the *Ḥudūd al-ᶜālam* describes the capital of Khwarazm, the city of Kāth, as the Gateway to Turkestan of the Oghuz[13]). His caravan of 5,000 riding and pack animals (*dābba*, perhaps comprising horses, camels and mules) and 3,000 men[14] crossed the Üst-Urt plateau, the numerous rivers running down from the southern end of the Urals range into the Caspian Sea, such as the Emba and the Ural or Yayïq, and after then traversing the lands of the Bashkirs, finally reached the summer encampment of the Bulghar ruler on the middle Volga, in the modern Kuybyshev region.

Ibn Faḍlān's *Riḥla* is supremely valuable for its ethnographical and sociological information on the Oghuz people at that time. He relates that they lived in wretched conditions but were nevertheless strong and hardy, roaming 'like wild asses'. They had no religious sense as he conceived it, that is, a faith with a defined creed and a body of rituals, and they performed no religious ceremonies; they merely felt the vague sense of a Heavenly Supreme Power, Tengri, which we know was characteristic of much of the Inner Asian steppe peoples, Turks, Mongols and others.[15] We know, however, from the *Ḥudūd al-ᶜālam*'s chapter on the Oghuz/Ghuzz how they venerated and relied greatly on their shamans, which this geographical text calls *ṭabībān* and *pijishkān*, implying that they possessed magical powers of healing and exorcism.[16] Because of trading connections with Khwarazm, Ibn Faḍlān's Oghuz knew about Islam but had no liking for it. When one of their chiefs, the Lesser Yināl, became a convert to Islam he was given the choice of either adhering to his new-found faith or continuing to enjoy the status of a chief; he chose the prestige of chieftainship.[17] What Ibn Faḍlān describes of their funeral practices, involving the slaughter of up to 200 of a chief's horses into his tomb to serve as his mounts for his after-death journey to Tengri's heavenly domain, accords closely with what we know of such practices amongst Turkish and other Altaic peoples in general.[18]

These Oghuz had a multiplicity of chiefs of various kinds (*mulūk, ruʾasāʾ, arbāb*). This seems to have been a permanent characteristic of Oghuz social organisation. The *Ḥudūd al-ʿālam* comments that all the component groups of the Oghuz had their own chief, on account of the discords amongst them, and it remained a valid feature for the period of the Turkmens' overrunning of Ghaznavid Khurasan and northern Persia in the first half of the 11th century, when bands seem to have operated to a considerable extent independently of each other, the Seljuq family heading the main group but by no means controlling them all.[19] In Ibn Faḍlān's time there was, however, a generally acknowledged supreme chief, the Yabghu, this title having remained with the tribe since the events of the mid-8th century in Mongolia mentioned above, but significantly, he did not claim the exalted title of Qaghan/Khāqān; and indeed, these Oghuz of the Üst-Urt region seem to have had a subordinate relationship to the powerful kingdom of the Khazars on the lower Volga, since Ibn Faḍlān mentions that Oghuz hostages were held at the Khazar court, presumably as pledges for good behaviour. The Yabghu's deputy (*khalīfa*) was called the Kudherkin/Kül Erkin, and other leading figures were the Lesser Yināl, the army commander, *ṣāḥib al-jaysh*, that is, Sü-Bashï (whom Ibn Faḍlān specifically names, unusually, as Etrek, son of Qaṭaghān); the Ṭarkhān; and the Y.l.gh.z/Y.gh.l.z (this last name or title corruptly written in the mss). The Arab traveller describes the Ṭarkhān as the most influential and lofty of all these, his status obviously coming from his position in the tribal hierarchy (in Orkhon Turkish and Uyghur times, this title had denoted a high rank in the state, apparently just below that of Tégin and Shadh) rather than military prowess, since Ibn Faḍlān describes him as physically crippled and blind. This Ṭarkhān was reluctant to let Ibn Faḍlān's party pass through their lands, suspecting a stratagem on the part of the Islamic caliph to collaborate with the Khazar king against the Oghuz. He and his associates had to be placated by gifts of robes of honour in the shape of caftans fabricated in Merv, and of pieces of fine cloth, pepper and sheets of bread; textiles and spices must have been amongst the main products supplied by the *dār al-Islām* (the area under Islamic sovereignty) to the steppe peoples.[20]

The Islamic geographers concerned with Inner Asia and its peoples in the 10th century regarded the Oghuz with disfavour, reflecting their presence on the borders of Khwarazm and Transoxania and their harrying and plundering of these regions; in earlier times these could be generally contained by counter-raids into the steppes which could come back with such plunder as slave captives, like the annual raid of the kings of Khwarazm against the Oghuz at the onset of winter, mentioned by Bīrūnī as the *faghbūriyya* one,[21] but the problem became more acute by the later 10th century when the Khwarazmian and Samanid state powers were in palpable decline. Amongst what one might call the *mathālib* (vices) of the Turks, Ibn Faḍlān noted the shamelessness of Oghuz women, who were always unveiled, and their brazenly exposing their pudenda; the general aversion of all Oghuz to water and washing (the Muslim traders of the caravan had to perform their ablutions under the cover of night); and the fact that the men never took off their garments, which became encrusted with dirt, until they frayed away and disintegrated. He did, however, note that adultery was almost unknown amongst them and, when found out, was punishable by death, and that they abhorred pederasty, this last, when it occurred, being brought from the Iranian lands to the south.[22] The *Ḥudūd al-ᶜālam* describes the Oghuz as having arrogant faces and as being quarrelsome and malevolent.[23]

This last text was, however, wrong in describing the Oghuz as purely steppe dwellers in felt tents, with no towns, and in other parts of his work the author clearly contradicts this statement. In his chapter on the Transoxanian marches he mentions towns in the middle Syr Darya region, including Chāch and Ṭarāz or Talas, the latter being one of several places that had both Turkish and (Iranian) Muslim dwellers, mentioning specifically here the Oghuz' eastern neighbours, the Qarluq Turks, but it is probable that there were Oghuz there too. We also know of Sawrān and Sighnāq as urban centres here, the former being described in the *Ḥudūd* (as *Ṣabrān) as a centre of Oghuz traders. The towns along the lower Syr Darya were certainly resorts of the Oghuz; the *Ḥudūd* mentions here Jand, Khuvāra and 'the new settlement', Dih-i Naw (al-Qarya al-Ḥadītha in Ibn Ḥawqal, *Yengi-kent in Maḥmūd Kāshgharī), describing this last as the winter residence of the king of the Oghuz.[24] In particular, Jand (the modern Qyzyl-Orda, the Perovsk of Tsarist Russian times) became an important centre of the Oghuz towards the end of the 10th century. It plays a role in the semi-legendary accounts of Seljuq origins as recorded in what we know of the *Malik-nāma*.[25] According to these accounts, the eponymous founder of the family, Saljūq b. Duqāq/Toqaq, came to Jand with his followers and became a Muslim. Once converted to this new faith, he relieved the Muslim population of the town of the tribute laid on them by the still-pagan Yabghu of the Oghuz, and was ultimately buried there. From this time dates the hostility between the two branches of the Oghuz, the senior one of the Yabghu and the newer one of the Seljuq family, which is known to us from the history of the last Samanids and the early Ghaznavids. The Yabghus in Jand became Muslim at the turn of the millennium. Gardīzī places the event in 393/1003 when, he says, the Yabghu assumed the Islamic name of ᶜAlī and married a daughter of the last Samanid, Ismāᶜīl al-Muntaṣir.[26] The principality of the Yabghus, based on Jand, endured for almost fifty years until c. 435–6/1043–4, when the Seljuqs, having achieved a spectacular victory over the Ghaznavid sultan Masᶜūd at Dandānqān in 431/1040, expelled the Yabghu Shāh Malik b. ᶜAlī from Khwarazm, which he had briefly taken over as nominal tributary of the Ghaznavids, and then from Jand, Shāh Malik's flight and subsequent death marking the end of this branch of the Oghuz. The division of authority and the strong rivalry of the two families within the Oghuz thus ended with the triumph of Saljūq b. Duqāq's two grandsons Ṭoghrïl Beg and Chaghrï Beg and the inauguration of the Great Seljuq empire.[27]

The origins of the Seljuq family are, as has been noted, shrouded in at least semi-legend, having been embroidered by the compiler or compilers of the *Malik-nāma*, concerned to provide the Seljuq dynasty, as it became, with glorious antecedents. What can be gleaned from this source, apparently used by historians like Ṣadr al-Dīn Ḥusaynī and Ibn al-Athīr, with mentions of it in various other authors from Ibn al-ᶜAdīm to Barhebraeus, was examined in detail by Claude Cahen some sixty years ago,[28] and only the bare essentials need to be rehearsed here. The *Malik-nāma* attaches the Seljuq family to the Oghuz clan of the Qïnïq, which we know from the listing in Maḥmūd Kāshgharī, with variants in later sources like Rashīd al-Dīn, was one of the twenty-two to twenty-five component clans of the Oghuz, being part of the left wing of the Oghuz army host, the Üch Oq 'Three Arrows'. During Great Seljuq times, the Qïnïq accordingly enjoyed considerable prestige.[29]

The progenitor Duqāq is accorded in the *Malik-nāma* the sobriquet of Temür Yalïgh 'Iron Bow', bows and arrows being symbols of power amongst the Oghuz and known in *tamgha*s and on coins.[30] He is said to have been in the service of the 'Khazars', which Cahen thought here denoted a Turkish people nomadising between the Aral Sea and Lower Volga, in loose dependence on the Khazar kingdom proper, and to have quarrelled with the Yabghu over the launching of raids on the Muslims of the Oxus-Syr Darya region – clearly a back projection of the later role, in the later 11th and the 12th centuries, of the Islamised Seljuqs as foes of the still pagan Oghuz of the steppes. The connection of what became the Seljuq line and the ruling family of the Yabghus seems to have endured during this time, since Duqāq remained attached to the Yabghu and his military campaigns and there is no firm evidence that he became a Muslim, and it was only subsequently that the split and rivalry between the two Oghuz lines arose. The role of convert probably belongs to his son Saljūq, who, according to the *Malik-nāma*, had also been in Khazar service, perhaps as head of a tribal contingent, having the title of *sübashï*, but who likewise fell out with his Khazar suzerains and migrated, with a force of a hundred cavalrymen and thousands of sheep and camels, to Jand on the lower Syr Darya, where he became a Muslim. These events probably took place in the middle years or third quarter of the 10th century.[31] One of the sons of Saljūq bore the name Mikāʾīl, but there is no evidence that the appearance of this name, and other Biblical ones like Yūnus, Mūsā and Isrāʾīl, within the Seljuq family, points to connections in the past with the Judaism of the Khazar ruling elite or Nestorian Christianity.[32] The son of Saljūq, Mikāʾīl, was the father of Ṭoghrïl Beg, probably born in the early 380s/990s, and since this last bore the name Abū Ṭālib Muḥammad, Mikāʾīl was obviously a Muslim by then; another son of Saljūq, Mūsā, had a son with the equally Muslim name of Ḥasan. As for the original Yabghu in Jand, it is probable that he also became a Muslim in the 380s/990s, perhaps through friendly contacts with the last Samanids. Gardīzī mentions that the last Samanid, Ismāʿīl al-Muntaṣir, at one point sought refuge amongst the Oghuz and secured military aid from them, contracting a marriage alliance with the Yabghu, in his struggles to revive the fortunes of his house; the characteristically Samanid *kunya* of the last Yabghu of Jand, Abū l-Fawāris Shāh Malik, points to such connections.[33]

The *Malik-nāma* states that Saljūq remained at Jand and died there, having brought up Ṭoghrïl and Chaghrï on the premature death in battle of their father.[34] It was soon after this that the Seljuq family came on to the wider scene of Islamic history, appearing in Transoxania after being called in as auxiliary troops by the last Samanids, and then becoming involved in the Qarakhanid takeover of Transoxania and the rivalries of the Qarakhanids and early Ghaznavids, being forced further southwards by the pressure of events towards the fringes of northern Khurasan and of Gurgan. The sources bring a fresh set of problems for these early decades of the 5th/11th century, including the question of the relations between the branch of the Oghuz remaining at Jand under the original Yabghu, and the appearance of this title/office within the Seljuq family also, it being apparently adopted, in rivalry with the older branch of ruling Oghuz, by Saljūq's son Arslan Isrāʾīl; but the elucidation of these belongs to the wider history of the Eastern Islamic world at this time.

NOTES

1. For these early Byzantine-Turkish contacts, see René Grousset, *The Empire of the Steppes. A History of Central Asia*, English trans. Naomi Walford (New Brunswick, NJ, 1970), pp. 83–6.
2. Gyula Moravcsik, *Byzantinoturcica. I. Die byzantinischen Quellen der Geschichte der Türkvölker* (Berlin, 1958), p. 228.
3. Peter B. Golden, *An Introduction to the History of the Turkic Peoples* (Wiesbaden, 1992), pp. 95–7.

4. Ibid. p. 92ff.; P. B. Golden, 'Ethnogenesis in the tribal zone: the shaping of the Turks', *Archivum Eurasiae Medii Aevi* 16 (2008–9), pp. 83–7.
5. Ibid. pp. 205–6.
6. *Sharaf al-Zamān Ṭāhir Marvazī on China, the Turks and India*, ed. and English trans. V. Minorsky (London, 1942), text p. 18, English trans. p. 29, commentary pp. 94–5; and see Wilhelm Barthold, *Zwölf Vorlesungen über die Geschichte der Türken Mittelasiens* (Berlin, 1935), pp. 53–5.
7. Omeljan Pritsak, 'Von den Karluk zu den Karachaniden', *ZDMG* 101 (1951), pp. 273–4.
8. See C. E. Bosworth and Sir Gerard Clauson, 'Al-Xwārazmī on the peoples of Central Asia', *JRAS* (1965), pp. 6, 9–10; *EIr*, s.v. 'Jabğuya. ii. In Islamic sources', XIV, pp. 316–17 (C. E. Bosworth).
9. Ibn al-Athīr, *al-Kāmil fi 'l-ta'rīkh* (Beirut, 1385–7/1965–7), XI, p. 178; Narshakhī, *Tārīkh-i Bukhārā*, English trans. Richard N. Frye, *The History of Bukhara* (Cambridge, MA, 1954), pp. 68, 72; Gardīzī, *Kitāb Zayn al-akhbār*, ed. ᶜAbd al-Ḥayy Ḥabībī (Tehran, 1347/1968), p. 126, English trans. C. Edmund Bosworth, *The Ornament of Histories. A History of the Eastern Islamic Lands* AD *650–1041* (London, 2011), p. 34: 'infidel Turks'.
10. Anon., *Ḥudūd al-ᶜālam*, English trans. V. Minorsky, *'The Regions of the World'. A Persian Geography 372* A.H. – *982* A.D. (London, 1970), trans. p. 94, comm. p. 263ff.; cf. Golden, *Introduction*, pp. 145, 156, 206–7.
11. In Rashīd al-Dīn's *Jāmi ᶜ al-tawārīkh*, cited in Golden, *Introduction*, p. 207, note 109.
12. Barthold, *Zwölf Vorlesungen*, pp. 102–3; Grousset, *The Empire of the Steppes*, pp. 177–8; S. G. Agajanov, 'The States of the Oghuz, the Kimek and the Kïpchak', in *UNESCO History of the Civilizations of Central Asia. IV. The Age of Achievement:* A.D. *750 to the End of the Fifteenth Century. Part One. The Historical, Social and Economic Setting*, eds M. S. Asimov and C. E. Bosworth (Paris, 1998), pp. 63–5.
13. Anon., *Ḥudūd al-ᶜālam*, trans. Minorsky, p. 121.
14. A. Z. V. Togan, *Ibn Faḍlāns Reisebericht* (Leipzig, 1939), §29, text p. 14, German trans. p. 26, following Togan in his Excursus §29a in reversing the two figures (hence the figures should be thus corrected in C. Edmund Bosworth, *The Ghaznavids, their Empire in Afghanistan and Eastern Iran 994:1040* (Edinburgh, 1963), pp. 214–15).
15. Togan, *Ibn Faḍlāns Reisebericht*, §20, text p. 10, German trans. pp. 19–21; cf. Bosworth, *Ghaznavids*, pp. 216–17.
16. Anon., *Ḥudūd al-ᶜālam*, trans. Minorsky, §19, pp. 100–1, comm. pp. 311–12.
17. Togan, *Ibn Faḍlāns Reisebericht*, §28, text p. 13, trans. pp. 25–6.
18. Ibid. §31, text p. 14–15, trans. pp. 27–8, and Excursus §31a.
19. Anon., *Ḥudūd al-ᶜālam*, trans. Minorsky, §19, trans. p. 101. Regarding these Oghuz invasions, we have mention in a source like Bayhaqī of both the Seljuqiyān and Yināliyān, cf. Bosworth, *Ghaznavids*, pp. 226, 241
20. Togan, *Ibn Faḍlāns Reisebericht*, §§33–6, text 15–17, trans. pp. 28–31, and Excursus 33a, 34a, 36a.
21. Al-Bīrūnī, *al-Āthār al-bāqiya*, English trans. C. Edward Sachau, *The Chronology of Ancient Nations* (London, 1879), p. 224.
22. Togan, *Ibn Faḍlāns Reisebericht*, §§20–1, 24, 27, text pp. 10–11, 12, 13, trans. pp. 21–3, 25, and Excursus §§21a, 24a, 27a.
23. Ibid. §19, trans. p. 100.
24. Ibid. §§25, 26, trans. pp. 118–19, 122. See also on these settlements of the Oghuz,

Barthold, *Zwölf Vorlesungen*, pp. 80, 101–2, 104; Bosworth, *Ghaznavids*, pp. 212–13; Golden, *Introduction*, pp. 209–10.

25. See *EI2* Suppl., s.v. 'Djand' (C. E. Bosworth).
26. Gardīzī, *Zayn al-akhbār*, p. 176, trans. p. 83.
27. Claude Cahen, 'Le Malik-Nâmeh et l'histoire des origines seljukides', *Oriens* 2 (1949), p. 41ff.; Pritsak, 'Der Untergang des Reiches des Oġuzischen Yabġu', in *Fuad Köprülü armağanı* (Istanbul 1953), pp. 397–410 (English trans. 'The decline of the empire of the Oghuz Yabghu', in Pritsak, *Studies in Medieval Eurasian History* (London, 1981), no. XIX).
28. Cahen, 'Malik-Nâmeh', pp. 32–7.
29. M. T. Houtsma, 'Die Ghuzzenstämme', *WZKM* 2 (1888), p. 226; Cahen, 'Les tribus turques d'Asie occidentale pendant la période seljukide', *WZKM* 51 (1948–52), pp. 179–80; Golden, *Introduction*, pp. 207–9; Agajanov, 'States of the Oghuz', pp. 65–6.
30. For the *tamgha* of the Qïnïq on Ṭoghrïl Beg's coins, see the catalogue of Islamic coins in the Istanbul Archaeological Museum cited in *EI2*, s.v. 'Tamgha' (G. Leiser).
31. Cahen, 'Malik-Nâmeh', pp. 42–3.
32. Ibid. p. 42; Bosworth, *Ghaznavids*, p. 215.
33. Gardīzī, *Zayn al-akhbār*, p. 176, trans. p. 83. Bosworth, *Ghaznavids*, pp. 221–2, citing ᶜUtbī's *al-Taʾrīkh al-Yamīnī*, according to whom the Oghuz had a traditional bias in favour of the Samanids.
34. Cahen, 'Malik-Nâmeh', pp. 43–5.

CHAPTER

2

ASPECTS OF THE COURT OF THE GREAT SELJUQS

Carole Hillenbrand

Several quite distinct approaches to the study of the Seljuq court might be proposed. One could view it from the perspective of an apparently immemorial, quasi-mythical ancient Iranian tradition which found its most characteristic expression in Sasanian times but drew its inspiration from Parthian and especially Achaemenid models.[1] Or one could highlight the very different traditions inherited from the nomadic cultures of the Eurasian steppe, stretching back in historical times to the Turkic culture exemplified by the Orkhon inscriptions of the 7th and 8th centuries AD. In still earlier times these nomadic cultures may be glimpsed in the perhaps distorting mirror of the Chinese sources, so here too there is a taproot that extends to a very distant past.[2] Yet another approach to understanding the Seljuq court might be founded on a close study of Abbasid precedent; the court life in the golden prime of Hārūn al-Rashīd described in admiring detail in a multitude of Arabic sources.[3] It set a standard of luxury, ceremony and ostentatious display to which many a later Muslim court aspired. The Samanid and Ghaznavid courts in the eastern Iranian world took over many of the practices of the caliphal court;[4] this was the most readily available model for the Seljuqs to follow, adapting it where appropriate to their own preferences and needs. The topic of the Seljuq court, then, is a complex one with multiple ramifications to earlier cultures. Moreover, the very concept of a court in this period requires close examination. In the present chapter, restrictions of space make it appropriate to limit the discussion to certain key themes. Accordingly, this chapter will highlight a few aspects of the many ceremonial, intellectual and leisure activities pursued by the Seljuq sultans. Most of the evidence, though not all of it, will be drawn from the heyday of their rule, from the reign of Sultan Ṭughril (d. 453/1063) until that of Sultan Muḥammad (d. 512/1118).[5]

WHAT IS A COURT IN THE CONTEXT OF THE GREAT SELJUQS?

There has been much scholarly interest in the concept of medieval princely courts in recent years, from the context of Europe in the West to that of China in the East.[6] Vale's book on the cultural characteristics of 13th- and 14th-century north-western European courts, for example,[7] stresses the continuities from Carolingian times onwards. The book also examines such issues as the crucial elements of public display expected of rulers and the necessary material foundations of court life. In many European countries, the court of the medieval ruler was often peripatetic. How much more so was the case for nomadic military usurpers such as the Seljuq Turks, who travelled a great deal, often over vast distances, first to secure territories and then to defend and expand them. So the safest thing to say about the Seljuq 'court' is that it could be found wherever the sultan happened to be. Like other medieval courts, that of the Seljuqs followed a predictable routine wherever it went. The first two Seljuq sultans, Ṭughril and Alp Arslān, spent most of the time in the saddle, criss-crossing enormous tracts of land in pursuit of territory and booty. Alp Arslān went almost immediately from eastern Turkey, where he had gained his famous victory over the Byzantine emperor in 463/1071 at Manzikert, to Central Asia where he was assassinated the following year.

The twenty-year reign of Sultan Malikshāh represents an important transition in Seljuq history. At this point there seems to have been a greater tendency for the Seljuq sultan, and therefore the court attending him too, to stay in one place for at least certain periods of the year. With Malikshāh there is a clear attachment to Iṣfāhān,[8] although he too continued to travel around the empire but to a lesser extent. Such travel was nothing new in Iran. Indeed, since ancient times, the courts of the rulers of Iran had moved around. The Achaemenid court, for example, moved according to the season, spending autumn and winter in one place and spring and summer in another. At various times Susa, Hamadan and Persepolis served as a royal centre.

SOURCES

For most of our knowledge of the Seljuq period, we are dependent on a good number of Arabic and Persian chronicles which provide detailed information on the dynasty. However, these sources, by their dating and their very nature, have to be treated with caution. They date largely from 150 to 200 years after the heyday of Seljuq rule in the 11th century and they reflect the retrospective views of non-Turkish Muslim chroniclers – usually religious scholars or bureaucrats – who lived under the rule of later Turkish overlords in Syria, Egypt, Iraq and

Iran and who, without a second thought, cast Seljuq rule into a mould of Perso-Islamic statecraft. Moreover, these chronicles are written, not in Turkish, but in Arabic and Persian. The Seljuq Turks themselves have no authentic voice. Instead, they are seen in the Muslim sources, as it were, through a rosy Islamic prism.[9]

A very useful resource, however, for reconstructing the realities of Seljuq statecraft and court life is the 'mirrors for princes' literature, and the Seljuq period abounds in such material.[10] The letters in Persian written by al-Ghāzālī to contemporary rulers echo the same ethos.[11] But the material in the 'mirrors for princes' genre is problematic in that it speaks more often of a model court rather than an actual one. It describes what ought to be rather than what the author has actually experienced. This is especially true of the *Siyar al-mulūk*, the 'mirror for princes' work written by Niẓām al-Mulk, the most famous Seljuq vizier, dedicated to the third Seljuq sultan Malikshāh. In it Niẓām al-Mulk harks back to the halcyon days of the Ghaznavid court in Khurasan and he sees a fall in standards in Seljuq protocols and ceremonies as well as in government administration more widely.

To sum up this discussion of written sources, it is important to re-emphasise that they remain problematic. They date from later periods of Turkish rule. They are written by men who never milked a flock, never pitched a tent, never ate steak tartare, never strung a bow for battle, never galloped across the plain. So, as scholars and bureaucrats, they airbrush out the nomadic milieu. And they fit the Seljuqs onto the procrustean bed of Islamic 'mirrors for princes'.

When it comes to reconstructing the life of the Seljuq court, the scholar is faced with the need to seek supplementary information from material culture to amplify the fragmentary, often unexplained, snippets of relevant information scattered through the medieval Arabic and Persian written sources. With such concrete contemporary or near-contemporary evidence – such as pottery, sculpture and painting – it is important, where they exist, to consult artefacts as close as possible in date to the Seljuq period. It is worth pointing out that although the period of strong, unified Seljuq rule can be said to have lasted only until 485/1092, or at a pinch until 512/1118 when the Seljuq sultan Muḥammad Ṭapar died, military commanders and Atabegs founded smaller polities in eastern Turkey, Iraq and Syria in the 12th and 13th centuries. These small principalities – they can rightly be labelled Seljuq successor-states – modelled themselves on the government and court life of the Great Seljuqs. For such Turkish states as these – the Artuqids in eastern Turkey, the Burids in Syria and the Atabegs of Mosul in Iraq – there is additional and most useful visual evidence which can be brought into play.

RANK

The importance of rank was maintained at the Seljuq court. It was represented visually by all kinds of symbols. Already in the Sasanian period, in the *Letter of Tansar*, the necessity of maintaining differences between the common people and the nobility and of making the upper classes dependent on the patronage of the ruler is emphasised. Indeed, the sovereign is explicitly advised as follows:

> There is no wickedness or calamity, no unrest or plague in the world which corrupts so much as the ascending of the base to the station of the noble . . . You must make the heads of their first families and their men of rank and their lords and nobles rely on your position and patronage; and through favours and kindnesses you must banish the causes of vexation and care from their hearts.[12]

The anonymous author goes on to say that the King of Kings has established 'a visual and general distinction between men of noble birth and common people with regard to horses and clothes, houses and gardens, women and servants.' Indeed, the nobles are clearly differentiated from ordinary folk by their dress, horses, lofty dwellings, headgear, hunting and other characteristics related to their status.[13]

The same kind of 'pecking order' must have prevailed in Seljuq times when it is likely that the nobles had their own prescribed positions, according to rank and office held, and protocol dictated where they should stand on official occasions.

AN ARTISTIC OVERVIEW OF A TYPICAL MEDIEVAL TURKISH COURT

A telling visual evocation of rank and its importance can be seen in a well-known masterpiece of Arab painting which evokes with remarkable clarity many aspects of the court life of the Turkish-dominated Seljuq successor-states, and indeed it can be regarded as a reliable guide to actual Seljuq practice. Here we see the easy interplay between the domestic and the public, the formal and the informal, business activities and the life of leisure, which characterised these medieval Middle Eastern courts. The painting depicts this entire world in microcosm and it can therefore serve to frame this entire paper. And, as the adage has it, a picture is worth a thousand words. This particular picture, datable c. 648/1250 and probably hailing from northern Iraq, is a frontispiece – a kind of medieval equivalent to the modern dust jacket, with the same purpose of advertising the book itself – to a medical treatise dealing with antidotes to snakebite, a text based on the work of the Greek physician Galen (Figure 2.1).[14]

Figure 2.1 Frontispiece of the Kitāb al-Diryāq of Pseudo-Galen, probably Mosul, c. 648/1250 (Vienna, National Library) (after Hayes)

So here is a work of Greek science rendered into Arabic and given a full-page introductory illustration that has nothing whatever to do with snakes. But the respect for Greek learning is clear, and serves as a reminder of the ruler's commitment to intellectual pursuits. In fact the format of this image also has classical roots, for it ingeniously adapts the form of the late antique diptych, the wooden or ivory panel whose flip side was coated with wax on which the letter was incised. In other words, it was an endlessly re-usable envelope. In late Roman and early Byzantine times such diptychs bore an image of the ruler. And so does this – imitation is the sincerest form of flattery. The difference is that the classical letter has become the Arabic book.

But in place of the rigid formality of its classical source, here informality is the keynote. We see the ruler in relaxed mode. He wears a fur *sharbush* on his head and sits cross-legged on an ample bolster with a decorative L-shaped wooden backrest. No formal throne here. His elegant caftan, of Central Asian type with voluminous sleeves, seems to be trimmed with ermine and falls open to reveal a scarlet under-robe. He holds a glass beaker with a ruby-coloured liquid in it, presumably wine. A golden ewer on a shelf behind him, flanked by vases with flowers, promises easy refills. In front of it is an open dish piled high with fruit. Meanwhile a gorgeously clad, *sharbush*-crowned kneeling retainer – no kitchen boy, this – prepares two skewers of shish kebab on a fancy barbecue. Two bodyguards holding up tasselled swords keep watch. Like the other courtiers dancing attendance on the ruler, they perch uncomfortably on one leg. This central panel is set within an architectural framework that suggests an open-plan two-storey palace. The four side panels contain two men apiece. Several of them bear their symbols of office – the falconer, who was responsible for the hunt, is at nearside top left, while at top right the men holding a duck and a goblet respectively were charged with the provision of food and drink. Meanwhile at lower right is the *ḥājib* in pink with his staff of office and the polo-master in green with his polo stick. These are the *khāṣṣakiyya* or court officials in the immediate retinue of the sultan, each with his own designated responsibility. Those responsibilities often had an army dimension, and were not just confined to court life. Thus the polo-master oversaw the cavalry, and the man in charge of the court buttery was also the army quartermaster. Practically all the men, from the ruler downwards, wear their hair in long plaits.

The oblong panels above and below also have their parts to play in this microcosm of court life. Above is a hunting scene complete with a saluki and an onager being brought down by archers mounted on richly caparisoned horses with docked tails. Below, four heavily veiled ladies, one with a child, and mounted on camels, are led by an attendant on foot towards a group of horsemen with polo sticks. Thus the composite image contains references to hunting, polo, the harem and the family as well as evoking the functions of the principal court officials and depicting the ruler feasting at his ease. All this is put across in condensed form but with a wealth of corroborative detail in furnishings, accessories and costume so that we are vouchsafed a remarkably lifelike snapshot of the Seljuq court at play.

THE *NAWBA*

There were many visible ways in which the Seljuq sultan demonstrated his sovereignty over all his subjects, including those who ruled on his behalf in a subordinate capacity in other parts of his realm. Acknowledgement of the supreme authority of the sultan was demanded especially from members of his own family. From the very beginning of Seljuq power in the Muslim world, although the two brothers Chaghri and Ṭughril agreed to divide and share the lands they conquered, there would be only one overarching sovereign. This precept was enshrined in the conferring of the title of 'Sultan of East and West' on Ṭughril by the caliph al-Qāʾim (no doubt under duress) in 447/1055.[15] This title had never been used in an Islamic context before and it may well have had its roots in the nomadic concept of world dominion in the steppes – a symbol of Turkish sovereignty, extending from where the sun rose to where it set.[16]

Long before the coming of the Seljuqs the *nawba* ceremony was an integral part of court protocol at the caliphal court in Baghdad.[17] Amongst the multiple meanings of the word *nawba* the following definitions of the word are relevant in the context of this discussion: *nawba* could mean 'a drum struck at stated hours', 'drums beating at the gate of a great man at certain intervals' or 'a musical band playing at stated times before the palace of a king or prince'.[18] The *nawba* took place at the hours of prayer but its use was extended to other celebratory occasions, such as a military victory.[19] The visual evidence from 13th-century painting (Figure 2.2) indicates that wind and stringed instruments were also played in the *nawba* concert.[20]

The *nawba* was a crucial symbol of Muslim sovereignty.[21] According to Hilāl al-Ṣābiʾ, who devoted a short chapter to the *nawba* in his book on court protocol written just before the Seljuqs took power in Baghdad, the *nawba* was originally the prerogative of the caliph only. He implies, but does not state explicitly, that this would take place five times a day. Gradually, however, with the weakening of centralised caliphal power, the right to have the *nawba* was extended to other rulers. The number of times a day this was permitted depended on the recipient's status. Hilāl al-Ṣābiʾ explains how under the Buyids their rulers were allowed to beat the drum at the gate of their palace in Baghdad: 'A tent was pitched there for drummers, who beat at the time of each of the three prayers'.[22]

Figure 2.2 Al-Jazarī *nawba* scene, Kitāb fī Ma^crifat al-Ḥiyal al-Handasiyya, Iraq, 602/1206 (Topkapı Sarayı Library, Istanbul)

It is noteworthy that the Buyids were only to be allowed three *nawbas*, namely at the time of the early morning prayer and the two evening prayers. Hilāl al-Ṣābiʾ remarks too that it is important that, if the *nawba* ceremony takes place in honour of rulers other than the caliph, it should do so at a suitable distance from the caliphal palace. Although he does not state this overtly, Hilāl al-Ṣābiʾ implies that only the caliph was entitled to have five *nawba*s each day.

So the sounding of the *nawba* a certain number of times a day was jealously guarded as one of the signs of Islamic sovereignty; the more the *nawbas*, the greater the prestige of the ruler. The Seljuq viziers saw to it that the sultans embraced preceding court ceremonials. So they included the *nawba* as one of the marks of their sovereignty and they would also grant such a privilege to certain rulers subordinate to them. But the number of *nawba*s awarded could vary.

There are isolated references to the *nawba* in the Arabic and Persian sources that deal with the Seljuqs, but when such references do occur the chronicler sees no need to give details of what *nawba* means. For example, Nīshāpūrī writes simply that Sultan Muḥammad struck five drum beats (*panj nawbat*) in Hamadan.[23] Sibṭ b. al-Jawzī, however, is more explicit, mentioning under the year 457/1064–5 that amongst the honours Alp Arslān conferred on al-Faḍlūya Shabānkarāʾī, a Kurdish chief who had seized power from the Buyids in Fars,[24] was the prerogative that drums (*al-ṭubūl*) should be beaten outside his door at the times of prayer.[25]

There is evidence in an intriguing but unexplained passage in *Akhbār al-dawla al-saljūqiyya* that the supreme Seljuq sultan used the *nawba* prerogative as a mechanism for disciplining his subsidiary adjunct rulers when they came to visit him, as they were obliged to do, in order to pay him allegiance, or when he came, in threatening mode, to see them. Sultan Maḥmūd, for example, was summoned by his uncle Sultan Sanjar and was instructed by Sanjar's vizier on how he should enter into the presence of the Great Sultan. According to al-Ḥusaynī,[26] the vizier instructed Maḥmūd as follows:

> He should give up the sultanate formalities (*rusūm*) of the red military band fanfare (*al-nawba al-ḥamrāʾ*), he should dismount with two black and white fanfares (*fī nawbatayn sawdāʾ wa-bayḍāʾ*), he should renounce the beating of five fanfares and he should kiss the ground in front of Sanjar when he went in to see him.

So Maḥmūd followed these instructions. It is clear from this narrative that Maḥmūd had arrogated to himself the full five *nawba*s and that Sanjar was most displeased with this. He alone amongst the Seljuq rulers wanted this privilege.

What is unusual in this passage is the mention of coloured *nawba*s – red, black and white. As already mentioned, five *nawba*s were the highest sign of kingship and here Sanjar is denying Maḥmūd the privilege of the red *nawba.* Is this a usage inherited from Turkic steppe tradition? The Russian scholar Kononov mentions that one of the ways of determining orientation amongst the Turks, as well as the Indians and the Chinese, was a 'finely elaborated system wherein the cardinal points are designated by colours'.[27] Unfortunately he does not discuss what he calls this 'colour geo-symbolism' in any detail. However, other specialists, such as Sinor and Pullyblank,[28] have argued that in nomadic Turkic societies orientation labels played an important role in public claims to universal world domination and in this context colours were important. Red was associated with the south, white with the west, black with the north and blue with the east.[29] The supreme ruler was in the north, facing the south (the colour 'red'). And these colours continued to be used long afterwards to denote divisions of territory amongst the steppe peoples. Hence too, such terms as Kara Deniz (Black Sea) for the north and Ak Deniz (White Sea) for the Mediterranean to the west.

To return to the quotation in the chronicle of al-Ḥusaynī, the mention of red, black and white fanfares may well be a reference to this ancient Turkic tribal colour symbolism. Yet it has to be admitted that the Arab world itself had made public use of colours to fulfil certain social and political agendas. De Slane comments that 'even before the promulgation of Islamism, red or scarlet tents indicated that their possessors were princes'.[30] But how would the colours red, black and white be demonstrated publicly in the *nawba*? Would the musicians wear clothes of special colours? Would they have carried flags of different colours? Or would the horses be decorated in special coloured trappings? Perhaps it is too fanciful to suggest that horses of various colours would be used but Figure 2.3 certainly shows horses coloured red and blue.

MEN OF LETTERS AT THE SELJUQ COURT

For the Abbasid caliphs in Baghdad, as Kennedy writes, 'the patronage of scholars was part of the exercise of elite power and the caliphs led the way'.[31] After the fragmentation of the Abbasid realms in the 9th and 10th centuries, the little courts of upstart military barons and provincial governors that sprang up in the eastern Islamic world followed Abbasid models closely. For such rulers too it was an intrinsic sign of the prestige of their court to have an entourage of public intellectuals, even if the rulers themselves were unschooled. The Turkish ruler Maḥmūd of Ghazna collected intellectual elites from the areas he conquered and could boast of scholars of the calibre of the great polymath al-Bīrūnī at his court in Ghazna. The Seljuqs and their advisers wished to carry on that tradition. And indeed al-Ghazālī was the jewel in the crown of the intellectual elite that flocked to the entourage of the Seljuq sultan Malikshāh and his vizier Niẓām al-Mulk.

Figure 2.3 Illustration from Varqa va-Gulshāh by ᶜAyyūqī, probably Konya, c. 648/1250 (Istanbul Sarayı Library) (after Grube)

A key role in medieval Muslim courts was played by poets, some of whom fulfilled the role of *nadīm* (the boon companion of the ruler), whose task it was to amuse and entertain his royal master.[32] Malikshāh, for example, had ᶜUmar Khayyām as one of his *nadīms*.[33] Like the Samanids and Ghaznavids[34] before them, the Seljuq sultans attracted a good number of poets, seeking their patronage and the contents of their purse.[35] A veritable galaxy of poets flocked to the Seljuq court and their presence proved to be beneficial to the sultans who wished their renown to be spread across their realms through poetry declaimed at their courts. As Niẓāmī-yi ᶜArūḍī puts it: 'A king cannot dispense with a good poet, who shall conduce to the immortality of his name . . . his name will endure forever by reason of the poet's verse'.[36]

Particularly noteworthy was the poet Muᶜizzī who wrote panegyrical poems in Persian addressed both to Niẓām al-Mulk and to Malikshāh.[37] In one poem he called Malikshāh 'the Khusraw of the age'.[38] His verses addressed to the sultan could be very grandiose, praising his military victories, or sometimes more lyrical. When speaking of a visit paid by Malikshāh to Iraq in 479/1087, he declares: 'It is the season of the *ᶜīd*, the banks of the Tigris are joyful with the scent of sweet basil and the brightness of the goblets of ruby wine'.[39]

But it was not just Persian poetry that was declaimed at the Seljuq court. Arab literary figures came too. Take the Arab poet al-Ṭughrāʾī (d. 514/1120–1), [40] for example. He was obviously a polymath – he composed at least six works on alchemy and served as the court astrologer, as well as vizier to the Seljuq sultan

Mas^cūd. The masterpiece of al-Ṭughrāʾī, a poetic ode entitled *Lāmiyyat al-ʿajam* (*The verses rhyming in lām of the non-Arabs*), bemoans the corrupt times in which he lived and berates the inferior brand of politicians who now rule in the corridors of power. The work aroused great admiration for its use of rare words and was a deliberate parallel to the more famous *Lāmiyyat al-ʿarab* (*The verses rhyming in lām of the Arabs*) of al-Shanfarā; indeed, all the lines of both works rhyme in the letter *lām*.[41]

Another Arab poet, nicknamed Ḥayṣa Bayṣa (d. 574/1179), because he once uttered the phrase *fī ḥayṣa bayṣa* ('in dire straits'), cut a dashing figure at the Seljuq court, always wearing Bedouin dress and speaking 'the purest Arabic'.[42] He also wrote ornate epistles so convoluted that the recipients could not understand them, as well as an ode dedicated to Sultan Maḥmūd in which every line rhymed in 'd'.[43] Perhaps not surprisingly, his collection of poetry is still unedited. Yet another poet, al-Abīwardī (d. 507/1113), served one of the sons of the great Seljuq vizier, Niẓām al-Mulk. His poetry, both panegyrical and pastoral, found favour until he incurred the displeasure of the Seljuq sultan Muḥammad who had him poisoned.[44] Seljuq poets had to produce celebratory odes on demand. On one occasion a scribe composed verses to celebrate the arrival of the head of a defeated enemy at Sanjar's court.[45]

Not all the poets who frequented the Seljuq court spent their energies on eulogising the sultans and their viziers. Following long-established Abbasid traditions, Ibn al-Qaṭṭān (d. 498/1105)[46] and Ibn al-Ḥabbāriyya (d. 504/1110–11),[47] and no doubt others besides, wielded their pens and tongues in satirical verses. In his obituary of Ibn al-Qaṭṭān, Ibn Khallikān breaks away from his customarily bland laudatory comments to describe the poet in juicy terms as 'excessively licentious and dissolute, full of humour and pleasantry, pertinacious in flattering and in satirizing the proud and haughty'.[48]

Ibn Khallikān goes on to say that Ibn al-Qaṭṭān was dreaded for the 'virulence of his tongue' and that nobody, not even the caliph, was immune from his attacks. He was locked into poetic skirmishes, often acrimonious no doubt, with Ḥayṣa Bayṣa. As for Ibn al-Habbāriyya, one of the poets in the retinue of Niẓām al-Mulk, his verses are described by Ibn Khallikān as satirical, humorous and obscene. He was not popular at court and he had to put up with much malice from the pages and other members of the entourage of Niẓām al-Mulk.

The rivalry between poets at court must have been disagreeably vicious at times. To gain the sultan's favour was thrilling; to fall from grace was terrible. When Anvārī, another Persian poet, was banished in disgrace from the Seljuq court, he wrote strong words condemning the sycophancy of its poets, speaking of poetry as 'male menstruation'.[49]

The bureaucratic class were also distinguished men of letters; two famous examples were al-Bākharzī (d. 467/1075) and ᶜImād al-Dīn al-Iṣfahānī (d. 597/1201). Al-Bākharzī wrote in prose as well as verse; his most famous work was a piece which he wrote to comfort his patron, the Seljuq vizier al-Kundurī, after his castration.[50] Stretching credulity to its limits, he quips: 'He is now increased in virility since the removal of his testicles'. Here, the poet has sacrificed verisimilitude for the sake of a pun.

As for ᶜImād al-Dīn al-Iṣfahānī, he is best known for his historical writings once he had moved to Syria and entered the service of Saladin, but his extremely informative work, the *Kharīdat al-qaṣr*, is a massive anthology of 6th/12th-century poets who wrote in Arabic.[51]

THE SULTAN AT PLAY: HUNTING – THE SPORT OF KINGS

As Daryaee has mentioned recently, the hunt was a favourite pastime of the nobility in Sasanian Persia. He points out that 'the hunt mirrored warfare in the off season, and symbolically signified the battle readiness of the warriors'.[52] He draws attention to similar ideas in Europe amongst the Germanic tribes for whom hunting also became the accepted activity of the warrior aristocracy.[53] So too with the incoming Seljuq chiefs. Malikshāh is singled out in the sources for his love of the hunt; indeed, in his eulogy of Niẓām al-Mulk, Ibn Khallikān writes sweepingly that the vizier had all the power, 'whilst the sultan (Malikshāh) had nothing more to do than show himself on the throne and enjoy the pleasures of the chase'.[54]

In his obituary of Malikshāh, Ibn Khallikān elaborates on this theme, describing the sultan's fondness of the chase as excessive.[55] He is said to have killed ten thousand game beasts in one day.[56] A more realistic figure is given by Nīshāpūrī who reports that one day Malikshāh shot seventy gazelles; in each hunting place he made towers (*manārhā*) of the hooves of gazelles and wild asses. Fear of offending God led him to give a Maghribī gold coin in alms for every animal that he had killed.[57] The sultan would hunt in a party with his vizier and his military commanders and when visitors came to his court he would invite them to attend too. Hunting duties went alongside religious obligations; in one trip in 479/1086–7, as Ibn al-Athīr relates, Malikshāh went hunting in the desert, visited the shrines of ᶜAlī and al-Ḥusayn, and then went into the hinterland, where he hunted many gazelles and other animals. Thereafter, he constructed a beacon of horns between the two shrines at Najaf and Kufa.[58] Indeed, according to Rashīd al-Dīn, 'at Isfahan and in those districts, wherever a hunting-ground is found, he (the sultan) had left traces, and they remained for a long time'.[59]

A later Seljuq sultan, Maḥmūd, had an especially acute obsession with hunting and it apparently led to his neglecting the affairs of the realm. He had four hundred hunting dogs with gold collars and 'he spent all his time on baits and traps'. He was devoted to pigeons, caged birds, sparrowhawks, dogs, cheetahs and all sorts of other hunting animals.[60] Drums also accompanied hunting expeditions. A loud drum role made sure that any birds roosting in the trees flew into the air so that the hunters could shoot them more easily. Usāma b. Munqidh devotes much space to his hunting experience and provides valuable detail on how the chase was organised in Syria, Mesopotamia and Egypt in the 6th/12th century.[61]

FINAL REFLECTIONS

In a discussion of three themes connected with the court of the Seljuq sultans this chapter has shown that these newcomers to Iran, no doubt under the skilful tutelage of their sophisticated Persian viziers, equipped themselves with one of the key status symbols of the Perso-Islamic ruler – an entourage of distinguished literati and scholars. This formal intellectual milieu was something new for the Seljuq tribal chiefs.

Hunting, 'the sport of kings', on the other hand, came easily to these sultans. Here, however, the tough exigencies of survival on the steppes were exchanged for lavish court hunting parties in a style which harked right back to pre-Islamic Iran.

As for the traditional Muslim *nawba* ceremony, in Seljuq times it was given a Turkic gloss, as was shown in the above preliminary analysis of a short enigmatic passage in *Akhbār al-dawla al-saljūqiyya*. In this passage the colour 'red' is used to accompany the privilege of five *nawba*s – the prerogative of the supreme sultan – whilst the right of subordinate rulers to two *nawba*s is called 'black' or 'white'. This system of colours would seem to denote cardinal points. Here the Seljuq Turks have adopted the *nawba* ceremony and tweaked it to fit their own ancient and familiar colour geo-symbolism. Thus the gradual process of assimilation of the nomadic Turks was now fully in train.

NOTES

1. Cf. Ernst Diez, *The Ancient Worlds of Asia* (London, 1961), pp. 78–99; Touraj Daryaee, *Sasanian Persia. The Rise and Fall of an Empire* (London, 2009).
2. Edouard Chavannes, 'Notes additionnelles sur les Tou-Kiue (Turcs) occidentaux', in *Documents sur les Tou-Kiue (Turcs) Occidentaux*, ed. Edouard Chavannes (Paris, 1900).
3. Cf. Hugh Kennedy, *The Court of the Caliphs. The Rise and Fall of Islam's Greatest Dynasty* (London, 2004).
4. Clifford Edmund Bosworth, *The Ghaznavids. Their Empire in Afghanistan and Eastern Iran 994:1040* (Edinburgh, 1963).

5. I will be writing about other themes concerned with the Seljuq court in a later publication.
6. Cf., for example, Elias Norbert, *The Court Society*, trans. Edmund Jephcott (Oxford, 1983).
7. M. G. A. Vale, *The Princely Court: Medieval Courts and Culture in North-west Europe, 1270–1380* (Oxford, 2001).
8. This has been persuasively argued in David Durand-Guédy, *Iranian Elites and Turkish Rulers. A History of Iṣfāhān in the Saljūq Period* (London, 2010).
9. Carole Hillenbrand, 'Some reflections on Seljuq historiography', in *Eastern Approaches to Byzantium*, ed. A. Eastmond (Aldershot, 2000), pp. 73–88.
10. Cf., for example, Pseudo-Ghāzālī (6th/12th century), *Nasīḥat al-mulūk*, trans. by F. R. C. Bagley as *Ghāzālī's Book of Counsel for Kings* (Oxford, 1971); Abū ᶜAlī Ḥasan Ṭūsī Niẓām al-Mulk (d. 485/1092), *Siyar al-mulūk*, ed. Hubert Darke (Tehran, 1347/1928), and trans. by Hubert Darke as *The Book of Government or Rules for Kings* (Henley-on-Thames, 1978); Anon. (6th/12th century), *The Sea of Precious Virtues* (*Baḥr-i favā'id*). *A Medieval Mirror for Princes*, trans. Julie Scott Meisami (Salt Lake City, UT, 1991).
11. Al-Ghāzālī, Abū Ḥāmid Muḥammad, *Faḍā'il al-ānām*, trans. Abdul Qayyum as *Letters of al-Ghazzali* (Lahore, 1976).
12. Anon., *The Letter of Tansar*, trans. M. Boyce (Rome, 1968), pp. 27–8.
13. Ibid. p. 44.
14. The illustration is the frontispiece of the Pseudo-Galen, *Book of Antidotes.* A picture of it can be found in *The Genius of Arab Civilization. Source of Renaissance*, ed. John R. Hayes (Oxford, 1978), p. 115. The contents of the painting are described by Holter who makes no comment on their significance; Kurt Holter, 'Die Galen-Handschrift und die Maqamen des Harîrî der Wiener Nationalbibliothek', *Jahrbuch der Kunsthistorischen Sammlungen in Wien* N.F.XI (1937), pp. 1–15 and Plate 1. Grabar provides a short but useful analysis of the picture in Hayes, *Genius*, p. 114.
15. Ṣadr al-Dīn Abū l-Ḥasan ᶜAlī al-Ḥusaynī (7th/13th century), *Akhbār al-dawla al-saljūqiyya*, ed. M. Iqbal (Lahore, 1933), p. 18.
16. The Turkic empire in the 6th century was organised on a bipartite, east-west principle; cf. Peter B. Golden, 'War and warfare in the pre-Cinggisid western steppes of Eurasia', in *Warfare in Inner Asian History*, ed. Nicola di Cosmo (Leiden, 2002), p. 112.
17. Cf. *EI2*, s.v. 'Marāsim. 3. In Iran', VI, pp. 521–9 (A. K. S. Lambton); s.v. 'Ṭabl-khāna', X, pp. 34–8 (H. G. Farmer).
18. F. Steingass, *Persian-English Dictionary* (London, 1892), p. 1431.
19. Cf. Bertold Spuler, *Iran in früh-islamischer Zeit. Politik, Kultur, Verwaltung und öffentliches Leben zwischen der arabischen und der seldschukischen Eroberung 633 bis 1055* (Wiesbaden, 1952), pp. 349–50.
20. Figure 2.2 illustrates a *nawba* band.
21. Cf. M. Quatremère, *Histoire des Sultans Mamlouks de l'Egypte* I (Paris, 1837), p. 139, note 18.
22. Hilāl al-Ṣābi', *Rusūm dār al-khilāfa*, trans. by Elie A. Salem as *The rules and regulations of the ᶜAbbasid court* (Beirut, 1977), p. 115.
23. Ẓāhir al-Dīn Nīshāpūrī (d. mid-6th/12th century), *Saljūqnāma*, ed. A. H. Morton (Chippenham, 2004), p. 41.
24. Clifford Edmund Bosworth, *The New Islamic Dynasties* (Edinburgh, 1996), p. 154.
25. Abū l-Muẓaffar Yūsuf b. Kizoghlu Sibṭ b. al-Jawzī (d. 654/1257), *Mir'āt al-zamān fī ta'rīkh al-aᶜyān*, ed. Ali Sevim (Ankara, 1968), p. 121.

26. Al-Ḥusaynī, *Akhbār al-dawla al-saljūqiyya*, p. 89.
27. A. N. Kononov, 'Terminology of the definition of cardinal points at [sic] the Turkic peoples', *Acta Orientalia Academiae Scientiarum Hungaricae* 31 (1977), pp. 61–2.
28. Denis Sinor, 'Some components of the civilization of the Turks', in *Altaistic Studies*, eds G. Jarring and S. Rosén (Stockholm, 1985), p. 147; Edwin G. Pullyblank, 'The Hsiung-nu', in *History of the Turkic Peoples in the pre-Islamic Period*, ed. Hans Robert Roemer (Berlin, 2000), pp. 52–75.
29. Edwin G. Pulleyblank, 'The nomads in China and Central Asia in the post-Han period', in Roemer (ed.), *History*, p. 92.
30. Aḥmad b. Muḥammad Ibn Khallikān (d. 681/1282), *Wafayāt al-aᶜyān wa anbāʾ ibnāʾ al-zamān*, trans. by Baron MacGuckin de Slane as *Kitāb Wafayāt al-Aᶜyān: Ibn Khallikān's Biographical Dictionary* (Paris, 1843–71), I, p. 641, note 2.
31. Hugh Kennedy, *The Court of the Caliphs* (London, 2004), p. 260.
32. Cf. Julie Scott Meisami, *Medieval Court Poetry* (Princeton, NJ, 1987), pp. 3–40.
33. G. E. Tetley, *The Ghaznavid and Seljuk Turks. Poetry as a Source for Iranian History* (London, 2009), p. 13.
34. Maḥmūd of Ghazna was said to have had four hundred poets in regular attendance at his court; Bosworth, *Ghaznavids*, p. 131.
35. Cf. ᶜAlī Jawād al-Ṭāhir, *Al-shiᶜr al-ᶜarabī fī l-ᶜIrāq wa balad al-ᶜajam fī l-ᶜaṣr al-saljūqī* (Baghdad, 1958); R. A. Nicholson, *A Literary History of the Arabs* (Cambridge, 1969), pp. 326, 329–36; Meisami, *Medieval Persian Court Poetry*; Tetley, *Ghaznavid and Seljuk Turks*.
36. Aḥmad b. ᶜUmar Niẓāmī-yi ᶜArūḍī (2nd half of 6th/12th century), *Chahār Maqāla*, trans. by E. G. Browne as *The Four Discourses* (Cambridge, 1921), p. 45.
37. Tetley, *Ghaznavid and Seljuk Turks*, ch. 4.
38. Ibid. p. 96.
39. Ibid. p. 121.
40. Muʾayyid al-Dīn al-Ṭughrāʾī (d. 514/1120–1), *Dīwān*, ed. ᶜAlī Jawād al-Ṭāhir and Yaḥyā al-Jubūrī (Baghdad, 1976).
41. Al-Fatḥ b. ᶜAlī al-Bundārī (d. 7th/13th century), *Zubdat al-nuṣra wa-nukhbat al-ᶜuṣra*, in *Recueil de textes relatifs à l'histoire des Seldjoucides*, ed. M. T. Houtsma (Leiden, 1889), pp. 110, 116, 132–3; cf. also ᶜAlī Jawād al-Ṭāhir, *Lāmiyyat al-Ṭughrāʾī* (Baghdad, 1962).
42. Ibn Khallikān, *Wafayāt*, trans. de Slane, I, p. 559; III, pp. 337, 584–6; IV, pp. 119–21; ᶜImād al-Dīn al-Iṣfahānī, al-Kātib (d. 597/1200), *Kharīdat al-qaṣr*, ed. M. B. al-Atharī (Baghdad, 1980), pp. 202–366.
43. Ibn Khallikān, *Wafayāt*, trans. de Slane, III, p. 337.
44. Ibid. III, pp. 144–8.
45. Rashīd al-Dīn, *Jāmiᶜ al-tawārīkh*, partial ed. by A. Ateş as *Cami' al-tavarih (Metin), II. Cild, 5. Cuz, Selçuklar tarihi* (Ankara, 1960); trans. by K. A. Luther as *The History of the Seljūq Turks from the Jāmi' al-tawārīkh. An Ilkhanid Adaptation of the Saljūq-nāma of Ẓahīr al-Din Nīshāpurī* (London, 2001), p. 86.
46. Ibn Khallikān, *Wafayāt*, trans. de Slane, III, pp. 583–9.
47. Al-Bundārī, *Zubdat*, pp. 64–5, 103–5; Sibṭ b. al-Jawzī, *Mirʾāt*, VIII/I, pp. 58–62; Ibn Khallikān, *Wafayāt*, trans. de Slane, III, pp. 150–3.
48. Ibn Khallikān, *Wafayāt*, trans. de Slane, III, p. 583.
49. Bernard Lewis, *Music of a distant drum* (Princeton, NJ, 2001), p. 16.
50. Ibn Khallikān, *Wafayāt*, trans. de Slane, III, p. 294.

51. ʿImād al-Dīn al-Iṣfahānī, *Kharīdat al-qaṣr*, ed. M. B. al-Atharī (Baghdad, 1980); this volume of the anthology deals with the poets of Iraq.
52. Daryaee, *Sasanian Persia*, pp. 51–2.
53. For a fascinating and detailed account of hunting in 7th/13th-century North Africa, cf. *Al-Mansur's Book on Hunting*, trans. Sir Terence Clark and Muawiya Derhalli (Warminster, 2001).
54. Ibn Khallikan, *Wafayāt*, trans. de Slane, I, p. 413.
55. Ibid. III, p. 441.
56. Ibid. III, p. 441.
57. Nīshāpūrī, *Saljūqnāma*, p. 30.
58. ʿIzz al-Dīn Abū l-Ḥasan ʿAlī Ibn al-Athīr, *Al-Kāmil fī l- taʾrīkh*, ed. C. J. Tornberg (Leiden and Uppsala, 1851–76), partial trans. by D. S. Richards as *The Annals of the Seljuk Turks. Selections from al-Kāmil fi'l-Ta'rīkh of ʿIzz al-Dīn Ibn al-Athīr* (London, 2002), p. 228; cf. also Abū l-Faraj ʿAbd al-Raḥmān b. ʿAlī Ibn al-Jawzī, *al-Muntaẓam fī tārīkh al-mulūk wa-l-umam* (Hyderabad, 1357–8/1938–40), IX, pp. 35, 70; Sibṭ b. al-Jawzī, *Mirʾāt*, p. 243.
59. Rashīd al-Dīn, *Jāmiʿ*, trans. Luther, p. 61.
60. Ibid. p. 99.
61. Usāma b. Munqidh (d. 584/1188), *Kitāb al-iʿtibār*, trans. by Philip. K. Hitti as *Memoirs of an Arab-Syrian Gentleman* (Beirut reprint, 1964), pp. 222–54.

CHAPTER

3

'SOVEREIGN AND PIOUS': THE RELIGIOUS LIFE OF THE GREAT SELJUQ SULTANS

*D. G. Tor**

The Seljuqs were, for much of history, remarkably successful in propagating the view of themselves as Sunni heroes: generous supporters of Sunni religious scholarship, staunch champions of the Abbasid caliphs, and indefatigable defenders of Islam against heresy, heretics and Infidels. Their success in projecting this image is reflected in the medieval historiography; the *Tārīkh-i guzīda*, for instance, after enumerating the flaws of every Muslim dynasty from the Umayyads through the Khwarazmshahs, asseverates: 'But the Seljuqs were free of these defects: they were Sunni, and of pure religion and good beliefs . . .'[1]

Similarly fulsome praise of the Seljuqs as the saviours and renewers of Sunni Islam can be found in, for instance, the *Saljūqnāma*, which states:

> It is well known that in the Islamic community after the *Ṣaḥāba* and the *Rāshidūn* caliphs . . . there were no kings who were greater, or more worthy of ruling over humanity, than the kings of the House of Seljuq . . . How many good [works] were manifested in the days of their dynasty: the revival of the signs of religion, the raising high of the articles of faith of the Muslims; the building and creating of mosques, madrasas, *ribāṭ*s, bridges and stipends . . . and [the bestowal of] *awqāf* upon the *ʿulamāʾ*, sayyids, ascetics and holy people [which] had never been in any period [before] . . .[2]

* The author gratefully acknowledges the contributions of Christian Lange and Jürgen Paul, who read and commented upon this article; and of the German-Israeli Foundation for Scientific Research (GIF); the Israel Science Foundation (ISF); and the National Endowment for the Humanities (NEH), which generously funded this research.

Indeed, even the very origins of the dynasty are presented in various sources as steeped in Islamic piety; from the legend that Duqāq, the Infidel father of Saljūq, the dynasty's eponymous founder, refused to raid the lands of Islam;[3] to the tradition that Saljūq himself was supposedly a holy warrior near Jand who relieved the Muslims of having to pay tribute to pagan Turks;[4] to the assertion that Saljūq's son Mīkāʾīl is said to have 'died a martyr in the path of Allah' while raiding some pagan Turks.[5]

Moreover, there is evidence in the sources that this pious Islamic image was one that the Seljuq sultans themselves actively sought to cultivate. In the very first letter the Seljuqs wrote to the caliph, they presented themselves as devout Muslims: 'We, your slaves of the House of Seljuq, are a band continually obedient, friends of the [Abbasid] dynasty and holy Prophetic presence. We are perpetually striving in *ghazw* and *jihād*, and evincing assiduity in pilgrimage to the Kaᶜba.'[6]

Until fairly recently, the historical accuracy of this pious image was never doubted; the traditional scholarly appraisal of most important facets of religious life in the Seljuq period closely followed the official Seljuq presentation of themselves as the saviours of the caliphate, defenders and patrons of Sunni religious learning and the religious clerics (*ᶜulamāʾ*), and enemies of all *bidᶜa* (religiously reprehensible innovation), especially Ismaᶜili Shiᶜism.[7]

Cracks in the scholarly consensus first appeared with George Makdisi's revisionist work in the 1970s, which cast doubt on some aspects of the Seljuq claim to religious revitalisation.[8] Several decades passed, however, before other scholars took up the challenge and began to subject the Seljuqs' model Sunni religious reputation to renewed scrutiny and criticism, in areas ranging from the seriousness of the Seljuq effort to combat the Ismaᶜili heresy,[9] to the relations between the Seljuqs and the religious classes,[10] and relations between the Seljuqs and the caliphs.[11]

As a result of this welcome revisionist effort, serious doubt has arisen regarding the religious nature of Seljuq rule. If, as this recent scholarship has shown, the Seljuqs were a greater scourge of the Abbasid caliphs than were the Buyids; behaved in a Machiavellian fashion toward the religious classes; prosecuted only a desultory and half-hearted war against the Ismaᶜilis; and were not responsible for the much-vaunted Sunni Revival, why do so many medieval Islamic sources – including ones written after the fall of the Seljuqs – nevertheless perpetuate the Sunni aura of the Seljuq sultans? Even a good propaganda campaign coupled with political muscle cannot account for the enthusiastically positive, reverent and virtually unanimous religious verdict passed upon the Seljuqs by posterity.

The aim of this chapter is to try to solve this puzzle, at least in part, by examining one somewhat neglected but key aspect of the Seljuqs' religious life and the way in which they were perceived by the Muslim public: the personal piety, beliefs and practices of the sultans themselves, and the extent to which the sultans' religious outlook influenced their actions and policies. Such an examination reveals that the lives of the Great Seljuq sultans evince a significant degree of personal religiosity, particularly among the rulers through the time of Sanjar, manifested in areas ranging from personal devotional practices and expressed beliefs, through the veneration of holy men and shrines and the incorporation of religious figures into the state, to the active role of personal belief in the formulating of public policy.

THE PERSONAL BELIEFS AND PRACTICES OF THE SULTANS

Regarding the first issue – the religious sensibilities and practices of the sultans – the sources are strewn with anecdotes that reveal the fundamentally devout outlook of many of the Seljuq sultans. Obviously, our knowledge relies mainly upon literary descriptions, raising the question of whether, or to what degree, these sources are tendentious. One point that would seem to validate the authenticity of the characterisations of particular sultans is that not all sultans were invariably described as devout; that is, this was by no means an automatic hagiographic appellation or a topos.

Also, it is significant that the piety portrayed in the sources is not uniform, but varied in its manifestations – another indication that the depictions of the sultans' religiosity are most likely genuine rather than stock. Interestingly, the earlier sultans seem, by and large, to have been more pious than the later ones, particularly the shadowy post-Sanjar epigones; it is unclear whether this reflects reality or is merely the outcome of the circumscribed field of action of these later sultans and, perhaps, a lack of information on the part of the medieval historians.

Looking in chronological order, we see that the descriptions of Ṭughril Beg, while varying in some fundamental points, all seem to agree on his assiduity in prayers and supererogatory fasting. Several accounts describe him as follows:

> He was valiant, mild, noble; diligent in good deeds, Friday prayer, and fasting on Mondays and Thursdays; and perfuming himself with precious morals . . . He was great in pious benefactions, avid for building mosques; and he used to say: 'I should be ashamed before God . . . if I were to build a house and not build next to it a mosque.'[12]

Elements, at least, of this paean are given credibility by more balanced appraisals such as the following, in which the description of Ṭughril's personal religious qualities appears to be quite impartial: 'He used . . . to be heedful of his prayers, to fast on Mondays and Thursdays, and he wore [plain] white garments; but he was [also] tyrannical, unjust, and merciless.'[13]

The claim about Ṭughril's high regard for prayer is borne out in some unlikely places; one 6th/12th-century hagiography of a Sufi master, for instance, relates an anecdote in which Sultan Ṭughril, after reprimanding an official, Abū Manṣūr Variqānī, for his religiously motivated absenteeism, relents and accepts Variqānī's shirking of his duties, since this neglect is occasioned by the latter's zealousness in prayer and Qur'ān recitation.[14]

Furthermore, Ṭughril is described as having undergone mystical experiences. In one source, Ṭughril recounts a vision he experienced at the beginning of his career in Khurasan, in which he was lifted up in a fragrant mist to Heaven, and offered a boon. Upon requesting a long life, the sultan was informed that he would live for seventy years.[15]

The second sultan, Alp Arslān, is similarly singled out for his strong religious beliefs and devout practices:

> He was of good life; stern, devout, just, and righteous . . . and of many *ghāzī* raids and *jihād*. He would have slaughtered and cooked every day 50 heads of sheep, and the *fuqarā'* fed.[16]

In fact, one of Alp Arslān's closest associates, Niẓām al-Mulk, has left a powerful description of the strong religious convictions of this sultan, which appear to have bordered on the fanatical:

> The Martyr Sultan, may God have mercy on him, was so firm and wholehearted in his *madhhab* that many a time upon his tongue there proceeded [the words]: 'Alas! If only my vizier were not a Shāfiᶜite!' He was possessed of great authority and dignity; and I – because he was in his *madhhab* so earnest and such a believer, and reprobated the Shāfiᶜite *madhhab* – I lived in continual fear of him.[17]

Later in Niẓām al-Mulk's narrative, when he learns that the ambassador of the Khān of Samarqand had falsely accused him, Niẓām al-Mulk, of being a Shīᶜite, Niẓām al-Mulk informs the reader:

> I became greatly afflicted at heart from terror of the sultan. I said [to myself]: 'He holds the Shāfiᶜite *madhhab* shameful and at every opportunity reproaches me [about it]. If he should in any fashion hear that the Chigils[18] describe me as *Rāfiḍī*, and that this [description] came before the Khān of Samarqand, he will not grant me protection of my life.'

Accordingly, Niẓām al-Mulk, by his own account, spent thirty-thousand dinars in hush money in order to ensure 'that this talk never reached the ear of the sultan'.[19]

This account is particularly valuable because Niẓām al-Mulk relates it not in order to prove anything about Alp Arslān and his religiosity, but, rather, as an illustration of the tendency of ambassadors to find fault with their hosts, and the consequent necessity for a king and his men to be on their best behaviour when such emissaries come to visit. The light it sheds on Alp Arslān's apparently genuine religious zeal – for his religious partisanship in this context would not redound to his credit – is incidental to Niẓām al-Mulk's purpose, and is therefore less likely to have been manufactured for didactic purposes.[20]

In a similar vein, Niẓām al-Mulk, writing in the time of Malikshāh, informs us that the previous two sultans (thus implicitly contrasting their behaviour with that of his own employer) took great care, both to properly humiliate (from an Islamic point of view) Zoroastrians, Christians and Shiᶜites,[21] as well as to exclude from power and public service anyone not a Ḥanafite or Shāfiᶜite. While one might be inclined to dismiss this as mere pandering aimed at scoring cheap popularity, rather than a conviction-based policy, the description of Alp Arslān's vehement reaction to a violation of that policy belies this assumption.

According to Niẓām al-Mulk, when Alp Arslān learned that one of his nobles, Ardam, had hired a certain Shīᶜite as his personal secretary, he had the Shīᶜite beaten until he was half dead, and severely reprimanded the noble publicly before the whole royal entourage, explaining that the Turks had been able to conquer Transoxiana and Khurasan only because of their pure religious beliefs.[22] Alp Arslān was supposedly so incensed by Ardam's gaffe that he not only refused to speak with him for an entire month, but refused even to look at his erring magnate until the other nobles intervened on his behalf.[23]

Additionally, it is reported of Alp Arslān that he did not impose non-canonical taxes, but contented himself with the religiously sanctioned *kharāj*, which he collected semi-annually in order to make payment less onerous for the populace. He is also said to have had read aloud to him frequently the regulations of Islamic law, in order to guide and improve his own conduct. So meticulous was he in preventing his soldiery from appropriating the property of his subjects, that he is said once to have had gibbeted one of his own personal *mamlūk* (military slave) guards upon learning that the man had snatched a waist-wrapper from one of the farmers.[24]

Although this last action strikes one as a topos, it should not therefore be dismissed out of hand: first, because many of the motifs which became topoi were not only originally 'securely anchored to real historical referents',[25] but also continued to be so, because such topoi referred either to behaviour which, though reprobated, is extremely common among mankind generally (i.e. fornication, drinking or any other sin); or, conversely, to behaviour considered so paradigmatic that many people aspiring to holiness actually consciously and deliberately emulated the topological action (e.g. use of the *takbīr* (the phrase *Allāhu akbar*) by, for instance, modern Islamist airplane hijackers, consciously emulating the pious early Muslims).

Second, what is important for our present purposes – evaluating the piety or lack thereof of specific sultans – is not whether or not a sultan actually committed one specific act or another, but the fact that the historical memory of him is of a pious or impious individual, the kind of person who *would do* something of that sort. Then the question becomes one of the veracity of the overall historical characterisation, rather than of a particular assertion. This methodological point holds true for all of the other topoi-like actions that will be discussed throughout this article.

In one of the spheres most prominently featured in the religious praise of the Seljuqs – 'the establishment of pious foundations and stipends, and consideration of the religious clerics (*ᶜulamāᵓ*), pious people (*ṣulaḥā*), judges, descendants of the Prophet, ascetics, holy men (*ᶜibād*), and the religious and pious ones (*akhyār ū abrār*)'[26] – Alp Arslān scores highly. He is said to have distributed fourteen or fifteen thousand dinars in alms every Ramadan, 'and kept in his *dīwān* the names of a great number of religious mendicants throughout all his realms, upon whom [he bestowed] abundantly [stipends] and blessings'.[27] Regarding Alp Arslān's charitable activities, another eulogy asseverates that he 'was of merciful heart; a friend of the *fuqarāᵓ*; frequent in prayer for the continuation of the blessings Allah had bestowed upon him. One day in Marv he passed by the poor ordure-workers. He wept, and asked of God that from His bounty he make him free from want.'[28]

Alp Arslān was probably also the most *ghāzī* of the sultans; as one source epitomises his reign: 'He occupied himself with *ghazwa*s in Turkestan and Rum . . . and entered into the service of the caliph from pure and sincere faith.'[29] While his defeat of the Byzantines at Manzikert is surely the most renowned of his *jihād*s,[30] he was extremely active in the Caucasus as well,[31] and on some of these raids he is reported to have built mosques and sent religious instructors for the newly Islamised areas.[32]

The sultan's fundamental religious outlook on life, however, is best revealed in his reported reactions to difficult situations. For instance, several years prior to the battle of Manzikert, while Alp Arslān was leading a campaign into Georgia, the sultan would not interrupt his prayers even when the Georgians attacked the Muslims and the latter fled; rather, he continued his orisons with due deliberation, and only after their conclusion went out to rally his troops and repel the Christian forces.[33] That is, not even a political and military emergency was allowed to interrupt his devotions.

In a similarly pious vein was the sultan's reaction to being fatally stabbed, in Rabīᶜ I 465/November 1072. While lying on his deathbed, Alp Arslān is recorded as having voiced the following (admittedly topological-sounding) musings:

> There was no goal I turned towards, and no enemy I pursued, but that I called upon God for help; but yesterday I ascended a hill and the earth shook beneath me from the greatness of the army, and I said to myself: 'I am king of the world and no one can stand against me.' So His decree forsook me, and I ask Allah's aid and forgiveness for this idea.[34]

Alp Arslān was succeeded by his son Malikshāh, who appears to have followed in his father's footsteps, both in actions and outlook. He, like his father, is noted as having marked Ramadan by bestowing alms upon religious mendicants and other religious practitioners, as well as by freeing prisoners.[35] His pious benefactions included building water cisterns on the road to Mecca, as well as houses (presumably for shelter) in the desert on the Ḥajj route; removing the customs and protection fees from the Ḥajj by giving *ᶜiqṭāʾ*s (revenue-producing land grants) and stipends, both to the *Amīr al-Ḥaramayn* and the Arab desert tribes, from his own personal fortune;[36] establishing gardens and charitable foundations;[37] building *ribāṭ*s;[38] and commencing construction of the third of the great Friday mosques of Eastern Baghdad.[39]

While the above-named acts could be construed as public relations ploys, it is much harder to explain away in this fashion Malikshāh's personal reactions to the challenges he faced. On one occasion, two men came before Malikshāh to ask redress for having been unjustly mulcted of money by one of his emirs. Malikshāh thereupon dismounted from his horse, and ordered the men to drag him by the sleeves before Niẓām al-Mulk. Upon the astonished vizier's inquiring as to the meaning of this spectacle, the sultan replied:

> What will be my condition tomorrow before God, if I am called to account for the rights of the Muslims? I have invested you with your power in order to spare me this kind of situation. If the subjects are harmed, you are accountable; have a care for me and for yourself.[40]

Nowhere is Malikshāh's religious sensibility revealed so clearly, and with so little possible alternative ulterior motivation, as in his scruples over his own inveterate hunting. Obviously anguished about his own behaviour, yet equally unable to modify it, he kept inventing means of penance to expiate his guilt for killing God's creatures for mere sport. After one hunting spree, in which he and his *mamlūks* reportedly bagged 10,000 animals, Malikshāh, overwhelmed by remorse, ordered that 10,000 dinars be distributed in charity, stating: 'I fear before Allah . . . on account of the spilling of the blood of his creatures for amusement'.[41] However, he apparently could not resist this pastime, and therefore invented various methods of trying to assuage his own racked conscience, ranging from giving a Maghribī dinar to the poor for every piece of game he shot, to building towers or minarets throughout the Middle East from the horns of the gazelles and onagers that had fallen victim to his bow.[42]

Among the fourth generation of Seljuq rulers, not all of Malikshāh's sons inherited his religious sensibility – only two, in fact, both from the same mother: Sultans Muḥammad Ṭapar and Sanjar. The first of these two, Muḥammad Ṭapar, is said to have been of godly life,

> endowed with religion and piety; right-thinking, true to his word, of sound faith. In the strengthening of religion and suppressing of the accursed heretics he was diligent and a *mujāhid*. In guarding the territory of Islam he showed a pure hand, and with the sickle of chastisement he mowed the thorn of Unbelief and Innovation.[43]

He is also, most unusually, lauded for his chastity, as well as for being true to his word.[44] Descriptions of him include encomia such as: 'He was a God-fearing, religious, beneficent man in the extreme; and chaste of soul, abstemious, continent, pure';[45] 'a just, God-fearing friend of the religious cleric';[46] and 'He was of right opinion, sound belief, and truthful promise; diligent and a *mujāhid* in the strengthening of religion and [achieving] victory over and smiting the accursed heretics'.[47] Other sources describe him as 'pious to a great extreme [*be ghāyat-i buzurg dīndār*]',[48] and 'a king who was characterized by justice and equity, and renowned for religion and piety', adding moreover that 'He made a great effort in repelling the heretics who at that time had become very strong; he [also] pursued the aim of raiding India, battled with the Infidels and was victorious'.[49] Virtually all the sources note that Muḥammad abolished the non-canonical taxes, and loathed heretics.[50]

Muḥammad's full brother Sanjar is also cited for pious practices – but for very different ones. In Sanjar's case, it was his own cultivation of religious knowledge, close ties with the *ᶜulamāᵓ*, ascetics and hermits,[51] as well as his personal ascetic practices – for example, simplicity in dress – which caught the attention of historians.[52] Rashīd al-Dīn describes him as 'God-fearing, modest, a munificent benefactor';[53] while Jūzjānī states that during Sanjar's reign, 'affairs were managed upon the straight path of the Sunna and good policy, and the high road of justice; the commands of the Sharīʿa of Muḥammad, and the ordinances of the religion of Islam, in accordance with divine commands and prohibitions, all acquired freshness'.[54] Similarly, we are told that in his time, 'Khurasan was . . . the source of religious sciences and the fountain of virtues, and the mine of knowledge and wisdom; and he manifested the utmost veneration and assistance toward the *ʿulamāʾ* and the wise men of religion'.[55]

One of the local histories of Herat writes of Sanjar's accession to rule of the city as a deliverance, stating that '[he] commanded that the people of these lands be freed from the wickedness of the accursed Ḥabashī b. Altūtiyāq [*sic*][56] and his reprobated companions, and made Islam victorious'. The source alleges that the said Ḥabashī was a Bāṭinī, and that Sanjar accordingly saved orthodox Islam in the area, in this case if not in others, by defeating Ḥabashī's armies and killing their heretical leader.[57]

Once again, these descriptions are credible because of the fact that not all the sultans are indiscriminately portrayed as pious individuals; and also because the sources balance their praise with free criticism – for instance, Muḥammad is accused of having had a tendency toward hoarding money,[58] and Sanjar is described as having engaged in the serial purchase of male sex slaves.[59] Equally important, the descriptions of piety are clearly individual, varying from one sultan to the next, rather than fitting some preconceived formula – Muḥammad Ṭapar, for instance, is never credited with any ascetic practices or cultivation of religious knowledge, while Sanjar is never stated to have engaged in devotional practices such as Ṭughril Beg's supererogatory fasting or Malikshāh's charitable penances.

Intriguingly, the level of personal piety of the Seljuq sultans definitely appears to have tapered off by the fifth generation; very few of them – all sons of Muḥammad Ṭapar - are described as pious in the sources, however positive the descriptions are in other respects; for example, Sultan Maḥmūd b. Muḥammad Ṭapar is said to have been gentle-natured and intelligent, but he seemed to have been far more interested in his hundreds of hunting dogs than in religion, and is said to have suffered from sexually transmitted diseases as a result of unbridled promiscuity.[60]

Maḥmūd's brother Ṭughril, similarly, while credited with justice, generosity, modesty and valour, is not described as having been particularly religious.[61] Their brother Sultan Sulaymān b. Muḥammad is actually depicted as downright impious; he was supposedly killed because of his violation of moral and religious norms, including, for instance, drinking during the day during Ramadan.[62] In fact, the only sultan of this generation to whom the sources attribute any positive religious interest is Sultan Masʿūd b. Muḥammad, who is described as 'a friend of the *ᶜālim* and a giver to the religious poor [*darvīsh*], and bearing love toward the insane and the lunatic'.[63] Ṣibt Ibn al-Jawzī states that he heard 'the Shaykhs of Baghdad' relating from their fathers and grandfathers that Sultan Masᶜūd 'loved to visit the *ᶜulamāʾ* and the righteous, and to seek [knowledge from] the Shaykhs'.[64]

The next generation was similarly mixed. Sultan Malikshāh b. Maḥmūd b. Muḥammad, although he is said to have been generous and good-natured, is also portrayed as having been 'addicted to drink and hunting and carnal relations'. He was eventually deposed because he was said to have spent all his time in bibulous and frivolous pursuits in the company of ignoble companions.[65] His brother Sultan Muḥammad b. Maḥmūd b Muḥammad, in contrast, is stated to have been 'of sound faith, confirmed merit, pious [*dīndār*], and a lover and honourer of the *ᶜulamāʾ*'.[66]

Of the penultimate generation of Seljuq sultans, the very brief reign of Sulaymān or Sulaymānshāh b. Muḥammad b. Malikshāh was forcibly ended after the magnates tired of his unremitting inebriation;[67] on the other hand, this same drunkard's brother, Arslān or Arslānshāh b. Ṭughril b. Muḥammad b. Malikshāh, while not singled out in the sources for his piety,[68] is however noted to have been an ardent *jihād* fighter, against both Christian Infidels and Ismaᶜili heretics.[69]

His son, Ṭughril b. Arslān, was the last of the Great Seljuq sultans. The contemporaneous author Nīshāpūrī writes of Ṭughril's 'perfect judgment; complete knowledge; comprehensive clemency; diffusing of justice; vigilance; caution; personal chastity; and love of the *ᶜulamāʾ*', among various other qualities such as good calligraphy and skilled horsemanship.[70] While one might be tempted to dismiss this eulogium as somewhat suspect, since it was penned during Ṭughril's actual reign, it is harder to discount the similar evaluation of Nīshāpūrī's continuator, quoted by Rashīd al-Dīn as one Abū Ḥāmid Muḥammad b. Ibrāhīm, who composed his addendum more than eight years after the final downfall of both Ṭughril b. Arslān and the Seljuq dynasty itself. Despite the limited scope and opportunity Ṭughril would have had for demonstrating any personal piety he may have possessed, Abū Ḥāmid appraises him and the quality of his rule as follows:

> Ṭughril was a king [who ruled] with justice and good policy . . . In manliness he was the Rustam of the age, and in justice, liberality, and eloquence the nonpareil of the time; a friend of the *ᶜālim* and protector of the *darvīsh* without limit – but he had one defect: that he came in the rear guard [i.e. at the end of the dynasty].[71]

RELATIONSHIPS BETWEEN THE SELJUQS AND SUNNI MEN OF RELIGION, SAINTS AND SHRINES

Another notable component of the religiosity of several of the Seljuq sultans was their reverence for, and association with, Sunni religious figures and shrines. Charismatic holy men and other Sunni religious figures constituted a prominent feature of public life generally in the Seljuq era, and the Seljuq sultans, by and large, evinced the same desire to obtain the blessing of holy men – living and dead – as did the general populace.[72]

One form this association with holy men assumed was that of pilgrimage.[73] In one such instance, when Ṭughril Beg came to Hamadan in the beginning of his reign he paid a personal visit to three Sufi masters. When enjoined by one of them to behave in accordance with God's commands, Ṭughril Beg wept and vowed to do so. The Sufi master then gave the sultan a piece of a broken jug from which he had made the ritual ablutions for years, and Ṭughril reportedly added it to 'the other amulets he had', and would take this talisman with him into battle.[74]

Similarly, Ṭughril and Chaghri Beg together made a pilgrimage to the great Sufi mystic Abū Saᶜīd Abī l-Khayr Mayhanī, during the course of which they treated the shaykh with the utmost reverence. According to the hagiography written by one of this Sufi saint's descendants, Abū Saᶜīd bestowed his stamp of approval upon these two Seljuq sultans, using his mystical powers to confer dominion upon each of them over, respectively, Iraq and Western Iran, and Khurasan.[75]

The sultan most renowned for his cultivation of holy men, however, was undoubtedly Sultan Sanjar; in fact, he is described (no doubt with some exaggeration) as 'using to converse and keep company entirely with hermits, ascetics, and holy men'.[76] One such figure with whom Sanjar surely did consort was the greatest holy man of his day, Shaykh Aḥmad-i Jām (known as the *Zhanda Pīl*), whose spiritual patronage and protection the sultan enjoyed. The account we have of this relationship is particularly valuable, since it was written by an eyewitness, Khwāja Sadīd al-Dīn Muḥammad Ghaznavī, one of the Shaykh's own disciples, during Sanjar's lifetime. Not only did Sanjar make pilgrimages to the saint,[77] but, more importantly, Ghaznavī relates several stories illustrating the mutuality of the relationship: that is, not only the veneration Sanjar felt for the saint, but also the positive light in which both the saint and his disciple viewed Sanjar, thus indicating that he met their religious standards.

Divine religious approval (and, by extension, the Sufi's approval) of Sanjar is perhaps expressed most clearly in an episode said to have occurred at the time of Malikshāh's death. Aḥmad-i Jām, while praying for Sultan Barkyāruq, was supposedly visited by an angel, who ordered him to pray for Sanjar instead

(Barkyāruq is slighted here for having been too tolerant of the Ismaᶜilis). The angel states: 'Pray for [Sanjar], for repose will come to the Muslims from him; and these others will die, but he shall remain in place'.[78]

Several anecdotes emphasise the divine protection accorded to Sanjar, and the Shaykh's divinely assigned duty to protect Sanjar with his supernatural powers. In one such story, two mysterious beings (presumably angels) appeared one day before Shaykh Aḥmad-i Jām and revealed to him that one of Sanjar's emirs was plotting to murder the sultan. They charged the saint with protecting Sanjar, in the following terms: 'O Aḥmad, know that the King of the Age, Sanjar b. Malikshāh, has been entrusted to you. You must remain informed of his doings and his circumstances, and you must say prayers for him; we have spoken to you.'[79]

This theme of Aḥmad-i Jām's concern for Sanjar, and his divine mission to protect the sultan, appears in several other incidents as well. In one, the Shaykh encourages Sanjar and bestows upon him victory in battle.[80] In another episode, the Shaykh holds a disputation with the Ismaᶜilis in front of Sanjar, and when Sanjar fears to kill the heretics as instructed, the Shaykh reprimands him in the following terms:

> What a strange thing this is, seeing that you clearly know that you have been entrusted to me; and by the grace of God, may He be exalted, and by His leave, may His power be strengthened, I have been and am guarding you, and in many times in various situations you have witnessed this . . . As long as I am alive, you should fear no one and should not be afraid.[81]

It is immaterial here whether or not these stories are complete fictions. What is of the essence for our purposes (as opposed to the hagiographer's, which were quite different, obviously) is that Aḥmad-i Jām's closest associates – and, presumably, the Shaykh himself – viewed themselves as being in a divinely ordained partnership with Sanjar; he had their approbation, and they regarded themselves as closely concerned in the preservation of his rule. Note that this is a hagiography of the saint, not of the sultan – and is therefore much more valuable, because its attestation to Sanjar's passing religious muster is incidental to the purpose of the author.[82]

This approval is also seen in Sanjar's correspondence and personal contact with Aḥmad-i Jām – apparently authentic – which shows him seeking religious knowledge and guidance from the Shaykh.[83] Moreover, even before this close association with Aḥmad-i Jām, Sanjar also corresponded, and subsequently consorted, with the other great figure of his day, al-Ghazālī, whom Sanjar treated with great honour once he had met him, and whose preaching whilst at Sanjar's court apparently has also been preserved.[84]

The personal reverence of the Seljuq sultans toward holy men also extended to dead saints, as demonstrated by their numerous pilgrimages to the shrines of holy men. Malikshāh in 479/1087, upon coming to Baghdad, is reported to have made pilgrimages in the company of Niẓām al-Mulk to the shrine of Mūsā b. Jaᶜfar, Aḥmad b. Ḥanbal, Abū Ḥanīfa, al-Ḥusayn, ᶜAlī and others.[85]

Interestingly, the graves of al-Ḥusayn, ᶜAlī and Mūsā al-Kāẓim were not the only ᶜAlid tombs that Malikshāh and Niẓām al-Mulk visited. While in Ṭūs once, the pair also betook themselves to pray at the tomb of ᶜAlī al-Riḍā; when they left, the following conversation supposedly took place:

> [The sultan] said to [Niẓām al-Mulk], 'O Ḥasan, for what did you pray? [Niẓām al-Mulk] replied: I prayed that Allah would give you the victory over your brother Tekesh' - for this was at the time when he rebelled against him and made war upon him. Then [Malikshāh] said to him: 'I did not ask for this; rather, I said: "O God, if my brother would be better for the Muslims, then give him the victory over me; but if I will be better [for them], then make me victorious over him."'[86]

While one might attribute associations and pilgrimages of this kind to mere folk custom or superstition, many of the Seljuq sultans also demonstrated an active cultivation of living Sunni religious figures: they desired their presence in court, and assigned them official tasks and roles in much the same way that the caliph or other pious Sunni rulers did.

Both general statements and concrete information are given regarding the predilection of various sultans for consorting with clerics. Alp Arslān apparently routinely surrounded himself with Sunni men of religion in his court; they are frequently mentioned off-handedly in our sources as having been present among the sultan's companions and in his retinue. Thus, Niẓām al-Mulk relates an incident in which this sultan had present among his entourage not only his official judge Abū Bakr – which one might expect – but also the prominent Ḥanafī *imām* Mushaṭṭab b. Muḥammad al-Farghānī.[87] In another instance, a different source mentions that Alp Arlsan 'had among his companions the judge Abū ᶜAmr Muḥammad b. ᶜAbd al-Raḥmān'.[88]

Sultan Muḥammad, apart from being described as 'a just, God-fearing friend of the *ᶜālim*',[89] is reported as having had frequent contact with various specific clerics, for instance with 'a group of the Imāms of Isfahan, such as Qāḍī Ṣadr al-Dīn and ᶜAbd Allāh Khaṭībī'.[90] Similarly, Sanjar is noted throughout his sixty-year reign for his habit of frequenting men of religion: 'He showed the utmost veneration for the religious clerics and learned [*ᶜulamā va ḥukamā*], and with the ascetics and hermits held speech';[91] 'He was the best of the House of Saljūq in terms of wisdom, religious knowledge, and love for the religious clerics [*ahl al-ᶜilm*]'.[92] Once again, the general assertion is bolstered by specific evidence of reverential behaviour toward, and close ties with, Sunni religious figures.

For instance, according to one report, a terrible *fitna* (civil war among Muslims) occurred between the Shāfiᶜiyya and Ḥanafiyya in Nishapur, in the course of which seventy Ḥanafites were killed. Sultan Sanjar was in his army camp nearby; and, when the news reached him, he immediately sent for his chief chamberlain (*ḥājib*), Maḥmūd al-Qāshānī, and, enraged, ordered him to go immediately to Muḥammad b. Yaḥyā, the leading Shāfiᶜite religious figure in Nishapur,[93] and issue to him an ultimatum to quit the city.

However, when the chamberlain arrived at the mosque, he lost his nerve and instead treated the offending cleric with marked deference. Instead of delivering the belligerent message with which the sultan had charged him, he took a seat in the circle around the legal scholar, and falsely asserted to Muḥammad b. Yaḥyā that the sultan sent him, Muḥammad b. Yaḥyā, greetings; gave him full carte blanche to resolve the inter-confessional conflict in whatever manner he should see fit; and, finally, requested of the cleric '[his] blessing and the treasures of [his] prayers'.[94]

What follows is quite instructive; when the chamberlain returned to Sanjar, the sultan was anxiously awaiting him in an agony of suspense, rueing 'with very deep regret' that he had sent him with such a disrespectful and imperious message to the cleric. When the chamberlain explained what he had done on his own authority, therefore, Sanjar, instead of being angry, exclaimed in relief: 'What an excellent man you are!' and promoted him.[95]

Sanjar also sought men of religion to serve in his administration; he even appointed actual clerics to the position of vizier. For instance, Sanjar raised Shihāb al-Islām ᶜAbd al-Razzāq al-Ṭūsī to the vizierate in the year 511/1117.[96] Of this cleric it is said that 'most of the days of his youth he employed in investigating questions of Muslim religious ordinances, and he learned by heart many of the Prophetic traditions, writing them upon the tablets of his mind'. In fact, Sanjar is described as having hauled him out of 'the corner of the madrasa' in order to appoint him vizier, 'submitting the affairs of the vizierate to the grasp of his knowledge, and placing the keys of the affairs of the kingdom in the palm of his competence'.[97] Other pious clerical viziers include the Shāfiᶜite 'the *ᶜālim* Naṣīr al-Dīn Maḥmūd b. al-Muẓaffar b. Abī Tawba al-Khwārizmī', who is eulogised as having been 'virtuous, very learned, and especially in the branches of the religious sciences, a master of and expert in the jurisprudence of the legal school of Shāfiᶜī'.[98]

Sanjar, like his grandfather Alp Arslān and father Malikshāh, also brought Ḥanafite clerics with him into battle. One such cleric was the foremost shaykh of the Ḥanafites, Abū Ḥafs ᶜUmar b. ᶜAbd al-Azīz Ibn Māza al-Bukhārī, of whom we are told that 'his standing with the sultan [Sanjar] grew strong . . . until God rewarded him with martyrdom at the hands of the Infidels' after the disastrous battle of Qatwan in 536/1141, to which he had accompanied his patron.[99]

So closely was Sanjar associated with the religious clerics, that his political enemies, quite exceptionally, wreaked their wrath upon them as in some way embodying or representing his rule. Thus, after Sanjar's defeat at the battle of Qatwan, the Khwarazmshah, who invaded Khurasan, seized and imprisoned 'Abū'l-Faḍl al-Kirmānī, the leader of the Ḥanafites, and a group of the *fuqahāʾ*'.[100] Similarly, after Sanjar fell captive to the Oghuz in 548/1153, the Oghuz singled out the *ʿulamāʾ*, together with government functionaries, to bear the brunt of their anti-Sanjar displeasure.[101]

In short, the Seljuq sultans maintained ongoing close contact, in a variety of ways, with Sunni clerics and holy men: as pilgrims and beseechers of their blessings; by placing themselves under their spiritual protection and guidance; and by employing them or keeping them in the court. Above all, the sultans treated venerable religious figures with a respect and humility they rarely showed anyone else outside the family – certainly the sultans were willing to submit to behaviour and speech from Sunni religious figures that they would tolerate from no one else.

THE EFFECT OF RELIGIOUS CONVICTIONS ON PUBLIC POLICY

While one could, perhaps, argue that the more dramatic and public religious statements and gestures, if they really occurred, were merely staged to burnish the image of the Seljuqs, there is other evidence which cannot be so easily dismissed. Most strikingly, there are those notable occasions when Seljuq sultans changed their political policies or behaviour due to religious conscience. For instance, in the year 448/1056–7, Sultan Ṭughril Beg's year-long stay in Baghdad greatly inconvenienced the populace, due to the unruly behaviour of Ṭughril's largely Turkmen troops. The caliph al-Qāʾim finally sent a written remonstrance to Ṭughril Beg 'reminding him of his duty to God'. Ṭughril, unfazed by this reprimand, offered the prevarication that his troops were so numerous that he could not control them.

However, Ṭughril was soon to reverse his attitude completely:

> That very night in his dream the sultan saw the Prophet . . . at the Kaʿba, and it seemed to him as though he was greeting the Prophet, who turned away from him and would not look at him, but said, 'God gives you dominion over His lands and His servants, but you do not observe Him in your dealings with them, nor are you ashamed before His glorious Majesty on account of your wicked treatment of them, and you are misled by His forbearance when you oppress them.'[102]

As a result of this dream, Ṭughril is described as having awoken in terror, summoned his vizier and sent him to the caliph to announce instead that he would obey his injunction in the matter – and Ṭughril actually kept his word, ending the billeting of his troops in private homes. Note that Ṭughril did not fear anything from the caliph himself, nor did he accord him any special religious status – indeed, Ṭughril had no problem, the very next year, of ending the Buyid practice of granting refuge status to the caliphal precinct, much to al-Qāʾim's chagrin.[103] Ṭughril's about-face in the former case therefore appears to have been genuinely religiously motivated.

Another instance of a sultan's radically altering political policy from religious motives transpired around the year 515/1121, when two fires broke out in the same week, one in the sultan's palace in Baghdad, the other in the largest and most beautiful mosque of Isfahan. According to Ibn al-Athīr, 'The sultan [Maḥmūd] had intended to take a sales tax, and to renew other non-canonical taxes in Iraq on the advice of the vizier . . . but the occurrence of these two fires terrified him. He acceded to the admonition and abandoned [the idea].'[104]

Perhaps the most spectacular instance of religious sensibility causing a reversal of policy occurred in the year 521/1127. Sultan Maḥmūd b. Muḥammad, in the midst of hostilities against the caliph, fell desperately ill, 'and [the conviction] came into his heart that the reason for the sickness which had befallen him was his war upon the Commander of the Faithful al-Mustarshid'. Maḥmūd thereupon abruptly ceased hostilities, and had himself borne upon a litter to the fortress where the caliph was holed up, in order to apologise to him and to ask him to pray on his behalf.[105]

We even see battle timing being decided on the basis of religious considerations. In 463/1071, when Alp Arslān was about to fight the fateful battle of Manzikert, his personal imam, Abū Naṣr Muḥammad b. ʿAbd al-Malik al-Bukhārī al-Ḥanafī, whom he had brought along with him, advised him to wait until the hour of Friday prayers to hold the battle, saying, 'Meet them on Friday, at the hour when the preachers will be in the pulpits, praying for victory for the *mujāhidīn* over the Infidels; for prayer is linked to a favourable answer.' Alp Arslān accordingly waited until Friday, then the imam led the sultan and his army in prayer, and the sultan is reported to have wept and rubbed his face in the dust before setting out to the battle.[106]

In conclusion, while there is no doubt that much of what Omid Safi appositely described as 'the Great Seljuq myth' is indeed just that – a myth – this should not blind us to the fact that the Seljuq sultans – or at least most of them until the death of Sanjar in the mid-6th/12th century – were indeed genuinely pious Sunnis; the first pious Sunnis, in fact, to control Iraq and western Iran since the caliphs had lost political control of these areas in the 10th century, and the greatest Sunni rulers of their time.

It is an incontrovertible fact that, whatever might be their own abuse of the Abbasid caliphs, they did save them from being replaced entirely by the Fatimid caliphate at a critical juncture; however desultory and erratic the Seljuq efforts against heretics and Infidels may have been, they did contain the former – in the case of the Buyids, they actually brought an end to Shīᶜite political dominance in Western Iran and Iraq – and bring about the Byzantine collapse; and however lacklustre the actual financial contributions of the Seljuq sultans to the establishment of madrasas may have been, they were indeed fervently partisan Sunnis.[107]

Again, this is not to say that the revisionist scholarship is incorrect in debunking many of the foundations upon which the Seljuq religious reputation has rested until now; on the contrary: the sultans did indeed oppress, manipulate and occasionally murder Abbasid caliphs; the sultans definitely attempted to subsume the *ᶜulamāʾ* into their own state apparatus; and the sultans were unquestionably less interested in fighting the Ismaᶜilis during the critical period of the late 11th and early 12th centuries than they were in fighting their own rivals. But to recognise that the Seljuq sultans were not saints does not mean that they were not real – often devout – Sunnis; this is a false dichotomy.

We must also recognise that many of the Seljuq trappings of piety or religious fervour were indeed geared toward burnishing their public image, at least secondarily if not primarily; in fact, they appear to have been markedly interested in emphasising their religious credentials. Edmund Bosworth long ago noted that the Seljuqs were the first rulers to adopt titles with the component 'dīn'[108] – although here it should be noted that the sources, whether disingenuously or not, attribute this use of such titles to the grateful initiative of the Abbasid caliph al-Qāʾim, after Ṭughril Beg had saved him from durance vile at the hands of al-Basāsīrī, and restored recognition of the Abbasid dynasty to Baghdad after several years of Fatimid allegiance.[109]

In the same vein, the Seljuq sultans also prominently employed titles with the word Islam or 'dīn' in them. Thus, Ṭughril Beg marketed himself on his coins as *Rukn al-Dīn*;[110] Malikshāh called himself variously *Rukn al-Islām*,[111] *Muᶜizz al-Dunyā wa l-Dīn*,[112] and *Muᶜizz al-Dīn wa-Rukn al-Islām*;[113] Barkyāruq entitled himself *Rukn al-Dunyā wa l-Dīn*;[114] Muḥammad Ṭapar, *Ghiyāth al-Dunyā wa l-Dīn*;[115] Sanjar, *Muᶜizz al-Dunyā wa l-Dīn*;[116] and so forth.

Similarly, the sultans' use of religious personal mottoes was probably also intended for public consumption. This practice began with Alp Arslān, who adopted the *tawqīᶜ* (motto) 'Allah renders victorious'[117] – no doubt most appropriate for a *ghāzī* sultan. From Barkyāruq onward the next six sultans all adopted such mottoes before the practice fell into desuetude.[118] These mottoes included such pious platitudes as: 'My trust is in God';[119] 'I look to God for help';[120] 'I rely upon God';[121] 'I ask assistance from God alone',[122] and so forth.

But when we leave aside such obvious public relations ploys, there remains a body of evidence which indicates that, wholly apart from the propaganda at which the Seljuqs apparently excelled, many of the sultans exhibited pious Sunni religious beliefs and behaviour. And, despite the many situations in which political expediency or personal wants trumped religious principle for the Seljuq sultans, there remain those instances in which the opposite happened: belief trumped expediency, and religious principle shaped their lives, actions and political policies, rather than the other way around.

NOTES

1. Ḥamdallāh b. Abī Bakr b. Aḥmad b. Naṣr Mustawfī Qazvīnī (d. c. 740/1339), *Tārīkh-i guzīda*, ed. ᶜAbd al-Ḥusayn Navāʾī (Tehran, 1339/1960), p. 426.
2. Ẓahīr-al-Dīn Nīshāpūrī (d. c. 582/1182), *The Saljūqnāma*, ed. A. H. Morton (Chippenham, 2004), pp. 2–3. A similar paean can be found in Rashīd al-Dīn Faḍlallāh, *Jāmiᶜ al-tavārīkh*, ed. A. Āteş (Ankara, 1999), II, pp. 249–50.
3. Ṣadr-al-Dīn Ḥusaynī, *Akhbār al-dawla al-saljūqiyya*, ed. M. Iqbāl (Beirut, 1984), p. 1.
4. ᶜIzz al-Dīn Abū l-Ḥasan Alī b. Muḥammad Ibn al-Athīr (d. 630/1233), *al-Kāmil fī l-ta'rīkh*, ed. Tornberg (reprinted Beirut, 1979), IX, p. 474; Zayn al-Dīn ᶜUmar b. Muẓaffar Ibn al-Wardī (d. 749/1348), *Taʾrīkh Ibn al-Wardī* (Baghdad 1389/1969), I, p. 481, speaks of his 'going on *ghazwas* against the Infidel Turks'.
5. Ibn al-Wardī, *Ta'rīkh* I, p. 481. Similarly, al-Ḥusaynī, *Akhbār al-dawla al-Saljūqiyya*, p. 2, expatiates that the Seljuq family 'became fortunate in the Ḥanīfī religion (*al-dīn al-ḥanīfī* – i.e. Islam), and chose [to settle in] the area of Jand, then chased away the officials of the Unbelievers from it'. Rāvandī, for his part, claims that the Seljuqs' migration to Khurasan was motivated by their wish 'to avoid the Abode of Unbelief and to draw near the House of Islam, to make pilgrimage to the Kaᶜba and frequent the leaders of religion'. See J. Meisami, *Persian Historiography to the End of the Twelfth Century* (Edinburgh, 1999), p. 242, citing Muḥammad b. ᶜAlī b. Sulaymān Rāvandī (d. after 600/1204), *Rāḥat al-ṣudūr wa-āyat al-surūr dar tārīkh-i Āl Saljūq*, ed. Muḥammad Iqbāl (Tehran, 1364/1985), p. 86.
6. Nīshāpūrī, *Saljūqnāma*, pp. 13–4; also Rāvandī, *Rāhat al-Sudūr*, pp. 102–3.
7. To paraphrase Julie Meisami, *Persian Historiography*, pp. 142–3.
8. For example George Makdisi, 'The marriage of Ṭughril Beg', *IJMES* 1 (1970), pp. 259–75; George Makdisi, 'The Sunni revival', in *Islamic Civilization, 950–1150*, ed. D. H. Richards, *Papers on Islamic History III* (Oxford, 1973), pp. 155–68; George Makdisi, 'Les rapports entre calife et sulṭân à l'époque saljūqide', *IJMES* 6 (1975), pp. 228–36.
9. Carole Hillenbrand, 'The power struggle between the Saljūqs and the Ismāᶜīlīs of Alamut, 487–518/1094–1124: the Saljūq perspective', in *Mediaeval Ismāᶜīlī History and Thought*, ed. F. Daftary (Cambridge, 1996), pp. 205–20.
10. Omid Safi, *The Politics of Knowledge in Pre-Modern Islam: Negotiating Ideology and Religious Inquiry* (Chapel Hill, NC, 2006), passim.
11. D. G. Tor, 'A tale of two murders: power relations between caliph and sultan in the

twelfth century', *Zeitschrift der Deutschen Morgenländischen Gesellschaft* 159 (2009); Eric. J. Hanne, *Putting the Caliph in his Place: Power, Authority, and the Late Abbasid Caliphate* (Madison, NJ, 2007), *passim.*

12. Al-Ḥusaynī, *Akhbār al-dawla al-Saljūqiyya*, pp. 22–3; repeated in al-Fatḥ b. ᶜAlī b. Muḥammad al-Bundārī (d. after 639/1241), *Zubdat al-nuṣra wa-nukhbat al-ᶜuṣra*, ed. T. Houtsma (Leiden, 1889), p. 27. Yaḥyā b. ᶜAbd al-Laṭīf al-Qazvīnī (d. 964/1555), *Lubb al-tavārīkh* (Tehran, 1364/1984), p. 174, elaborates on this picture, noting that 'he would always at the fifth hour attend divine service in the mosque, and he would fast on Thursdays and Mondays; and every time he wished for his own sake to build a house he first would build a mosque; only after that would he finish building [his own house]'.
13. Ibn al-Athīr, *al-Kāmil*, X, p. 28.
14. Muḥammad b. Munavvar b. Abī Saᶜd b. Abī Ṭāhir b. Abī Saᶜīd Mayhanī (fl. 1157–1202; hereinafter referred to as Ibn Munavvar), *Asrār al-tawḥīd fī maqāmāt al-Shaykh Abī Saᶜīd*, ed. M. R. Shafīᶜī Kadkanī (Tehran, 1381), I, pp. 319–20. To be precise, the Sultan originally chides the official in the following terms: 'Every time I have some work for you and I call you, they say that you are reciting the Qurᵓān or praying, and my matter remains neglected.' Shafīᶜī Kadkanī correctly points out that, *pace* Ibn Munavvar, Variqānī was not a vizier, but a Nishapurian financial official. See ibid. II, pp. 680–1.
15. Al-Ḥusaynī, *Akhbār al-dawla al-Saljūqiyya*, p. 22.
16. Ibid. p. 54.
17. Abū ᶜAlī al-Ḥasan b. ᶜAlī b. Isḥāq al-Ṭūsī Niẓām al-Mulk (d. 485/1092), *Siyar al-mulūk*, ed. Hubert Darke (Tehran, 1378/1999), p. 129. The present author finds unconvincing Khismatulin's contention that the book 'is the work of [the scribe] Maghrebī from beginning to end'. See A. A. Khismatulin, 'To forge a book in the Medieval [*sic*] Ages: Nezām al-Molk's *Siyar al-Moluk* (*Siyāsat-Nāme*)', *Journal of Persianate Studies* 1 (2008), p. 46.
18. Technically, the Chigils were one of the important constituent Turkic tribes or tribal groupings forming the Qarakhanid confederation. See R. N. Frye, *The Heritage of Central Asia: From Antiquity to the Turkish Expansion* (Princeton, NJ, 1996), p. 237. However, as Barthold already noted, 'at the end of the eleventh century . . . the kernel of the army of the Qarā-Khānids bore the name of jikils, but we are told by the contemporary Maḥmūd Kāshgharī . . . that all the Eastern Turks were called jikil (or chikil) by the Turkmens of the Saljūq empire'. See W. Barthold, *Turkestan Down to the Mongol Invasion* (3rd edn, Taipei, 1968), p. 254 note 6. As Madelung has pointed out, 'the militant Ḥanafism of the Turks, rulers as well as common soldiers, their dislike of Šāfiᶜism, their distinct hostility towards Ašᶜarism . . . are basic factors in the religious situation of the Seljūq age'. See W. Madelung, 'The spread of Māturīdism and the Turks', *Actas do IV Congreso de Estudos Àrabes e Islāmicos, Coimbra-Lisboa 1968* (Leiden, 1971), p. 126.
19. Niẓām al-Mulk, *Siyar al-mulūk*, p. 131.
20. Note also Ṭughril Beg's similar leanings, confirmed by the notorious Ḥanafī partisanship of his vizier al-Kundurī, particularly as expressed in the latter's animus against the Shāfiᶜites; Ibn al-Athīr, *al-Kāmil* X, p. 33, for instance, states that 'he was violently prejudiced against the Shāfiᶜites'. His institution of the cursing of the latter *madhhab* from the pulpits of the mosques in Khurasan, which resulted in the flight of Imām al-Ḥaramayn al-Juwaynī, is too well-known to require recapitulation here. See, for example, Tilman Nagel, *Die Festung des Glaubens: Triumph und Scheitern des*

islamischen Rationalismus im 11. Jahrhundert (Munich, 1988), pp. 85–99; George Makdisi, 'Ashʿarī and the Ashʿarites', *SI* 17 (1962), p. 47, among many others, both primary and secondary. Of course, there was a complete volte-face during the vizierate of Niẓām al-Mulk, to the point where Malikshāh supposedly sent al-Juwaynī as his emissary to Byzantium. See Muʿīn al-Dīn Muḥammad Zamchī Isfizārī (d. 915/1510), *Rawḍat al-jannāt fī awṣāf madīnat Harāt*, ed. Sayyid Muḥammad Kāẓim Imām (Tehran, 1338), I, p. 285

21. Using pejorative terms for the three: '*Gabrī ū Tarsāʾī ū Rāfiḍī*'.
22. Niẓām al-Mulk, *Siyar al-mulūk*, p. 217.
23. Ibid. p. 223.
24. Ibn al-Athīr, *al-Kāmil*, X, p. 75. On the common use of this form of punishment, see Christian Lange, *Justice, Punishment, and the Medieval Muslim Imagination* (Cambridge, 2008), pp. 62–6.
25. Albrecht Noth, *The Early Arabic Historical Tradition: a Source-Critical Study*, trans. Michael Bonner (Princeton, NJ, 1994), p. 109.
26. Rashīd al-Dīn, *Jāmiʿ al-tavārīkh*, II, p. 250.
27. Al-Ḥusaynī, *Akhbār al-dawla al-Saljūqiyya*, pp. 29–30; Ibn al-Athīr, *al-Kāmil*, X, p. 75.
28. Ibid. X, p. 74. Note that 'the founding of mosques, madrasas, and *ribāṭ*s' constitutes another prominent component of Rashīd al-Dīn's religious evaluation of the Seljuqs (*Jāmiʿ al-tavārīkh*, II, pp. 249–50).
29. Abū ʿAmr Minhāj al-Dīn ʿUthmān b. Sirāj al-Dīn Jūzjānī (aka Minhāj-i Sirāj, d. 664–86/1265–87), *Ṭabaqāt-i Nāṣirī*, ed. ʿAbd al-Ḥayy Ḥabībī (Tehran, 1363), I, p. 252. This same source, in fact, gives him the title 'Alp Arslān Ghāzī'.
30. On Manzikert see now Carole Hillenbrand, *Turkish Myth and Muslim Symbol: the Battle of Manzikert* (Edinburgh, 2007).
31. On these raids and those of other early Seljūq sultans in the Caucasus, see Andrew C. S. Peacock, 'Nomadic society and the Seljūq campaigns in the Caucasus', *Iran and the Caucasus*, 9, 2 (2005), pp. 205–30.
32. For example, al-Ḥusaynī, *Akhbār al-dawla al-Saljūqiyya*, pp. 34–40, 44–5. Qazvīnī, *Lubb al-tavārīkh*, p. 175.
33. Al-Ḥusaynī, *Akhbār al-dawla al-Saljūqiyya*, p. 37.
34. Ibid. p. 45; repeated in Ibn al-Athīr, *al-Kāmil*, X, p. 74 and Bundārī, *Zubdat al-nuṣra*, p. 47.
35. Al-Ḥusaynī, *Akhbār al-dawla al-Saljūqiyya*, p. 58.
36. Nīshāpūrī, *Saljūqnāma*, pp. 29–30; Muḥammad b. ʿAlī b. Muḥammad Shabānkāraʾī (d. 759/1358), *Majmaʿ al-ansāb*, ed. Mīr Hāshim Muḥaddis (Tehran, 1376), pp. 103–4; Rashīd al-Dīn, *Jāmiʿ al-tavārīkh*, II, p. 294; Qazvīnī, *Lubb al-tavārīkh*, p. 178.
37. Nīshāpūrī, *Saljūqnāma*, pp. 30–1; echoed in Rāvandī, *Rāḥat al-ṣudūr*, p. 132.
38. Qazvīnī, *Lubb al-tavārīkh*, p. 178. It is unclear if the structures to which the text refers were intended for Sufis or border warriors.
39. Le Strange, *Baghdad During the ʿAbbasid Caliphate* (London, 1924), p. 240.
40. Ibn al-Athīr, *al-Kāmil*, X, p. 212.
41. Al-Ḥusaynī, *Akhbār al-dawla al-Saljūqiyya*, p. 73; Bundārī, *Zubdat al-nuṣra*, p. 69.
42. Ibid. p. 69; Shabānkāraʾī, *Majmaʿ al-ansāb*, pp. 103–4; Nīshāpūrī, *Saljūqnāma*, p. 30; echoed in Rāvandī, *Rāḥat al-ṣudūr*, p. 132; Bundārī, *Zubdat al-nuṣra*, p. 69; Rashīd al-Dīn, *Jāmiʿ al-tavārīkh*, II, p. 294, and so forth.

43. Nīshāpūrī, *Saljūqnāma*, p. 44; Rāvandī, *Rāḥat al-ṣudūr*, p. 153; Rashīd al-Dīn, *Jāmiᶜ al-tavārīkh*, II, pp. 313–14.
44. Sexual abstemiousness was apparently in very short supply among medieval Islamic rulers, given the extreme infrequency with which it appears in eulogies; for another rare exemplar of this quality, Yaᶜqūb b. al-Layth al-Ṣaffār, see D. G. Tor, *Violent Order: Religious Warfare, Chivalry, and the ᶜAyyār Phenomenon in the Medieval Islamic World* (Würzburg, 2007), p. 179.
45. Rashīd al-Dīn, *Jāmiᶜ al-tavārīkh*, II, p. 314.
46. Ibid. II, p. 321.
47. Rāvandī, *Rāḥat al-ṣudūr*, p. 153.
48. Shabānkāraʾī, *Majmaᶜ al-ansāb*, p. 108.
49. Al-Qazvīnī, *Lubb al-tavārīkh*, p. 178.
50. Al-Ḥusaynī, *Akhbār al-dawla al-Saljūqiyya*, p. 82; Rashīd al-Dīn, *Jāmiᶜ al-tavārīkh*, II, p. 314; Rāvandī, *Rāḥat al-ṣudūr*, p. 153.
51. This point will be discussed at greater length, *infra*.
52. Nīshāpūrī, *Saljūqnāma*, p. 56; Shabānkāraʾī, *Majmaᶜ al-ansāb*, p. 110; al-Ḥusaynī, *Akhbār al-dawla al-Saljūqiyya*, p. 125. G. E. Tetley, *The Ghaznavid and Seljuk Turks: Poetry as a Source for Iranian History* (London, 2009), p. 188, notes that Muᶜizzī's poetry depicts both Sanjar and his mother as 'notably devout'.
53. Rashīd al-Dīn, *Jāmiᶜ al-tavārīkh*, II, p. 325.
54. Jūzjānī, *Ṭabaqāt-i Nāṣirī*, I, p. 257.
55. Abū l-Qāsim Jamāl al-Dīn al-Qāshānī, *Pseudo-Saljūqnāma*, ed. Ismāᶜīl Afshār (Tehran, 1332/1913), p. 45.
56. That is, Altūntāq, Barkyāruq's general.
57. Zamchī Isfizārī, *Rawḍat al-jannāt*, I, p. 391. For more on this episode, see Marshall S. G. Hodgson, *The Secret Order of Assassins: the Struggle of the Early Nizārī Ismāᶜīlīs Against the Islamic World* (Philadelphia, 2005), pp. 86–7. The author is grateful to Christian Lange for pointing out the Hodgson reference.
58. Nīshāpūrī, *Saljūqnāma*, p. 50; Rashīd al-Dīn, *Jāmiᶜ al-tavārīkh*, II, p. 321.
59. Bundārī, *Zubdat al-nuṣra*, p. 271.
60. Nīshāpūrī, *Saljūqnāma*, p. 70; Rashīd al-Dīn, *Jāmiᶜ al-tavārīkh*, II, p. 352.
61. Nīshāpūrī, *Saljūqnāma*, p. 72.
62. Ibn al-Athīr, *al-Kāmil*, XI, p. 266. On the historicity or lack thereof of seemingly topological actions, see infra, pp. 43–4.
63. Nīshāpūrī, *Saljūqnāma*, p. 74. Similarly, Rashīd al-Dīn, *Jāmiᶜ al-tavārīkh*, II, pp. 358–9, declares that 'he was a friend of the *ᶜālim* [and] the ascetic, and a giver to the religious poor; and toward people who were simple of heart and crazy, and caged birds, he bore an intimate friendship'.
64. Shams al-Dīn Abū l-Muẓaffar Yūsuf b. Qizoghlu Ṣibt Ibn al-Jawzī (d. 654/1256), *Mirʾāt al-zamān fi taʾrīkh al-aᶜyān* (Hyderabad, 1371/1951), p. 216.
65. Nīshāpūrī, *Saljūqnāma*, p. 87; Rashīd al-Dīn, *Jāmiᶜ al-tavārīkh*, II, p. 382; Qazvīnī, *Lubb al-tavārīkh*, p. 184.
66. Nīshāpūrī, *Saljūqnāma*, p. 89; Rashīd al-Dīn, *Jāmiᶜ al-tavārīkh*, II, p. 386; his fondness for religious clerics is mentioned also in Qazvīnī, *Lubb al-tavārīkh*, p. 185.
67. Nīshāpūrī, *Saljūqnāma*, pp. 101–2; Rashīd al-Dīn, *Jāmiᶜ al-tavārīkh*, II, p. 401.
68. Nīshāpūrī, *Saljūqnāma*, p. 104; Rashīd al-Dīn, *Jāmiᶜ al-tavārīkh*, II, p, 403.

69. Nīshāpūrī, *Saljūqnāma*, pp. 108–9; Rashīd al-Dīn, *Jāmi*ᶜ *al-tavārīkh*, II, pp. 409–12, 419–20.
70. Nīshāpūrī, *Saljūqnāma*, p. 122.
71. Rashīd al-Dīn, *Jāmi*ᶜ *al-tavārīkh*, II, pp. 427–8. The part about justice, at least, is corroborated by Al-Ḥusaynī, *Akhbār al-dawla al-Saljūqiyya*, p. 196.
72. See for instance the mass frenzy and adulation accompanying a Khurasani *ᶜālim* and holy man, including a stampede to obtain water from the same well from which the man drew water to perform his ablutions; Abū al-Faraj ᶜAbd al-Raḥmān b. ᶜAlī b. Muḥammad Ibn al-Jawzī (d. 597/1200), *al-Muntaẓam fī taʾrīkh al-umam wa l-mulūk*, ed. M. ᶜA. ᶜAṭā (Beirut, 1412/1992), XVII, pp. 3–5.
73. The chronicles are littered with the death notices of pious men who, while living, used to be visited by the sultans, who wished to benefit from their sanctity; e.g. Ḥassān b. Saᶜīd b. Ḥassān al-Makhzūmī, who died in 463/1071, Ibn al-Athīr, *al-Kāmil*, X, p. 69; Ibn al-Jawzī, *al-Muntaẓam*, XVI, p. 135.
74. Rāvandī, *Rāḥat al-ṣudūr*, pp. 98–9.
75. Ibn Munavvar, *Asrār al-tawḥīd*, I, p. 156. While the purpose of the story is undoubtedly to demonstrate the shaykh's spiritual power and *baraka*, it has the derivative consequence of showing that the shaykh actually approved of these men – a piece of information all the more reliable precisely because the author's primary purpose was not to convey that fact.
76. Al-Qāshānī, *Pseudo-Saljūqnāma*, p. 45.
77. Khwāja Sadīd al-Dīn Muḥammad Ghaznavī, *Maqamāt-i Zhanda Pīl*, ed. Ḥeshmat Allāh Muʾayyad Sanandajī (Tehran, 1345), pp. 55–6.
78. Ibid. p. 237.
79. Ibid. p. 35.
80. Ibid. p. 238.
81. Ibid. p. 74.
82. This sympathetic, almost proprietary attitude of Aḥmad-i Jām's toward the Seljuq sultan stands in stark contrast to that of prominent early Sunni clerics toward their rulers, e.g. Abū Isḥāq al-Fāzārī, who would eject from his *majlis* anyone who had any dealings with the government, and ᶜAbdallāh Ibn al-Mubārak, who is quoted by Aḥmad b. Ḥanbal as having enjoined the pious to stay away from the caliphs. See Tor, *Violent Order*, ch. 2.
83. In Aḥmad-i Jām's *Risāla-yi Samarqandiyya*, printed in the back of the *Maqamāt-i Zhanda Pīl*, p. 331ff.
84. Abū Ḥāmid Muḥammad b. Muḥammad b. Aḥmad al-Ghazzālī, *Makātīb-i Fārsī-yi Ghazzālī*, ed. ᶜAbbās Iqbāl (Tehran, 1333/1915), letter pp. 3–5, exhortation pp. 6–10.
85. Ibn al-Athīr, *al-Kāmil*, X, p. 156; Ibn al-Jawzī, *al-Muntaẓam*, XVI, p. 259.
86. Al-Ḥusaynī, *Akhbār al-dawla al-Saljūqiyya*, p. 74; Ibn al-Athīr, *al-Kāmil*, X, p. 211.
87. Niẓām al-Mulk, *Siyar al-mulūk*, p. 218.
88. Ibn al-Jawzī, *al-Muntaẓam*, XVI, p. 86.
89. Rashīd al-Dīn, *Jāmi*ᶜ *al-tavārīkh*, II, p. 321
90. Ibid. II, p. 318.
91. Ibid. II, p. 328; similarly, Nīshāpūrī, *Saljūqnāma*, p. 56; Shabānkāraʾī, *Majma*ᶜ *al-ansāb*, p. 110.
92. Al-Ḥusaynī, *Akhbār al-dawla al-Saljūqiyya*, p. 125.
93. See his laudatory entry in Dhahabī, *Siyar a*ᶜ*lām al-nubalā*ʾ, XX, pp. 312–15. He was

later killed during the rampage of the Oghuz in 548/1153, after Sanjar was taken captive. Ibn al-Athīr, *al-Kāmil*, XI, p. 181, writes: 'The Oghuz killed many of the Imāms and the *ᶜulamāʾ* and the righteous, among them Muḥammad b. Yaḥyā, the Shāfiᶜī *faqīh* who had no equal in his time.' Nīshāpūrī, *Saljūqnāma*, p. 65, calls him 'the model of the Imams of Iraq and Khurasan and the prince of the *ᶜulamāʾ* of the world'.

94. Al-Ḥusaynī, *Akhbār al-dawla al-Saljūqiyya*, pp. 125–6.
95. Ibid. p. 126.
96. Carla Klausner, *The Seljuk Vezirate: a Study of Civil Administration 1055–1194* (Cambridge, MA, 1973), p. 107.
97. Ghiyāth al-Dīn b. Humām al-Dīn Khwānd Mīr, *Dastūr al-vuzarāʾ*, ed. Saᶜīd Nafīsī (Tehran, 1317/1938), p. 189. Corroborated by Nāṣir al-Dīn Munshī Kirmānī (d. 725/1325), *Nasāʾim al-asḥār min laṭāʾim al-akhbār dar tārīkh-i vuzarā*, ed. Mīr Jalāl al-Dīn Ḥusaynī Armavī (Tehran, 1338/1959), pp. 58–9, who states that he was 'Renowned among the princes of the imams of his time and the nobles of the religious clerics'. The fact that this pious cleric was corrupted by the courtly life of the vizierate – or, as our first source would have it, 'due to the blandishments of the devil' – and became a drinker does not change the fact that Sanjar specifically and deliberately chose a reputable religious cleric as his vizier.
98. Kirmānī, *Nasāʾim al-asḥār min laṭāʾim al-akhbār*, pp. 69–72; Bundārī, *Zubdat al-nuṣra*, p. 268, who lists him under the *nisba* of 'al-Marwazī', mentions only his close relations with the clerics, without, however, noting the fact that he himself was also an *ᶜālim*.
99. Al-Dhahabī, *Siyar aᶜlām al-nubalāʾ*, XX, p. 97; mentioned also in Bundārī, *Zubdat al-nuṣra*, p. 278 and al-Ḥusayni, *Akhbār al-dawla al-Saljūqiyya*, p. 95, together with two other leading clerics who had apparently also been involved in the battle.
100. Ibn al-Jawzī, *al-Muntaẓam*, XVIII, p. 17.
101. For example Nīshāpūrī, *Saljūqnāma*, p. 65; Mīrkhwānd, Muḥammad b. Burhān al-Dīn Khwāndshāh (d. 1498), *Tārīkh rawḍat al-ṣafā* (Tehran, 1339/1920f.), IV, p. 318.
102. Ibn al-Athīr, *al-Kāmil*, IX, pp. 626–7; also Ibn al-Jawzī, *al-Muntaẓam*, XVI, pp. 2–3.
103. Ibn al-Athīr, *al-Kāmil*, IX, p. 635.
104. Ibid. X, p. 595.
105. Al-Ḥusaynī, *Akhbār al-dawla al-Saljūqiyya*, p. 97–8.
106. Al-Ḥusaynī, *Akhbār al-dawla al-Saljūqiyya*, p. 49. Hillenbrand (*Turkish Myth and Muslim Symbol*, pp. 121–3) dismisses this as a topos, but, again, as noted above, it is extremely problematic to do so, since (a) such a dismissal fails to take into account the fact that Muslims tried to realise the sacred topoi in their own lives and actions; and (b) the introduction of the topos reveals that Alp Arslān was close enough to the model of a *ghāzī* sultan to be clothed in the chroniclers' imaginations in the trappings of one; they would not have done so had the historical memory of him not been of a pious individual.
107. In the words of Nīshāpūrī, *Saljūqnāma*, pp. 2–3: 'Clear and shining are the endeavour they evinced and the waging of religious war that [they] commanded through the suppressing and conquering of the People of Innovation [*ahl-i bidᶜa*] and wickedness . . . and their claim of service to the house of the honoured caliphate by rescuing the Imam of the Muslims al-Qāʾim bi-amr Allāh.' Similarly, Qazvīnī, *Lubb al-tavārīkh*, p. 174, succinctly adumbrates Ṭughril Beg's achievements as follows: 'He freed the caliph al-Qāʾim from the durance of al-Basāsīrī, such that [al-Basāsīrī] died, and cast down the Būyid dynasty.'
108. C. E. Bosworth, 'The titulature of the Early Ghaznavids', *Oriens* 15 (1962), p. 216.

109. Rashīd al-Dīn, *Jāmiʿ al-tavārīkh*, II, pp. 268–9.
110. Tübingen coin collection [=TÜ] 91-25-36; FB4 A4.
111. TÜ FB6 B3; 2002-16-52; 96-37-21.
112. TÜ 2001-13-100.
113. TÜ FB5 D5.
114. TÜ FB8 A3.
115. TÜ FC1 A6.
116. TÜ 93-9-20; FC1 E4.
117. Nīshāpūrī, *Saljūqnāma*, p. 25.
118. The last four – Muḥammad b. Maḥmūd, Sulaymān b. Muḥammad, Arslān b. Ṭughril, and Ṭughril b. Arslān – ceased to employ such mottoes. See Nīshāpūrī, *Saljūqnāma*, pp. 99, 103, 119, 122–3.
119. Barkyāruq: Nīshāpūrī, *Saljūqnāma*, p. 43; Rāvandī, *Rāḥat al-ṣudūr*, p. 138.
120. Muḥammad Tapar: Nīshāpūrī, *Saljūqnāma*, p. 53; Rāvandī, *Rāḥat al-ṣudūr*, p. 152.
121. Sanjar: Nīshāpūrī, *Saljūqnāma*, p. 69
122. Ṭughril b. Muhammad: Nīshāpūrī, *Saljūqnāma*, p. 73.

CHAPTER

4

KINGSHIP AND IDEOLOGY UNDER THE RUM SELJUQS*

Songül Mecit

This chapter will give a short outline of the evolution of the official ideology of kingship of the Rum Seljuqs. It will be argued that the Rum Seljuq concept of legitimate kingship was formulated for the first time under the fifth Rum Seljuq ruler ᶜIzz al-Dīn Kılıç Arslan II (r. 551–88/1156–92) and re-formulated and completed under his two grandsons ᶜIzz al-Dīn Kay Kāwūs I (r. 608–16/1211–20) and ᶜAlāʾ al-Dīn Kay Qubādh I (r. 616–34/1220–37). Rum Seljuq ideology of kingship was thus formulated at a time when the new dynasty had been consolidated as an independent dynasty in Anatolia following the disintegration of the state of their Great Seljuq cousins and rivals. At the same time the ideology of kingship was formulated in order to defend their new-found status against Muslim rivals who appeared on the eastern borders of their realm, the atabegs of the Great Seljuq princes and commanders, as well as Turkish warlords not attached to the Great Seljuqs who founded principalities usurping the remains of the Great Seljuq empire in Iraq, northern Syria and upper Mesopotamia. Among these, Nūr al-Dīn Maḥmūd (r. 541–69/1147–74) the son of the Great Seljuq atabeg Zangī (r. 521–41/1127–46) and the former's Kurdish lieutenant and successor Saladin (r. 564–89/1169–93) were to become the main rivals of the Rum Seljuqs in the east.

The Rum Seljuq rulers did not commission treatises to elaborate their ideology and the source material for the Rum Seljuqs in general is far from rich.[1] However, we can find the concept of legitimate kingship articulated in

* I am very grateful to Professor Carole Hillenbrand for reading and commenting on the final draft of this article.

monumental inscriptions, coinage, diplomacy (letters and embassy ceremonies) and literary works (chronicles, 'mirrors for princes', poems). The epigraphic evidence is the most valuable for an analysis of ideology, as it is the most contemporary evidence available to us.[2] This evidence has however been largely ignored and we have no collection of the Rum Seljuq epigraphy.[3] It should be kept in mind, however, that all the works extant, including the texts of the inscriptions and coins, were composed by Persian and Arab officials in Persian and Arabic and thus they reflect predominantly their ideas and attitudes. These officials were all adherents of the Perso-Islamic concept of rule and were anxious to mould their alien Turkish Seljuq masters into this ideal, thereby remaining silent about their Turkish side. It is therefore not possible to prove how far the Rum Seljuq rulers themselves wanted to be autocratic kings or how far they remained attached to their Turkish traditions. We can be certain, however, that from the time of Kılıç Arslan II onwards they realised the importance of the ideology of kingship for the legitimisation of their rule. Epigraphic evidence starts to appear during his reign and he seems to be the first Rum Seljuq ruler to have minted coins. Limitation of space does not allow us to discuss here all the epigraphic as well as other sources available for all Rum Seljuq rulers. For an understanding of the Rum Seljuq ideology of kingship a case study is sufficient in which we will discuss the first formulation of that ideology under Kılıç Arslan II, when the Rum Seljuq sultanate was established, and its re-formulation during the reign of his two grandsons Kay Kāwūs I and Kay Qubādh I and the zenith of power of the sultanate.

Ideology of kingship will be understood here as the set of ideas which a ruler employs to define himself as a sovereign and to legitimise his rule. The study of ideas defining sovereign rule is important, as these were not just abstract concepts but were decisive for the formation of a state.[4] Every sovereign from the most powerful king to the petty prince had to justify to different groups within his realm and outsiders his control over territories, people, armies and resources.[5] Hence rulers employed ideologies of kingship to sustain their power over their lands and at the same time as an ideological weapon against internal and external rivals who contested their power. Consequently, ideologies of kingship were formulated to mark the consolidation of a sovereign's power or as was more often the case to oppose rival claims to power.

THE GREAT SELJUQ MODEL

It is generally assumed that the Rum Seljuq sultans adopted the government system and institutions established by their Great Seljuq cousins and consequently the Perso-Islamic concept of legitimate kingship.[6] This concept was the result of the synthesis of the ancient Iranian concept of kingship and Islamic notions and norms which resulted in the ideology usually called 'Perso-Islamic autocracy'.[7] While it is true that Islamic notions and norms were especially static and resistant to change, it cannot be said that they remained the same. Different ideological options, though not entirely novel, were developed as the result of historical, political and economical changes. The Rum Seljuqs adopted the Perso-Islamic concept of the ideology of kingship as it was formulated under their Great Seljuq cousins, but they had to adapt it taking into account the political realities of their time. A compact formulation of the Perso-Islamic ideology as promoted by the Great Seljuqs is given in an inscription of the third Great Seljuq sultan Malikshāh on the Friday Mosque in Isfahan:

> The mighty sultan, the greatest *shāhānshāh*, the king of the West and the East, the pillar of Islam and the Muslims, the glory of the world and religion, Abū l-Fatḥ Malikshāh b. Muḥammad, b. Dāwūd, the support of the caliph of God, the commander of the faithful, may God glorify his victory![8]

The honorific titles used here are stereotypical for the description of a Perso-Islamic ruler and were used by the Great Seljuqs and their successor states to express their ideology of kingship. This ideology accommodated three important elements according to which the Great Seljuq sultan was an autocratic monarch, the guardian of Islam and the Muslims, and the loyal ally and deputy of the Abbasid caliph. The resulting duties of the sultan were the support of the Sunni Abbasid caliph and the protection of Islam and Muslims against heresy and unbelievers. He was obliged to uphold Islamic law, ascertain that the Muslim lands prospered and that justice prevailed in them. This concept of legitimate kingship remained the same down to the times of the Rum Seljuq successor states. Yet this concept was not static, though the Islamic notions and norms were unchangeable. Different ideological options were developed in reaction to the changes in the historical, political and economical circumstances. Hence the options available to the Rum Seljuqs were in some aspects different from the options adopted by the Great Seljuqs. For the Great Seljuqs their ideological and political rivals were Muslim heretics, namely the Shiᶜi Buyids, the Shiᶜi Fatimid caliphs in Cairo, and the Assassins. They therefore sought to legitimise their usurpation of power in Iran and Iraq and their expansionist policy towards Syria and Egypt with the claim to protect Islam from heresy.

The Rum Seljuq sultanate was founded by the rebellious branch of the Great Seljuq family, the descendants of Kutalmış b. Arslan Isrāᵓīl, who revolted against the second Great Seljuq sultan Alp Arslan in 456/1064. Kutalmış based his claim to the throne on the ancient Turkish tradition of 'collective sovereignty' and the fact that his father Arslan Isrāᵓīl had been the eldest of the family.[9] Following the death of Alp Arslan in 465/1072 the son of Kutalmış, Sulaymān escaped Great Seljuq captivity, fled westward to the border of the Great Seljuq empire and came to Byzantine Anatolia. Here he established a principality in Nicaea/Iznik which lay opposite the Byzantine capital Constantinople. Hence, as direct neighbours of the Christian Byzantine enemy who had conquered new territory for Islam, the Rum Seljuqs could claim to be frontier warriors who safeguarded the *dār al-Islām* from the Christian enemy. However, despite the proximity to the 'Christian enemy' Sulaymān did not aim to expand towards the west but towards the east into Syria where he came into conflict with Tutuş, the brother of the Great Seljuq sultan Malikshāh, and was killed in 478/1086. Sulaymān's son Kılıç Arslan in turn was taken captive by the Great Seljuq sultan Malikshāh and escaped to Nicaea after the latter's death in 588/1092. When in 490/1097 the armies of the First Crusade re-conquered Nicaea the Seljuqs were pushed into the interior of Anatolia where Kılıç Arslan I established himself in Iconium/Konya. Kılıç Arslan I did not seek revenge against the Christians. Like his predecessors he was more interested in the east. Because of the weakened position of the Great Seljuq empire he went on an expedition against it but was defeated by the armies of Muḥammad I Ṭapar b. Malikshāh and died. Following the death of Muḥammad Ṭapar in 511/1118, however, the Great Seljuq empire finally disintegrated and the Rum Seljuqs used this opportunity to consolidate their power in Anatolia. The way to the east was closed off to them by the successor states of the Great Seljuqs who became their new fellow Sunni rivals. Therefore the defence of Islam from heresy was not an integral part of Rum Seljuq policy and ideology.

ᶜIZZ AL-DĪN KILIÇ ARSLAN II (551–88/1156–92)

The first extant piece of evidence for the ideology of kingship of the Rum Seljuqs is the dedication inscription[10] in the name of Kılıç Arslan on the *minbar* (pulpit) which originally had been commissioned by his father Masᶜūd for his great mosque. According to the foundation inscription the *minbar* was the work of a craftsman from Ahlat and was finished in 550/1155[11] but the *minbar* was placed later in the ᶜAlāᵓ al-Dīn Kay Qubādh mosque[12] which was built on the site of an earlier building and completed in 616/1219.[13] It should be mentioned here that the *minbar* itself was a symbol of the sovereignty of the ruler, as every Friday in the *khuṭba* his sovereignty was acclaimed to the believers of the town.[14] The titles claimed by Kılıç Arslan suggest that he commissioned his inscription to be added probably at a later date after he had firmly established his power. The inscription reads:

> The mighty sultan, the greatest *shāhānshāh*, lord of the Arab and Persian kings, possessor of the neck of nations, glory of the world and religion, pillar of Islam

> and the Muslims, pride of the kings and sultans, experienced protector of justice, destroyer of the infidel and idol worshipers, helper of the warriors of *jihād*, guardian of the lands of God, supporter of the Caliph of God, sultan of the lands of Rum, Armenia, the Franks and Syria, Abū'l-Fatḥ Kılıç Arslan b. Mas'ūd b. Kılıç Arslan, helper of the Commander of the Faithful, may God make his reign endure and his empire everlasting and his fortunes doubled.[15]

The catalogue of honorific titles used here reveals that the Rum Seljuq sultan adopted the Perso-Islamic ideology of kingship, as the inscription includes all integral elements of that concept. The Rum Seljuq sultan is presented as an autocratic monarch, as the guardian of Islam and the Muslims, and as the loyal ally and deputy of the Abbasid caliph. Added here, however are elements which reflect the political realities of Kılıç Arslan's time. Hence the *jihād* epithets claiming that the Rum Seljuq sultan is 'the warrior who strives to expand the realm of Islam' and the composite *jihād* epithets 'helper of the warriors of *jihād*' and 'destroyer of the infidels and idol worshipers'. The adoption of *jihād* epithets reveals that the Rum Seljuq ideology was re-formulated as a direct response to the ideological challenges posed by his Muslim rivals. Kılıç Arslan's Muslim rivals Nūr al-Dīn and Saladin were fellow Sunni rulers but they were upstarts and military warlords who had usurped power in Syria, upper Mesopotamia and Egypt. They had no real legal base for their rule. Kılıç Arslan's claim to rulership was not very different from that of a warlord but he was of noble lineage, as he was a member of the Seljuq house and thus could easily link himself to the Great Seljuq dynasty to legitimise his rule. Under the 'Counter Crusaders' Nūr al-Dīn and Saladin the ideology of *jihād* with an extensive propaganda machine was developed presenting them as warriors for the faith who waged *jihād* against the Crusaders.[16] The ideology of *jihād* was used most probably as an alternative concept to compensate for their lack of lineage and to legitimise their rule. Kılıç Arslan, on the other hand, did not depend as much on *jihād* propaganda as the 'Counter Crusaders' and he did not in fact care so much for *jihād*. Indeed he used the ideology of *jihād* first and foremost in order to compete with Nūr al-Dīn and Saladin.

The claim of imperial rule made in this inscription must also be seen in the context of the inter-Muslim rivalry. The Rum Seljuq sultan is styled as the 'Lord of the Arab and Persian Kings', 'Conqueror of Nations', and 'Glory of the Kings and Sultans'. He thus regarded himself as overlord of all Muslim rulers, including the Christian rulers of the region, though it is noteworthy that neither the Great Seljuq empire nor the Byzantine empire is referred to directly. The regions claimed to be under Kılıç Arslan's rule are then specified as the towns of 'Rum, Armenia, the Franks and Syria'. Important to note here too is that the specification 'Rum' proves that from the time of Kılıç Arslan onwards the Seljuqs in Anatolia regarded themselves as a new independent dynasty, the Seljuqs of Rum. The Rum Seljuq sultan is thus presented among others as ruler over territories held by the 'Counter Crusaders' but as Nūr al-Dīn and Saladin did not regard themselves as his subordinates, he was not in a position to demand authority over these territories.

The inscriptions on Kılıç Arslan's coins propagate the same image of the great Muslim sultan. The title on the couple of dinars and several dirhams extant is *al-sulṭān al-muᶜaẓẓam.*[17] It might be an accident of survival but the earliest coins of Kılıç Arslan are a dirham minted in Konya in 571/1175 and a dinar from the year 573/1178, one year after the battle of Myriokephalon. On both of these coins Kılıç Arslan is styled as the great sultan and on the dinar the name of the caliph al-Mustaḍīᵓ (r. 566–75/1170–80) is added.[18] There is no extant evidence of an investiture by the caliph which can help us to ascertain the date when exactly Kılıç Arslan was recognised officially as sultan. It seems probable that the title was first self-assumed and that he was probably invested with the title after 571/1175 but which territories were officially recognised as under his rule is not clear.

Yet the titles assumed in the inscription and his coins must be seen in the first instance as part of the ideological warfare between Kılıç Arslan and the 'Counter Crusaders'. An account given by the anonymous Rum Seljuq chronicler hints in this direction:

> At the beginning of his reign Kılıç Arslan founded Aksaray, caravansarais and market places. The tyranny of Malik Dhu'l-Nūn in Kayseri had extended all boundaries, he spent his time drinking wine. The sultan marched with his army against Dhu'l-Nūn and in 560 took Kayseri from him and seized all the fortresses of that province and put them under the command of his emirs . . . The Artuqids in Diyarbakır read the *khuṭba* in the name of the sultan and the rulers of Amid from the house of the Nisanids came to kiss the sultan's hand. The rulers of Erzurum and Erzincan submitted to the sultan. In short he dominated all regions.[19]

This account betrays the claims made in the inscription as imperial propaganda and reveals that Kılıç Arslan's actual aim was the submission of the Turkish-held Anatolian territories. Hence his main targets were to take his immediate neighbours the Danishmendids under his direct control and to be formally recognised as overlord by the Artuqids and Nisanids. The use of *jihād* epithets in the inscription and Kılıç Arslan's claim to have submitted Christian lands to his rule should therefore not be overemphasised,[20] especially since the same author gives a report of the battle of Myriokephalon without exploiting the ideological potential of this struggle between the Muslim sultan and the Christian emperor.[21] Besides, the relations between the Rum Seljuqs and the Byzantines were for prolonged periods friendly and they regarded each other as allies. The battle of Myriokephalon was in a sense an exception.[22]

Kılıç Arslan's long reign is decisive for Rum Seljuq history, as he consolidated the independent Rum Seljuq house and as under him the official ideology was formulated designating him as 'the sultan of Rum' and as a Perso-Islamic king. He was, however, not an autocratic king and we cannot be sure if he actually wanted to be one or if this was the image his Persian advisers thought appropriate. What is certain is that he realised the importance of the ideology of kingship for the legitimisation of his rule. At the same time however, it is certain that Turkish traditions from the steppe were still influential and that their Turkishness was relevant to the Rum Seljuq rulers, though the sources are silent about this. Besides, Turkish traditions were not expressed in public and remained an internal affair of the Seljuq house and their Turkmen followers.[23] Be that as it may, like all Seljuq rulers Kılıç Arslan could not ignore the ancient Turkish tradition of 'collective sovereignty' and divided his realm among his eleven heirs who already ruled their respective territories as semi-independent provinces. The death of Kılıç Arslan led to succession struggles among his many heirs, and only with the return of his son Kay Khusraw I from his exile in Constantinople and second accession to the throne in 601/1205 was the Rum Seljuq state re-united, reaching its apogee under his grandsons Kay Kāwūs I and Kay Qubādh I.

Drastic transformations in the political landscape contributed to the success of these two Rum Seljuq sultans. The Crusaders turned against Byzantium and the armies of the Fourth Crusade conquered Constantinople in 1204. On the other hand, the 'Counter Crusade' lost its momentum and the Ayyubid state was divided among Saladin's successors. In the power vacuum that developed Kay Kāwūs I and Kay Qubādh I transformed the Rum Seljuq state into a maritime state and the strongest power in Anatolia. The conquest of the important sea outlets of Attaleia (Antalya) in 603/1207, Sinope (Sinop) in 611/1214 and Kalon-Oros (ᶜAlāʾiyya, modern Alanya) in 620/1223 led to the economic expansion of the Rum Seljuq state and made it the wealthiest power in the region.[24] Hence it was during this period that the real development of the Rum Seljuq state took place, cities, especially the capital Konya, were developed and mosques, madrasas and caravansarais constructed.

This political and economic transformation was accompanied by the transformation of Rum Seljuq culture. The number of Iranian bureaucrats, scholars, Sufis and craftsmen from Persian territories and especially Khurasan who fled the Mongols and sought refuge in Anatolia grew substantially during the reign of Kılıç Arslan, and under their influence the Rum Seljuq sultanate was

Persianised.[25] The names given to Kılıç Arslan's sons and grandsons are almost all derived from the ancient epic Iranian tradition and are the most visible testament for this. As a result, the Rum Seljuq ideology of kingship was altered. Kay Kāwūs I and his brother and successor Kay Qubādh presented themselves as imperial rulers and laid special emphasis on the elements derived from the Persian model of autocratic kingship.

ᶜIZZ AL-DĪN KAY KĀWŪS I (608–16/1211–20)

Kay Kāwūs continued the expansionist policy of his father and transformed the Rum Seljuq state into a maritime power. In 611/1214 he seized the northern port of Sinop from the Byzantine state of Trebizond and in 612/1215 re-conquered Antalya which had been recaptured by the Christians. Following this success the self-image of the sultan was altered and the new role of the Rum Seluq sultan was symbolised and propagated to internal and external audiences through architectural constructions and inscriptions in their old strongholds, Konya and Sivas, as well as in the newly acquired towns, Sinop, Alanya and Antalya. The first expression of the re-formulated ideology of kingship can be found on an inscription on the citadel in Sinop which is dated Rabi 612/August 1215:

> The king of the east and the west, the master of the kings of the world, the ruler of the Arabs and the Persians . . . the sultan of the continents and the two seas.[26]

Kay Kāwūs is described as 'the sultan of the continents and two seas (*al-baḥrayn*)' thus alluding to the maritime power of the Rum Seljuq state. The epithet of the sea was also used in the inscriptions on monuments built in the inner Anatolian strongholds of the Rum Seljuqs, such as Sivas ('the sultan of the land and the sea')[27] and Konya in the ᶜAlāᵓ al-Dīn mosque ('the sultan of the land and the two seas').[28] This formula reappears on the city walls of Antalya where following the rebellion of the Christian people and the re-conquest by the sultan a long inscription was ordered by him to be placed on the city walls. In a self-laudatory fashion Kay Kāwūs' victory over the Christians is described and his full protocol is given to demonstrate his sovereignty to the Christians and rival Muslim rulers.[29] Here Kay Kāwūs is designated as:

> The shadow of God on the two horizons . . . the great *shāhānshāh*, the sovereign of the neck of the nations, the master of the Arab and Persian sultans, the king of the kings of the world, ᶜIzz al-Dunyā wa'l-Dīn, the refuge of Islam and the Muslims, the pillar of the triumphant empire (*dawla*), the glorifier of the eminent community, the rescuer of the flourishing nation, the sultan of the two seas,

> Abū'l-Fatḥ Kay Kawūs the son of the martyr (*shahīd*) Sultan Kay Khusraw, the son of the most happy Sultan Kılıç Arslan, the proof of the Commander of the Faithful.[30]

As usual, the sultan is presented as the guardian of Islam and the helper of the Abbasid caliph. Special emphasis, however, is laid here on attributes of legitimacy and sovereignty derived from ancient Persian titles of sovereignty and from Muslim titles received from the caliph. The Rum Seljuq sultan is styled not only as an exemplary Muslim ruler but the epithet 'pillar of the empire' seems to suggest that he is the supreme ruler of the Muslim world.

The invocation of *jihād* on the other hand seems somewhat anachronistic and superficial, as the war between Laskaris and Kay Khusraw was the last serious military conflict between the Byzantine empire of Nicaea and the Rum Seljuqs. As for the other Christian principalities, the state of Trebizond, Georgia and Cilician Armenia, the main aim of the Rum Seljuq sultans was to be recognised as suzerains, to secure their grasp over Anatolia and not to wage *jihād*. In connection with the conquest of Sinop, the main motive of the Rum Seljuqs was not *jihād* or defence of the Muslims but to secure important sea outlets. It is thus surprising that, whereas in the inscriptions of Sinop the *jihād* epithet was used only once, now *jihād* epithets are adopted and Kay Khusraw is referred to as *shahīd*. Hereby it is implied that Kay Khusraw, the father of Kay Kāwūs, died waging 'holy war' against the Christians and that the latter is continuing the 'holy war'. Kay Khusraw is designated as *shahīd* in all subsequent inscriptions. Yet for Kay Kāwūs, as for his predecessors, the control of Anatolia and influence over his Muslim neighbours in the east played a greater role than the seizure of Christian territories. He continued the traditional Rum Seljuq policy of expansion towards the east. Like his predecessors, he sought the alliance of his immediate neighbours in Anatolia in order to receive support against the Ayyubids ruling in Mesopotamia and northern Syria. For this reason most probably he concluded a matrimonial alliance with the Mengücük dynasty and married the daughter of Dāwūd II Bahrām Shāh, the ruler of Erzincan, before his campaign into Syria.[31]

ʿALĀʾ AL-DĪN KAY QUBĀDH I (616–34/1219–37)

Kay Qubādh, who followed his brother Kay Kawūs on the Rum Seljuq throne, is regarded as the greatest Rum Seljuq sultan under whom Rum Seljuq power reached its peak. Ibn Bībī who devotes the greatest part of his work to his reign presents him as the personified ideal Perso-Islamic ruler. Yet Kay Qubādh owed much of his success to the farsighted policies of his predecessor Kay Kawūs, and he did not expand the Rum Seljuq territories much further. But he secured the maritime frontiers by conquering Kalon-Oros, which he rebuilt giving it his name ᶜAlāᵓiyya, and by restraining the domination of the Black Sea by the Byzantine state of Trebizond, and he established himself as the overlord of Trebizond, Cilician Armenia and Georgia.[32] On the other hand he consolidated himself as the paramount Muslim ruler as he secured an alliance with the Ayyubid princes and defeated Jalāl al-Dīn Khwārazmshāh at Yazıçimen in 628/1230. The reason why he was remembered as the last great sultan of the Seljuq dynasty and why later rulers tried to link themselves to him is not so much a result of his success than his luck to have died before the Mongol invasion of Anatolia.[33] It was his successor and son Kay Khusrāw II who was defeated by the Mongols in 639/1242 at Kösedağ and made a vassal. Therefore the fact that the Mongol raids had begun under Kay Qubādh and that he was cautious with the Mongol demand for tribute and was prepared to pay it in order to keep them at bay seems not to have tarnished the picture of him as the ideal ruler.

In the inscription on the Red Tower (Kızıl Kule) of ᶜAlāᵓiyya or Alanya dated Rabīᶜ 623/March 1226 he is portrayed as:

> ᶜAlāᵓ al-Dunyā wa'l-Dīn, the shadow of God in the two earths, the outshining splendour of the empire, the eminent helper of the community of the faithful, the enlivener of justice [in the two worlds], the sultan of the continent and the two seas, the holder of the two horizons, the crown of the house of Seljuq, the master of the kings and the sultans, Abū'l-Fatḥ Kay Qubādh b. Kay Khusraw b. Kılıç Arslan, the proof of the Commander of the Faithful . . .[34]

The protocol of Kay Qubādh is similar to that of his predecessor but one important title appears here for the first time. Kay Qubādh is designated as 'the crown of the house of Seljuq'. This affirms the noble lineage of the sultan and at the same time puts him above all members of that house. It can thus be interpreted as an allusion to the delayed Rum Seljuq victory over their Great Seljuq rivals. In contrast to their grandfather Kılıç Arslan II whose expansionist ambitions were specified in his inscription as Rum, Armenia and Syria, the ambitions of his grandsons seem to have no limits. The portrayal of Kay Qubādh to whom Ibn Bībī dedicated his work and whose reign makes the bigger part of the chronicle is even more glorifying. It is a eulogy in which Ibn Bībī threads all characteristics expected of an exemplary ideal Perso-Islamic ruler:

> From the extreme east to the extreme west the banners of Islam have not shaded a ruler like Sultan ᶜAlāᵓ al-Dīn Kay Kubādh b. Kay Khusraw b. Kılıç Arslan b. Masᶜūd b. Kılıç Arslan b. Sulaymān b. Kutalmış b. Arslan Isrāᵓīl b. Saljuq.

> 'Truly, the banner of Islam shaded no other sultan, who was better suited through personal achievement, and through inheritance and who was better in matters of religion and sincere in strong faith, with wider knowledge . . . who was a greater protector of Islam and its followers and a greater opponent of polytheism and its professors than him'. His rank had risen to such heights that the kings of the lands of the believers and unbelievers, from the farthest Abhāz to the regions of the Hijaz . . . from the steppes of the Qipchaq to the lands of Iraq, especially the kings of Syria, regarded themselves as his chessmen and acknowledged his name in the *khuṭba* and on their coins.[35]

Firstly, our author demonstrates Kay Qubādh's noble lineage by listing his descent down to the ancestor of the Seljuq dynasty Seljuq. The noble lineage is further affirmed with the statement that Kay Qubādh was king also by right of inheritance. Secondly, Kay Qubādh I is designated as the greatest protector of Islam and the Muslims and ranked above all other Muslim rulers. This claim is strengthened through the description of the exemplary piety and religious zeal of Kay Qubādh. Thirdly, the sultan is portrayed as the best leader of *jihād* in Muslim history, but *jihād* epithets are not used. Fourthly, Kay Qubādh is described as the supreme king who has subordinated all neighbouring rulers, Muslim and Christian alike. Consequently, Ibn Bībī describes in his narrative every small-scale campaign against Muslims as world conquest. In the tradition of the Persian ideology of kingship, this was the duty and prerogative of the king. At the same time, Ibn Bībī describes every campaign against Christians, regardless of the real motives behind it, as Holy War. It could be suggested that Ibn Bībī's specification 'especially the kings of Syria regarded themselves as his chessmen' can be taken as a hint that Kay Qubādh had no real interest in either world conquest or *jihād*. It is more likely that Kay Qubādh wanted to be nominally recognised as suzerain in Syria, Georgia, Trebizond and Cilician Armenia and not to take them under his direct control. Therefore, in contrast to the claims made in the inscriptions and by Ibn Bībī, Kay Qubādh should be understood as a ruler fully aware of *realpolitik*.

This is not immediately evident from Ibn Bībī's chronicle because he does not aim to give an account of events but looks back especially on the period of Kay Qubādh, who for him most fully exemplified Iranian ideals of kingship as the lost Golden Age. His aim was that the sultans of his time who were powerless puppets dominated by the Mongols and their equally incompetent advisers should take it as an example from which to learn. Ibn Bībī's work and especially his account of Kay Qubādh's reign is a 'mirror for princes',[36] which the author wrote with the intention that future kings would read and learn from it.

CONCLUSION

To conclude, the ideologies of kingship formulated in the inscriptions and other sources describe an ideal and not the reality. There certainly existed a gap between the ideology which was employed to justify and legitimise the authority of the Rum Seljuq sultans and the political realities of their rule. Nevertheless, the ideological statements made in the inscriptions and by Ibn Bībī were not just mere window dressing but significant political tools. Moreover, they were decisive for the development of the Seljuq principality in Anatolia into the new dynasty of the Rum Seljuqs or 'the House' of Sulaymān b. Kutalmış b. Arslan Isrāʾīl b. Saljuq. Thus this rebellious branch of the Turkish Seljuqs was transformed into a 'Perso-Islamic state' with a developed court and capital.

NOTES

1. There are no contemporary historical works extant from the period of the Rum Seljuqs and it will suffice here to mention briefly the four chronicles which have come down to us. These were all composed in Anatolia but after the disintegration of the Rum Seljuq state between the late 13th and late 14th century. The most important among these is Ibn Bībī's *Al-Awāmir al-ʿAlāʾiyya fī l-umūr al-ʿAlāʾiyya* which narrates the history of the Rum Seljuqs from the end of the reign of Kılıç Arslan II c. 581 to c. 679/c. 1185 to c. early 1281: *Histoire des Seldjoucides d'Asie Mineure d'après Ibn Bībī, (Recueil de texts relatives à l'histoire des Seldjoucides)*, III, ed. M. T. Houtsma (Leiden, 1902); facsimile reproduction of the Ayasofya transcript, A. S. Erzi (Ankara, 1956). The other two chronicles give very brief surveys of Seljuq history: the *Musāmarat al-akhbār wa musāyarat al-akhyār* of Karīm al-Dīn Maḥmūd Aqsarāʾī, ed. O. Turan, *Müsâmeret ül-Ahbâr Moğollar zamanında Türkiye Selçukluları Tarihi* (Ankara, 1944); the *Tārīkh-i āl-i Saljūq* written by an anonymous author, ed. N. Jalali, *Tārix-e Āl-e Saljuq dar Ānāṭoli* (Tehran, 1999). The Al-walad al-shafīq of Qāḍī Aḥmad of Niğde remains in manuscript and has so far not received much attention. These chronicles, except the work of Qāḍī Aḥmad of Niğde, are discussed in: C. Cahen, 'The historiography of the Seljuqid period', in *Historians of the Middle East*, eds B. Lewis and P. M. Holt (London, 1952), pp. 59–78; C. Melville, 'The early Persian historiography of Anatolia', in *History and Historiography of Post-Mongol Central Asia and the Middle East*, eds J. Pfeiffer, S. A. Quinn and E. Tucker (Wiesbaden, 2006), pp. 135–66. For Qāḍī Aḥmad, see A. C. S. Peacock, 'Ahmad of Niğde's *al-Walad al-Shafīq* and the Seljuk past', *Anatolian Studies* 54 (2004), pp. 95–107.
2. As Carole Hillenbrand rightly points out, however, one should be aware that there is 'the danger of attributing too much historical value to inscriptions and to their highly stylised modes of expression'. C. Hillenbrand, 'Jihad propaganda in Syria from the time of the First Crusade until the death of Zengi: the evidence of monumental inscriptions', in *The Frankish Wars and their Influence on Palestine*, eds K. Athamina and R. Heacock (Birzeit, 1994), p. 62.
3. The compendium of Arabic inscriptions with French translations, published by a group of French scholars is outdated but remains an important work of reference: E. Combe, J. Sauvaget and G. Wiet (eds), *Répertoire chronologique d'épigraphie arabe*, 16 vols

(Cairo, 1931–64) (hereafter cited as *RCEA*). Volumes 8–11 published between 1936 and 1939 include the epigraphy of the Great Seljuqs and Rum Seljuqs. There are also even older works extant which contain some of the Rum Seljuq and other medieval Islamic inscriptions. Some of these works are unfortunately difficult to access and use: C. Huart, *Epigraphie arabe d'Asie Mineure* (Paris, 1895); İsmail Hakkı, *Kitabeler* (Istanbul, 1827); J. H. Löytved, *Konia. Inschriften der Seldschukischen Bauten* (Berlin, 1907), p. 21; Max van Berchem, *Inschriften aus Syrien, Mesopotamien und Kleinasien: gesammelt im Jahre 1899* (Leipzig, 1909); H. Hilmi, *Sinop kitabeleri* (Sinop, 1925); İ. Hakkı Konyalı, *Abideleri ve Kitabeleri ile Konya Tarihi* (Konya, 1964). Remzi Duran's work on the Rum Seljuq inscriptions in Konya is more modern but unfortunately it is descriptive and uncritical: Remzi Duran, *Selçuklu Devri Konya Yapı Kitâbeleri İnşa ve Ta'mir* (Ankara, 2001). A useful discussion of the inscriptions on the citadel walls in Antalya that also considers the question of ideology has been published more recently by S. Redford and G. Leiser, *Taşa Yazılan Zafer Antalya Içkale Surlarındaki Selçuklu Fetihnâmesi: Victory Inscribed the Seljuk Fetiḥnāme on the Citadel Walls of Antalya, Turkey* (Antalya, 2008).

4. As Claessen and Oosten aptly point out, 'There must exist an ideology, which explains and justifies a hierarchical administrative organization and socio-political inequality. If such an ideology does not exist or emerges, the formation of state becomes difficult, or even outright impossible'; H. J. M. Claessen and J. G. Oosten (eds), *Ideology and the Formation of Early States* (Leiden, 1996), p. 5. See also H. J. M. Claessen and P. S. Skalník (eds), *The Study of the State* (The Hague, 1981), p. 479.
5. See R. S. Humphreys, *Islamic History: A Framework for Inquiry* (London, 1991), p. 148. In Chapter 6 entitled 'Ideology and propaganda religion and state in the early Seljukid period', Humphreys gives a general definition of ideology and propaganda, discusses the literature which was written on other dynasties and concludes that: 'There is no general survey of ideology as such in the Seljukid period; that is, we have no broad study devoted not only to the political ideas of that age, but also to rhetoric, symbolism, and propaganda' (ibid. p. 159). He finishes his chapter with a brief analysis of the ideology of the early Great Seljuqs (ibid. p. 164–8). Humphreys' statement is still valid but in recent times the importance of research on ideology has been recognised and a very interesting work on kingship and ideology has been written by A. F. Broadbridge, *Kingship and Ideology in the Islamic and Mongol Worlds* (Cambridge, 2008). Fortunately, the ideology of the Great Seljuqs has also received some attention in recently published monographs: Omid Safi, *The Politics of Knowledge in Premodern Islam. Negotiating Ideology and Religious Inquiry* (Chapel Hill, 2006); Christian Lange, *Justice, Punishment and the Medieval Muslim Imagination* (Cambridge, 2008).
6. Niẓām al-Mulk, arguably the greatest Seljuq vizier and architect behind the new state, who served under Alp Arslan and his son and successor Malikshāh, was commissioned by the latter to write a treatise on good government. The result was the 'Book of Government' (*Siyāsat-nāma*), in which Niẓām al-Mulk elaborated the Perso-Islamic concept of government. This book, even though it is not a treatise specifically commissioned or designated as the formulation of the Great Seljuq ideology of kingship, can be regarded as such. Niẓām al-Mulk was a member of the Persian bureaucracy of Khurasan who changed from Ghaznavid into Great Seljuq service; indeed, members of that bureaucracy developed the Perso-Islamic concept of kingship under the Ghaznavids and refined it further under the Great Seljuqs and their successor states. See A. K. S. Lambton, 'The dilemma of

government in Islamic Persia: the *Siyasat-nama* of Nizam al-Mulk', *Iran* 22 (1984), pp. 55–66; E. I. J. Rosenthal, *Political Thought in Medieval Islam. An introductory outline* (Cambridge, 1958), esp. p. 82 for Niẓām al-Mulk's description of the ideal king.

7. Humphreys, *Islamic History*, p. 154.
8. *RCEA*, VII, p. 247 (inscription no. 2775).
9. The tribe or tribal confederation was ruled by a paramount noble family or house. Within the ruling house one member, in most cases the eldest of the family, was merely designated as *primus inter pares*. The Seljuq sultans could not and probably did not wish to eliminate this tradition and thus partitioned their realm to allot it as autonomous appanages to their relatives. See W. Barthold, *Turkestan Down to the Mongol Invasion*(3rd edn, London, 1968), p. 268; J. E. Woods, *Aqquyunlu: Clan, Confederation, Empire* (Minneapolis, MN, 1976); Humphreys, *Islamic History*, p. 166.
10. Löytved, *Konia*, p. 23; *RCEA*, IX, pp. 11–12 (inscription no. 3218).
11. See Löytved, *Konia*, p. 23; *RCEA*, VIII, p. 289 (inscription no. 3200); O. Aslanapa, *Turkish Art and Architecture* (New York, 1971), p. 107. This carved wooden *minbar* is the earliest extant Rum Seljuq work of art. The authors of the *RCEA* do not discuss the date of the dedication inscription but list the foundation inscription under the year 550/1155, the last year of Masᶜūd's reign and the dedication inscription of Kılıç Arslan II under the year 551/1156, the first year of his reign.
12. This was the main mosque in Konya and the modern Turkish spelling of its name is Alaeddin Keykubad Cami.
13. See Aslanapa, *Turkish Art and Architecture*, p. 109.
14. The symbolic function of the *minbar* has so far not received much scholarly attention, except for two works dealing with the Umayyad period: Carl H. Becker, *Vom Werden und Wesen der islamischen Welt* (Leipzig, 1924), pp. 450–71; Jean Sauvaget, *La Mosquée omeyyade de Médine* (Paris, 1947), pp. 139–44. For a brief outline see R. Hillenbrand, *Islamic Architecture* (Edinburgh, 1994), pp. 46–8. See also Yasser Tabbaa, 'Monuments with a message: propagation of jihād under Nūr Al-Dīn (1146–1174)', in *The Meeting of Two Worlds Cultural Exchange between East and West during the Period of the Crusades*, ed. V. P. Goss (Michigan, 1986), pp. 230–1; S. Auld, 'The minbar of al-Aqsa. Form and function', in *Image and Meaning in Islamic Art*, ed. R. Hillenbrand (London, 2005), pp. 42–60.
15. As translated by Löytved, *Konia*, p. 23 and also by C. Hillenbrand, *Turkish Myth and Muslim Symbol: the Battle of Manzikert* (Edinburgh, 2007), p. 161.
16. See E. Sivan, *L'Islam et la Croisade* (Paris, 1968); M. C. Lyons, *Saladin. The Politics of the Holy War* (Cambridge, 1982); M. Köhler, *Allianzen und Verträge zwischen fränkischen und islamischen Herrschern* (Berlin, 1991).
17. Halit Erkiletlioğlu/Oğuz Güler, *Selçuklu sultanları ve sikkeleri* (Kayseri, 1996), pp. 49–52, (hereafter cited as Güler, *Selçuklu Sikkeleri*).
18. See Güler, *Selçuklu Sikkeleri*, p. 50; Şevki N. Aykut, *Türkiye Selçuklu Sikkeleri vol. 1. I. Mesud'dan I. Keykubad'a kadar (510–616/1116–1220)* (Istanbul, 2000), pp. 190–1.
19. Anonymous, Jalali, *Tārix-e*, pp. 81–2. See also the translation by Uzluk, Anonymous, *Ta'rīkh-i āl-i Saljūq dar Anaṭulyā*, facsimile reproduction and Turkish trans. by F. N. Uzluk as *Anadolu Selçukluları Devleti Tarihi. III. Histoire des Seldjoucides d'Asie Mineure par un anonyme* (Ankara, 1952), pp. 25–6.
20. See Köhler, *Alianzen und Verträge*, p. 240. Köhler's suggestion that the *jihād* epithets used by Kılıç Arlsan II and the Artuqids of Hartbirt and Mayyafariqin are more

impressive than the epithets used for *jihād* propaganda by Nūr al-Dīn is only true for the Artuqids but not for Kılıç Arlsan.

21. See Hillenbrand, *Manzikert*, p. 154.
22. Magdalino states that: 'Byzantine texts which celebrate the rebuilding of Dorylaion and Soublaion show that Manuel advertised this as the start of holy war of re-conquest in which he declared himself willing to lay down his life'; Paul Magdalino, *The Empire of Manuel I Komnenos, 1143–1180* (Cambridge, 1993), p. 96. Lilie gives a similar argument and writes: 'Manuel proposed a crusade and declared publicly that he intended to come to the aid of the crusaders'; R.-J. Lilie, 'Twelfth-century Byzantine and Turkish states', *Byzantinische Forschungen* 16 (1991), p. 40. However, that Manuel propagated the expedition against Kılıç Arslan as a crusade does not mean that Byzantium embraced the idea of the 'Holy War'. The warfare between emperor and sultan is hardly ever presented as a religious struggle. The histories of Choniates and Kinnamos do not reflect the idea of 'Holy War' and crusade in the connection with the fortification of Dorylaion and Soublaion or Myriokephalon. Manuel's crusade propaganda was directed towards the west and the Latin east. Manuel did not aim to re-conquer Asia Minor or lead a 'Holy War' against the infidel sultan. He wanted to re-establish the land route leading through Asia Minor to the Holy Land and bring the Crusader States under his authority. It seems therefore safe to suggest that the events leading to Myriokephalon were part of the ideological warfare between the two Christian emperors and did not necessarily aim to eliminate the Rum Seljuq sultanate. Cf. the discussion in S. Mecit, *The Rum Seljuqs (473–641/1081–1243): Ideology, Mentality and Self-Image* (PhD Edinburgh, 2010), pp. 221–37.
23. Turkish cultural traditions can be found in art; the use of bow and arrow as symbols of power was later incorporated into the *ṭughrā* as one example of this. See C. Cahen, 'La tugrā seljukide', *Journal Asiatique* 234 (1943–5), pp. 167–72.
24. The wealth of the Rum Seljuq sultanate was even recognised by medieval European authors. Jean de Joinville writes: 'At the time of our arrival in Cyprus the Sultan of Iconium [Konya] was the richest ruler in all the pagan world'. Simon de St Quentin states: 'Erat quidem illud Turquie regnum nobilissimum et opulentissimum. Ibi civitates fere .C. exceptis castris et villis et casalibus.' Jean de Joinville, *Sire de Jean de Joinville*, trans. by M. R. B. Shaw as *The Life of Saint Louis* (Harmondsworth, 1963), p. 199; Simon de St Quentin, *Historia Tartarorum*, ed. J. Richard, *Histoire des Tartares* (Paris, 1965), p. 66.
25. C. Hillenbrand, 'Rāvandī, the Seljuk court at Konya and the Persianisation of Anatolian cities', in *Les Seldjoukides d'Anatolie*, ed. G. Leiser (Paris, 2005), pp. 157–69.
26. *RCEA*, X, p. 114 (inscription no. 3761).
27. *RCEA*, X, pp. 146–7, (inscription no. 3809).
28. *RCEA*, X, p. 163 (inscription no. 3835); Löytved, *Konia*, p. 32.
29. For a translation and discussion of the long inscription which as Redford states equals a *fatḥnāma*, see Redford and Leiser, *Victory Inscribed*, pp. 107–18.
30. *RCEA*, X, pp. 109–12 (inscription no. 3757); see also the translation in Redford and Leiser, *Victory Inscribed*, p. 112.
31. Ibn Bībī does not give the political background of this marriage alliance but it is interesting that he argues that the sultan wanted to marry the daughter of the Mengücük ruler because of her noble lineage as she was 'of the brilliant descent of the sultan Kılıç Arslan and the root of Saljuk'. See Duda's German translation of the epitome of Ibn Bībī's work: H. W. Duda, *Die Seltschukengeschichte des Ibn Bībī* (Kopenhagen, 1959), p. 77.

32. Andrew Peacock has written some interesting articles on the Rum Seljuqs and their Christian neighbours: A. C. S. Peacock, 'Nomadic society and the Seljuq campaigns in Caucasia', *Iran and the Caucasus* 9, 2 (2005), pp. 205–30; Andrew Peacock, 'The Saljuq campaign against the Crimea and the expansionist policy of the early reign of 'Ala' al-Din Kayqubad', *JRAS* 16, 2 (2006), pp. 133–49; Andrew Peacock, 'Georgia and the Anatolian Turks in the 12th and 13th centuries', *Anatolian Studies* 56 (2006), pp. 127–46.
33. For a discussion of how the Ottomans sought to legitimise their rule through a link to the Rum Seljuq sultan, see Chapter 5 in this volume.
34. *RCEA*, X, pp. 240–1 (inscription no. 3957); R. M. Riefstahl, *Turkish Architecture in Southwestern Anatolia* (Cambridge, 1931), p. 96.
35. Ibn Bībī, Al *Awāmir*, trans. Duda, p. 99.
36. See E. I. J. Rosenthal, *Political Thought*, pp. 68–81; A. K. S. Lambton, 'The theory of kingship in the Naṣīḥat ul-mulūk of Ghazālī', in *Theory and Practice in Medieval Persian Government* (Collected studies series), ed. A. K. S. Lambton (London, 1980), V, pp. 47–55; A. K. S. Lambton, 'Islamic Mirrors for Princes', in *Theory and Practice*, VI, pp. 419–22; C. Hillenbrand, 'A little-known mirror for princes of al-Ghazali', in *Words, Texts and Concepts Cruising the Mediterranean Sea*, eds R. Arnzen and J. Thielmann (Leuven, 2004), pp. 593–601.

CHAPTER

5

SELJUQ LEGITIMACY IN ISLAMIC HISTORY

A. C. S. Peacock

Even if such influential developments in the history of the Middle East as madrasas, Sunnism, and the use of Persian for official purposes did not originate in the Seljuq period, it was then that they grew and spread. Yet to what extent the Seljuq dynasty itself deserves credit for them is debatable, and one could argue that in many ways the sultans were but bystanders to historical processes over which they had little control. The institution of the atabegate, the guardians for royal princes, was perhaps a more genuinely Seljuq contribution, although its origins are so obscure that even this is questionable.[1] More durable, and more certainly Seljuq, was the political legacy of the dynastic name itself, by linking themselves to which later rulers sought to add lustre to stories of their own origins. Throughout history, rulers have grappled with the question of how to justify their existence, and for new dynasties needing to explain the processes by which they have acquired the right to rule, this problem is always particularly acute. For centuries after the demise of the last Seljuq rulers of Anatolia, the Ottomans promoted their own legitimacy by claiming that they had inherited sovereignty from their predecessors, while their opponents tried to establish that they themselves were the Seljuqs' true heirs. In this chapter, we shall explore how the Seljuqs came to have such a lasting political influence on subsequent generations. In addition, nostalgia for the dynasty as well as political necessity gave rise to an important literature, with the composition of numerous *Saljūqnāma*s or 'Books of the Seljuqs' commemorating the dynasty's deeds, some of which are major historical sources.

In the early days, the Seljuq family's position was that of tribal chiefs, and their support was dependent on their success in providing pasture and plunder for their followers, who if dissatisfied would break away to join some rival chief.[2] Nonetheless, a certain aura of prestige was already attached to membership of the dynasty, as is illustrated by the comments addressed to Sulaymān b. Qutlumush, Saljūq's great grandson and founder of the Anatolian branch of the Seljuq family, by Shaklī, a tribal leader in Syria in the late 5th/11th century. Shaklī invited Sulaymān to lead his Türkmen in place of the chief Atsız, saying:

> You are of the Seljuq dynasty and the royal house. If we obey you and serve you, we will be honoured by you and be proud. Atsız was not from the royal house so we did not like to follow and obey him.[3]

For Ṭughril and Alp Arslān too, the Seljuq name held a prestige that was worth capitalising on, as is reflected in some of the literary works dedicated to the first two sultans. Ibn Ḥassūl, who composed the *Kitāb Tafḍīl al-atrāk*, 'The book of the superiority of the Turks', for Ṭughril, compared the nobility of the sultan's descent from Saljūq favourably to the pedigree of rival dynasties.[4] Another lost work, the *Maliknāma*, dedicated to Alp Arslān, recorded tales of Seljuq origins and the heroic deeds of the dynasty's progenitor; this was in essence the first *Saljūqnāma*.[5] However, later Great Seljuq sultans showed less interest in their pre-Islamic roots and sought legitimacy among their subjects largely through the trappings of Islamic kingship, such as the title *sulṭān* first claimed by Ṭughril. That the tribes were not necessarily impressed is illustrated by the notorious rebellion in Central Asia of 548/1153–4 by the Oghuz, who captured and imprisoned Sultan Sanjar. The Seljuqs gained a reputation for having betrayed their tribal followers which was still alive in the 11th/17th century: Abū 'l-Ghāzī Bahādur, genealogist of the Turks and prince of Khīva, recounts how the Seljuqs sought to deny their tribal roots and instead link themselves to the Turanian ruler Afrāsīyāb of Firdawsī's *Shāhnāma*:

> The Seljuqs are Türkmen; they used to say [to them], 'You are our brothers,' but they were no use to their tribe or people. Until they became kings, they claimed to be from the Qiniq tribe of Türkmen. After they became kings they said, 'A son of Afrāsīyāb fled from Kaykhusraw, and took refuge with the Qiniq Türkmen where he stayed. We are his descendants and come from the line of Afrāsīyāb.'[6]

The Seljuqs' reputation fared better in the Middle East, where their political legacy was perpetuated though the atabegate. A senior military figure would be appointed as a ward (*atābeg*) of a Seljuq prince. The latter would hold the nominal position of governor of a given appanage, but in fact real power would be exercised by the atabeg. The position of these atabegs would often become hereditary, and sometimes, as with the most powerful of these atabeg dynasties, the Ildegüzids, they would further boost their legitimacy by marrying into the Seljuq family.[7]

Yet Seljuq rule was certainly not uniformly viewed positively. An enthusiastic assessment is given in the chronicle attributed to Ṣadr al-Dīn Ḥusaynī, composed in the early 7th/13th century:

> The prosperity of the land was secured by their presence and the populace were richly endowed by their bounty and generosity, and justice and security spread throughout the land. Khurasan was ruined by the death of Sultan Sanjar b. Malikshāh and Iraq by the killing of Sultan Rukn al-Dīn Ṭughril b. Arslanshāh.[8]

Writing around 603/1206–7, probably in Kāshān in Iran, the bureaucrat Jurbādhqānī was much less keen. According to him, disaster was brought on the region not by the end of Seljuq rule, but by the death of the Ildegüzid atabeg Jahān Pahlavān in 582/1186–7.[9] The Seljuqs would soon be forgotten, for 'men of learning did not prosper in their days'.[10] This uncertain legacy is reflected in the Ildegüzid atabegs' experimentation with various means of legitimation. The atabeg Qizil Arslān (Jahān Pahlavān's son) at first proclaimed as sultan in place of Ṭughril III the infant Seljuq, Sanjar b. Sulaymānshāh. However, he later decided this was an unnecessary expedient and himself adopted the title of sultan, as did his successor and brother, Muẓaffar al-Dīn Uzbek.[11] In Iran, Iraq and Central Asia, Seljuq rule was followed (after the brief interlude of the Khwarazmian empire) by the Mongols. Old Perso-Islamic political ideas were sidelined as Chinggisid descent became a crucial factor in establishing a ruler's political legitimacy, and remained so into Timurid times.

In time, the breakaway branch of the Seljuq dynasty in Anatolia gradually acquired a prestige unmatched by their relatives in other territories. In the 5th/11th and 6th/12th centuries, the Seljuqs were just one Muslim dynasty among many others in Anatolia, and not necessarily the most powerful. However, following the elimination of their main rivals, the Danishmendids, by the late 6th/12th century the Seljuqs were able to establish themselves as the major power in Anatolia. As far as our inadequate sources can tell us, it was not until the 7th/13th century that Seljuq descent itself became a source of pride for the Anatolian dynasty. The first hint of this comes in the reign of ᶜAlāᵓ al-Dīn Kay Qubādh I (616–34/1219–37), for whom the court poet Qāniᶜī composed a vast verse *Saljūqnāma*, today lost apart from a few extracts preserved in Ibn Bībī's chronicle. The work took him forty years to complete, and allegedly ran to thirty volumes.[12] Its contents must remain a matter of surmise, but clearly the author would not have lacked space to detail the history and achievements of the Seljuq dynasty. Even this did not sate ᶜAlāᵓ al-Dīn's enthusiasm for the genre, for he also is said to have commissioned the poet Dahhānī to compose a 20,000 verse work on a similar theme, modelled on the *Shāhnāma*.[13]

This was an age when the Seljuq sultanate of Rum was emerging as a power of first rate importance in the eastern Mediterranean, and it is natural that its ruler should have sought to affirm his place in history. Nonetheless, ᶜAlāᵓ al-Dīn's successors did not – as far as we can tell – emulate his lead in commissioning *Saljūqnāma*s. For Ibn Bībī, writing in the late 7th/13th century, who composed a detailed history of the Seljuq state in Anatolia which idealised ᶜAlāᵓ al-Dīn Kay Qubādh I, the ancestry of the dynasty barely merits a passing mention.[14] Ibn Bībī does allude to Arslan Isrāᵓīl b. Saljūq, the father of Qutlumush from whom the Anatolian branch of the Seljuq family was descended. However, Ibn Bībī is not interested in him for the nobility of his ancestry, but as a means of linking the Seljuqs to the Banū Isrāᵓīl, the Israelites of the Qurᵓān; like the Seljuqs of Rum when Ibn Bībī was writing, they were a group that had lost God's former favour.[15]

Yet even if the sultans themselves did not always feel the need to emphasise their lineage, dubious claims to legitimacy based on Seljuq descent had already started their long career. A good example of this is the court official Saᶜd al-Dīn Köpek, who, not content with the absolute power he briefly seized after ᶜAlāᵓ al-Dīn Kay Qubādh I's death, even sought to arrogate to himself the title of sultan. He claimed to be the illegitimate son of ᶜAlāᵓ al-Dīn's father, Ghīyāth al-Dīn Kay Khusraw I, 'and by this report and fabrication, it became established in people's minds that he was of Seljuq descent (*kih ū az nizhād-i Saljūq ast*)'.[16] Köpek then tried to persuade the sultan (Ghīyāth al-Dīn Kay Khusraw II b. ᶜAlāᵓ al-Dīn Kay Qubādh) to change the colour of the royal standard from the Sunni, Abbasid black. Köpek hoped to use this symbolic abandonment of the Abbasids to persuade the caliph to grant him the sultanate in place of ᶜAlāᵓ al-Dīn's son, the rightful heir. The usurper was himself soon overthrown, but his example shows that in Anatolia, aspiring claimants to the throne now had to prove they were of Seljuq descent. This contrasts strongly with the earlier situation, when dynasties like the Danishmendids and Saltukids ruled without boasting of any Seljuq blood (even if in practice, Anatolian rulers were connected to one another through a web of marriage alliances; these, however, seem to have been made for purely practical political purposes).

Indeed, the very survival of the Seljuq dynasty in the second half of the 7th/13th century is itself testimony to the aura of legitimacy it gave to the business of ruling Anatolia. After the defeat of Ghīyāth al-Dīn Kay Khusraw II by the Mongols at the battle of Köse Dağ in 641/1243, Rum was subject to the descendants of Chinggis Khān. Although the Seljuq sultan's ignominious flight from the field of battle, leaving his vizier to seek what terms he could, hardly redounded to the dynasty's credit, Ghīyāth al-Dīn and his successors were maintained in office, if not in power. While the Mongols used their own network of officials to rule Anatolia, they were not apparently ready to dispense entirely with the Seljuq dynasty, although succession to the sultanate was dependent on Mongol support. Of course, the Seljuq sultanate was preserved primarily because this suited the Mongols, who used the rival Seljuq claimants as puppets in their own internal power struggles, just as they did in neighbouring Georgia with its Bagratid kings. Yet for all the Seljuqs' political impotence in the late 7th/13th century, with many sultans but children, a certain prestige still adhered to the dynastic name.

The potency of Seljuq descent is vividly illustrated by the events of 675/1277, when a man nick-named Jimrī appeared in Anatolia. It was claimed that he was the son or grandson of Sultan ᶜIzz al-Dīn Kay Kāwūs II, who had been forced to flee to the Crimea following disputes with the Mongols. This Jimrī fell into the hands of Mehmed Beg, son of the Türkmen leader Karaman who dominated south-central Anatolia and founded an eponymous dynasty that was to succeed the Seljuqs. Mehmed Beg seized the opportunity to buy himself some political legitimacy through his own tame Seljuq. He wrote to the senior Seljuq official, the *nāᵓib al-salṭana* Amīn al-Dīn Mīkāᵓīl, saying,

> The son of Sultan ᶜIzz al-Dīn Kay Kāwūs is with us. A group of reliable people have testified to the truth of his descent. You should hasten to do homage to him and kiss hands. If there is any doubt or suspicion about him in this respect [i.e. his lineage] send a reliable old court official of this family, who can inspect this king and offer you a complete and clear report. If he is of the true lineage, both you and we must obey him.[17]

Although it was Mehmed Beg b. Karaman who held real power, he did so only as vizier, hiding behind the fiction (as Ibn Bībī would have it) that he was serving a Seljuq. It is interesting to note that even according to Ibn Bībī's hostile account, Mehmed Beg tried to strengthen his legitimacy by seeking the hand of the daughter of Sultan Rukn al-Dīn Kılıç Arslan IV, not for himself but for Jimrī.[18] Evidently, there were limits to Mehmed Beg's presumptions and he felt not only unable to rule without the sanction of a member of the Seljuq family (whether real or not is another matter), but did not even dare to aspire to marry into it. Mongol intervention eventually assured the fall of Jimrī and Mehmed Beg and the restoration of the Mongol puppet Seljuq sultan, Ghīyāth al-Dīn Kay Khusraw III. Yet the Karamanids remained an important force, and they soon seem to have got over their modesty about claiming a blood link to the Seljuqs.

It was not only Anatolian rivals of the Seljuqs who sought to connect themselves to the dynasty. Around the same time as Jimrī's revolt, the Mamluk ruler of Egypt and Syria, Baybars, succeeded in occupying Kayseri briefly. He was careful to present himself as a legitimate successor to the dynasty, continuing the Seljuq style of military band (*nawba*), sitting under a Seljuq parasol (*chatr*, one of the symbols of rule) and seating himself on the Seljuq throne in Kayseri.[19] Even for the ruler of an established and powerful dynasty, then, the regalia of his defeated Seljuq opponents retained a certain prestige.

Ghīyāth al-Dīn Masᶜūd, probably the last Seljuq sultan,[20] died in 708/1308. The Ilkhanid ruler Ghāzān had evidently already decided that the newly Muslim Mongols could dispense with the Seljuqs, for he had started minting coins in his own name across Anatolia, even in Konya itself, in the last years of the 7th/13th century. This contrasts with the previous practice which had been to allow the Seljuq sultans to continue striking their own coins without even mentioning the Mongol ruler on them.[21] The political irrelevance of the Seljuqs is underlined by the fact that relatively few chroniclers even thought Ghīyāth al-Dīn Masᶜūd's passing worth mentioning, and indeed the sources do not even agree on the last member of the dynasty to reign, some claiming it to have been ᶜAlāᵓ al-Dīn Farāmarz,[22] or perhaps a certain ᶜAlāᵓ al-Dīn Kılıç Arslan b. Kay Khusraw who may have ascended the Seljuq throne in 710/1310.[23] Ḥamdallāh Qazvīnī, writing in the mid-8th/14th century, states that members of the Seljuq household survived as rulers on the frontiers of Anatolia and on its coasts.[24] Indeed, according to the 9th/15th-century Ottoman historian Yazıcızade Ali, Ghīyāth al-Dīn Masᶜūd had installed his children in Simre near Amasya and at Sinop on the Black Sea, where they escaped the Mongol attempts to destroy the family.[25] Whether or not these individuals were really of Seljuq descent is more difficult to say, as we shall see.

Despite their murky end, the Seljuqs remained a focus for local political loyalties. For instance, Qāḍī (Judge) Aḥmad of Niğde (b. 685/1286) wrote a history of the Seljuq dynasty, now lost, in addition to his sole extant (but unpublished) work mixing history, *ḥadīth* and sundry geographical information entitled *al-Walad al-Shafīq*.[26] Qāḍī Aḥmad's *Saljūqnāma* was written for a certain emir Shams al-Dīn Dündar Beg b. Ḥamza of Niğde,[27] otherwise unknown to history, which suggests a certain popular appeal of tales of the Seljuq dynasty beyond the political purposes of legitimation. The sections on the Seljuqs that survive in *al-Walad al-Shafīq* serve to give an impression of the Qāḍī Aḥmad's treatment of the dynasty. He is anxious to establish the legitimacy of transfer of power, first from the Ghaznavids to the Seljuqs, and then from the Great Seljuqs to the Seljuqs of Rum. The latter transfer is described in terms that some Ottoman historians would themselves use to explain the Ottomans' own inheritance of sovereignty from the Seljuqs of Anatolia: the weakness of the dynasty meant they forfeited their right to rule, and the symbols of power were transferred to the new ruler, in this case Kılıç Arslan, sultan of Rum.[28] The awkwardness of the often hostile relations between the Great Seljuqs and their relatives in Anatolia is glossed over, and the latter are provided with a falsified genealogy that links them directly to Malikshāh, omitting the rebel Qutlumush. Qāḍī Aḥmad goes out of his way to stress the purity of the Seljuq lineage, emphasising that as his ancestors had served the Seljuq state in Anatolia since its inception, he was in a position to know: 'in their descent there is no illegitimacy (*valad al-zinā nīst*)' he remarks, and slightly later reaffirms the point: from the whole length of dynasty from beginning to end there was no blemish on their lineage and no unknown person had infiltrated it (*bīgāna-yi mutadākhil nīst*).[29] It is interesting that Qāḍī Aḥmad should go out of his way to deny the 'lies'[30] about the dynasty's lineage, given he was writing in 733/1333, quarter of a century after the last Seljuq sultan had died (at least in his view, for he emphasises that the dynasty had come to an end with Ghīyāth al-Dīn Masᶜūd's death). The target of these comments is unclear, but could well have been the Karamanids, whom Qāḍī Aḥmad's father had played a prominent role in fighting and who were a continuing threat to the security of Niğde;[31] as we shall see, they claimed Seljuq descent. At any rate, it is clear that long after the dynasty's demise, even outside of court circles (for Qāḍī Aḥmad is very much a provincial author), questions of how the Seljuq sultanate had come to be established and who had the right to call himself a Seljuq remained emotive.

The death of the last sultan did not immediately result in the extinction of the dynasty. In the very year that he completed *al-Walad al-Shafīq*, Qāḍī Aḥmad records the death of Sultan Rukn al-Dīn Kılıç Arslan's daughter, who was buried in Niğde[32] – perhaps the town, with figures like Dündar Beg and Qāḍī Aḥmad himself, was a stronghold of Seljuq loyalists. Later in the 8th/14th century, another prose *Saljūqnāma* was composed for 'the descendant of the Seljuqs, the residue of the Seljuq sultans, the sultan ᶜAlāᵓ al-Dīn b. Saljūq Sulaymānshāh b. Saljūq Malik Rukn al-Dīn b. Sulṭān Ghīyāth al-Dīn Kay Khusraw'.[33] The prevalence of the name 'Saljūq' among ᶜAlāᵓ al-Dīn's immediate progenitors rather suggests that they were striving – or he was – to prove a point, perhaps rather too hard. Certainly 'sultan' ᶜAlāᵓ al-Dīn, unattested in any other source, is unlikely to have exerted the power implied by his grandiose title of *shāhzāda-yi jahān*, 'prince of the world'.[34] Indeed, the only way of dating him even approximately is by the death of his brother – also called Saljūq – which occurred on 6 Muḥarram 765/15 October 1363.[35] Probably he lived in Konya, which seems to have been where the anonymous *Saljūqnāma* was compiled by various hands.[36] His father may have been the Sulaymānshāh who was taken prisoner by the Mongol general Timurtaş in 726/1326,[37] suggesting that the surviving members of the dynasty were not entirely politically quiescent. This is confirmed by Yazıcızade

Ali, who states that when Timurtaş came to Anatolia to suppress revolts, he had the descendants of the Seljuq family in Akşehir and Konya strangled,[38] in accordance with Turco-Mongol traditions for ensuring royal blood was not spilt. The existence of these individuals confirms what Qāḍī Aḥmad suggests, that pretenders to the Seljuq throne remained active in 8th/14th century Anatolia, even if the veracity of their claims was far from universally accepted. Any attempts they may have made to revive Seljuq rule were of such little consequence as to be ignored by our admittedly limited sources.

Seljuq claimants persisted into the 9th/15th century too, even if their activities were usually of only local importance. In 821/1418, a certain Ḥusayn Beg b. Alp Arslān seized the Black Sea *beylik* (principality) of Canik, claiming that he was 'one of the descendants of the Seljuqs (*min awlād al-Salājiqa*)'.[39] The governors of ᶜAlāʾīya, today's Alanya, on the Mediterranean coast, also purported to have a Seljuq lineage through 'a daughter of the Seljuq family', although the historian Müneccimbaşı sceptically notes, 'it is also reported that they are descended from one of their [i.e. the Seljuqs'] commanders.'[40] In fact they were probably of Karamanid origin, but the second ruler of this dynasty was known by the self-consciously Seljuq-sounding name of Kılıç Arslan Beg.[41] It was not just petty rulers who sought to bask in the reflected glory of an association with the Seljuq house. The historian Shukrullāh, himself a native of Amasya, proudly asserts that Sultan Masᶜūd made his home in the city, and built the nearby town of Simre, along with mosques and *khānqāhs*, 'and [the Seljuqs'] tomb in Simre remains a place of pilgrimage [*mazār*] for Muslims to this day'.[42] In so far as the tale has any historical basis, Shukrullāh must be referring to Ghīyāth al-Dīn Masᶜūd, who is recorded by Aḥmad of Niğde to have been buried in Simre.[43] Although the idea that this helpless Mongol puppet would have embarked on large-scale construction programmes may seem improbable, the continuing veneration for the Seljuq family by an author writing in the Ottoman lands in the early 9th/15th century is symptomatic of its enduring prestige. It is in this context that we must consider the attempts of two of the principal powers of late medieval Anatolia, the Ottomans and the Karamanids, to portray themselves as legitimate successors to the Seljuqs.[44]

For the Ottomans, the enduring power of the Seljuq political legacy seems to have presented both an opportunity and a threat. It was an opportunity in that if the Ottomans could establish a connection with the Seljuqs, then they could gain legitimacy for their rule in Anatolia, which initially was probably rather tenuous. It was a threat in that in reality the Ottomans had had very little to do with the Seljuqs. Although the early Ottoman chroniclers generally treat Seljuq history only fairly briefly, a deeper interest in the dynasty is reflected by the Turkish translations and adaptations of works on Seljuq history complied by Yazıcızade Ali for Sultan Murad II (824-55/1421–51).[45] These comprised, firstly, an account of the Oghuz, derived from Rashīd al-Dīn's *Jāmi*ᶜ *al-Tawārīkh*. The latter had aimed to provide both Mongols and Turks with a common ancestry in the figure of Oghuz-khān, who was a thinly veiled, mythologised, disguise for Chinggis Khān. Membership of the Oghuz tribe became a source of legitimacy for 9th/15th- and 10th/16th-century rulers, and the Ottomans as much as their Akkoyunlu and Karakoyunlu rivals sought to vaunt their Oghuz ancestry,[46] ironically in view of the negative associations of the Oghuz in Seljuq times.[47] The following two sections of Yazıcızade Ali's work were Turkish extracts from Rāvandī's *Rāḥat al-ṣudūr* and abridgements of Ibn Bībī's *al-Awāmir al-ᶜAlāʾīya*.[48] The former was intended to supply the Great Seljuq background, the latter the connection with the Seljuqs of Rum. Yazıcızade Ali's intent, in what is perhaps the earliest extant prose work of Ottoman historiography, was to link the Ottomans to their predecessors and to affirm the dynasty's place in both Islamic history and that of the Turko-Mongol peoples.

Early Ottoman historians adopted a variety of approaches to the Seljuq connection, although all centre around the transfer of power to Osman, the founder of the dynasty, from Sultan ᶜAlāʾ al-Dīn (who becomes a legendary figure in the Ottoman sources, variously identified as ᶜAlāʾ al-Dīn Kay Qubādh I and ᶜAlāʾ al-Dīn Kay Qubādh II or even ᶜAlāʾ al-Dīn Farāmarz).[49] Aşıkpaşazade (d. late 9th/15th century) implies that the Ottomans' ancestor Ertuğrul had reached Anatolia before the Seljuqs had,[50] a theme developed by Karamanlı Mehmed Paşa, who served Mehmed the Conqueror as vizier between 881/1476 and 886/1481. He claimed that the Seljuqs only arrived in Rum in the aftermath of the Mongol conquest of Baghdad, and that Qiniq Alp, descendant of Oghuz-khān, who was the ancestor of Ertuğrul, was already settled in the area around Akhlāṭ.[51] Nonetheless, even these accounts accept the Seljuqs as the legitimate sultans of Rum. ᶜAlāʾ al-Dīn is portrayed as recognising Osman's merits, especially after the latter's success in capturing the castle of Karacahisar from the Byzantines, and handing over to him the symbols of sovereignty, the standard and the drums, 'as befits a sultan', as Mehmed Paşa puts it.[52] A different version, found in Oruç (9th/15th century) and Cenabi (10th/16th century), claims that the Seljuqs eventually lost their right to rule by the oppression of the last sultan, Ghiyāth al-Dīn, and Osman was chosen as the new ruler by the consensus of the *ghāzī*s.[53] The most widely accepted version of these narratives of Ottoman origins was established by Neşri, writing around 895/1490, who claimed that the Seljuq ᶜAlāʾ al-Dīn II had planned to appoint Osman his heir, but died before he could formally bestow the position on Osman. Nonetheless, the insignia of rulership had already reached the latter.[54]

By the 10th/16th century, the Ottoman empire had become a world power, with military commitments across the Mediterranean and deep into Africa and central Europe. However, the Seljuq connection remained an important part of the dynasty's efforts to gain acceptance.[55] Particularly telling in this respect is the collection of diplomatic correspondence gathered by Feridun Beg under the title of *Münşeat ül-Selatin*, which was presented to Murad III in 982/1575. The collection starts with a number of Persian documents in fact forged by Feridun Beg himself which purport to be Sultan ᶜAlāᵓ al-Dīn's grant of the town of Söğüt, the first Ottoman power-base, to Osman.[56] Another mark of the continuing importance of the Seljuq past was Aḥmad b. Maḥmūd's Ottoman translation of the Arabic history of the Seljuqs attributed to Ṣadr al-Dīn Ḥusaynī, which he supplemented with material drawn from other medieval historians such as Ibn al-Athīr.[57] The work concentrates, as the Arabic original had, on the Great Seljuqs; only a short concluding section deals with the Seljuqs of Rum, bringing matters down to their collapse and the transfer of power to Osman. The purpose of the translation is mysterious; the author seems to suggest his aim is to show that the Ottomans were the best and most just rulers,[58] and perhaps the choice of Ṣadr al-Dīn's work, which devotes much attention to the unedifying and destructive struggles between the Seljuqs and the Ildegüzids, is meant to remind the audience of their good fortune to live under the Ottoman dynasty. The Ottomans were fond of vaunting their superiority over their predecessors, as is suggested by a verse inscribed in the Topkapı Palace comparing the building to ᶜAlāᵓ al-Dīn I's famous palace of Kaykubādīya: 'Beside this royal arch, the envy of Caesar, the palace of Kay Qubādh is but an old tent.'[59]

Nonetheless, Ottoman historiography continued to feel the need to stress the legitimacy of the transfer of power from the Seljuqs. Even at the end of the 11th/17th century Müneccimbaşı repeats the story of ᶜAlāᵓ al-Dīn's investiture of Osman.[60] For similar reasons, probably, Yazıcızade Ali included a story about the Ottoman sultan Bayezid I's conquest of Salonica in the late 8th/14th century, in the course of which he seized the nearby town of Berrhoea/Karaferia from a descendant of ᶜIzz al-Dīn Kay Kāwūs II named Leyizkus, who was a Christian. Leyizkus was recruited into the Ottoman army, serving in eastern Anatolia, and requested a 'diploma of exemption'. 'When Bayezid realised he was of Seljuq origin, he accepted his request and granted him [the diploma]', after which Leyizkus retired to Macedonia and became a priest.[61] Thus the Seljuq descendant is shown accepting Ottoman suzerainty, as well as implicitly forfeiting any political legitimacy of his own by his attachment to Christianity.

Thus this continued interest in the Seljuqs should not be seen as some sort of indulgent antiquarian nostalgia. The legitimacy provided by membership, real or fabricated, of the Seljuq house, remained potent long after the establishment of the Ottomans. At the beginning of the 9th/15th century, the Qāḍī Bedreddin of Simavna led a major revolt against Ottoman rule in the Balkans. The hagiography written by Bedreddin's grandson stresses the nobility and prestige of the *qāḍī*'s ancestry: Bedreddin's grandfather had himself been not just a famous *ghāzī*, a disciple of the mystic Jalāl al-Dīn Rūmī, and a vizier to the Seljuqs, but was also himself of Seljuq descent.[62] 'Know that his lineage [*nesl*] is to Sultan ᶜAlāᵓ al-Dīn/there is no doubt in this statement.'[63] Clearly, the grandson's aim was to demonstrate the illustriousness of Bedreddin's ancestry in contrast to the Ottomans, who had eventually captured and executed him.

Challenges based on the superiority of the rebel's connections to the Seljuq house persisted for centuries, especially in the south of central Anatolia, the Seljuq and Karamanid heartland. An illustration of this is presented by our main source for the Karamanids, the history by Şikari which was composed in the 11th/16th century (although perhaps drawing on older sources). Şikari, whose sympathies clearly lay with the defunct Karamanid dynasty rather the Ottomans, demotes Osman to the lowly position of the chief shepherd to the Seljuqs.[64] For Şikari, it was the Karamanids, not the Ottomans, who were the legitimate heirs to the Seljuqs. As in the Ottoman legends, a semi-mythical ᶜAlāᵓ al-Dīn played the key part in transferring the right to rule on his successors. The sultan bestows the royal gifts of drums and the standard, as well as robes of honour, on Karaman, son of Nūr-i Ṣūfī, the founder of the Karamanid dynasty.[65] Şikari's presentation of ᶜAlāᵓ al-Dīn is often quite negative, stressing his treacherous murder of Karaman through poisoning,[66] and attributing the eventual loss of his throne to his treachery and injustice (*ẓulm*) towards the Karamanids. On the other hand, Şikari emphasises the Karamanids' blood link to the Seljuqs through ᶜAlāᵓ al-Dīn's cousin, Melik Arslan, who granted his daughter in marriage to Karaman; through her the Karamanid rulers Mehmed Beg and Mahmud traced their descent.[67] The Karamanids' Seljuq blood was reinforced by the marriage of the Karamanid ᶜAlāᵓ al-Dīn Mehmed to the great grand-daughter of Kay Khusraw (presumably Ghīyāth al-Dīn Kay Khusraw II),[68] from whom the Karamanid Ibrāhīm Beg was descended. That these tales were current long before Şikari's time and probably reflect the official propaganda of the Karamanid house is suggested by Yazıcızade Ali, who, writing while the dynasty was still in power, remarks that the Karamanids' claim to Seljuq descent derives from their marriage to a daughter of the Seljuq family who had escaped Timurtaş's massacre of the Seljuqs by fleeing to Karaman.[69]

Thus Ottoman rule over Karaman does not seem to have diminished a certain sense of loyalty to its erstwhile rulers, which may have served as a means for expressing local dissatisfaction. As late as 1004/1596, the Ottoman chronicler

Selaniki reports that another Seljuq pretender raised the banner of revolt during the so-called Celali rebellions:

> In the region of Turgut and in Karaman, an impious, low man from the clan called Davud claimed to be a descendant of the last Seljuq ᶜAlāᵓ al-Dīn Farāmarz, whose line became extinct three hundred years ago. He got a rabble to flock to him, saying, 'The Ottomans have gone down the road of oppression and aggression, I will provide justice.'[70]

Continuing interest in the pre-Ottoman past is reflected in the copies of Şikari's work produced in the early 12th/18th century, a time of troubles for the empire as it was racked by revolts such as the Patrona Halil rebellion of 1115/1704. The oldest extant manuscript dates to 1119/1707, the next to 1153/1740.[71] As if in response, in 1161/1748, a curious work which also clearly has roots in the Konya region was copied, the *Saljūq Shāhnāma* of Ünsi.[72] Written in a rather strange Persian, this little verse chronicle purports to have been composed in Aleppo in 785/1383, a claim which should perhaps be treated with a measure of scepticism. To date only one manuscript has been discovered, the wherabouts of which are today unknown.[73] Ünsi's theme is also the transfer of power, but his aim is to discredit the Karamanids as usurpers of the Seljuq throne. He starts by tracing the Seljuqs' ancestry back to Oghuz-khān,[74] which is perhaps a reaction to Karamanid boasts of a more noble lineage than the Seljuqs through their own pretensions to Oghuz descent.[75] The Seljuqs are thus given the same mythological Oghuz descent as the Ottomans, with whom their common ancestry is underlined. A completely legendary history of the foundation of Seljuq rule in Anatolia follows, but much of the text is taken up with an account of the Seljuq-Karamanid wars. Osman Ghāzī only features briefly in the narrative, but where he does it is to contrast his courage and loyalty with the despicable Karamanids who were attempting to overthrow ᶜAlāᵓ al-Dīn.[76] In constrast to Şikari's hostile depiction of the last Seljuq sultan, Ünsi calls him 'of good character, pious behaviour, a scholar and an ascetic.'[77] Despite the massive destruction caused by the Mongols, the sultan was able to return to his throne, fortified by the tidings of the Ottoman victory over the infidel at the fortress of Karacahisar.[78] However, the Karamanids' love of plunder could not be restrained,[79] and they repeatedly but vainly sought to overthrow the sultan. Despite ᶜAlāᵓ al-Dīn's efforts to act as a good ruler, restoring the ruined mosque of his predecessor Kaykhusraw, 'fate was treacherous and the fire of strife swiftly appeared' (*līk nakard dahr vafā/ ātish-i fitna tīz shud numā*).[80] Another Mongol attack caused further devastation, and the Karamanids allied themselves with the invaders. Although ᶜAlāᵓ al-Dīn sought Ottoman help against the rebels, Ibn Karaman saw the opportunity to trick the sultan's underage son, Ghīyāth al-Dīn, and the latter was lured on by the promise of the sultanate to murder his father. The text concludes with the lamentations of the people of Konya at the loss of the Seljuq sultan.

Ünsi at no point states explicitly that the Karamanids succeeded the Seljuqs. As with Şikari, the reader is clearly meant to conclude that the dynasty forfeited its right to rule by its own behaviour, in this case by Ghīyāth al-Dīn's murder of his father. The presentation of the Ottomans as the Seljuqs' relatives and loyal supporters is clearly meant to underline the legitimacy of their rule, even if their rise is nowhere directly described. The references to Osman's victory at Karacahisar suggest the author was acquainted with the traditions of the Ottoman chronicles, although why the work was composed in Persian, evidently not the author's native language, remains a mystery. Whenever and why ever it was originally written, Ünsi's *Saljūq Shāhnāma* illustrates the continuing vitality of debates about the origins of the Seljuqs, Ottomans and Karamanids, and legitimate succession to the Seljuqs right into the 12th/18th century. Perhaps Ünsi's work was intended to counter the pro-Karamanid stance evinced by Şikari, whose work was clearly being circulated roughly contemporaneously. The upkeep of the tomb of Nūr-i Ṣūfī, ancestor of the Karamanid dynasty, into the same comparatively late period also underlines the continued relevance of pre-Ottoman dynasties.[81]

It was suggested at the outset that the power of Seljuq legitimacy was restricted to Anatolia. This is probably connected with the comparatively late Islamisation of Anatolia and the shortage of other political traditions upon which Muslim rulers could establish a popular appeal, in contrast to other areas of the Middle East where the heritage of the Abbasids and even the Umayyads remained the focus for legitimacy. Yet empires may facilitate the spread of ideas, and in the early 11th/17th century in Ottoman Basra, the local governor, Afrāsīyāb, claimed mixed Seljuq and Arab descent. Although Afrāsīyāb, probably a local tribal chief, contented himself with the title of Paşa, he achieved a de facto independence from both Baghdad and Istanbul.[82] However useful a forged Seljuq lineage might be to a local politician on the make seeking to aggrandise his status, one must remember that by no means everyone who claimed Seljuq ancestry sought to do so as means of undermining Ottoman rule. The Ottoman archives record several Anatolian tribes with the name Seljuq, presumably self-consciously linking themselves to the dynasty.[83] In the 19th century the Ottoman official Cevdet Paşa recorded, presumably on the basis of what he was told locally, that the Varsak Türkmen tribes of the Kozan mountains in Cilicia were 'left over from Seljuq times'[84] – another deliberate identification with the Seljuq past. Indeed, the reign of the Ottoman sultan Abdülmecit II (1839–61) witnessed a resurgence of interest in things Seljuq as government officials restored medieval monuments.

For instance, in the Cappadocian town of Ürgüp, where local legends claimed that Sultan Rukn al-Dīn Kılıç Arslan IV fought a heroic last stand against the Mongols in 663/1265, the governor of Kayseri Vecihi Paşa restored the place thought to be his tomb and erected an inscription dated 1852 commemorating the ill-fated sultan's association with the town.[85] Elsewhere, restoration concentrated on mosques, but the repair inscriptions often take care to refer to the structure's orginal Seljuq patron, as at the Alaeddin mosque at Sinop.[86]

Despite the astonishing longevity of the political potency of the Seljuq name, it is wise to close with a note of caution. Even in Anatolia, the Seljuq connection was but one means of seeking legitimacy, and one should be wary of overestimating it. Many of the beyliks of post-Mongol Anatolia were based in areas that were on the peripheries of Seljuq control, or outside of it. Even in the core Seljuq lands, links with the Mongols were probably of greater relevance to the legitimacy of some beyliks like the Eretnids of Kayseri. When Yazıcızade Ali remarks that the emirs of Karasi and Saruhan (in western Anatolia) had been servants of the Seljuq sultan, he is not trying to pay them a compliment.[87] In time, even Amasya seems to have forgotten its Seljuq connection as the alleged burial place of Ghīyāth al-Dīn Mas^cūd, or at least it lost any political significance. As regions where the Seljuq name remained a political rallying point until the eve of modernity, Konya and Karaman stand out as exceptions rather than the rule. Nonetheless, they suggest that the most lasting influence of the Seljuq dynasty itself may have derived less from any specific achievements than in the uses to which its name could be put by later generations.

NOTES

1. *EI2*, s.v. 'Atabeg' (C. Cahen); Ann K. S. Lambton, *Continuity and Change in Medieval Persia: Aspects of Administrative, Economic and Social History, 11th–14th Century* (London, 1988), pp. 229–33.
2. A. C. S. Peacock, *Early Seljūq History: A New Interpretation* (London, 2010), pp. 60–8.
3. Sibṭ b. al-Jawzī, *Mirʾāt al-zamān*, ed. Ali Sevim (Ankara, 1968), p. 174.
4. Ibn Ḥassūl, *Kitāb Tafḍīl al-atrāk ʿalā sāʾir al-ajnād* (İbni Hassulün Türkler hakkındaki eserinin arapça metni), ed. A. Azzavi, *Belleten* 4 (1940), pp. 49–50.
5. See the discussion in Peacock, *Early Seljuq History*, pp. 8–9, 27–31.
6. Ebugazi Bahadır Han, *Şecere-i Terākime (Türkmenlerin Soykütüğü)*, ed. Zuhal Kargı Ölmez (Ankara, 1996), p. 205.
7. Ṣadr al-Dīn al-Ḥusaynī, *Akhbār al-dawla al-Saljūqīya*, ed. Muḥammad Iqbāl (Beirut, 1984), pp. 133, 140.
8. Ibid. p. 196.
9. Jurbādhqānī, *Tarjuma-yi Tārīkh-i Yamīnī*, ed. Jaʿfar Shiʿār (Tehran, 1966), p. 5.
10. Ibid. p. 9; cf. Julie Scott Meisami, *Persian Historiography to the End of the Twelfth Century* (Edinburgh, 1999), p. 258.

11. *EIr*, s.v. 'Atabakān-e Ādarbāyjān' (K. A. Luther).
12. Mehmed Fuad Köprülü, *The Seljuks of Anatolia: their History and Culture According to Local Sources*, trans. and ed. Gary Leiser (Salt Lake City, UT, 1992), pp. 15–17.
13. Ibid. pp. 17–18; Şikari, *Karamanname (Zamanın Kahramanı Karamaniler'in Tarihi)*, eds Metin Sözen and Necdet Sakaoğlu (Karaman, 2005), f. 5a–b.
14. Ibn Bībī, *al-Awāmir al-ʿAlāʾīya*, facsimile edn by Adnan Sadık Erzi (Ankara, 1956), pp. 3–4.
15. Sara Nur Yıldız, 'Mongol rule in thirteenth century Seljuk Anatolia: the politics of conquest and history writing' (PhD University of Chicago, 2006), pp. 540–1.
16. Ibn Bībī, *al-Awāmir al-ʿAlāʾīya*, p. 475.
17. Ibid. p. 691.
18. Ibid. pp. 696–7.
19. Al-Qalqashandī, *Ṣubḥ al-aʿshā* (Cairo, 1338/1919), XIV, pp. 154–5; Faruk Sümer, *Yabanlu Pazar: Selçuklular Devrinde Milletlerarası Büyük Bir Fuar* (Istanbul, 1985), pp. 83, 122–3.
20. Aḥmad of Niğde, *al-Walad al-Shafīq*, Süleymaniye Library, Istanbul, MS Fatih 4518, f. 151a–b; Aqsarāʾī, *Musāmarat al-akhbār*, ed. Osman Turan (Ankara, 1944), p. 301.
21. Ömer Diler, *Ilkhans: Coinage of the Persian Mongols* (Istanbul, 2006), pp. 360, 363. In 698/1298–9, there was a joint issue in the names of ʿAlāʾ al-Dīn Farāmarz and Ghāzān, but the experiment does not seem to have been repeated; ibid. p. 375.
22. Cf. *Tārīkh-i āl-i Saljūq dar Anaṭūlī*, ed. Nādira Jalālī (Tehran, 1999), p. 132.
23. Osman Turan (ed.), *İstanbulʾun Fethinden Önce Yazılmış Tarihî Takvimler* (Istanbul, 1984), pp. 78–9.
24. Ḥamdallāh Qazvīnī, *Tārīkh-i guzīda*, ed. ʿAbd al-Ḥusayn Navāʾī (Tehran, 1960), p. 480; cf. Osman Turan, *Selçuklular Zamanında Türkiye: Siyasi Tarih Alp Arslan'dan Osman Gazi'ye* (Istanbul, 2002 [1971]), pp. 644–5 on the last Seljuqs.
25. Yazıcızâde Ali, *Tevârîh-i âl-i Selçuk*, ed. Abdullah Bakır (Istanbul, 2009), p. 907.
26. On the author and his work see A. C. S. Peacock, 'Aḥmad of Niğde's *al-Walad al-Shafīq* and the Seljuk past', *Anatolian Studies* 54 (2004), pp. 95–107.
27. Aḥmad of Niğde, *al-Walad al-Shafīq*, f. 141a.
28. Ibid. f. 146b; Peacock, 'Aḥmad of Niğde's', p. 102.
29. Aḥmad of Niğde, *al-Walad al-Shafīq*, ff. 150b, 152b.
30. Ibid. f. 151a.
31. On this see Peacock, 'Aḥmad of Niğde's', pp. 99, 106.
32. Aḥmad of Niğde, *al-Walad al-Shafīq*, f. 152a.
33. *Tārīkh-i āl-i Saljūq*, p. 39.
34. Ibid. p. 39.
35. Ibid. p. 134.
36. Charles Melville, 'The early Persian historiography of Anatolia', in *History and Historiography of Post-Mongol Central Asia and the Middle East: Studies in Honor of John E. Woods*, eds J. Pfeiffer, S. Quinn and E. Tucker (Wiesbaden, 2006), pp. 150–1.
37. *Tārīkh-i āl-i Saljūq*, p. 132.
38. Yazıcızâde Ali, *Tevârîh-i âl-i Selçuk*, pp. 907–8.
39. Müneccimbaşı, *Jāmiʿ al-duwal*, Nuruosmaniye Library, Istanbul, MS 3172, f. 133a.
40. Ibid. f. 133a.
41. On the Alanya dynasty, see İsmail Hakkı Uzunçarşılı, *Anadolu Beylikleri ve Akkoyunlu, Karakoyunlu Devletleri* (Ankara, 1937), pp. 92–5.

42. Shukrullāh, *Bahjat al-tawārīkh*, Süleymaniye Library, Istanbul, MS Fatih 4203, f. 347a. On Shukrullāh's own connection with Amasya see Theodore Seif, 'Der Abschnitt über die Osmanen in Šukrüllāh's persischer Universalgeschichte', *Mitteilungen zur Osmanischen Geschichte* 2 (1923–6), p. 66. Müneccimbaşı, however, attributes the tomb and the town to Rukn al-Dīn Masᶜūd (d. 551/1156): see Müneccimbaşı Ahmed b. Lütfullah, *Câmiu 'd-Duvel: Selçuklular Tarihi II: Anadolu Selçukluları ve Beylikler*, ed. Ali Öngül (Izmir, 2001), Arabic text p. 14–15. For more on Simre, Amasya and their Seljuq connection, see Abdi-zade Hüseyin Hüsameddin, *Amasya Tarihi* (Ankara, 1986), I, pp. 333–42.
43. Aḥmad of Niğde, *al-Walad al-Shafīq*, f. 151b.
44. On the competition for legitimacy in this period, see Hasan Basri Karadeniz, *Osmanlılar ile Beylikler Arasında Anadolu'da Meşruiyet Mücadelesi (XIV–XVI Yüzyıllar)* (Istanbul, 2008).
45. On this work, see Paul Wittek, 'Yazijioghlu Ali on the Christian Turks of the Dobruja', *BSOAS* 14, 3 (1952), pp. 642–7.
46. Barbara Flemming, 'Political genealogies in the sixteenth century', *Osmanlı Araştırmaları* 7–8 (1988), pp. 123–7.
47. Peacock, *Early Seljūq History*, pp. 48–53.
48. The text published as *Histoire des Seldjoucides d'Asie Mineure d'après Ibn Bībī: texte turc*, ed. M. T. Houtsma in *Recueil des Textes Relatifs à l'Histoire des Seldjoucides*, vol. 3 (Leiden, 1902) is only a partial edition; the complete text has now been made available in the edition by Abdullah Bakır (Istanbul, 2009) used here.
49. Colin Imber, 'The Ottoman dynastic myth', *Turcica* 19 (1987), p. 14.
50. Aşıkpaşazade, *Osmanoğullarının Tarihi/Tevârîh-i âl-i Osman*, eds Kemal Yavuz and M. A. Sekta Saraç (Istanbul, 2007), pp. 273–4.
51. Karamanlı Mehmed Pasha, *Risāla fī taʾrīkh al-salāṭīn*, Süleymaniye Library, Istanbul, MS Aya Sofya 3204, ff. 1b–2a.
52. Aşıkpaşazade, *Tevârîh-i âl-i Osman*, p. 281; Karamanlı Mehmed, *Ta'rīkh al-Salāṭīn*, f. 3a–b.
53. *Oruç Beğ Tarihi*, ed. Necdet Öztürk (Istanbul, 2007), pp. 10–12; Cenabi, *al-Ḥāfil al-wasīṭ wa-l-aylam al-ẓāhir*, Süleymaniye Library, Istanbul, MS Hamidiye 896, f. 416a–b.
54. Imber, 'Ottoman dynastic myth', p. 14; Mehmed Neşri, *Kitab-ı Cihan-Nüma (Neşri Tarihi)*, eds Faik Reşit Unat and Mehmed A. Köymen (Ankara, 1949), I, p. 53.
55. For a discussion of other Ottoman Persian works including sections on the Seljuqs see *EIr*, s.v. 'Historiography. XIV. The Ottoman Empire' (S. N. Yıldız).
56. Imber, 'Ottoman dynastic myth', p. 15; Feridun Beg, *Münşeat ül-Selatin* (Istanbul, 1264), I, pp. 48–64.
57. Aḥmad b. Maḥmūd, *Selçuk-name*, ed. Erdoğan Merçil (Istanbul, 1977), I, pp. xiv–xv.
58. Ibid. II, p. 157.
59. Abdurrahman Şeref, 'Topkapu Saray-i Humayunu', *Tarih-i Osmani Encümeni Mecmuası*, p. 282, cited in Scott Redford, 'The Alaeddin mosque at Konya reconsidered', *Artibus Asiae* 51, 1–2 (1991), p. 70.
60. Müneccimbaşı Ahmed b. Lütfullah, *Camiü'd-Duvel: Osmanlı Tarihi (1299–1481)*, ed. Ahmet Ağırakça (Istanbul, 1995), Arabic text pp. 17–18.
61. Yazıcızâde Ali, *Tevârih-i Âl-i Selçuk*, p. 856; Paul Wittek, 'La descendance chretienne de la dynastie Seldjouk en Macedonie', *Échos d'Orient* 33 (1934), pp. 409–12; Wittek, 'Yazijioghlu Ali', p. 650.
62. Abdülbaki Gölpınarlı, *Simavna Kadısıoğlu Şeyh Bedreddin ve Manâkıbı* (Istanbul, 2008 [1st edn 1967]), pp. 237–8.

63. Ibid. p. 238.
64. Şikari, *Karamanname*, f. 63a.
65. Ibid. ff. 15b, 17b–18a, 23b.
66. Ibid. f. 25a.
67. Ibid. ff. 10b, 12b.
68. Ibid. f. 129a.
69. Yazıcızâde Ali, *Tevârîh-i âl-i Selçuk*, p. 908 (see note 1792, not present in all manuscripts).
70. Selânikî Mustafa Efendî, *Tarih-i Selânikî*, ed. Mehmet İpşirli (Ankara, 1999), II, p. 581.
71. Şikari, *Karamanname*, pp. 69–72.
72. *Ünsi'nin Selçuk Şehnamesi*, ed. Mes[c]ud Koman (Konya, 1942).
73. The work's editor, Mes[c]ud Koman, was a library director in Konya in the 1940s, and claims to have shown the work to President İnönü on his visit to the city, along with a number of other unique works on the history of Karaman and Konya (ibid. introduction). A search through the manuscript libraries of Konya and extensive enquiries revealed no trace of any of them. If they ever do resurface, the Persian *Saljūq Shāhnāma* written by Lutfi for Sultan Bayezid II would be of great interest for our theme, as would the Persian history of the Seljuqs and Karaman composed by one [c]Abd al-Qādir b. Aḥmad b. Sulaymān of Efsus in 929/1522, and the Turkish *Karamanname* of 1143/1730.
74. Ünsi, *Selçuk Şehnamesi*, p. 2.
75. Şikari, *Karamanname*, f. 29b.
76. Ünsi, *Selçuk Şehnamesi*, pp. 12, 13.
77. Ibid. p. 12.
78. Ibid. p. 13.
79. Ibid. p. 14.
80. Ibid. p. 17.
81. İbrahim Hakkı Konyalı, *Abideler ve Kitabeler ile Karaman Tarihi: Ermenek ve Mut Abideleri* (Istanbul, 1967), pp. 680–1.
82. Stephen Helmsley Longrigg, *Four Centuries of Modern Iraq* (Oxford, 1925), pp. 100–1.
83. Cevdet Tükay, *Başbakanlık Arşivi Belgelerine Göre Osmanlı İmparatorluğu'nda Oymak, Aşiret ve Cemaatler* (Istanbul, 2001), p. 567.
84. Cevdet Paşa, *Tezakir* (Ankara, 1963), pp. 21–39.
85. The medieval sources agree that Rukn al-Din was poisoned in Aksaray by the Pervane and his body was taken to Konya to be buried in the ancestral tomb. Vecihi Paşa's inscription has been removed from the *türbe* on Temenni Hill in Ürgüp and is now in the town museum.
86. M. Şakır Ülkütasır, 'Sinop'ta Selçukiler Zamanına Ait Tarihi Eserler', *Türk Tarih, Arkeologya ve Etnografya Dergisi* 5 (1949), pp. 139–40; for more on the fate of Seljuq monuments in Ottoman times see Zeki Atçeken, *Konya'daki Selçuklu Yapılarının Osmanlı Devrinde Bakımı ve Kullanılması* (Ankara, 1998).
87. Yazıcızâde Ali, *Tevârîh-i âl-i Selçuk*, p. 907.

PART II

. . .

SOCIETY

CHAPTER
6

ARSLĀN ARGHŪN – NOMADIC REVIVAL?

Jürgen Paul

Succession struggles in dynasties of Turkic or Mongolian stock are known to have been frequent and complicated: on principle, all male members of the ruling family had an equal right to rule. Many a time, the empire was divided up into appanages – territories where individual members of the dynasty ruled, often on a hereditary basis. The Seljuqs were no exception. Khurasan, the eastern Iranian region which had been the first basis of Seljuq power, seems to have been divided into a number of appanages by the end of the 5th/11th century, much to the disappointment of those who still thought that Khurasanis ought to stay in control of the Seljuq empire as a whole.

In this chapter, a succession struggle is the narrative background. The thesis is that pretenders for the throne were mobilising different sets of resources, above all of military manpower, and that the Turkmen (Ghuzz) warriors who had formed the backbone of the primordial Seljuq fighting force had by no means disappeared from the scene. The succession struggle also reveals political rifts within the empire. However, the last acts of the struggle were not staged because the hero disappeared in a kind of historical anticlimax.

When Malikshāh b. Alp Arslān died on 15 Shawwāl 485/20 November 1092, a number of Seljuq princes and also some other persons were eligible for his succession, or at least thought they might have a chance to win the sultanate.[1] Among these, the following pretenders vied for power over the three or four following years: two of Malikshāh's sons, (a) Maḥmūd, four years old, from Tarkān Khātūn, a Qarakhanid princess; (b) Barkyāruq, twelve years old and the eldest of Malikshāh's surviving sons, from Zubayda Khātūn, a Seljuqid princess. (The other sons, such as Sanjar and Muḥammad who later were to play prominent roles, were from lesser wives and not important in the initial stages of the succession struggle.) Since both sons who were active at this point, but in particular Maḥmūd, were minors, and since it was by no means clear that the succession would go to Malikshāh's offspring, two or three of the surviving brothers of the deceased sultan cast in their lot too: (c) Tutush b. Alp Arslān, regional lord in Syria (Damascus); (d) Tekesh b. Alp Arslān (he was, however, blinded and in prison when the sultan died, and did not advance a personal claim for the sultanate, but was considered dangerous nevertheless); (e) Arslān Arghūn b. Alp Arslān, who was a minor fief-holder in western Iran when his brother Malikshāh died and whose story is the main subject of this chapter.

The surviving brothers were all grown men, Tutush being in his mid-thirties and Arslān Arghūn having passed twenty. Other pretenders included Ismāᶜīl al-Yāqūtī, Barkyāruq's uncle on his mother's side (and therefore Zubayda Khātūn's brother) who held much power in Ādharbayjān, and the great emir Öner who legitimised his claim by stressing that Malikshāh had adopted him as a son.

Most of the fighting during the first three or four years after Malikshāh's death went on between the parties supporting Maḥmūd and Barkyāruq, respectively, and between Barkyāruq and Tutush. As is well known, in the end, Barkyāruq succeeded in establishing his rule over much of the territories which had formed the empire of his father, even if, as Bosworth says, the fighting came to an end only with his death in 498/1105. The campaigns led by Barkyāruq's party against Arslān Arghūn are retold, in the sources as well as in research literature, as a mere episode, and Arslān Arghūn's bid for power is as a general rule treated as a 'revolt' in both the sources and in scholarly literature.

In this chapter, I propose another look at the succession struggle, viewing it 'from the edge', that is, from the vantage point of one of the losers, in fact a rather improbable player in the game, Arslān Arghūn. For that, I will first recount his story in some detail, and then I will show the resources he used in his undertaking. The final questions will be whether his attempt at gaining at least regional power in Khurasan – which was quite successful for a while – was due to some nomadic influence, and whether he lost out by mere chance or whether his attempt was in a way doomed to failure.

ARSḶĀN ARGHŪN AS A PRETENDER

When Malikshāh died, Arslān Arghūn had a fief (*iqṭāᶜ*) worth seven thousand dinars in the region of Hamadan and Sāwa. This information probably is intended to convey the impression that he had not been ambitious previously and had not held any serious military or political position; otherwise, he might have claimed more than this small appanage as his due. He was in Baghdad when his brother died, but did not join any of the parties which quickly formed under the influence of the two wives of Malikshāh and the factions in the bureaucracy (sons and grandsons of Niẓām al-Mulk who had been killed just a few weeks before Malikshāh's death, and enemies of that towering figure). One source says that Arslān Arghūn was incited to seek power – an unnamed person asked him: 'How long do you plan to sit idle and to content yourself with what you have, how long will you renounce the sweetness of power?'[2]

All sources concur that he did set out at some point, but we do not learn with whom he was moving east quickly. His retinue cannot have been very numerous, though, since he neither held an important position in the imperial army (his name is never quoted before Malikshāh's death), nor did he have a regional power base. As suggested above, this could be behind the information in the sources that he had only a small fief. Ibn al-Athīr[3] states that at first, he did not have more than seven *mamlūk*s, a topical number for a small personal retinue. On his way, more people (of unspecified background) joined him, probably because he was one of the legitimate pretenders and as such, a man who would attract adventurers and others. Ḥusaynī apparently saw a problem here; he tends to explain this stage in Arslān Arghūn's career by stating that Arslān Arghūn 'gathered people/troops' (*ḥashada*), and that he profited from the struggle between his two nephews and the division of the troops between the two of them.[4]

The sources then say that he reached Nishapur, and laid siege to the city which he was however unable to take. There is some confusion in the sources about the situation at Nishapur at this point. Ibn al-Athīr says that in Dhū l-Ḥijja of 488/December 1095 one of the great emirs of Khurasan 'gathered a great host and marched with them to Nishapur, which he besieged' for forty days, but without being able to take the city.[5] One is at first tempted to identify this emir with Arslān Arghūn, but for two reasons, this identification would make things complicated: the chronology would be difficult to maintain, since we have the date of 488/1095 for the second battle between Arslān Arghūn and Böri Bars (see below), and this must be accepted; and second, Ibn Funduq's report about an emir called Qızıl Sārıgh who came to Bayhaq in Muḥarram 489/January 1096 after having fought the people of Nishapur makes one prefer to identify this person with the emir mentioned in Ibn al-Athīr.[6] Thus, I propose that Arslān Arghūn's unsuccessful siege of Nishapur, if it took place at all, must be dated earlier than 488/1095; it is possible, though, that the western Iranian sources mix up the emir Qızıl Sārıgh and Arslān Arghūn, and that the only siege of Nishapur which took place in that period was the one by Qızıl Sārıgh. This emir was indeed one of the great emirs in Khurasan; he had been fighting the Isma^{c}ilis in Quhistan some time before, in 485/1092, on Malikshāh's behalf.[7]

Even if it is difficult to establish a date for Arslān Arghūn's arrival in Khurasan, he must have been a powerful figure there by spring 487/1094, or perhaps even earlier. This is made plausible by the information that Fakhr al-Mulk b. Niẓām al-Mulk left Balkh when Arslān Arghūn took over there, and Fakhr al-Mulk met Tutush in Hamadan probably during the summer of 487/1094. Another vizier, Muʾayyid al-Mulk b. Niẓām al-Mulk, is said to have fled from Khurasan because of the fighting between Arslān Arghūn and Böri Bars; he was appointed as vizier to Barkyāruq in Dhū l-Ḥijja 487/December 1094.[8] ʿAbbās Iqbāl says that Arslān Arghūn's *fitna* lasted from 485/1092 until Muḥarram 490/December 1096–January 1097, that is, around four years.[9] This would mean that Arslān Arghūn started his bid for power very soon after Malikshāh's death, and this is in keeping with the chronological hints we get in the sources (see below).

It was through the support of the regional power-holder in Merv, the emir Qudun (Qawdan in al-Ḥusaynī[10]) that Arslān Arghūn rose to a prominent position. The reasons why this emir supported precisely this prince are linked to his role in the murder of Niẓām al-Mulk – this is not at all surprising, since many of the individuals having to decide which faction to join after Malikshāh's death took their decision according to how they had been treated by the old vizier and how they had acted towards him.[11] After one of the regional power-holders had joined his cause, more regionally important people apparently went over to Arslān Arghūn: he was now accepted in Merv, Balkh, and Tirmidh, and 'all of Khurasan'. Ibn al-Athīr adds Nishapur to the cities now under Arslān Arghūn's control[12] – which is improbable given the following. It seems clear that the base for Arslān Arghūn's ephemeral rule which now began was in northern Khurasan, along the Amu Darya, between Merv and Balkh, and that his influence sometimes extended to more westerly regions – he is said to have come to Sabzawar twice (Ibn Funduq)[13] – but never reached Herat.

Tirmidh may have been of particular value. The place had been heavily fortified at Niẓām al-Mulk's command – it had been recaptured from the Qarakhanids in 466/1073, and according to Müneccimbaşı, it was the emir Sāwtegin who received the order to rebuild and fortify the place.[14] Tirmidh – more precisely 'one of the fortresses of Tirmidh' – also was the starting point of Tekesh b. Alp Arslān's 473/1080–1 'revolt' and was likewise the place from where Malikshāh returned to Isfahan after he had crushed the movement.[15] Tirmidh apparently also was an important fortress for Arslān Arghūn: this was where he incarcerated his brother Böri Bars after he had defeated him. Tirmidh also was the place where Barkyāruq went after the Arslān Arghūn affair was over.[16] So, we may conclude that Tirmidh was one of the strongest places in northern Khurasan during this period. The mountains of Tukharistan were the last refuge of Arslān Arghūn's followers, and I take this to be the mountains just south of Balkh.

This region, northern Khurasan and Tukharistan, previously had been the focus of another 'rebellious' Seljuqid prince, Tekesh b. Alp Arslān, who had been in prison at Tikrit since around 477/1084–5 and was now murdered (in Rabīᶜ I 487/March–April 1094) because Barkyāruq suspected that he would join the fighting on either Tutush's[17] or perhaps Arslān Arghūn's side. There were rumours that he wanted to go to Balkh 'because the people there wanted him',[18] but Balkh most probably was under Arslān Arghūn's control at that point, so some kind of agreement between the two brothers may have been in the offing. Tekesh had a long history of opposition to Malikshāh, and his base had been in Khurasan, and in particular the northern part of it, with Merv and the upper Murghab as centre and Tirmidh as a stronghold. We have two reports on 'rebellions', dated to 473/1080–1 and 477/1084–5. Tekesh's commitment to northern Khurasan goes back to his appointment as governor there as a replacement for Ayāz b. Alp Arslān (in 466/1073–4); he had served as governor in Balkh without problems until 473/1080–1. Ayāz, it is said, had received his grandfather Chaghrı Beg's share of the imperial revenues, half a million dinar per annum.[19] Even if we do not know whether Tekesh was equipped with a similar revenue, it can be surmised that Balkh was a prestigious position.

It should be noted likewise that Tekesh's troops must have included a large body of Turkmen pastoralists, in particular from the Balkh region. In the report on his 473/1080–1 rebellion, placed under the events of 474 by Sibṭ b. al-Jawzī, the final stage is described like this:

> Tekesh's followers had hidden their belongings and their flocks in the inaccessible mountains,[20] but nevertheless, the sultan's army found them, routed them and drove them away [as booty]. Then Tekesh's followers came to him and told him: Our belongings have been taken away. If now you asked for a truce they would be returned to us. If not, we'll leave you for the sultan and serve him.[21]

Then, of course, Tekesh gave up; he had to open the gates of Tirmidh to his brother, but finally he was restored to his former position at Balkh. The event which triggered Tekesh's 473 rebellion was – in all of the sources apart from Sibṭ who seems to imply that the Turkmens incited Tekesh to action – the dismissal of 7,000 men from the imperial payroll, and it was these disgruntled soldiers (professional soldiers, as the sources have Niẓām al-Mulk stress) who went to Tekesh and made him revolt. Since this version has a clear message, namely to underline Niẓām al-Mulk's political acumen – professional soldiers should not be easily fired, they are liable to cause trouble – I think that Sibṭ's version should be preferred.[22]

The 477/1084–5 rebellion is depicted as a typical Ghuzz raid to the point that the description could be transferred without problem to the mid-540s/1150s. Sibṭ follows Ibn Hilāl in stating that Tekesh thought the time might be propitious for a revolt, since Malikshāh was busy in Syria. He first went to Marw ar-rudh, where destruction and pillaging ensued after a siege, then he proceeded to Merv where people were so afraid that they opened up the city to him, with the unpleasant result that three days of unrestricted looting followed. Ibn Hilāl stresses the anti-Islamic character of the looting which, according to him, included drinking bouts in the Friday mosque in stark daylight during Ramaḍān (Ramaḍān 477/beginning on New Year's Day 1085; this could well be a set piece to show how very far from civilised Muslim behaviour these people were). The cavalcade ended at Sarakhs where the governor held out long enough to allow Malikshāh to regain the initiative. Again, the final scenes took place around Balkh.[23]

Both reports seem to indicate that northern Khurasan, and in particular the region around Balkh, was heavily populated by Turkmen or Ghuzz pastoralists who made their influence felt every now and then. The main indicator is that Tekesh's followers seem to have cared more about their herds than about anything else. The insecure position of the region on the Qarakhanid frontier may have increased Turkmen or Ghuzz leverage.

To return to the story: with Arslān Arghūn established at Merv, Barkyāruq in the west had to be concerned about a new regional power forming in Khurasan. And this is exactly what the sources quote as Arslān Arghūn's aim: he is said to have asked his nephew to recognise him as a vassal ruler in the east, on the same basis as Ṭughrıl had accepted Chaghrı Beg Dā'ūd, their common ancestor (Arslān Arghūn's grandfather and Barkyāruq's great-grandfather), to rule over Khurasan. However, Arslān Arghūn excepted Nishapur (this shows that he had never been well established there, if at all, and did not pretend to be). Arslān Arghūn offered to pay tribute, and he promised not to claim the supreme sultanate for himself. It is not quite clear how Barkyāruq responded to this proposal. Some sources say that he seemingly agreed,[24] others say that he never answered, being too busy in Iraq fighting first his brother Maḥmūd and then his uncle Tutush and still other pretenders. In the end, Arslān Arghūn stopped these diplomatic advances. The sources say that he was unwilling to accept Majd al-Mulk – whose complete name was Abū l-Faḍl Asᶜad b. Muḥammad al-Qummī or al-Balāsānī[25] – as interlocutor. Even if Fakhr al-Mulk held the title of vizier, it was in fact Majd al-Mulk who had replaced Mu'ayyid al-Mulk b. Niẓām al-Mulk soon after Ṣafar 488/March 1095 when Barkyāruq had deposed Mu'ayyid al-Mulk, and was seen as a representative of the non-Khurasani bureaucrats, religiously unreliable (he was a Shiᶜi), and in every respect a person a dignified Khurasani could only look upon in contempt.[26] Thus, Arslān Arghūn had been ruling in Khurasan, based at Merv, for next to three years when he came to understand that Barkyāruq would be unwilling to share power and accept him as regional lord.

War ensued; Barkyāruq, we are told, sent his uncle Böri Bars b. Alp Arslān to Khurasan. Böri Bars had been governor at Herat for quite a while; he had been appointed there at the same time as Tekesh had become governor in Balkh.[27] Since we do not know what he had done in the meantime and what his position had been until then in the succession struggle, it is not evident that he had to travel east in order to confront his brother Arslān Arghūn – it is also possible that he started out from Herat, using regional forces at his disposal. Böri Bars must have had his own reasons to fight Arslān Arghūn, because if the latter had been appointed to a position like their grandfather Chaghrı Beg, this would have made his own position as governor at Herat quite delicate.

Böri Bars at first won a victory over his brother, and Arslān Arghūn had to flee to Balkh, whereas Böri Bars established himself in, or rather went back to, Herat; Ḥusaynī adds that he also took over Merv and the rest of Khurasan, and it is clear from the following that Arslān Arghūn lost his base at Merv as a consequence of this defeat.[28] It is not said what kind of troops either had at their disposal; in the case of Arslān Arghūn, we can make an informed guess: his main support until now had been the emir Qudun, and it would be reasonable to suppose that at this point, the regional troops from Merv – or from Merv and Balkh – formed the mainstay of his army. As for Böri Bars, it is not excluded that he had some troops from the imperial army with him, but it seems clear that the main body of his fighting force was constituted by regional troops from Khurasan, since on his way, 'the troops from Khurasan gathered around him'.[29] Herati forces are not mentioned explicitly.

We do not have a date for this first battle between Böri Bars and Arslān Arghūn, but I would suggest mid-488/summer 1095 because of the dates on record for the coming to power of Majd al-Mulk and the ensuing breakdown of diplomatic relations. Arslān Arghūn's takeover at Merv must consequently be dated quite a bit earlier, because of the dates for the two sons of Niẓām al-Mulk leaving Khurasan (see above) as a consequence of the fighting. It is therefore quite possible that he arrived in Khurasan by 485/1092.

In the next stage of confrontation during the summer of 488/1095, Arslān Arghūn had to build up a new army. It seems that he had lost the regional support from Merv and now had to rely on forces from Balkh. Ibn al-Athīr says that 'he gathered a large force and went to Merv';[30] al-Bundārī states that he 'sent envoys to the regions and environs and gathered troops'.[31] Al-Ḥusaynī alone gives an explanation as to who these troops were: Arslān Arghūn mobilised some Turkmen tribes, so that numerous troops gathered around him.[32] It is quite possible that this explanation was added later on, but then, this is what people in al-Ḥusaynī's times could imagine from which quarters a beaten pretender might get support – such was their experience. On the other hand, there is no contradiction between this bit of information and what we get from other sources, so we may assume that Turkmen (Ghuzz) tribal warriors were quite numerous in the body of troops Arslān Arghūn now had at his disposal.

At any rate, Arslān Arghūn laid siege to Merv (therefore, he must have lost this city before), and took it 'by force' (*ᶜanwatan*),[33] but we do not learn who was in command in the city at that point. And then apparently there are traces of a dramatic shift in politics. Not only did large-scale killings take place in Merv, but Arslān Arghūn also ordered the walls of the city to be demolished, something he is not reported to have done before when he had taken a city. We will come back to this point later.

A second confrontation with Böri Bars ensued, and this time Arslān Arghūn emerged victorious. This confrontation is dated 488/1095 in Ibn al-Athīr[34] and located in the environs of Merv in al-Ḥusaynī.[35] The date makes sense, since Böri Bars was taken prisoner and kept in Tirmidh for a year or so before he was strangled (in both Ibn al-Athīr and al-Ḥusaynī, with no precise details about how long he was incarcerated in al-Bundārī).[36] It is not clear, however, how the battle should be related to the siege of Merv.

There is a story about why Arslān Arghūn was able to win in this encounter. In the army Barkyāruq had sent east together with Böri Bars or in support of him, two senior emirs were serving. One of these was the 'Master of Horse' (to use Richards' terms)[37] Altūntāsh,[38] and the second was the emir Masᶜūd b. Tājir (this is the form under which the name appears in Ibn al-Athīr, but other forms are also quoted).[39] Tājir had been Commander of the troops in Khurasan under Chaghrı Beg Dāʾūd, and it was possibly for this reason that his son enjoyed a high reputation in that province.[40] Altūntāsh did not have confidence in him; the reasons can be surmised: Masᶜūd would have fitted perfectly into a scheme to revive Khurasan as a regional power, with Arslān Arghūn as regional lord, and Masᶜūd in the same position as his father had held. It probably is not by chance that Arslān Arghūn is said to have referred to the days of Chaghrı Beg Dāʾūd in his dealings with Barkyāruq: Chaghrı had been a lord in his own right, and it is quite possible that he had dealt on a par with his brother Ṭughril.[41] However that may be, we are told that there was 'old friendship' between Arslān Arghūn and the Master of Horse, and therefore Arslān Arghūn tried to win him over. Altūntāsh 'responded favourably' to these overtures. In the end, Altūntāsh killed Masᶜūd b. Tājir and his son.

As for the motives for the murder, we are left to speculate. As suggested in Ibn al-Athīr, Altūntāsh killed Masᶜūd in order to weaken Böri Bars, and this was what ensued (so the explanation could be given in hindsight). In al-Bundārī's version, Altūntāsh was completely in charge after Masᶜūd's death,[42] and the most probable motif would then be ambition or a pre-emptive action on Altūntāsh's part: both Altūntāsh and Masᶜūd were possible candidates for a leading position in what promised to become Arslān Arghūn's regional state in Khurasan, and the loyalty of both men for Böri Bars and Barkyāruq may be questioned. Ḥusaynī does not have the murder story; his account simply says that Böri Bars was put to flight. As a result of this killing (in Ibn al-Athīr's version),[43] Böri Bars' army dispersed, and apparently battle was not joined.

Arslān Arghūn was now again in control over much of Khurasan, and it is difficult to see what could have prevented him from establishing regional rule there. Therefore, Barkyāruq decided to deal with this threat in person. The statements in Nīshāpūrī and Rāvandī on Barkyāruq's concern about the situation should probably be referred to at this moment: Arslān Arghūn was fearless and had innumerable forces (Rāvandī);[44] 'he was a courageous, bold, magnificent ruler' (Nīshāpūrī).[45] It must also be during this period that Arslān Arghūn continued what he had begun at Merv: he had many fortifications demolished all over Khurasan. The sources name the walls of Merv, the citadel at Sarakhs, the citadel (*quhandiz*) at Nishapur, 'and all the fortresses there were in Khurasan'.[46] Ibn al-Athīr adds Sabzawar, and this is confirmed by Ibn Funduq.[47] All this is dated to 489/1096. In none of the lists given in the sources are the fortifications of Balkh and Tirmidh mentioned, and in both cases, it is probable that they were left intact.

Barkyāruq enlisted the help of his brother Sanjar to fight Arslān Arghūn. In the meantime, Maḥmūd, Tarkān Khātūn, Tekesh and Tutush were all dead (Tarkān Khātūn died in autumn 487/1094; Maḥmūd a little later the same year; Tekesh was killed in prison in spring 1094; Tutush fell in battle, 17 Ṣafar 488/15 March 1095). It is improbable that the Iraqi forces would have been able to start action in Khurasan if one of the erstwhile pretenders had still been alive. Barkyāruq's departure for the east has been calculated to 489/1095–6[48] which is quite in keeping with what follows.

In Muḥarram 490/19 December 1096–17 January 1097 Arslān Arghūn was killed by a slave, apparently for personal reasons. In order to fill out this story, Bundārī adds that in his moment of victory, an astrologer had told Arslān Arghūn that he had better conceal himself until a certain danger was over, and therefore he had isolated himself to the point that a slave could stab him. The motif given by the slave – he had wanted to eradicate Arslān Arghūn's injustice (*ẓulm*) – is perhaps best referred to the way Arslān Arghūn behaved in his private quarters, not to his rule of the province.[49]

Barkyāruq and his brother Sanjar, on their way east, learned about this situation, and that the emirs of the murdered prince had elevated his minor son (age seven) to the throne (no name given for the boy), but now had fled to the mountains of Tukharistan. The emirs asked for pardon, and having received a positive answer, they came to Barkyāruq's camp near Balkh; Barkyāruq had taken the city without a fight. The sources say that 15,000 warriors accompanied the infant, and that within a short time, all of them had left him, having joined other masters. Barkyāruq restored, it is said, the fief Arslān Arghūn had held to the child and treated him kindly. Ibn Funduq, however, mentions a son of Arslān Arghūn by name, a man called Alp Arghūn; he had been blinded (*al-masmūl*), and this man's descendants are known to live in Merv.[50] So perhaps Barkyāruq's magnanimity had its limits.

RESOURCES

It is difficult to say if the outcome of a succession struggle like the one under study here can be predicted. Contemporaries thought that either chance or God's will was at work, and even Ibn al-Athīr muses about God's strange and inscrutable ways in a paragraph inserted (as an auctorial comment) after his account of Tutush's death. In the scenes he had described before, the fortunes of the different actors rose and fell at dramatic speed, and it seems that he thought that Barkyāruq's final victory was so improbable that it could not be explained otherwise than by God's direct intervention. It is not necessarily the person most favoured at the outset who will win the race. Nevertheless, a look at the resources seems in order.

Legitimacy may be understood as a resource besides other more material assets. In spite of the general wisdom that in Turkic dynasties, all male descendants of the founder have an equal right to rule, the sons of the deceased sultan seem to have been a much more evident choice for many people than 'collateral' pretenders (e.g. the late sultan's brothers), and the question of whether the right to ascend the throne should be restricted to the late ruler's sons or else whether the senior male of the whole clan had a better claim was hotly debated. Personal aptitude to rule, however, was a must, and thus infants and infirm persons were not really considered to be eligible. Out of Malikshāh's agnatic kin, thus, at least his son Maḥmūd and his brother Tekesh suffered from a legitimacy gap. Tekesh is not reported to have made a bid for the sultanate for himself after Malikshāh's death, but still he was seen as a danger, possibly because his support could have tipped the balance in either Tutush's or Arslān Arghūn's favour. In order to enhance Maḥmūd's legitimacy, Tarkān Khātūn sought a caliphal investiture which she finally obtained, but this proved to be comparatively unimportant.

Out of the five or so pretenders coming from Malikshāh's immediate family involved in the succession struggle after his death, resources besides legitimacy were very unevenly distributed. In particular, this concerns military manpower which of course is required in a succession struggle, and money which can serve to buy it. Military manpower, I assume, was of several kinds: first, the imperial army and personal retinue of the sultan, for a large part *mamlūks*; second, regional forces under the command of emirs (*iqṭā*ᶜ-holders), these forces in a way also are part of the imperial army in that they are on the payroll (cf. the story about larger groups of soldiers being 'cashiered' in 473/1080–1 because they or their equipment was deemed insufficient – the story presupposes that they were professional soldiers); third, regional forces not on the payroll, and these include urban militias as well as rural or nomad groups.[51] Out of these, the Turkmen nomads have a particular position because they had been the founding force of the empire. Turkmen forces must have been very numerous indeed,[52] and they were mobile. Urban militias were a major asset in siege warfare, and many a time a city could hold out against its enemies – if it was well fortified and if its inhabitants were resolved to fight. Urban militias were of no use in the open country.

Maḥmūd, backed by his mother Tarkān Khātūn, had the largest part of the imperial treasury and of the imperial army. The money was used up very quickly – it was expensive to buy military support for a pretender who so very evidently was not a good choice, being but a young boy. Moreover, as Durand-Guédy has rightly observed, the succession struggle in itself served the interests of the great emirs: their support could be sold to the highest bidder, and a plurality of pretenders made the prices go up.[53] When Tarkān Khātūn and her son came to Isfahan (end 1092), the army at their disposal is said to have numbered no more than 10,000. Barkyāruq at first had the support of the Niẓāmiyya *mamlūks*, and also part of the imperial army, numbering 20,000 in all;[54] his financial resources were no match for Maḥmūd's. Neither of the two, however, had any solid regional base, both vied for control over Isfahan, Hamadan and Rayy, the centre-west of the sultanate. Apparently, they had not had time to establish any kind of regional roots anywhere.

Tutush, on the contrary, had a more or less secure regional power base in Damascus, which he succeeded at least temporarily to extend by winning the leading emirs in the Fertile Crescent (the Aleppo-Edessa-Mossul half-circle). It is not clear what his financial resources may have been, but we may suppose that even if he was unable to reach into the imperial treasury, he could of course dispose of the Syrian tax emoluments. His successes and his temporary recognition by the caliph earn him a nearly unanimous appreciation that he was by far the most important and most dangerous rival for Barkyāruq.

The most improbable pretender was Arslān Arghūn, so improbable that he is not even mentioned by some authors who deal with the period in question.[55] Of all the three factors we have considered so far, a share in the imperial army, financial means, that is, access to the imperial treasury, or a regional power base, he had nothing worth mentioning. It was one of Malikshāh's senior emirs, Qudun, who first made Arslān Arghūn's claim into a serious affair.

However, as the story has shown, he was a danger for Barkyāruq, even if his aims, as Bosworth states, were limited, and he strove first of all to establish Khurasan as an autonomous province for himself.[56] This would have meant that he occupied the position of his grandfather Chaghrı Beg, and thus would have been a major player in the two Iraqs as well. Thus, to all intents and purposes, he was very successful at first, starting from next to nothing (he had nothing but his genealogical position to his merit), and ending as ruler over much of Khurasan, regionally without rival, and probably ready to confront his nephew Barkyāruq.

If one tries to assess how he achieved this surprising and unexpected career, the following factors come to mind. First, he encountered regional support, or perhaps he was used as a stalking horse by regional power-holders. Qudun was one example; we do not know who held power at Balkh. Balkhī emirs may have inclined towards Tekesh b. Alp Arslān, and may therefore have been willing to join anybody who would fight Barkyāruq. If Arslān Arghūn stood for any particular programme at this point, it would have been the re-establishment of Khurasan as an autonomous province, with himself as regional ruler. This could have been achieved, though only as long as Barkyāruq was weak, and it surely ran counter to the interests of other Khurasani power holders, among them Böri Bars.

Second, if we consider where his military manpower may have come from, the Turkmen tribes are an obvious place to turn to. There is little direct evidence to prove that Arslān Arghūn in fact was supported by Turkmen tribes, indeed the passage in al-Ḥusaynī quoted above is all I have found: after his first defeat, when he had to look for new military partners, Arslān Arghūn mobilised, so the source says, some Turkmen tribes, so that a numerous army gathered around him. His brother Tekesh, on the other hand, was in a way his predecessor, and in that case, there is evidence that his attempts at regional or even imperial power were inspired by Turkmen leaders.

As suggested above this moment was some kind of turning point in Arslān Arghūn's career. From then on, he started demolishing a number of city fortifications and fortresses, but apparently did not touch those cities where he planned to establish his rule, viz. Balkh and Tirmidh. Is this evidence that Arslān Arghūn was some kind of precursor of the Ghuzz who, more or less in the same region, brought about the end of the Seljuq sultanate in Khurasan some sixty years later?

Local Khurasani power-holders may have seen with growing discontent the rise of 'Iraqi' figures to positions of influence in the west, and some influential circles perhaps thought that the Khurasanian character of the Seljuq empire was in jeopardy. In support of this, I would quote the long series of 'rebellions' in northern and north-eastern Khurasan, led by Tekesh during Malikshāh's reign, and continued by Arslān Arghūn. The revolts, however, did not stop at that point, and regional emirs took up where Arslān Arghūn had been defeated. It is tempting to see an alliance of Turkmen tribal leaders and regional power-holders behind this long history of Khurasani assertiveness. This does not have to mean that anybody aspired to Khurasani 'independence';[57] it may also be that both Tekesh and Arslān Arghūn thought of Khurasan as the 'realm of Chaghrı Beg' with all that meant for the province's position in the Seljuqid empire at large. This in a way is reminiscent of the appanage policies of later Turko-Mongolian rulers, and we are perhaps not too far off the mark if we think of this regional state in Khurasan as a kind of '*ulus* Chaghrı'.

RE-NOMADISATION – IN LIEU OF CONCLUSION

Andrew Peacock has discussed the demolition of city walls and fortresses by the Seljuqs in Caucasia and Eastern Anatolia in a recent article.[58] He comes to the conclusion that the devastation wrought by the Seljuqs, including the sultans, in Caucasia and Eastern Anatolia as reported not only by Islamic but also by Armenian and Georgian sources, was due neither to a frequently assumed effort by the sultans to direct the rough instincts of their tribal warriors outside of the *dār al-islām*, nor was it just wistful and planless destruction brought about by a quasi innate appetite for plunder. Peacock points out that some regions were victims to Seljuq-Turkmen destruction much more than others, and he establishes a geographical pattern to show that the Seljuq Turkmen were interested in pasture, both winter and summer grazing grounds. He summarises his findings:

> [These campaigns] were to a large extent concerned with securing pasture land for the Seljūqs' nomadic followers. This explains why the Seljūqs destroyed so many fortifications and cities without ever intending to occupy them permanently: they were interested not in the cities but in the pastures around them, but to secure control of the pastures they had to ensure that the cities could not be used by anyone else to threaten their control of the surrounding countryside.[59]

There are differences and commonalities with what we can surmise for Arslān Arghūn and northern Khurasan. First, the areas around Merv and Balkh were old Turkmen regions, with Turkmens (or Ghuzz or any other kind of Turkic nomadic population) present there for centuries. For the Merv region, for instance, we have evidence from the geographical literature, starting with the 4th/10th century, that Turkmens were present there. For the more easterly region, Balkh and Tirmidh, Turks are evident there since the Arab conquest or perhaps even earlier. This of course is a contrast to the situation in Caucasia and Eastern Anatolia, where the Turks were newcomers in the 5th/11th century.

Second, Balkh and Merv were big cities until the Mongol conquest, two of the four capital cities of Khurasan (the other two being Herat and Nishapur), and therefore, the Turkmens were interested in these cities themselves. Cities were one of the major points of contention and also one of the major assets to be fought over. Lesser urban sites like Sabzawar and Sarakhs could be more easily compared to the Caucasian towns the Seljuqs destroyed. But still, the selection of places where Arslān Arghūn chose to have the fortifications destroyed is telling: apparently, he did not want them to 'be used by anyone else to threaten [his] control of the surrounding countryside'.

For Sabzawar, we can establish a record of demolitions and reconstructions of the city wall all over the Seljuq period thanks to the local history of Ibn Funduq. The city walls had suffered from an earthquake in 444/1052; twenty years later, they were reconstructed under Niẓām al-Mulk. It was this wall that Arslān Arghūn destroyed. The next reconstruction is not dated, and the following report thus is again one about demolition: it was Sanjar's spouse Terken Khātūn who ordered the destruction of the city walls in 543/1148–9. The following reconstruction took place in 548/1153–4.[60] Certainly, not all of these demolitions can be linked to Turkmen policies, and it would be rash to draw the conclusion that wherever a city wall is demolished, the people behind it are pastoralists interested in grazing grounds and not in cities. We have to consider, on the contrary, that even a well-established imperial power would sometimes be more interested in razing fortifications rather than in constructing them.

Yet, it is also true that Balkh and its region, the whole northern slope of the Hindukush down to the Amu-Darya, is very well suited for pastoral nomadism, with the winter pastures in the plain near the river and the summer pastures uphill, and an agricultural (oasis) zone in between. The corresponding political pattern in the late medieval and early modern periods (from the Mongols down to the 19th century) shows local political units arranged like stripes, each including a section of the river bank, one or more oasis towns, and summer pastures in the mountains.

For Merv and its environs, it is harder to pinpoint a migration pattern, and it is not at all certain that a 'vertical' yaylaq-qishlaq pattern applied here. Nevertheless, from the earliest Seljuq times on until today, this region was and is basically Turkmen, even if the city itself may not have been Turkic-speaking before the Mongol period.

And last but not least, it certainly is no mere coincidence that the Balkh area (at times including the city itself) was 'Ghuzz country' from the later period of Sanjar's reign more or less until the Mongol invasion. The power of the Turkmen tribes in this particular region must have been strong even in Malikshāh's day, and therefore, the people cooperating with Arslān Arghūn after his initial sponsor Qudun apparently had left him, may well have been Turkmen chieftains. The political aim of winning Khurasan as an autonomous province for himself, to take up Bosworth's formula again, was one Arslān Arghūn could achieve only with the backing of the Turkmen warriors. Even if we know that pastures of legendary quality were to be found in Khurasan (besides the slopes of the Hindukush, one might mention the imperial summer grazing grounds at Rādkān-i Ṭūs, so prominent in the Khwarazmian and later in the Mongol and Timurid periods), the evidence in the sources for this region is too flimsy to apply Peacock's analysis there. And there is one very basic argument that makes the whole difference – the Turkmens controlled the grazing grounds already, and the city fortifications Arslān Arghūn demolished did not stand in their way in this respect.

The sources do not offer any evidence for another explanation, unfortunately. So, at the end, the question of whether Arslān Arghūn was a nomadic leader and his short rule in Khurasan one of nomadisation or re-nomadisation, must be left open.

Arslān Arghūn has certainly been much underestimated by modern scholarship. His attempt at recreating a regional state in Khurasan was no mere episode. He succeeded in establishing his rule, first at Merv, later at Balkh, for about four years. During the last period, he seems to have relied on support from Turkmen (Ghuzz) warriors which led him to the policies of tearing down city walls and fortresses in numerous places for which he has earned ambivalent fame. His end did not come in the confrontation with his nephew Barkyāruq which had however become inevitable – he was murdered by a slave before, without apparent link to the political and military situation.

It is difficult to assess his chances of success. He was not the first to aim at establishing the '*ulus Chaghrı*' – his brother Tekesh had done so before, and there were others after him. All of these 'rebellions' failed, however, and it was not until Sanjar's day that Khurasan once more became the centre of Seljuq power.

NOTES

1. For a general introduction into the political situation at this point, see C. Edmund Bosworth, 'The political and dynastic history of the Iranian world', in *CHI5*, pp. 1–202, in particular pp. 102–7. The story of Arslān Arghūn has been known to European scholarship from early on: M. C. Defrémery, *Recherches sur le règne de Barkiarok* (Paris, 1853), pp. 47–53.
2. Al-Fatḥ b. ᶜAlī b. Muḥammad al-Bundārī, *Zubdat al-nuṣra wa-nukhbat al-ᶜuṣra*, ed. M. T. Houtsma (Leiden 1889), p. 256.

3. ᶜIzz al-Dīn Abū l-Ḥasan ᶜAlī Ibn al-Athīr (d. 630/1233), *al-Kāmil fī l-tārīkh*, ed. Tornberg (Beirut, 1385–/1965–), X, p. 262. The source does not specify which kind of people joined Arslān Arghūn: 'A number of people gathered around him' (*wa-ttaṣala bihi jamāᶜa*).
4. Ṣadr al-Dīn Abū l-Ḥasan ᶜAlī b. Nāṣir Al-Ḥusaynī (wrote 622/1225), *Akhbār al-dawla al-saljūqiyya*, ed. Muḥammad Iqbāl (Lahore, 1933), 85f.
5. Ibn al-Athīr, *al-Kāmil*, X, p. 171.
6. Abū l-Ḥasan ᶜAlī b. Zayd-i Bayhaqī Ibn Funduq (d. 564/1169), *Tārīkh-i Bayhaq*, ed. Aḥmad Bahmanyār (n.p., n.d.), p. 270.
7. Bosworth, 'The political and dynastic history', p. 94.
8. ᶜAbbās Iqbāl, *Vizārat dar ᶜahd-i salāṭīn-i buzurg-i saljūqī* (Tehran, 1338 HSh), p. 104; Bundārī, *Zubdat*, p. 85.
9. Iqbāl, *Vizārat*, pp. 205, 206. Iqbāl quotes a *qaṣīda* saying that the troubles in Khurasan lasted four years.
10. Al-Ḥusaynī, *Akhbār*, p. 85.
11. Qudun remained an important figure later on, and a restive one at that. Together with one emir Yaruqtash he killed the governor Ekinchi b. Qochqar who had had held Khwarazm for the Seljuqs, and was dislodged from there by Ḥabashi b. Altuntaq (Bosworth, 'The political and dynastic history', p. 107; Ibn al-Athīr, *al-Kāmil*, X, pp. 181–2). The source does not link this episode to Qudun's previous involvement in the first stages of Arslān Arghūn's bid for power.
12. Ibn al-Athīr, *al-Kāmil*, X, p. 263.
13. Ibn Funduq, *Tārīkh-i Bayhaq*, p. 270.
14. Müneccimbaşı, Ahmed, *Cami'ü d-düvel* [Jāmiᶜ al-duwal], ed. Ali Öngül (İzmir, 2000), text p. 42, trans. p. 49.
15. Shams al-Dīn Abū l-Muẓaffar Yūsuf b. Qızoğlu Sibṭ b. al-Jawzī (d. 1257), *Mirʾāt al-zamān fī tārīkh al-aᶜyān*, ed. Ali Sevim (Ankara, 1968), p. 209.
16. Ibn al-Athīr, *al-Kāmil*, X, p. 181.
17. There is one remark that Tutush wrote to Tekesh and invited him to join him. But it makes more sense to have him join Arslān Arghūn because of his regional attachments in Balkh.
18. D. S. Richards, *The Annals of the Saljuq Turks: Selections from* al-Kāmil fī l-Tārīkh *of ᶜIzz al-Dīn Ibn al-Athīr* (London, 2002), p. 276. The Arabic is *wa-qīla annahu arāda al-masīr ilā Balkh li-anna ahlahā yurīdūnahu.*
19. Bosworth, 'The political and dynastic history', p. 105.
20. This may have been the same 'mountains of Tukharistan' where later Arslān Arghūn's followers took refuge, although it is not quite clear on which side of the Amu the scene is set.
21. Sibṭ b. al-Jawzī, *Mirʾāt*, ed. Sevim, p. 209.
22. For example, al-Bundārī, *Zubdat*, p. 71.
23. Sibṭ b. al-Jawzī, *Mirʾāt*, ed. Sevim, p. 231.
24. Al-Ḥusaynī, *Akhbār*, p. 85.
25. Iqbāl, *Vizārat*, p. 55.
26. Ibid. p. 110. David Durand-Guédy, *Iranian Elites and Turkish Rulers: a History of Isfahān in the Saljūq Period*, (London, 2010) has shown how important the divide between Khurasanis and western Iranian people was at this point.
27. The *Mujmal at-tawārīkh wa-l-qiṣaṣ*, ed. Malik ash-Shuᶜarā Bahār and Muḥammad Riḍāʾī (Tehran, 1309 HSh), p. 408, has Malikshāh entrust Khurasan to Arslān Arghūn from the

start with his centre at Herat; I take this to be a confirmation that Khurasan was given to one of Malikshāh's brothers, and apart from that, as a conflation of the various brothers: *Arslān-Arghūn-rā Khurāsān dād ba-Harī wa dīgar barādarān-rā hamchunīn wilāyathā dād.* There is no further mention of Arslān Arghūn in this source.

28. Al-Ḥusaynī, *Akhbār*, p. 85. There is no information about the fate or role of Qudun in this affair, but since we meet him again at Merv a couple of years later, it may be that he had come to terms with either Böri Bars or Barkyāruq so that he could retain his position in the Murghab region. Özaydın devotes a paragraph to his 'revolt'. Abdülkerim Özaydın, *Sultan Berkyaruk Devri Selçuklu Tarihi (485–98/1092–1104)* (Istanbul, 2001), pp. 53–4.
29. Al-Bundārī, *Zubdat*, p. 257: *wa-jtamaᶜat ilayhi ᶜasākir Khurāsān.*
30. Ibn al-Athīr, *al-Kāmil*, X, p. 263: *jamaᶜa Arghūn ᶜasākira jammata.* There are no details in this source as to who responded to his call.
31. Al-Bundārī, *Zubdat*, p. 257: *arsala ilā l-aṭrāf wa l-awsāṭ wa-ḥashada wa-ḥashara.* This makes it clear that regional people are intended, but there is no hint in this source as to their social background.
32. Al-Ḥusaynī, *Akhbār*, p. 85: *ḥashada Arslān Arghūn umaman min at-turkmān wa-jtamaᶜa lahu jamᶜun min al-ajnād.*
33. The expression is in Ibn al-Athīr: *fataḥahā ᶜanwatan wa-qatala fīhā wa-akthara*, 'he took the city by force and had its inhabitants killed in great numbers'.
34. Ibn al-Athīr, *al-Kāmil*, X, p. 263, trans. Richards, *Annals*, p. 290.
35. Al-Ḥusaynī, *Akhbār*, p. 86.
36. Ibn al-Athīr, *al-Kāmil*, X, p. 264; al-Ḥusaynī, *Akhbār*, p. 86; al-Bundārī, *Zubdat*, p. 257.
37. Richards (trans.), *Annals*, p. 290. The original term is *mīrākhūr.*
38. This name is only given in al-Bundārī, *Zubdat*, p. 257. No more information about him is available.
39. Iqbāl, *Vizārat*, p. 81; Ibn al-Athīr, *al-Kāmil*, X, p. 263.
40. Ibn al-Athīr, *al-Kāmil*, X, p. 207. He had been 'lord of Balkh' (*ṣāḥib Balkh*) before reaching the position of Commander of the Khurasani troops.
41. Shabānkāraʾī treats Khurasan consistently as a separate dominion. About Barkyāruq's eastern campaign, he says he wanted to take the throne of Khurasan and sent his younger brother Sanjar ahead with a huge army in 489/1096. The sultanate of Khurasan at that moment was in the hands of one of Alp Arslān's sons, his name was 'Arslan Arghū', and he was an awe-inspiring and famous man – Muḥammad b. ᶜAlī Shabānkāraʾī, *Majmaᶜ al-ansāb*, ed. Mīr Hāshim Muḥaddith (Tehran, 1363 HSh.), pp. 106–7. For the statement about Arslān Arghūn as a person, see the quotes from Rāvandī and Nīshāpūrī (notes 44 and 45).
42. Al-Bundārī, *Zubdat*, p. 257: *fa-ammā Masᶜūd fa-inna Altūntāsh tawahhama minhu bi-mā qīla lahu fa-fataka bihi wa-bi-waladihi wa-ṣāra l-amr kulluhu fī yadihi.*
43. Ibn al-Athīr, *al-Kāmil*, X, p. 264.
44. This may serve as further indication that many Turkmen warriors had joined Arslān Arghūn, but Rāvandī's account (based on Ẓahīr al-Dīn) already is too far from the events, and at any rate, he is one of those writers who systematically link nomadic warfare to mindless and heedless destruction. Muḥammad b. ᶜAlī b. Sulaymān Rāvandī (wrote in 1202–4), *Rāḥat al-ṣudūr wa-āyat al-surūr*, ed. Muḥammad Iqbāl (Leiden, 1921), p. 143.
45. Ẓahīr al-Dīn Nīshāpūrī, *The History of the Seljuq Turks*, trans. Kenneth A. Luther (Richmond, 2001), p. 68.
46. Al-Ḥusaynī, *Akhbār*, p. 86.

47. Ibn al-Athīr, *al-Kāmil*, X, p. 264; Ibn Funduq, *Tārīkh Bayhaq*, p. 269.
48. Durand-Guédy, *Iranian Elites*, p. 148.
49. The date of Arslān Arghūn's death is given according to Ibn al-Athīr. Other sources give 17 Ṣafar 490/3 February 1097. Özaydın, *Berkyaruk*, p. 50, with detailed references.
50. Ibn Funduq, *Tārīkh Bayhaq*, p. 72.
51. Ayalon's claim that the Seljuq armies were manned by *mamlūk*s and that the Turkmen tribal warriors were 'auxiliaries' is, of course, true in a certain way. He does not make a difference between 'imperial' and 'regional' armies. I use this difference here in order to stress that the leading emirs had their own military following, composed of *mamlūk*s in the first place, but including free-born men as well. See David Ayalon, 'The mamlūks of the Seljuqs: Islam's military might at the crossroads', *JRAS* 3rd series 6, 3 (1996), pp. 305–33. Özaydın proposes a similar repartition of Seljuq armed forces: after the Saray *mamlūk*s, he has 'Hassa ordusu' (corresponding to my 'imperial army'), after that 'Troops of Imperial officials, of emirs issued from military slavery, and of [other] statesmen' ('Hanedan Mensuplarıyla Kölelikten Yetişme Emîrlerin ve Devlet Adamlarının Askerleri', corresponding roughly to my 'regional armies', and finally 'Turkmen forces' ('Türkmen Kuvvetleri'). See Özaydın, *Berkyaruk*, pp. 208–12. He stresses that the 'regional forces' could play an important role when the central government was weak, particularly in fratricidal warfare (ibid. p. 210). The question of whether the 7,000 warriors which Malikshāh cancelled from the payroll in 473/1080–1 were Turks or Armenians (as Müneccimbaşı has it, *Câmi 'ud-düvel*, text p. 44, trans. p. 51) is completely irrelevant for our purpose.
52. İbrahim Kafesoğlu, *Sultan Melikşah Devrinde Büyük Selçuklu İmparatorluğu* (Istanbul, 1953), pp. 162–3, quoted in Bosworth, 'The political and dynastic history', p. 84. The figure given by Kafesoğlu is 300,000 Turkmen warriors.
53. Durand-Guédy, *Iranian Elites*, p. 149.
54. Ibid. p. 146–7.
55. S. G. Agadshanow, *Der Staat der Seldschukiden und Mittelasien im 11.–12. Jahrhundert* (Berlin, 1994).
56. Bosworth, 'The political and dynastic history', p. 105.
57. Özaydın takes a programme of 'bağımsızlık' for granted, *Berkyaruk*, p. 47.
58. Andrew Peacock, 'Nomadic society and the Seljuq campaigns in Caucasia', in *Research Papers from the Caucasian Centre for Iranian Studies* 9, 2 (2005), pp. 205–30.
59. Ibid. pp. 224–5.
60. Ibn al-Athīr, *al-Kāmil*, IX, p. 591; Ibn Funduq, *Tārīkh-i Bayhaq*, p. 269; see also Jürgen Paul, *Herrscher, Gemeinwesen, Vermittler: Ostiran und Transoxanien in vormongolischer Zeit* (Stuttgart/Beirut, 1996), p. 122.

CHAPTER

7

CONTROLLING AND DEVELOPING BAGHDAD: CALIPHS, SULTANS AND THE BALANCE OF POWER IN THE ABBASID CAPITAL (MID-5TH/11TH TO LATE 6TH/12TH CENTURIES)

*Vanessa Van Renterghem**

Seljuq Iraq, though a central Islamic land and the heart of the Abbasid caliphate, has not received the full scholarly attention it deserves;[1] in comparison, the Buyid rule over Iraq has been studied more extensively by historians.[2] Descriptions of Iraq under Seljuq rule are mainly to be found in studies devoted to the social and religious life in Baghdad,[3] and many questions concerning the history of Iraq from the middle of the 5th/11th until the middle of the 6th/12th century are still unanswered. Studies comparing the role and position of Iraq in the Great Seljuq empire with other areas under Seljuq rule, such as Iran, Syria and the Jazīra, likewise remain a desideratum. The nature and extent of Seljuq domination over Iraq requires further research in terms of the exact territories under Seljuq control,[4] the relationship between Seljuq agents and local powers, the nature of urban and extra-urban control exerted by the sultans, or the forms of taxation and the evolution of *iqṭā*ᶜ (revenue-producing land grants) granting. Issues like the degree of the Turkmen presence, contacts with local nomadic and sedentary populations and acculturation have not been examined for Iraq. As in the case of Seljuq Iran, the available sources concern urban agglomerations rather than the countryside, and as a result, economic questions are difficult to deal with.[5]

Different issues will be discussed in this chapter, which concentrates on the

---

* The author would like to thank Christian Lange, Marianne Boqvist and Stephen McPhillips for their highly valuable readings and suggestions about the first versions of this paper.

Abbasid capital and its relations with Seljuq sultans and officials in a local perspective, from Ṭughril Beg's first entry into Baghdad in 447/1055 until the beginning of the reign of the caliph al-Nāṣir (575–622/1180–225).[6] This perspective is linked to the sources used for the study: local biographical dictionaries[7] and chronicles,[8] as well as non-Baghdadi Arabic sources[9] and Seljuq dynastic histories in both Arabic and Persian, which provide a more imperial perspective.[10]

As the caliphal capital, Baghdad had a special status compared to other cities in the Seljuq empire; in consequence one cannot study Seljuq Baghdad without questioning the power balance between the caliphs and the sultans, whose policy in Baghdad was strongly shaped by the nature of the relationship they intended to establish with the Abbasids. The 'Sunni-Abbasid' policy of the Seljuqs is usually considered as part of the 'Sunni revival' which in turn is regarded as a critical evolution of the period. But a careful study of the case of Baghdad shows that this notion must be discussed and cannot be considered as the key explanation of all evolutions of this period.

THE BALANCE OF POWER BETWEEN CALIPHS AND SULTAN: FROM SELJUQ DOMINATION TO ABBASID RECOVERY

The relation between the caliphs and the sultans was essentially a balancing act, evolving from the actual Seljuq domination of the caliphate and over large areas of Iraq, which was to culminate in Malikshāh's reign, to a slow but effective recovery of Abbasid power and authority over the course of the 6th/12th century.

The relationship between caliphs and sultans was of a contractual kind: sources refer to a 'pact' or 'contract' (*ᶜahd*) regulating the rights and duties of each party. A written document called *ᶜahd*, signed by the caliph, was bestowed to the Seljuq sultans during the ceremony of investiture at the Abbasid court, fictively treating them as Abbasid officials.[11] Such *ᶜahd*s are mentioned concerning Ṭughril Beg,[12] Alp Arslān,[13] Malikshāh,[14] Barkyāruq[15] and Maḥmūd;[16] the last sultan mentioned as being linked to the caliphate by an *ᶜahd* is Masᶜūd.[17]

ᶜAhd documents certainly contained the titulature given to the sultans, but it is doubtful that it openly listed the duties of the caliph towards them. It is nevertheless obvious that the *ᶜahd* had implicit stipulations, one of the most important being the interdiction made to the caliph to raise an army, as in Buyid times.[18] In situations of military need, Abbasid caliphs had to rely on Seljuq forces. This allowed the sultans to repeatedly claim for caliphal money in exchange for their military services. Huge sums were sent, usually gathered from Iraqi urban and rural taxes, and occasionally from exceptional, non-canonical taxation.[19]

The caliphs remained deprived of military power until the reign of al-Mustarshid, the first Abbasid ruler to lead an army since Buyid times. In

516/1123, he gathered troops to fight the Mazyadid Dubays.[20] The existence of an Abbasid army is from then on occasionally attested. It allowed the caliphs to lead a regional policy without the help of the Seljuqs, sometimes even against them. This resulted in a slow recovery of Abbasid authority over Iraq. In 572/1176, the soldiers of caliph al-Mustaḍīʾ expelled the last Seljuq armies trying to loot the Sawād.[21] These troops left for Khurasan, and Seljuq presence in Iraq was effectively ended.

This military recovery was paralleled by a major transformation of Abbasid administration that had been drastically reduced during Buyid times. In the first decades of Seljuq rule, civil administration was limited to the chancellery (*inshāʾ*) whose main task was to administer the caliph's private domains. The Abbasid administration (*dīwān*) was located inside the Dār al-Khilāfa, on the east bank of Baghdad. Al-Qāʾim was assisted by a vizier, who acted as the intermediate between him and the Seljuq sultans. He was also surrounded by agents called *ḥujjāb* (plural of *ḥājib*), who were in charge of local administration and of the day-to-day urban control of Baghdad. The *ḥujjāb* remained the main agents of the Abbasid government during the second half of the 5th/11th century; contemporary chronicles depict them as auxiliaries of the caliph's vizier. In addition the caliph had many servants (*khādim*, pl. *khadam*) in his private service. With the Seljuq conquest, the provincial administration of Iraq (primarily tax collection) passed directly from Buyid to Seljuq control.

As indicated by the greater number of state employees (*aṣḥāb al-dīwān* or *arbāb al-manāṣib*) mentioned in the sources, the role of central Abbasid administration increased during the 6th/12th century. Simultaneously, Abbasid independence from Seljuq influence became increasingly obvious. If, in 471/1078, Malikshāh did not hesitate to interfere in the choice of a vizier by the caliph al-Muqtafī,[22] from the reign of his successor al-Mustaẓhir (r. 487–512/1094–118), nomination and dismissal of officials by the caliphs are regularly mentioned in the chronicles. Al-Mustaẓhir was also the first caliph to suspend, even if temporarily, the Seljuq *khuṭba* (sermon) in Baghdad.[23]

From his reign on, more administrative services are mentioned by the sources: financial departments headed by the *ṣāḥib al-makhzan*, and inspection services (*dīwān al-zimān*). These administrations themselves were more strongly structured, and the hierarchy of employees gained in complexity, with the appearance of inspectors (*nāẓir*, pl. *nuẓarāʾ*). Under the reign of the son and successor of al-Mustaẓhir, al-Mustarshid (r. 512–29/1118–35), a very important office appeared: the *ustādh al-dār* (or *ustādār*). At the same period some civil lineages, of local or eastern origin, slowly began to control the most important administrative offices in Baghdad.

The Seljuq-Abbasid struggle for the control of state prerogatives (tax collection, urban rule, the mint) came into the open during the reign of caliph al-Muqtafī (r. 530–55/1136–60), increased by the fact that the Seljuq sultan Masᶜūd was residing intermittently in Baghdad at this time. In 541/1146, Masᶜūd opened a new mint (Dār al-Ḍarb) in Baghdad; the caliph immediately closed it and imprisoned its head-officer (*ḍarrāb*). In response, agents of the sultan put the *ḥājib al-bāb* and some private guards (*khawāṣṣ*) of the caliph in jail.[24] Two years later, Masᶜūd had to acknowledge the right of the caliph to assemble an army to defend Baghdad against Seljuq emirs competing for the sultanate. As a result, al-Muqtafī was able to reconquer Iraq from the rivals of Masᶜūd and in particular his nephews Malikshāh b. Maḥmūd and Muḥammad Shāh.

Consequently, al-Muqtafī's successors, al-Mustanjid (r. 555–66/1160–70) and al-Mustaḍīᵓ (r. 566–75/1170–80), never had to deal with Seljuq sultans or candidates to the sultanate in Baghdad. The members of the Seljuq family, weakened by heavy internal feuding, focused their attention on the eastern provinces of their empire and lost interest in Iraq and Baghdad. After 556/1161, there was no Seljuq *khuṭba* in Baghdad anymore.[25] Caliphal administration seems to have functioned smoothly, and at least two Abbasid officials held a very high social rank: the vizier and the *ustādh al-dār*. Al-Mustanjid and al-Mustaḍīᵓ are even presented by the sources as fighting corruption inside the administration. Although unverifiable, this statement nonetheless indicates that administrative services were developed and active at that time. The 'renaissance' of the caliphate that took place under the reign of al-Nāṣir,[26] who put an end to the eastern Seljuq sultanate by killing Ṭughril III in 590/1194, was therefore partly set on structures built by his predecessors over the previous half century.

QUESTIONING THE 'SUNNI REVIVAL'

Pro-Seljuq medieval sources present the sultans as the strong Sunni force who rescued a weak Abbasid caliphate oppressed by Shiᶜi rulers, emphasising the role of Ṭughril Beg as the saviour of the Abbasid caliph al-Qāᵓim, who had been expelled from Baghdad by the pro-Fatimid Turkish emir al-Basāsīrī. This view influenced 20th-century research on the period, to the point that the expression 'Sunni revival', first used by modern historians to qualify different periods of Islamic history, is since the 1960s mainly used to indicate the reign of the Great Seljuqs and of later Sunni dynasties such as the Zangids and Ayyubids.[27]

When referring to Seljuq times, the term has been used in reference to very different kinds of facts: the Seljuq political and military struggle against Shiᶜi powers (chiefly the Fatimid caliphate and other Ismaᶜili movements such as the 'Assassins' of Alamut), the supposed sultans' desire to eradicate Shiᶜism as a religious movement, the Seljuq 'official' patronage of Sunni institutions of learning, as well as the internal reorganisation of Sunni movements of thought (in law and theology)[28] and even social communities. In itself, the term is blurred and imprecise. Some historians even contested the implication that Sunnism was dead or dying before the 5th/11th century: Makdisi proposed replacing 'revival' by 'awakening',[29] and Bulliet preferred to consider the period a time of Sunni standardisation, a time when institutions and doctrines principally originating from the East were disseminated and adopted by the main branches of Sunnism.[30]

Most analyses present the 'Sunni revival' as the result of a central state policy: a movement initiated and led by rulers. Historians initially attributed it to the Seljuq sultans and their Persians officials, in particular the vizier Niẓām al-Mulk, in connection with the foundation of Sunni madrasas. The emphasis was subsequently placed on the role of the Abbasid caliphs, prior to the arrival of the Seljuqs, going back to the public profession of faith close to traditional Ḥanbalī views made by the caliph al-Qādir (r. 381–422/991–1031) in times of Buyid domination. This allowed Makdisi to push back the Sunni revival by half a century; he also argued that a crucial force of what he prefers to call the 'Sunni *traditional* revival' (emphasis is mine) was the Baghdad *ᶜulamāᵓ* (religious scholars) and in particular the Ḥanbalī scholars, whom he sees as the main contributors to the content and orientation of the policy later applied by the Abbasid state – not always with full Seljuq support.[31]

The problem of the actors of the 'Sunni revival' has been discussed controversially, but the question of these actors' means of actions is even less clear. The foundation of institutions such as colleges of law (madrasas) and 'Sufi convents' (*ribāṭ*s), patronage of Sufism or Ashᶜarism, state control over the *ᶜulamāᵓ* and popular preachers (*wuᶜᶜāẓ*), various intellectual output, monumental inscriptions, and even architectural and artistic style, have all been considered elements of the Sunni policy of Seljuq times; but the only topic fully investigated by historians is the foundation of madrasas.[32]

Most historians have considered the madrasa the principal instrument of the 'Sunni revival' understood as a state policy; an abundant bibliography has been produced on this topic since the 1960s. The numerous foundations of madrasas by Seljuq officials and the spread of this institution from the Eastern part of the *dār al-islām* towards the West are well established, but it has been understood in different ways. Gibb, followed by Klausner, interpreted it as the result of a Seljuq desire to establish a system of training for state employees,[33] a theory largely disproved by the fact that few officials in the administrative field were trained in madrasas, but nevertheless found even in recent literature.[34] Madrasas have also been seen as an instrument used by Seljuq officials to spread Ashᶜarism.[35] Based on the analysis of the local situation in certain Iranian cities, Bulliet gave another interpretation of the madrasa as a political tool used by the Seljuqs to control local factions of *ᶜulamāᵓ* by providing them with positions and stipends.[36] Though Bulliet provided the institution a new *raison d'être*, in such a view the madrasa was still considered the instrument of a deliberate Seljuq policy of strengthening their hold on the cities of their empire. The validity of such hypotheses can only be evaluated through careful examination of local cases.

After the foundation of the first Baghdad madrasa, the Niẓāmiyya, in 459/1066, up to the end of the 6th/12th century, around thirty madrasas were founded in the Abbasid capital, unequally distributed among the three main local schools of law (the Ḥanbalī, Shāfiᶜī and Ḥanafī *madhhab*s).[37] The first madrasas established in Baghdad – the Niẓāmiyya was followed immediately by a similar institution attached to the mausoleum (*mashhad*) of Abū Ḥanīfa, founded by the Seljuq official Abū Saᶜd, *ᶜamīd* and *mustawfī*, in 459/1067 – were devoted respectively to Shāfiᶜī and Ḥanafī *fiqh* (Muslim jurisprudence). Ḥanbalī *fuqahāᵓ* (jurists), even though they were the most numerous locally, had to wait another half century before the first madrasa attributed to their *madhhab* was built. In consequence, the transmission of Ḥanbalī *fiqh* continued to take place mainly in private circles or inside local mosques and oratories (*masjid*s), and some families, such as the Banū al-Farrāᵓ, maintained an important role in this process. In the second half of the 6th/12th century, nevertheless, new foundations provided Ḥanbalī *fuqahāᵓ* with a network of institutions comparable to that of the Shāfiᶜī and Ḥanafī rites. Before the end of this century, at least eleven Shāfiᶜī, nine Ḥanbalī and seven Ḥanafī madrasas had been set up in Baghdad – some of which, it is true, would not survive more than a few years because they had been granted insufficient endowments (*waqf*s). The identity of the founders also changed. The first sponsors of madrasa foundations were Seljuq officials, followed by Abbasid notables, and ultimately other inhabitants of Baghdad, the first to endow Ḥanbalī institutions.[38]

The impact of these foundations on the *fuqahāᵓ* of Baghdad greatly differed according to their legal affiliation.[39] The main local *madhhab*, the Ḥanbalī, was the last one to benefit from the madrasa system, and kept a strong local character.[40] Ḥanafī scholars, the lowest in number in Baghdad, enjoyed the sponsorship of Seljuq sultans and some of their officials. They were the first to benefit from a solid network of madrasas, and local Ḥanafī families like the Zaynabī and the Lamghānī consolidated their position in society. The proportion of local *fuqahāᵓ* among Ḥanafī madrasa teachers was higher at the end of the 6th/12th century than before, which proves the efficiency of the Ḥanafī networks. The situation was different for Shāfiᶜī *fuqahāᵓ*: their madrasas were numerous and had the support of influent Seljuq and Abbasid officials, but the status of the Niẓāmiyya was such that this institution attracted great numbers of foreign Shāfiᶜī madrasa-teachers (*mudarrisūn*), in particular from the Seljuq East. This generated a fraught competition inside the Shāfiᶜī milieus that paradoxically weakened the position of local *fuqahā*ᵓ. As a result, only a quarter of the Shāfiᶜī *mudarrisūn* were *fuqahā*ᵓ from local origin, compared to around three thirds local teachers in the Ḥanafī and Ḥanbalī madrasas.[41] Hence the foundation of madrasas cannot be considered a unified movement identified with the 'Sunni revival'. Moreover, since foundations were acts of individual patronage, it is difficult to interpret the multiplication of madrasas as the result of a deliberate and organised policy, be it Seljuq or Abbasid.

URBAN DEVELOPMENT OF BAGHDAD IN SELJUQ TIMES

The first Seljuq sultans did not usually visit Baghdad for periods longer than a few months, as they seem to have preferred their Iranian settlements to the hot and outlying Abbasid capital.[42] In the subsequent period, Seljuq sultans or candidates to the sultanate needed to be more present in the Abbasid capital, to make sure that the *khuṭba* was pronounced in their name or to exert pressure on the caliph.[43]

Despite this irregular presence in Baghdad, the first sultans undertook urban development projects during the second half of the 5th/11th century, intermittently followed by their main civil and military officials, who are responsible for as many foundations as the sultans. The Seljuq impact on Baghdad was thus stronger than one would think. The initial consequence of this was the urbanisation of vacant areas situated on the east bank, north of the caliphal districts and south of al-Ruṣāfa.[44] But the main impact on the city was the foundation of long-lasting institutions such as madrasas and *ribāṭ*s, endowed with *waqf*s which implied the construction of markets, *ḥammām*s, shops and private houses which provided steady incomes. Although these constructions are seldom mentioned by the sources, they played a dynamic role in the development of the city.

Despite their financial weakness, Abbasid caliphs were also important actors in the development of Baghdad, even during the strongest era of Seljuq dominance over the caliphate. From the second quarter of the 6th/12th century, Abbasid officials and Baghdad civilians played an increasing role in urban development, and sponsored the same kind of institutions (*ribāṭ*s, mosques and madrasas) that Seljuq officials had founded some decades earlier.[45]

Ṭughril Beg had planned a large-scale construction project in Baghdad. During his first (and longest) stay in 448/1056, he founded an urban settlement called by the chronicles 'The City of Ṭughril' (*madīnat Ṭughril*). Descriptions of this settlement are brief, but it was intended to be independent from other areas of the city since it was surrounded by walls and included markets and its own Friday mosque (*jāmi*ᶜ).[46] The construction material used to build Ṭughril's city was taken from ruined buildings of the west bank, as was often the case in Baghdad. Ṭughril Beg also founded a palace that the Baghdadis called Dār al-Mamlaka. It was fortified in 449/1057 to repel the expected arrival of al-Basāsīrī. The vizier of the sultan ᶜAmīd al-Mulk al-Kundurī supervised its construction and all inhabitants of the city were forced to participate.[47] On the west bank, Ṭughril sponsored the restoration of two hospitals[48] and the construction of markets, houses and caravanserais (*khāns*) in the Shiᶜi neighbourhood of al-Karkh[49] – possibly in order to contain its inhabitants and prevent them from circulating in other areas of the city.

Malikshāh continued the programme initiated by Ṭughril Beg. He built a new Friday mosque in the same area in 485/1092 and had luxurious residences constructed around it for his main officials: the vizir Niẓām al-Mulk, the financial minister (*mustawfī*) Tāj al-Mulk, and the most important emirs.[50] As a result, the district became popular among Seljuq elites, and wealthy Seljuq officials sponsored private and public foundations, including the first Baghdadi madrasas.[51] These foundations were to last longer than the sultan's administrative buildings, destroyed by Tigris floods or demolished by later Abbasid caliphs emancipating from Seljuq control.

Another palace, the Dār al-Sulṭāniyya, was built by Sultan Muḥammad b. Malikshāh. Inaugurated with great pomp in 509/1115,[52] it was destroyed by a fire six years later. The last important official Seljuq building in Baghdad was the new palace ordered by Maḥmūd in 515/1121.[53]

Seljuq sultans and officials were not the only actors in Baghdad's urban development. Abbasid caliphs also commissioned official buildings,[54] public works[55] and religious monuments.[56] Until the first decades of the 6th/12th century, they left the areas surrounding the Dār al-Mamlaka to total Seljuq control. Al-Mustarshid was powerful enough to order the destruction of some former Seljuq officials' private buildings at the end of his reign,[57] but it is only after the effective Seljuq presence in Baghdad was ended that Abbasid caliphs ventured their own building projects in the former Seljuq districts: al-Mustaḍīᵓ built a large mosque there in 573/1177 and symbolically bestowed it to the Ḥanbalīs. In the second half of the 6th/12th century, the caliphs also sponsored new palaces and Turkish-style pavilions (*kishks*) linked to hunting activities.[58]

Finally, ordinary Baghdadi civilians with no links either to Seljuq or Abbasid milieus must be mentioned as the third group of actors in the urban development process. More than a quarter of the sponsors of urban foundations from this period belong to this category; they founded eight madrasas, seven *ribāṭ*s and six *masjids*, almost all of them on the city's east bank, which was already favoured by sultans and caliphs.

A SHARED CONTROL OVER THE CITY

Baghdad's situation was unique in the Seljuq lands: as the Abbasid capital, it was supposedly under caliphal control and protection; but as a part of the Seljuq territories, the sultans also had a right of control over the city. As a result, the question of local administration and urban control was a complex one, with shared responsibility for the main political authorities, outside of the role played by the local militias led by the representative (*naqīb*) of the Hashemites.[59]

Seljuq Baghdad was governed like other urban centres of the empire, where the sultans were represented by an official called *shiḥna*,[60] chosen among their emirs or *khādims*, in most cases Turks.[61] In Baghdad, as stressed by Lambton, the *shiḥna* had a special position:[62] in addition to his function as the head of the Turkish soldiers responsible for urban control,[63] he also represented the Seljuq sultan before the caliph, and thus sometimes played a role comparable to the Seljuq vizier. On occasion, the *shiḥna* was explicitly called 'delegate' or 'representative' (*nāʾib*) of the sultan in Baghdad. His functions were not only of a military nature, as he could make the oath of allegiance (*bayʿa*) to a caliph in the name of an absent sultan,[64] and had to make sure that the *khuṭba* included the name of the ruling sultan. He could also levy taxes on Baghdad and its region in his name.[65]

The first *shiḥna*s of Baghdad were Turkish emirs nominated by the sultans, but it is not clear if *shiḥna*s played a role in urban control before the reign of Malikshāh. From 465/1072 until the end of the 5th/11th century, the chronicles report frequent interventions by the Seljuq *shiḥna*s in riots opposing Sunni and Shiʿi Baghdadis, leading Turkish armed forces against the Shiʿi elements of the population.[66]

Seljuq *shiḥna*s also had political functions: in 471/1078, the *shiḥna* Kawharāʾīn was in charge of the negotiations with al-Muqtadī when Niẓām al-Mulk commanded the caliph to dismiss his vizier Ibn Jahīr.[67] Frequently, they had to protect Ashʿarī preachers sent by Niẓām al-Mulk to lecture to the public in the Abbasid capital, where they met with great Ḥanbalī reluctance and resistance.[68]

Powerful *shiḥna*s in this period included Saʿd al-Dawla Kawharāʾīn (d. 493/1099),[69] a former *khādim* of the Buyids who entered the service of the Seljuqs and held the position of *shiḥna* of Baghdad under Alp Arslān and Malikshāh. Saʿd al-Dawla was renowned for his fierce repression of opponents of the Seljuq order; he would not hesitate to interfere directly in Abbasid policy. He owned a luxurious palace in Baghdad that the locals knew by his name (*dār Saʿd al-Dawla*).

Another well-known *shiḥna* of the first decades of the 6th/12th century was Bahrūz al-Ghiyāthī, surnamed Mujāhid al-Dīn (d. 540/1145).[70] This white *khādim* held different positions in Iraq where he was successively *shiḥna* or *wālī* (governor) of Baghdad, Tikrit and al-Hilla. He was first sent to Baghdad by Sultan Muḥammad to supervise the building of Dār al-Mamlaka and Jāmiᶜ al-Sulṭān. He was also patron of some public works, such as the provisioning of water in Baghdad and its surroundings, and he sponsored the foundation of a famous *ribāṭ* which was named after him (*ribāṭ Bahrūzī* or *ribāṭ al-khādim*),[71] and in which he was buried. This had such a positive impact on the capital that the Abbasid caliph himself rewarded him in 536/1141 for his works in Baghdad,[72] and that a street was named the Darb Bahrūz in his honor.

Not all Seljuq *shiḥna*s enjoyed the same popularity as Bahrūz. After his death, only emirs were appointed to this function, which consequently became less diplomatic and more military in character. As the representative of a foreign ruler, and above all as the leader of soldiers who would not hesitate to plunder areas of Baghdad or to carry out violence against its inhabitants, *shiḥna*s and their garrisons were often the subject of complaints from the population.[73] The caliphs' ability to intervene against them indicates their strength in the face of Seljuq power.

Abbasid authority over their capital was strongly challenged when competing candidates to the sultanate nominated their own *shiḥna*s in Baghdad,[74] even if in such situations, the role of *shiḥna*s was to symbolise the sultan's authority rather than to actually exert urban control. During the second quarter of the 6th/12th century, undisciplined and greedy *shiḥna*s were exacerbating Baghdad's internal instability instead of contributing to the security and public order, and *shiḥna*s of that time gained a reputation for tyranny. The last one of them, Masᶜūd Bilāl, had been nominated by Sultan Masᶜūd. When his master died in 547/1148, Masᶜūd Bilāl fled from Baghdad to Tikrit where the caliph al-Muqtafī would later meet him in battle.[75] Masᶜūd Bilāl's departure represents the end of direct Seljuq rule in Baghdad. There are some indications that Abbasid caliphs maintained the function of *shiḥna* after this period, though the sources rarely mention them during the second half of the 6th/12th century.[76]

The *shiḥna* was not the only official responsible for maintaining order in Baghdad. During the second half of the 5th/11th century, the chronicles regularly mention the head of the police forces, *ṣāḥib al-shurṭa*, whose role essentially was to arrest thieves and to combat everyday crime, including disorder caused by gangs of armed young men (*ᶜayyārūn*).[77] The *ṣāḥib al-shurṭa* was nominated and dismissed by the Abbasid caliphs;[78] only a small numbers of them are individuated by the sources. Baghdad's *shurṭa* is not mentioned anymore in the chronicles after 500/1106, but it seems that an official called *wālī* ('governor') took over the *ṣāḥib al-shurṭa*'s functions, in particular combating the *ᶜayyārūn*.[79]

Other Abbasid officials included the *ḥujjāb* (pl. of *ḥājib*), who were in charge of the different districts of Baghdad.[80] The sources also mention a *ḥājib al-bāb*, with duties very similar to those of the *ṣāḥib al-shurṭa*. He could assist the *shiḥna* or directly intervene if the Seljuq official was unable to re-establish order.[81] Seljuq and Abbasid officials actually collaborated in instances of Sunni-Shiᶜi confrontations. Officials in charge of governing Baghdad and repressing all kinds of riots also included the *muḥtasib* who was mainly in charge of controlling the markets and assuring the upkeep of Islamic morality in public spaces.[82] His powers were limited, and on some occasions he had to ask for the assistance of the *ḥājib al-bāb*.[83]

The Baghdadis themselves played a role in urban control: certain categories of the population, armed and organised under the direction of a leader, intervened in city affairs, sometimes upon caliphal request, sometimes apparently on their own initiative. This phenomenon is not specific to Baghdad: recent research shows that this kind of private militia operated in the great cities of Seljuq Iran, such as Isfahan.[84] But Baghdad was unusual in that the local armed forces were under the direction of an urban notable, the *naqīb* of the Hashemites.

The Hashemites (*Hāshimiyyūn* or *ashrāf*) were, in Seljuq as in Buyid times, divided into two groups: Abbasids (*ᶜAbbāsiyyūn*) and Alids or Talibids (*ᶜAlawiyyūn* or *Ṭālibiyyūn*), but the title 'Hashemite' was generally restricted to the Abbasids only.[85] Each of these groups was represented by a *naqīb* (pl. *nuqabāʾ*) of local origin,[86] appointed by the caliph.[87] In Seljuq times, supremacy was given to the Abbasid *naqīb*, who also held the title of 'chief *naqīb*' (*naqīb al-nuqabāʾ*).

The exact prerogatives of the *naqīb* are not known. According to the meagre bibliography on the subject,[88] his main task was to maintain the control of the Hashemites – he had to verify genealogies, supervise the morality of the *ashrāf*, and if necessary punish them, but evidence of this kind of action is scarce for the period.[89] On the other hand, we see the *naqīb*s holding a political and diplomatic position alongside the Abbasid caliphs on different occasions.[90] They seem to have exercised power on a territorial, rather than a religious basis: on different occasions, Abbasid *naqīb*s are mentioned as responsible for maintaining order in some districts on the west bank of the Tigris.[91] Throughout the Seljuq period, they were in charge of protecting Ashᶜarite preachers (*wuᶜᶜāẓ*) sent by the sultans, who were not welcome in Ḥanbalī neighbourhoods such as Bāb al-Baṣra.[92] The military functions of the *naqīb* are not clearly defined, but could have included the organisation of armed Hashemite militias,[93] called upon when the men of the Seljuq *shiḥna* and Abbasid *shurṭa* were not able to maintain the order, especially on the west bank of the city.[94] The *naqīb*s and possibly the Hashemites thus played an important part in urban control.

CONCLUSION: LOCAL CONSEQUENCES OF THE SELJUQ DOMINATION IN BAGHDAD

Seljuq domination over Baghdad was a complex and rich period in the history of the Abbasid capital. The city underwent crucial social and political changes during this century, but most of these changes cannot be ascribed to the 'Sunni revival'. Moreover, the notion itself, as discussed previously, is in need of clarification. The tensions and competitions inside Baghdad Sunnism, which are obvious in the sources, must be taken into consideration. The juridical or theological preferences of the main actors of the 'Sunni revival' also prevent us from considering this policy as monolithic or consensual. On the whole, the 'Sunni revival' appears more like a disparate ensemble of independent strategies. It seems indeed irrelevant to talk of a homogeneous 'Sunni community', a single 'Sunni camp' and a uniform 'Sunni policy' led by the Seljuq sultans or the Abbasid caliphs and their administrators. In addition, social, political and economical factors are essential to understand evolutions that religious policies, as complex as they may have been, cannot fully have caused.

Even though their causes and origins are not always clearly discernable, some developments can be seen as characteristic of the period. The first one is the drastic fading of Shiᶜi elites in Baghdadi society, or at least from the local sources. Of course, Shiᶜis did not disappear from Baghdad after the fall of the Buyids. Chronicles regularly mention the Shiᶜi parts of the city's population, notably in al-Karkh, in the context of riots between them and their Sunni neighbours. On the other hand, Shiᶜi scholars, jurists and thinkers are almost completely absent from the available sources. As most sources were written by Sunni authors, this does not mean that the Shiᶜi spheres were deprived of scholars and notables; but the mere fact that no important Shiᶜi work was produced in Baghdad during the period is in itself a clear sign of how Shiᶜi access to public space was reduced. This certainly contrasts with the Buyid period, but also with the uncertain period following the first Seljuq coming to Baghdad, when Sunni notables, including Ḥanbalī leaders, did not hesitate to pledge allegiance to the Fatimid caliph al-Mustanṣir.[95]

Non-Muslim communities seem to have witnessed the same kind of evolution. Muslim chronicles rarely mention the Christian and Jewish populations of Baghdad, whose presence is nevertheless attested by sources from within those communities.[96] Nestorian presence in the Abbasid capital was still important under Seljuq rule, with clerical elites conjured up by Nestorian chronicles, but high-status Christians were infrequent in Baghdad society, and their influence seems to have diminished during the period.[97]

The position of the Sunni populations is more variegated. The varied impact that the foundation of madrasas had on the three main Baghdadi *madhhab*s, as well as the personal preferences of Seljuq and Abbasid rulers and officials, affected the Sunni elites by strengthening the Ḥanafī *madhhab*, creating difficulties for local Shāfiᶜism, and transforming the political position of the Ḥanbalī *madhhab* from a strong opposition to the main powers of the time[98] to a reconciliation with the Abbasid milieus during the second half of the 6th/12th century. Ḥanbalī Baghdadis nevertheless remained a distinctly defined group in urban society, with their own scientific and social networks.[99]

The mystic milieu also underwent strong evolutions during the Seljuq period, which witnessed many foundations of *ribāṭ*s (or *khānqāh*s), buildings housing Sufis and dedicated to their activities.[100] Each *ribāṭ* was directed by a *shaykh* whose criteria of selection are vague. The distinguished title of *shaykh al-shuyūkh* was bestowed on the mystic Abū Saᶜd al-Nīsābūrī (d. around 477–9/1084–6) and on his descendants. This title seems to express social eminence (the successive *shaykh al-shuyūkh* all proved rich and influential) rather than corresponding to an actual position of control over mystic activities, as it did in later contexts.[101] Its appearance is representative of the general development of the period: an increasing proximity between mystical and political spheres, shown by the large number of officials, both Seljuq and Abbasid, who financed the foundation of Sufi institutions. One consequence was the appearance of new mystic lineages in 5th/11th- and 6th/12th-century Baghdad, many of them of Eastern origin, who came to dominate local Sufism.[102] The institutionalisation of Sufism, a phenomenon that was to develop in different areas of the *dār al-islām* during the later centuries, can thus be observed in Baghdad as early as the end of the 5th/11th century and notably accelerated during the following century.

Baghdad in the Seljuq period thus experienced not only a new political configuration – the domination of a foreign Sunni power over the caliphate, followed by a gradual Abbasid recovery – but also a deep social change partly due to this new political context, and partly to inherent endogenous tendencies already discernible in Buyid times.[103] From a local point of view, it is impossible to explain all the social changes merely in terms of the 'Sunni revival'. It is nevertheless true that the intellectual productivity that predominated in Baghdad at that time took the form of traditionalist works (treatises of *fiqh*, Quranic exegesis (*tafsīr*) and other religious sciences, collections of sermons (*waᶜẓ*), to which must be added a significant historiographical production) and the figure of active and prolific Ḥanbalī scholars such as Ibn ᶜAqīl (d. 513/1119) and Ibn al-Jawzī (d. 597/1201). On a larger scale, Baghdad was not the ruined and declining city that modern historians sometimes have depicted. Madīnat al-Salām was still attracting scholars from other parts of the *dār al-islām*. The connection with the

Iranian East is particularly apparent during the Seljuq period, but links with the Jazīra and Syria under Zangid and Ayyubid rule, and even with Egypt, can also be observed.[104]

It can therefore be stated that, in continuity with the Buyid period, Seljuq rule over Iraq increased the integration of Baghdad into the eastern Islamic world, until then predominantly Iranian in terms of culture, and from the Seljuq period on both Iranian and Turkish. This integration had important social and cultural consequences owing to the continuous arrival of scholars, officials and military elites from the East as well as to the new forms of political governance and religious patronage developed by the Seljuqs. Later developments, in particular those following the Mongol conquest of Iraq, must be considered in the light of this complex heritage.

NOTES

1. Iraq under Seljuq rule is usually dealt with in general studies of the Great Seldjuq empire, that is, the Seljuqs of Iran. For a good analysis see Claude Cahen, 'The Turkish invasion: the Selchükids', in *A History of the Crusades*, vol. 1, *The first hundred years*, ed. Marshall W. Baldwin (Philadelphia, PA, 1955), pp. 135–76. Elements of synthesis can also be found in Jean-Claude Garcin, 'Les Seldjukides et leurs héritiers', in *Etats, sociétés et cultures du monde musulman médiéval, Xe–XVe siècle, t. 1: L'évolution politique et sociale*, eds Jean-Claude Garcin *et al.* (Paris, 1995), pp. 123–49. Very few monographs are strictly dedicated to Iraq in the Seljuq period. Ḥusayn Amīn's *Taʾrīkh al-ʿIrāq fī-l-ʿaṣr al-saljūqī* (Baghdad, 1385/1965) is an exception, but it gives only a brief overview of the history of Seljuq Iraq drawn from Arabic historiographical sources (pp. 89–120).
2. In particular with the recent, if not innovative, study of John J. Donohue, *The Buwayhid Dynasty in Iraq 334 H./945 to 403 H./1012: Shaping Institutions for the Future* (Leiden, 2003).
3. See the unpublished PhD of Khidr Jasmin Duri, *Society and economy of Iraq under the Seljuqs (1055–1160) with special reference to Baghdad* (University of Pennsylvania, 1970), and the numerous works of George Makdisi, mainly *Ibn ʿAqīl et la résurgence de l'islam traditionaliste au XIe siècle (Ve siècle de l'Hégire)* (Damas, 1963). Many articles of Makdisi dealing with Baghdad in Seljuq times have been gathered in *History and Politics in Eleventh-Century Baghdad* (London, 1990).
4. A great part of Iraq was never fully controlled by the Seljuqs but remained under the rule of local dynasties such as the ʿUqaylids of Mosul and the Mazyadids of al-Hilla. See C. E. Bosworth, *The New Islamic Dynasties: a Chronological and Genealogical Manual* (Edinburgh, 1996), pp. 87–8, 91–2; George Makdisi, 'Notes on Ḥilla and the Mazyadids in Medieval Islam', *JAOS* 74, 4 (1954), pp. 249–62.
5. They can nevertheless be raised, on the model of the works of Stefan Heidemann on the Jazīra, combining text analysis with archaeological, numismatic and epigraphic evidences. See in particular *Die Renaissance der Städte in Nordsyrien und Nordmesopotamien* (Leiden, 2002).

6. A great part of the information used here is drawn from my PhD thesis (University of Paris 1 – La Sorbonne, 2004) entitled *Les élites bagdadiennes au temps des Seldjoukides* (to be published in Paris, *Éditions Les Indes savantes*).
7. See the monumental work of al-Khaṭīb al-Baghdādī (d. 463/1071), *Taʾrīkh Baghdād aw Madīnat al-Salām*, 14 vols, as well as its continuations by Ibn al-Najjār (d. 643/1245), *Dhayl taʾrīkh Baghdād*, 5 vols, and Ibn al-Dimyāṭī (d. 749/1348), *al-Mustafād min Dhayl taʾrīkh Baghdād*, 1 vol., all three of which were edited by Muṣṭafā ʿAbd al-Qādir ʿAṭā (Beirut, 1997). See also Ibn al-Dubaythī (d. 637/1239), *Dhayl taʾrīkh Madīnat al-Salām Baghdād*, ed. Bashshār ʿAwwād Maʿrūf, 2 vols (Baghdad, 1974); al-Bundārī (middle of the 7th/13th century), *Taʾrīkh Baghdād* (*unicum* manuscript), Paris, BnF, Fonds arabe no. 6152, 116 folios.
8. See the 'diary' of the Ḥanbalī scholar Ibn al-Bannāʾ (d. 471/1079) (Arabic edn and English translation in George Makdisi, 'Autograph diary of an eleventh century historian of Baghdād', *BSOAS* 18 (1956), pp. 9–31, 239–60; 19 (1957), pp. 13–48, 281–303, 426–43) and the chronicles of Ibn al-Jawzī (d. 597/1201), *al-Muntaẓam fī taʾrīkh al-umam wa-l-mulūk*, eds Muḥammad and Muṣṭafā ʿAbd al-Qādir ʿAṭā, 18 vols (Beirut, 1992), and of his grandson Sibṭ ibn al-Jawzī (d. 654/1256), *Mirʾāt al-zamān fī taʾrīkh al-aʿyān*. Of the latter, three editions have been used: ed. Ali Sevim, *Belgeler* 14/18 (1989–92), pp. 1–260 [years 448–80/1056–87]; ed. Musfir b. Sālim b. ʿArīj al-Ghāmirī, 2 vols (Mekka, 1987) [years 481–517/1088–1123]; (s.l., s.d. Hyderabad, 1955) [years 495–654/1101–1256].
9. Such as *al-Kāmil fī l-taʾrīkh* of Ibn al-Athīr (d. 630/1232), ed. Muḥammad Yūsuf al-Daqqāq, 10 vols (Beirut, 1998). See also the biographical dictionaries, in particular the ones dealing with Ḥanbalī authorities, such as Ibn Abī Yaʿlā's (d. 526/1132) *Ṭabaqāt al-ḥanābila* and Ibn Rajab's (d. 795/1392) *Dhayl ʿalā ṭabaqāt al-ḥanābila*, both edited, in two volumes each, by Abū Ḥāzim Usāma b. Ḥasan and Abū l-Zahrāʾ Ḥāzim ʿAlī Bahjat (Beirut, 1997).
10. In particular al-Rāvandī (d. after 599/1202), *Rāḥat al-ṣudūr* (in Persian), ed. Muḥammad Iqbāl (Tehran, 1985); al-Bundārī, *Zubdat al-nuṣra wa nukhbat al-ʿuṣra* (*Taʾrīkh dawlat Āl Saljūq*) (Beirut, 1980) and ʿAlī b. Nāṣir al-Ḥusaynī (second half of the 7th/13th century), *Zubdat al-tawārīkh* (*Akhbār dawlat Āl Saljūq*), ed. Muḥammad Iqbāl (Lahore, 1933; reprint Beirut, 1984); their information on Iraq in general and Baghdad in particular is nevertheless limited.
11. Written *ʿahd*s delivered by the Abbasid chancellery (*inshāʾ*) were bestowed to any important official during a ceremony of investiture (*taqlīd*).
12. Ibn al-Jawzī, *Muntaẓam*, XVI, p. 20; al-Bundārī, *Zubda*, p. 17.
13. Sibṭ ibn al-Jawzī, *Mirʾāt*, ed. *Belgeler*, p. 131.
14. Ibid. p. 259.
15. Ibn al-Jawzī, *Muntaẓam*, XVII, p. 10.
16. ʿAlī b. Nāṣir al-Ḥusaynī, *Zubda*, p. 96.
17. Ibn al-Jawzī, *Muntaẓam*, XVII, p. 263, and XVIII, p. 71. Here there is no direct reference to a written document, but the caliph al-Mustarshid mentions his mutual alliance with Masʿūd as 'sealed by a pact (*ʿahd*) and an oath (*yamīn*)'.
18. In 525/1131, al-Mustarshid recalls to Masʿūd that the *ʿahd* prevents him from raising an army: *wa-innī lā akhruju wa-lā udawwinu ʿaskar*[an]. See Ibn al-Jawzī, *Muntaẓam*, XVII, p. 263.
19. In 468/1075, an emissary was sent to Baghdad by Sultan Malikshāh to ask for 100,000 dinars in order to pay for the Seljuq troops. See Sibṭ ibn al-Jawzī, *Mirʾāt*, ed. *Belgeler*,

p. 197. In 493/1099, Sultan Barkyāruq asked from the Abbasid vizier 160,000 dinars for the same purpose. See Ibn al-Jawzī, *Muntaẓam*, XVII, p. 53. In 515/1121, Sultan Maḥmūd emptied the Abbasid treasure in response to the Abbasid claim to protect Baghdad from Dubays b. Mazyad. See Sibṭ ibn al-Jawzī, *Mir'āt*, edn Mekka, II, p. 721.

20. Ibn al-Jawzī, *Muntaẓam*, XVII, p. 207; Sibṭ ibn al-Jawzī, *Mir'āt*, edn Mekka, II, p. 738. It is not known how many soldiers this army numbered, but the same caliph is said to have gathered 30,000 men to fight Sultan Maḥmūd five years later, in 521/1127. See Ibn al-Athīr, *Kāmil*, IX, p. 239.
21. Ibn al-Jawzī, *Muntaẓam*, XVIII, p. 229ff.
22. Ibn al-Jawzī, *Muntaẓam*, XVI, p. 198; Ibn al Athīr, *Kāmil*, VIII, p. 417; Sibṭ ibn al-Jawzī, *Mir'āt*, ed. *Belgeler*, p. 213.
23. This occurred in 496/1102, in a context of strong rivalry between two Seljuq candidates to the sultanate. See Ibn al-Jawzī, *Muntaẓam*, XVII, p. 80. The Seljuq *khuṭba* was restored in Baghdad one year later.
24. Ibn al-Jawzī, *Muntaẓam*, XVIII, p. 49.
25. At least none is recorded in the chronicles. The *khuṭba* of 556/1161 was pronounced in favour of Arslān Shāh, another nephew of Masᶜūd and father of Ṭughril III.
26. On the reign of al-Nāṣir, see Angelika Hartmann, *An-Nāṣir li-Dīn Allāh (1180–1225): Politik, Religion, Kultur in der späten ᶜAbbāsidenzeit* (Berlin, 1975); summary in *EI2*, s.v. 'al-Nāṣir li-Dīn Allāh', VII, p. 996 (A. Hartmann).
27. French historians writing in the 1950s and 1960s used similar expressions to qualify the 3rd/9th century under Abbasid rule. Dominique Sourdel for example employed the expressions 'Sunni reaction' and 'Sunni restoration' to refer to the politics of the Abbasid caliph al-Mutawakkil (r. 847–61 CE) and his successors. See Dominique Sourdel, 'La politique religieuse des successeurs d'al-Mutawakkil', *SI* 13 (1960), pp. 5–21, 6, 9. Charles Pellat, on the other hand, spoke of the '*renaissance sunnite*' to refer to the times of Ibn Qutayba (d. 276/889). See Charles Pellat, 'La prose arabe à Baġdād', in *Baġdād, volume spécial d'Arabica, publié à l'occasion du 1200e anniversaire de la fondation* (1962), pp. 407–18.
28. In this case, the 'Sunni revival' has been interpreted as a reaction to Muᶜtazilism and other rationalist tendencies in Muslim theological thought, favoured or at least tolerated by the Buyids as stated by Joel L. Kraemer, *Humanism in the Renaissance of Islam: the Cultural Revival during the Buyid Age* (first publ. 1986, 2nd rev. edn Leiden, 1986).
29. George Makdisi, 'The Sunni revival', in *Islamic Civilisation, 950–1150*, ed. D. S. Richards (Oxford, 1973), p. 168.
30. Richard W. Bulliet, *Islam: the View from the Edge* (New York, 1994). An interesting synthesis on the question of the 'Sunni revival' has recently been provided by Jonathan Berkey. In a short but suggestive chapter of his book *The formation of Islam* (Cambridge, 2003), entitled 'A Sunni "revival"?' (pp. 189–202), he argues that the 5th–6th/11th–12th centuries should be seen less as a period of 'revival' than as a time of 'homogenization' of Sunni Islam (p. 189).
31. See George Makdisi, *Ibn ᶜAqīl*; George Makdisi, 'The Sunni revival'.
32. It is significant that, despite its promising title, Stephen Humphreys' article 'Ideology and propaganda: religion and state in the Early Seljukid period' (in *Islamic History: a Framework for Inquiry*, R. S. Humphreys (London, 1991), pp. 148–68) does not provide any actual information about the form of the 'propaganda' that the Seljuq sultans supposedly might have encouraged. Humphreys does list different means of propaganda,

including ceremonial, architecture, writings, monumental inscriptions, *khuṭba*s form and content; but he limits his discussion to the foundation of mosques and madrasas, stating that 'among the *ᶜulamāᵓ* and their followers, the dynasty's role as "defender of the faith" could be symbolized by its patronage of religious institutions'. See ibid. p. 165. Recently, Yasser Tabbaa has attempted to link artistic forms and patterns that spread in Iraq, Iran and Syria during the 5th–6th/11th–12th centuries to the Sunni revival. See his *The Transformation of Islamic Art during the Sunni Revival* (London, 2002). He considers Qurᵓānic calligraphy, building inscriptions, geometric patterns and *muqarnas* decoration as significant indicators of an allegiance to the Abbasid caliphate and to Sunni orthodoxy, although this notion is not clearly defined. His definition and chronology of the 'Sunni revival' is vague, sometimes ascribed only to the Abbasid caliphs, sometimes mainly attributed to other Sunni dynasties or rulers (in particular Niẓām al-Mulk, Nūr al-Dīn and Ṣalāḥ al-Dīn), sometimes related to al-Qādir's traditionalist profession of faith or to the supposed triumph of Ashᶜarism during the 5th/11th century.

33. Klausner gives the following definition of the purpose of the madrasas: 'These schools of higher learning were to be utilised, it seemed, as training colleges in the religious sciences for men who would fill positions in both the religious and administrative hierarchies'. See Carla Klausner, *The Seljuk Vezirate: a Study of Civil Administration, 1055–1194* (Cambridge, 1973), p. 5.
34. See for example Tabbaa, *The Transformation of Islamic Art*, pp. 18–19; Omid Safi, *The Politics of Knowledge in Premodern Islam: Negotiating Ideology and Religious Inquiry* (Chapel Hill, NC, 2006), p. 97.
35. Makdisi, 'The Sunni revival', contested this theory, underlining the fact that madrasas were devoted to the teaching of Muslim jurisprudence (*fiqh*) and not of dogmatic theology (*kalām*). But the case of the Niẓāmiyya madrasa should be further investigated in this regard, as *waᶜẓ* was one of the activities regularly hosted by this institution and included Ashᶜarite performances.
36. Richard W. Bulliet, 'Local politics in Eastern Iran under the Ghaznavids and Seljuks', *Iranian Studies* 11, 1–4 (1978), pp. 35–56. Bulliet thus asserted that madrasas 'were not designed to recruit bureaucrats for the central government; they were designed to exert imperial influence on local religious politicians'. See ibid. p. 52.
37. The following analysis is mainly based on my PhD research (Van Renterghem, *Les élites bagdadiennes*). Previous works on Baghdad madrasas in Seljuq times include Daphna Ephrat, *A Learned Society in a Period of Transition: the Sunni ᶜUlamaᵓ of Eleventh-Century Baghdad* (New York, 2000). Following the path opened by Michael Chamberlain studying 7th/13th century's Damascene madrasas (*Knowledge and Social Practice in Medieval Damascus, 1190–1350* (Cambridge, 1993)), Ephrat focused on the Baghdad madrasa as an instrument of the progressive self-definition of the *ᶜulamāᵓ* as an exclusive group.
38. Twenty-one founders of madrasas in Baghdad can be identified for the period under study. Eight belonged to the Seljuq entourage, and were active between 459/1066 and the first quarter of the 6th/12th century, when Sultan Muḥammad b. Malikshāh (d. 525/1131) founded the madrasa Ghiyāthiyya. Six of their endowments were devoted to Ḥanafīs and two to Shāfiᶜīs. Six individuals who did not belong to the Seljuq or Abbasid administration or military elite sponsored Ḥanbalī madrasas during the 6th/12th century, and seven Abbasid officials and princesses founded four Shāfiᶜī, two Ḥanbalī

and one Ḥanafī madrasas between the second quarter and the end of the 6th/12th century. See Van Renterghem, *Les élites bagdadiennes*, chs 4 and 15.

39. The statistics given hereafter are taken from the analysis of a prosopographical database created as a part of my PhD research. Mainly built from biographical dictionaries, it contains more than 2,600 records of individuals who died between 447/1055 and 600/1203 and lived in Baghdad, whether permanently or for shorter periods of time.
40. Out of the 262 Ḥanbalī *fuqahāʾ* of the database, 190 (73%) were Baghdadi by birth and residence, compared to 86 out of 211 Ḥanafīs (41%) and 104 out of 399 Shāfiʿīs (26%).
41. Eight of the twelve known *mudarrisūn* in Ḥanbalī madrasas for the period were Baghdadi by birth and residence; the proportion of local Ḥanafī teachers was even higher (nine out of twelve), but much lower for Shāfiʿīs (eleven Baghdadis out of the forty *mudarrisūn* and *muʿīdūn* identified).
42. Ṭughril Beg's first stay was the longest: he waited thirteen months to be received by caliph al-Qāʾim. The Abbasid sovereign finally allowed him the official investiture ceremony that he wished for in 449/1058. Subsequently, he stayed in Baghdad only briefly, from five months in 450/1058 to fifteen days in 452/1060. In ten years of reign, his successor Alp Arslān never visited the Abbasid capital. Malikshāh spent more time in Iraq, staying two or three months in Baghdad before going back to Isfahan (years 479/1086, 480/1087, 484/1091, and 485/1092 in the chronicles), and Barkyāruq briefly resided in Baghdad in 486/1093, 493/1099 and 494/1100.
43. To this end Muḥammad b. Malikshāh spent several months in Baghdad in 501/1107 and 502/1108, and the whole of 510/1116. The longest stay was Maḥmūd's of nineteen months, from Rajab 514/October 1120 to Rabīʿ I 516/May 1122. Masʿūd was the Seljuq sultan who visited the city most frequently (eleven stays between 526/1131, before he held the title of sultan, and 546/1131, his army conquering the city in 530/1135). The last candidate to the sultanate to visit Baghdad was Sulaymān Shāh, in 551/1136.
44. The choice of this location was motivated by the proximity of the caliphal quarters, and the distance to the Shiʿi district of Karkh, located on the other bank. Seljuq settlement on the east bank can also be explained by the fact that coming from eastern lands, it was thus not necessary to cross the wide and unpredictable Tigris.
45. Sixty-six sponsors of constructions, private (residences) or public (madrasas, *ribāṭ*s, *masjid*s), can be identified for the period: fifteen of them were Seljuq sultans, emirs, administrators or princesses; twenty-nine belonged to the Abbasid entourage, and eighteen were Baghdadi civilians, mainly *ʿulamāʾ* and wealthy merchants (half of whom were Ḥanbalīs). Cf. Van Renterghem, *Les élites bagdadiennes*, ch. 15.
46. The 'city of Ṭughril' still existed in the first half of the 7th/13th century according to al-Bundārī (*Zubda*, p. 13).
47. Ibn al-Jawzī, *Muntaẓam*, XVI, p. 18; Sibṭ ibn al-Jawzī, *Mirʾāt*, ed. *Belgeler*, p. 45.
48. The Bīmāristān ʿAḍudī, founded by the Buyid emir ʿAḍud al-Dawla, and the Bīmāristān situated in Bāb Muḥawwal. See Ibn al-Jawzī, *Muntaẓam*, XVI, p. 62.
49. Ibid. p. 62.
50. Ibn al-Athīr, *Kāmil*, VIII, p. 475.
51. The Ḥanafī madrasas founded by *ʿamīd* and *mustawfī* Abū Saʿd (459/1067) and Tāj al-Mulk (480/1087). Other Seljuq foundations include the *ribāṭ* founded by the *shiḥna* Bahrūz in 502/1108. The madrasa Niẓāmiyya was set outside of the 'Seljuq' area of Baghdad, south of the caliphal precincts, on the banks of the Tigris.

52. Ibn al-Jawzī, *Muntaẓam*, XVII, p. 509; Sibṭ ibn al-Jawzī, *Mirʾāt*, edn Mekka, II, p. 612.
53. Ibn al-Jawzī, *Muntaẓam*, XVII, p. 194.
54. A new Abbasid palace, called 'the precious' (*al-muthammina*), was built on the shore of the Tigris by al-Mustarshid, in order to replace the previous one, al-Tāj, that was about to collapse. The building was completed in 518/1124. See Ibn al-Jawzī, *Muntaẓam*, XVII, p. 224; Sibṭ ibn al-Jawzī, *Mir'āt*, edn Hyderabad, pp. 112–15.
55. Such as the edification of walls (*sūr*) around the caliphal precincts commissioned by al-Mustaẓhir in 488/1095. Ibn al-Jawzī, *Muntaẓam*, XVII, p. 16; Ibn al-Athīr, *Kāmil*, VIII, 506.
56. Like the *turba* shrine dedicated to the Baghdadi ascetic Maᶜrūf al-Karkhī sponsored by al-Qāʾim in 459/1066, and the re-building of the caliphal Friday mosque, Jāmiᶜ al-Qaṣr, by al-Muqtadī (r. 467–87/1075–94) in 475/1082. Ibn al-Jawzī, *Muntaẓam*, XVI, p. 102; Ibn al-Athīr, *Kāmil*, VIII, p. 380 (for the *turba*); Ibn al-Jawzī, *Muntaẓam*, XVI, p. 224 (for Jāmiᶜ al-Qaṣr).
57. He had the Bustān al-ᶜAmīd destroyed in 527/1133 in order to use its bricks to consolidate the city walls, and the following year he ordered the demolition of the old residence of Niẓām al-Mulk and the transfer of its furniture to the caliphal palaces. See Ibn al-Jawzī, *Muntaẓam*, XVII, pp. 276, 284.
58. The first palace, built in 559/1164 by caliph al-Mustanjid near Bāb al-Gharaba, north of the caliphal districts (ibid. XVIII, p. 160), was used subsequently to host a yearly reception of the main Baghdadi mystics and *ᶜulamāʾ*. The second was erected by al-Mustaḍīʾ in 570/1174, facing the treasury (*makhzan*) (ibid. XVIII, p. 213). These two caliphs and al-Mustanjid's vizier also sponsored costly pavilions (*kishk*s) in 558/1163 and 571/1175, including one in the former Seljuq district.
59. On the identification of the Hashemite *naqīb* with the *naqīb* of the Abbasids, see below. The following discussion derives from my PhD dissertation. See Van Renterghem, *Les élites bagdadiennes*, ch. 14.
60. The role of *shiḥna*s in different cities of the Seljuq empire has been discussed by historians. For a general discussion of the term in the Seljuq context, see *EI2*, s.v. 'Shiḥna', IX, pp. 437–8 (A. K. S. Lambton); A. K. S. Lambton, 'The administration of Sanjar's empire as illustrated in the *ᶜAtabat al-kataba*', *BSOAS* 20 (1957), pp. 367–88, particularly p. 380ff. On Baghdad, see also Simha Sabari, *Mouvements populaires à Bagdad à l'époque ᶜabbasside, IXe–XIe siècles* (Paris, 1981).
61. Among the twenty-one Seljuq *shiḥna*s of Baghdad I was able to identify, fourteen were emirs. The *shiḥnas* are usually mentioned by the chronicles, but rarely by biographical dictionaries (only seven of them are the subject of a brief biographical notice).
62. A. K. S. Lambton, 'The internal structure of the Saljuq empire', in *CHI5*, pp. 203–282, at p. 213.
63. These troops were supposed to maintain urban order in Baghdad, but in the beginning of the Seljuq rule, their mere presence occasionally caused incidents with the local population (for examples, see the events of years 450/1058, 461/1068, 464/1071 and 480/1087 in the main chronicles).
64. In 529/1135, Sultan Masᶜūd wrote to his *nāʾib* in Baghdad, the *shiḥna* Bakbah, to perform the *bayᶜa* in his name to the new caliph al-Rāshid. See Sibṭ ibn al-Jawzī, *Mirʾāt*, edn Hyderabad, p. 158.
65. A Seljuq *shiḥna* of Baghdad is first mentioned in the Arabic chronicles in 453/1061 when, in a context of crisis (the Abbasid caliph refusing to give him his daughter in

marriage), Sultan Ṭughril Beg ordered his *shiḥna* to levy taxes on the Baghdad population. See Ibn al-Jawzī, *Muntaẓam*, XVI, p. 69.

66. See the events of years 465/1072, 466/1073, 478/1085, 479/1086 and 482/1089, mainly in Ibn al-Jawzī, *Muntaẓam*.
67. The reason for this was that Ibn Jahīr had taken a pro-Ḥanbalī position in the conflict between Ashᶜarī preachers sent to Baghdad by Niẓām al-Mulk and the local Ḥanbalīs. See Ibn al-Jawzī, *Muntaẓam*, XVI, p. 198; Ibn al-Athīr, *Kāmil*, VIII, p. 417.
68. See the events of year 469/1076 as reported by Sibṭ ibn al-Jawzī: the *shiḥna* had to protect militarily the Ashᶜarī preacher al-Qushayrī who addressed the Friday mosque of al-Ruṣāfa, causing a *fitna* (civil war). See Sibṭ ibn al-Jawzī, *Mirʾāt*, ed. *Belgeler*, p. 205ff. Another Ashᶜarī *wāᶜiẓ* sent by Niẓām al-Mulk in 475/1082 publicly accused the Ḥanbalīs of being anthropomorphists. While preaching in the al-Manṣūr Friday mosque he needed protection from the *shiḥna*'s troops. See Ibn al-Jawzī, *Muntaẓam*, XVI, p. 224.
69. See Ibn al-Jawzī, *Muntaẓam*, XVII, p. 56 (#3694); Ibn al-Athīr, *Kāmil*, IX, p. 26; Sibṭ ibn al-Jawzī, *Mirʾāt*, edn Mekka, I, p. 340.
70. Ibn al-Jawzī, *Muntaẓam*, XVIII, p. 46 (#4116); Ibn al-Athīr, *Kāmil*, IX, p. 336; Sibṭ ibn al-Jawzī, *Mirʾāt*, edn Hyderabad, p. 186.
71. The foundation date of this building is not known, but it already existed in 510/1116. See Ibn al-Jawzī, *Muntaẓam*, XVII, p. 145.
72. Ibid. XVIII, p. 17; al-Dhahabī, *Taʾrīkh al-islām*, IX, p. 219ff.
73. See in the main chronicles (in particular Ibn al-Jawzī and Ibn al-Athīr) the events and riots of the years 479/1086, 487/1094, 495/1101 and 497/1103.
74. For example in 496/1102, when Barkyāruq as well as his brother Muḥammad both appointed a *shiḥna* in Baghdad (respectively the *khādim* Kumushtikīn al-Qayṣarī and the emir Īlghāzī). See Ibn al-Athīr, *Kāmil*, IX, p. 62ff.
75. Ibn al-Jawzī, *Muntaẓam*, XVIII, p. 85; Sibṭ ibn al-Jawzī, *Mirʾāt*, edn Hyderabad, p. 212; al-Dhahabī, *Taʾrīkh al-islām*, X, p. 34ff.
76. Among the notables who died in 589/1193, Sibṭ ibn al-Jawzī mentions a certain Qayṭarmash b. ᶜAbdallāh al-Mustanjidī (a *mamlūk* of the Abbasid caliph al-Mustanjid according to his name), *shiḥna* of Baghdad under al-Mustaḍīʾ and al-Nāṣir. See Sibṭ ibn al-Jawzī, *Mirʾāt*, edn Hyderabad, p. 423. Al-Dhahabī also states that al-Muqtafī nominated a *shiḥna* in Wāsiṭ in 547/1152. See al-Dhahabī, *Taʾrīkh al-islām*, X, p. 34ff.
77. See in particular Ibn al-Jawzī, *Muntaẓam*, years 448/1056, 458/1065, 474/1081, 487/1094, 497/1103 and 500/1106.
78. Ibid. XVII, p. 14; and Ibn al-Athīr, *Kāmil*, VIII, p. 498.
79. *Wālī*s are mentioned in the chronicles during the years 473/1080, 478/1085 and 529–38/1134–43. See in particular Ibn al-Jawzī, *Muntaẓam*, Ibn al-Athīr, *Kāmil*, and al-Dhahabī, *Taʾrīkh al-islām*.
80. Ibn al-Bannāʾ mentions the *ḥājib* of Bāb al-Marātib in 461/1069 ('Diary', §147) and Sibṭ ibn al-Jawzī the one of Bāb al-Nūbī who died in 478/1085 (*Mirʾāt*, ed. *Belgeler*, p. 250).
81. In 482/1089, the Abbasid *ḥājib* had to help the Seljuq *shiḥna* to stop a Sunni-Shiᶜi riot on the west bank of Baghdad. See Ibn al-Jawzī, *Muntaẓam*, XVI, p. 282.
82. Seventeen *muḥtasib*s are known in Baghdad for the period, both nominated and dismissed by the caliph; they were mainly *ᶜulamāʾ*, most of them with a juridical training (twelve led a judicial career as *shāhid* or *qāḍī*), one with commercial background. Each bank of the Tigris and possibly even each large district had its own *muḥtasib*.

83. See for example the events of the years 525/1131 and 563/1167 in Ibn al-Jawzī, *Muntaẓam*, XVII, p. 264 and XVIII, p. 177.
84. David Durand-Guédy, 'Iranians at war under Turkish domination: the example of pre-Mongol Isfahan', *Iranian Studies* 38, 4 (2005), pp. 587–606.
85. The chronicles sometimes mention 'Hashemites and Talibids' or 'Hashemites and Alids' as two distinct entities, the first of which must be identified with the Abbasid branch of the Banū Hāshim. See, for example, Ibn al-Jawzī, *Muntaẓam*, XVIII, p. 191. Belonging to an Alid lineage was not automatically an indication that an individual was Shiᶜi.
86. Of the twenty-three Abbasids or Talibid *naqīb*s known in Baghdad for the period, twenty were Baghdadi by birth and residence.
87. See for example the nomination of Abū ᶜAbdallāh ibn Abī Ṭālib, *naqīb* of Kufa, as *naqīb* of the Talibids, by al-Qāʾim in 450/1058. See Ibn al-Jawzī, *Muntaẓam*, XVI, p. 29; Sibṭ ibn al-Jawzī, *Mirʾāt*, ed. *Belgeler*, p. 52.
88. In particular *EI2*, s.v. 'Naḳīb al-ashrāf', VII, pp. 826–7 (A. Havemann).
89. Only one *naqīb* was noted for his knowledge of the science of genealogy (*ansāb*), and the authority of the *naqīb*s over their communities was frequently usurped by contradictory caliphal decisions. See for example Ibn al-Bannāʾ, 'Diary', §17; Ibn al-Jawzī, *Muntaẓam*, XVIII, p. 203.
90. For *naqīb*s sent in diplomatic missions by the Abbasid caliphs to Seljuq or Mazyadite rulers, see events of the years 479/1086, 501/1117 or 528/1133; for their role in Abbasid protocol, see years 513/1119 and 561/1165; for interventions in military contexts, mainly caliphal opposition to Seljuq sultans, see years 519–21/1125–7 and 528/1133.
91. Ibn al-Jawzī makes a clear reference to the territorial power of the *naqīb* of the Hashemites, mentioning that the area of al-Ḥarbiyya, on the west bank, was under his jurisdiction (*kāna amr*[u] *hādhihi l-maḥalla ilā al-naqīb*). See Ibn al-Jawzī, *Muntaẓam*, XVIII, p. 156. It can be hypothesized that the *naqīb* of the Talibids was in charge of the Karkh district; a distinct *naqīb* is also mentioned in relation to the Shiᶜi mausoleum (*mashhad*) of Bāb al-Tibn, north of the west bank.
92. See events of the years 461/1068 (Ibn al-Bannāʾ, 'Diary', §109), 475/1082 (Ibn al-Jawzī, *Muntaẓam*, XVI, p. 224), 546/1151 (ibid. XVIII, p. 81).
93. Groups of armed Hashemites are periodically mentioned by the chronicles. See for example the events of the year 467/1074, describing the Abbasid vizier Fakhr al-Dawla organising troops of Turks and Hashemites to prevent social troubles, in the context of the imminent death of the caliph al-Qāʾim (*rataba al-wazīr Fakhr al-dawla al-Atrāk wa l-Hāshimiyyīn bi-l-silāḥ yaṭūfūna*). See Ibn al-Jawzī, *Muntaẓam*, XVI, p. 163.
94. See events of the year 497/1103, when both *naqīb*s are called upon by the caliph to stop attacks of the *ᶜayyārūn* that both the *shiḥna* and the *shurṭa* proved unable to prevent. Ibid. XVII, p. 84ff.
95. See Ibn al-Jawzī, *Muntaẓam*, XVI, p. 44; Sibṭ ibn al-Jawzī, *Mirʾāt*, ed. *Belgeler*, p. 66. This must not be interpreted as a sign that the Sunni scholars were won over to Shiᶜism. Rather, it shows the political strength of Shiᶜism in a very confused political and military context. Ibn al-Athīr adds that the Sunni members of the *ᶜāmma* (populace) were mainly in favour of the Shiᶜi emir al-Basāsīrī because of the lootings they had suffered from Seljuq troops some months before. See Ibn al-Athīr, *Kāmil*, VIII, p. 342.
96. See in particular two Nestorian chronicles in Arabic: Mārī b. Sulaymān (middle of the 6th/12th century) and ᶜAmr b. Mattā (first half of the 8th/14th century?), *Akhbār faṭārika kursī al-mashriq*; both texts ed. Henricus Gismondi, *Maris, Amri et Slibae de*

Patriarchis Nestorianorum (Rome, 1896 and 1899). See also the travel narratives of western Jewish travellers like Benjamin of Tudela and Petachia of Ratisbonne (second half of the 6th/12th century). Muslim sources mention Christians and Jews primarily in reference to conflicts with their Muslim contemporaries, or discriminatory measures taken by the caliphs, frequently at the behest of traditionalist forces.

97. The only Christian notables mentioned by Muslim sources were Nestorian physicians working at the Abbasid court and the administrative lineage of the Banū l-Mawṣalāyā, who held the office of head of the Abbasid chancery (*kuttāb al-inshāʾ*). The main members of this family converted to Islam in 484/1091 under caliphal pressure.
98. This position was purely theoretical and must be considered more as a *posture* than as the reflection of reality. Ibn al-Jawzī's attitude towards the powerful is representative of this ambiguity. See Angelika Hartmann, 'Les ambivalences d'un sermonnaire hanbalite – Ibn al Jawzī (m. 597/1201), sa carrière et son ouvrage autographe, le *Kitāb al-Khawātīm*', *AI* 22 (1986), pp. 51–115.
99. See Vanessa Van Renterghem, 'Le sentiment d'appartenance collective chez les élites bagdadiennes des Ve-VIe/XIe-XIIe siècles', *AI* 42 (2008), pp. 231–58; Vanessa Van Renterghem, 'Structure et fonctionnement du réseau hanbalite bagdadien dans les premiers temps de la domination seldjoukide (milieu du Ve/XIe siècle)', in *Espaces et réseaux en Méditerranée VIe–XVIe siècle*, eds Damien Coulon, Christophe Picard, Dominique Valérian (Paris, 2010), vol. 2, pp. 207–32.
100. *Ribāṭ*s already existed in Baghdad before the coming of the Seljuqs (two at least are known during Buyid times), but thirty institutions of this type were founded during the second half of the 5th/11th and, mostly, the 6th/12th century. See Van Renterghem, *Les élites bagdadiennes*, ch. 3. *Ribāṭ*s were not totally dedicated to Sufism, since they also hosted activities involving non-Sufi travellers and local population.
101. For example in Damascus. See *EI2*, s.v. 'Shaykh', IX, p. 410 (E. Geoffroy).
102. Namely the Zawzanī and Nīsābūrī lineages during the second half of the 5th/11th century, followed by the Mīhanī and Suhrawardī in the following century. The phenomenon of consolidation of lineages was common to different spheres of activities in Seljuq Baghdad, such as the judiciary, administration and scholarship, but the main characteristic of the mystical milieu was the predominance of families coming from Khurasan and other Iranian and Kurdish areas.
103. Among these endogenous tendencies were the developments noted by Makdisi (the traditionalist trends of the caliphs al-Qādir and al-Qāʾim, the internal evolution of Baghdadi Ḥanbalism) and by Donohue (opposition between local Shāfiʿīs and Ḥanafīs). Detailed studies about Buyid Baghdad are still needed to evaluate the degree of social continuity with the Seljuq period.
104. See Vanessa Van Renterghem, 'Invisibles ou absents? Questions sur la présence kurde à Bagdad aux Ve–VIe/XIe–XIIe siècles', in *Les Kurdes – Écrire l'histoire d'un peuple aux temps pré-modernes*, ed. Boris James, *Etudes kurdes* 10 (2009) (special issue), pp. 21–52.

CHAPTER

8

THE SELJUQS AND THE PUBLIC SPHERE IN THE PERIOD OF SUNNI REVIVALISM: THE VIEW FROM BAGHDAD

Daphna Ephrat

During the late 5th/11th and 6th/12th centuries – a period often called the Sunni revival – a mainstream Sunni camp was emerging in the Islamic Near East. In their effort to end the religious ferment of the late classical period, Muslim scholars (the *ᶜulamāʾ*) and others combined to delimit a commonly accepted form of Islam, eliminate various sources of contention within the Islamic community, and set up the tone in the public sphere based on the Sunna and the Sharīᶜa.[1] The process of homogenisation of religious doctrine and practice had institutional and social dimensions as well. Associations and frameworks were developed to teach the Islamic religious and legal sciences, apply religious law, and harness mainstream Sufism. The four Sunni *madhhabs* consolidated as scholarly establishments, as pools for appointments to positions in the legal apparatus, as well as nuclei of public sphere arenas. The madrasas made their appearance as formally and lavishly endowed institutions of legal learning, and centres for devotion and learning (*khānqāh*s, *ribāṭ*s or *zāwiya*s) were founded for what may be labelled the mainstream Sufi tradition that brought together mystical and legal learning. Consequently, the space dominated by legal scholars and the 'righteous' Sufis was enlarged. These developments took place against the background of the Abbasid caliphate's disintegration and the subsequent rise to power of the sultanate of the Great Seljuqs.[2]

As a major scene in the crystallisation of the *madhhab*s and the development of the madrasa in its 'mature' form, Seljuq Baghdad figured prominently in the Sunnisation process. As the seat of the Abbasid caliphs and representatives of the Seljuq sultans, the caliphal city remained a major centre of government as well. Set in this context and drawing on accounts written in Arabic by native and other historians and observers, this chapter inquires into the role played by the Seljuqs in the process of forming the Sunna and consolidating its forms of organisation. It addresses the character and importance of endowments (*waqf*) made by members of the ruling elite for the benefit of legal scholars, the involvement or intervention of the ruling authorities in the sphere formed by leaders in Islamic learning and piety, and the nature of their relationships and encounters with the forces at work during the Sunni revival. Through this investigation, I seek to contribute to the study of the Seljuqs and the public sphere,[3] where research has often assumed the rise of military lords, separated and estranged from the society under their rule, and manipulating their resources to dominate society and the social order.

THE ROLE OF PATRONAGE

In one of the passages of *Zubdat al-nuṣra*, his classical history on the Seljuqs of Iraq, Fakhr al-Dīn al-Bundārī tells about the building of the first madrasa for adherents to the Ḥanafī legal school in Baghdad as early as 459/1066 (the same year in which the famous Niẓāmiyya madrasa was founded in the city for the Shāfiᶜīs):

> Sharaf al-Mulk Abū Saᶜd al-Mustawfī (the financial minister of Alp Arslān), having found that the lieutenants of the vizier Niẓām al-Mulk had already begun building the Niẓāmiyya madrasa, sought to duplicate it. He therefore built a shrine and a madrasa for adherents of his Ḥanafī *madhhab*, next to the tomb of Abū Ḥanīfa in the quarter of Bāb al-Tāq, thus giving evidence of the recompense he would receive from God due to its quality as a place of pilgrimage.[4]

His account refers to the complete reconstruction of the mausoleum of Abū Ḥanīfa, which involved a brick mausoleum, a madrasa, and other institutions which required considerable acquisitions of land and transfer of many tombs.[5] The *waqf* donation is presented as a personal gift and as an act of piety for which the endowing ruler will be rewarded in the hereafter. Ibn al-Jawzī, the famous Ḥanbalī preacher and historian of Baghdad, records that upon the completion of the building, the contemporary poet Abū Jaᶜfar Ibn al-Bayāḍī, on the occasion of his devotional visit (*ziyāra*) to the shrine of Abū Ḥanīfa, wondered at the beauty of the buildings and the considerable equipment placed at their disposal. Alluding to both the shrine and the madrasa that henceforth carried the name of the founder of the Ḥanafī school, the two verses he recited extemporaneously underline the prominence of the endowed buildings in the public sphere in the eyes of local observers. 'Do you not see that religious learning was lost until it was gathered by him who in this tomb reposes unseen? Likewise, this piece of land lay fallow until by the generosity of Abū Saᶜd it was revived.'[6]

Built in the east bank of the Tigris, adjacent to the great palaces in Dār al-Salṭana (the governmental residence, also called Dār al-Mamlaka) and Dār al-Khilāfa and housed in excellent buildings, the madrasas of Baghdad signified the role of the Seljuq dynasty in revitalising Sunni Islam in the caliphal city in the wake of the Shiᶜi century. At the same time, like other charitable foundations created for local communities of believers, madrasas were constructed in the urban public space and became an integral part of the city, together with mosques and shrines, the rulers' palaces, and the bazaars.[7] As such, accounts about madrasas – their foundation and inauguration, the buildings and the equipment set at their disposals – may afford us with a glimpse of the insertion of the endowing rulers into the space surrounding legal scholars, the guardians of faith.

The support granted by Seljuq ruling authorities to leaders of the emerging mainstream Sunni camp through the foundation of madrasas has been discussed in length in scholarly literature. George Makdisi, who was the first to demonstrate that madrasas were founded as private *waqfs* (rather than as acts of state as had been once thought), emphasised the personal piety and interest in religious learning of the endowing ruler as the prime motives of their foundation.[8] A later generation of historians stressed the political motives and uses of *waqf* established for madrasas. In the view of several historians, while enhancing the position of legal scholars and institutions in the public sphere, patronage by individual Seljuq sultans, emirs and other officials sowed the seeds for the creation of a religious establishment dependent on the military ruling elite and incorporated into the official sphere. To fulfil their religious and social roles, the *ᶜulamāᵓ* depended not only on the central government for protection against external enemies but also on gifts and endowments supplied by the military elite, who controlled and manipulated the main sources of the society.[9] More recently, a study by Omid Safi revises the view of the Seljuqs as benevolent Muslim rulers, and offers an innovative interpretation of the political uses of patronage and the nexus of politics and religion. He demonstrates the importance of the endowed madrasa as one of the institutions in the Seljuq state apparatus that managed to contribute to the larger process of legitimising and sustaining Seljuq rule. Established as a site of production of orthodox knowledge, the madrasas were designed to present the endowing rulers as champions of what they assumed to be an orthodox and normative view of Islam and propagate the state-sponsored orthodoxy. Negotiation and collaboration, this study suggests, rather than manipulation and domination by alien military lords, were the key elements of the relationships forged between the endowing rulers and the legal scholars who functioned under their patronage.[10] The study of these relationships in particular settings should be carried on further.

An inquiry into the pattern of appointments to the lucrative post of the professor of the law, the *mudarris*, in the great madrasas of Seljuq Baghdad and the prerogatives of its holder is one way to access the involvement or intervention of the ruling authorities in the institutions created by *waqf*. Surely, in theory, it was the Seljuq sultans and their officials who appointed the *mudarris*, paid his salary, and dismissed him at will. However, given the definition of *waqf* in *fiqh* (Muslim jurisprudence) as acquired private money and the fact that rulers constructed a large number of endowments with their own funds, appointments depended on relationships between an individual patron and a particular legal scholar, rather than on ties of patronage binding the *ʿulamāʾ* as a group to the state.[11]

Moreover, the biographies of the appointees indicate that in practice these appointments confirmed an existing leadership rather than created a new one. A considerable number of *mudarrisūn* in the madrasas of Seljuq Baghdad had already acquired renown as great scholars of religious law in their time. Their nomination by the endowing ruler proved his concern for excellence and prestige of the institution created through the endowment. In fact, appointments to the post of *mudarris* may even have been subject to the decision of the holders of this position. Whether or not *mudarrisūn* actually nominated their own successors, our sources attest that many disciples who were closely associated with their masters did eventually succeed them in their positions. Added to this was the phenomenon of inheriting the high-ranking religious posts of the *mudarris* and the *qāḍī* (judge), which was apparent already in the late 5th/11th century, and became more evident in the course of the subsequent century, a period which marked the decline of the Seljuq empire. The degree of intervention in the institution created by *waqf* varied over time and must have been dependent on the strength of the political regime and the relationships forged between the patrons and the beneficiaries. Members of the ruling elite continued to build and endow madrasas and assign religious scholars to teaching positions in them. However, as a result of the growing weakness of the central authorities, the ties of patronage between rulers and Baghdadi legal scholars loosened and the latter came to enjoy greater freedom in the choice of their successors and the administration of legal institutions in general.[12]

Once a scholar was appointed to the professorship in a madrasa he seemed to enjoy complete freedom in admission of students, the sequence and method of all instruction, and the choice of treatises. Apparently, the authority and leadership of the holder of the office of the *mudarris*, like that of holders of other administrative-religious offices (such as the various judges) was not derived from imperial authority of the office, but from the prestige of the office-holder. Outside of legal institutions – in mosques or private homes – there were many renowned legal scholars who attained religious authority and gained public esteem.

During the crucial period of Islamic revivalism, I propose, the mainstream Sunni camp in Baghdad emerged out of internal dynamics, independently of the official sphere, and was little affected by the policies of the Seljuqs. Leaders of this camp negotiated status and sorted out hierarchies among themselves, and extended their religious leadership to wider circles. Similarly, Sufi associations crystallised and extended their influence around renowned masters rather than around state sponsored institutions. Even though, the Seljuq rulers must have contributed to or at least facilitated the process of forming the Sunna and spreading its message. The role they played in this process was nowhere more clearly revealed than in the foundation of madrasas on substantial religious endowments for the teaching of the law in accordance with one or other of the Sunni legal schools and of *khānqāhs* for the cultivation of a deeper spiritual life based on the Sunna and the Sharīᶜa. By invoking the institution of the *waqf*, the founders – Seljuq men of the regime – ensured the perpetuity of these institutions and the permanent support of those who were considered representative of 'true' religion and who taught, studied or lodged in them. However, rather than serving as an instrument of control over the beneficiaries or as a tool for meddling in their affairs, the institution of the *waqf* worked in ways that strengthened the mainstream Sunni camp in Baghdad and enlarged the domain of a local elite of religious scholars with a degree of autonomy vis-à-vis the rulers.[13]

Foundations in the public sphere created by endowments in the pre-modern Muslim world were often used as instruments of public policy and helped enhance the ruler's power and prestige.[14] At the same time, endowments by rulers symbolised their adherence to the norms of proper social order inherent in the ideology of the *waqf*.[15] As in the case of *waqf* foundations in the public sphere, such as mosques and shrines, endowments of madrasas and *khānqāhs* must have also helped establish a bond of shared norms and values between the benefactors and the beneficiaries and generate a public opinion that approved of and even legitimised the rule of the endowing ruler in the territories he had conquered. The decision of individual Seljuq rulers to endow madrasas and *khānqāhs* throughout the lands they conquered from the Sunni Ghaznavids and Shiᶜi Buyids and their patronage of legal scholars and Sufis who functioned in them must be seen against this background. Here, as in other cases, the link between political legitimacy and the Sharīᶜa is highlighted.[16]

Moreover, the rules of the *waqf*, which withdrew ownership of the endowed assets from the endower and imposed legal restrictions upon the rulers, the necessity to secure the authorisation of the *qāḍī* for any transactions in *waqf* property,[17] the rulers' concern about the endowed institutions they founded, and the active involvement of religious scholars and the community in the way foundations were created and administered generated continuous discourse between rulers, religious scholars and the local community concerning major issues in the public sphere. As the endowed madrasas and *khānqāh*s proliferated and became an integral part of the Islamic city, they provided the rulers with an entry into the public space, and served as stages where rulers, religious scholars and other members of the community could interact.

The examples of the Niẓāmiyya madrasa and the Shrine College – the most magnificent institutions of learning of their kind in Baghdad – provide us with a glimpse of the practice of *waqf* endowment in the public sphere. Sibṭ Ibn al-Jawzī, whose *Mirʾāt al-zamān* preserves major lost works that provide eyewitness accounts, reports about the inauguration of the Niẓāmiyya more clearly and fully than any other historian known to us. He tells that on 10 Dhū al-Ḥijja 459/22 September 1067 the provincial governor (*ᶜamīd*) invited the general public, according to their various classes, to celebrate the inauguration of the madrasa. Niẓām al-Mulk was personally involved in the choice of the Shāfiᶜī legal scholar, Abū Iṣḥāq al-Shīrāzī, as the first professor of the Niẓāmiyya which he designed for adherents of the *madhhab*. When al-Shīrāzī refused to attend the ceremony and accept the office, since he heard about the misappropriation of materials of other buildings to construct the madrasa, the people invoked the blessing of God upon him, and praised him for that, thereby expressing their concern about the ruler's neglect of the norms and rules of the *waqf* and exercising their influence in the public sphere. Eventually al-Shīrāzī assumed the chair, largely due to Niẓām al-Mulk's personal intervention. On 26 Jumādā II 462/14 April 1070, in the third year of the Niẓāmiyya's operation, another *ᶜamīd*, Abū Naṣr, summoned the dignitaries of Baghdad, including the caliph's vizier and the chief judge, to the madrasa, wherein the public reading of the deed of endowment – as it was drawn up by Niẓām al-Mulk – took place.[18] The administration of the Niẓāmiyya was thereafter to remain in the hands of its famous founder, who, during his last visit to Baghdad, held a session for public dictating of prophetic traditions in the madrasa's library.[19] The Shrine College was built for Ḥanafī scholars in the quarter of Bāb al-Ṭāq (in west Baghdad), which, though populated by Shiᶜis, was the centre of the Ḥanafī school in Baghdad. The importance of its construction next to the tomb of Abū Ḥanīfa can be hardly overestimated. Ḥanafī scholars, including the distinguished Dāmaghānī family of judges and chief judges were normally buried beside the shrine which not only served as a centre for adherents to the *madhhab* but also developed into a major pilgrimage site in the public sphere.[20]

RULERS, SCHOOLS AND FACTIONS

During the period of Sunni revivalism, a religious public sphere was being formed in Baghdad in which a diversity of communities participated. This sphere was defined by the participation of Sufi associations and establishments, and intertwined networks of madrasas and *madhhab*s, at the intersection of religious, political and social life, set apart from the sphere of governmental authority. These networks were fixed and enduring, albeit not without occasional destructive tensions, notably the ongoing clashes between the 'traditionalists' (*ahl al-ḥadīth*) and the 'rationalists' (*ahl al-raʾy*) both between and within the schools of thought and law. In the course of this period Baghdad had become a major scene in the crystallisation of the Ḥanafī, Shāfiʿī and Ḥanbalī schools. Leaders of these three schools dominated the application of religious law and the transmission of the legal and traditional sciences, and emerged as principal actors in the public sphere. Their manifold functions – as judges, muftis, teachers, guardians of orphans, leaders of prayers, preachers – brought them into daily contact with the people, and made them natural leaders of public opinion and the informal representatives of the community.

Still, the various *madhhab*s differed in their internal coherence and organisation, and their status and roles in the public sphere, and consequently in their relation to political authority. Members of the Shāfiʿī and Ḥanafī schools held paid religious and administrative offices, often as professors in the madrasas founded for them by members of the ruling regime, as well as various positions in the judiciary. The Shāfiʿīs, who gained power under the vizierate of Niẓām al-Mulk, predominated in the office of the *mudarris*. But after his death (in 485/1092), and up to the mid-6th/12th century, the Ḥanafīs were the most favoured. As for the Baghdad Ḥanbalīs, they largely controlled the professorship in the great mosques of the city as well as the office of preacher, positions that were not subsidised by the state.[21] Naturally, acceptance of paid religious and administrative positions by many scholars of both the Shāfiʿī and Ḥanafī schools involved a certain degree of association with the rulers. The early model of the self-sufficient unworldly scholar who keeps a distance from the ruling authorities and rejects their offers and jobs persisted in the later period we are dealing with. But the biographies of well-respected Shāfiʿī and Ḥanafī scholars who held state-subsidised positions refrain from blame. Direct criticism of religious scholars who maintained close relationships with the rulers is likewise rarely pronounced in the biographies. Even Ḥanbalīs, normally praised for distancing themselves from all government, accepted the paid office of the *qāḍī* despite the fear of the pious man of being torn between his devotion to the religious law and his loyalty to the ruler who appointed him.[22] Moreover, scholars of the *madhhab*s competed over important *waqf* revenues – judicial positions, as well as teaching positions in the great mosques and madrasas – which extended to competition for governmental support.[23]

The majority of Shāfiᶜīs in Baghdad came from elsewhere, primarily the provinces of eastern Iran, as did many legal scholars of the Ḥanafī school.[24] To judge from a testimony by their leader al-Shīrāzī in his letter of complaint to Malikshāh, their school remained a minority in Baghdad, unable to put down roots in the city and attract a large local following, and dependent on the patronage and support of the ruling elite.[25] The inclination of several Shāfiᶜī scholars toward Ashᶜarism, and even more important, the patronage of members of the school by the rulers and their association with men of the regime, certainly did not contribute to their popularity, serving instead as a pretext for their criticism by the Ḥanbalīs and their followers (see below). But despite their dependence on the support of the regime, their liability to internal faction, doctrinal quarrels and status divisions, the Shāfiᶜī and Ḥanafī schools in Baghdad crystallised around renowned masters independently of the regime, and their scholars played significant social roles as teachers, muftis and judges, as well as patrons and leaders of social groups. It is noteworthy that the Baghdad Ḥanafīs were less dependent on the patronage of and recognition by the rulers. Not only did leading scholars within the school enjoy freedom in selecting their successors as judges and as *mudarrisūn* but the administration of the Ḥanafī madrasas was in their hands.[26]

Ḥanbalism – a school of law and theology – was the most localised and inclusive of the Baghdadi schools.[27] Relatively removed from the ruling elite and its resources, the Ḥanbalīs developed to a greater extent than the other *madhhab*s an autonomous social organisation around their networks of masters and disciples. Personal support provided by the school's wealthy adherents to finance its activities and to help the needy substituted for the patronage of political rulers, reinforcing the unity and self-sufficiency of the Ḥanbalī school at the same time. Shared theological and moral perspectives tied adherents to the school together. While debate still raged between the 'rationalists' (*aṣḥāb al-raᵓy*) and the 'traditionalists' (*ahl al-ḥadīth*) within the Ḥanafī and Shāfiᶜī schools, the Ḥanbalīs formulated a rather uniform position in matters of theology, dogma and morality. Though coming from different professional groups (*aṣnāf*) and consequently differing in their other identities, adherents to the *madhhab* seem to have had a shared common goal, both to find *ḥadīth* solutions to legal and theological questions, and to encourage moral and individual action aimed at combating religious and social innovations.[28] Radical Ḥanbalī theologians and preachers mobilised their large following in order to fight rationalism of all shades and enforce their rigid orthodoxy on Baghdadi society. During the second part of the 5th/11th century they fought primarily against Ashᶜarī preachers, deriving their support primarily from among the city's lower classes.[29]

The ongoing debates between radical Ḥanbalīs and Ashᶜarīs extended to Sufi circles and their establishment in Baghdad, the *ribāṭ*, which evolved both as a centre for the Sufi shaykh and his circle of disciples and followers, and as an arena of the public sphere. There were several *ribāṭ*s in Baghdad in the period of Sunni revivalism, most famously Ribāṭ al-Zawzanī and Ribāṭ Abū Saᶜd. While the former was associated with the native Ḥanbalīs, that of Abū Saᶜd housed Sufi-Ashᶜarīs from Khurasan. Settling in the *ribāṭ*, these immigrants and transients preached Ashᶜarī theology (*kalām*), thereby turning Ribāṭ Abū Saᶜd into a scene of several conflicts between Sufi-Ḥanbalīs and Sufi-Ashᶜarīs. At times, Sufi-Ashᶜarīs from Khurasan mixed praises of the sultanate with their sermon to the dismay of the Ḥanbalīs and the 'people of the Sunna' in general. This was the case of the Ashᶜarī preacher al-Ghaznawī who arrived in Baghdad in 516/1122 and enjoyed the patronage of Khātūn al-Mustaẓhiriyya, wife of the caliph and sister of sultan Sanjar. He owed to her the *ribāṭ* that bears her name and where he preached enthusiastically for support of the sultan.[30] Conversely, the preacher Abū l-Qāsim l-ᶜAlawī, who arrived in Baghdad in the same year and settled in Ribāṭ Abū Saᶜd, was praised and lavishly rewarded (probably by order of the caliph) after demonstrating his support of the Ḥanbalīs in his addresses to the people.[31]

I find, contrary to Jacqueline Chabbi, that such instances are no clear indication that the *ribāṭ*s of Baghdad associated with Ashᶜarism functioned primarily as bastions of Seljuq influence, or that political interests were promoted by Seljuq partisans under the disguise of religious sermons held in the Sufi establishment.[32] Significantly, in difference with the royal *khānqāh*s, which the Seljuqs established and endowed liberally for 'righteous Sufis' in their domain of Iran, the *ribāṭ*s of Baghdad were founded on the private initiative of a shaykh who presided over it, or erected by wealthy followers and supporters for the benefit of a particular shaykh, his followers, and his successors.[33] Having its origins with the foundations of the earliest *ribāṭ*s in the late 5th/10th century and persisting throughout the Seljuq period, this pattern of foundation may explain the development of the *ribāṭ* of Baghdad as the realm of its shaykh, and as an autonomous establishment set apart from the official sphere. Indeed, though Ashᶜarī preachers arrived in the city from time to time with permission of Niẓām al-Mulk, there is no evidence of direct intervention of the political authorities in the Sufi establishment that proliferated under their rule, using their personal funds to support a particular Sufi group or suppressing this group's opponents. Nor is there any indication of the Seljuq rulers dictating the functions and the content of sermons at the *ribāṭ* of Baghdad.

In contrast with the various schools of law and thought in the early period of Seljuq rule in Khurasan, the *madhhab*s of Baghdad were not directly affected by the policies and fate of their political patrons.[34] Members of the Baghdad legal schools were not persecuted or marginalised on account of their inclination to a particular school of thought. Nor were they favoured or patronised by a particular ruler in order to foster a particular theological current. Thus, the preference of the Shāfiᶜīs as beneficiaries of governmental patronage was not designed to establish the Ashᶜarī 'middle-road' orthodoxy, as has been once asserted.[35]

In general, members of the Seljuq ruling elite avoided the internal affairs of the schools of thought in the caliphal city. There, they did not try to define or articulate Sunnism according to a centrally espoused dogma; they refrained from taking an unequivocal stand in matters of local religious authority, and rarely intervened in controversies over proper creed and behaviour. Only when the rivalry between the religiously defined factions in Baghdad took a violent turn and public order was threatened, did rulers step in to restore peace and order. On such occasions, they usually acted in favour of the religious faction that had already gained the largest local following, fitting themselves into the existing balance of power.

Subduing (or at least reducing) conflicts in the public sphere, rather than spurring the rivalries between the religiously defined factions, seems to be a principal instrument of strengthening the position of the central government and securing its rule. This may explain why, while preferring the Shāfiᶜīs, Niẓām al-Mulk took the side of radical Ḥanbalīs, their rivals in Baghdad, yielding to their demand to frustrate any attempt to preach Ashᶜarism in the city's madrasas and mosques – obviously because of their greater popular appeal and the large following they succeeded in mobilising. One of the most serious incidents of this kind occurred when the famous Ashᶜarī theologian and preacher, Abū Naṣr al-Qushayrī, arrived in Baghdad from Khurasan in Shawwāl 469/March 1076. Preaching in the Niẓāmiyya madrasa, he mixed theological remarks with his sermon. Mobilising the masses, a group of Ḥanbalīs relentlessly attacked the Shāfiᶜīs, accusing them of leaning toward Ashᶜarism. The riots were so violent that they are described in the sources as *fitna* (seduction, or disputation of the proper order). As the *fitna* intensified and a member of the Shāfiᶜī school was killed, the Shāfiᶜīs fled to the Niẓāmiyya and closed its gates.[36] One poet, a witness to the violent riots, wrote to Niẓām al-Mulk pleading for him to put an end to the *fitna*. 'Order and security in the city have crumbled,' the poet warned, 'the soldiers are fighting one another . . . and the people of Baghdad are oppressed and their honour has been trampled.'[37] The vizier then ordered that the Ashᶜarī preacher be removed from his lectern in the Niẓāmiyya and sent back home.[38] Again, in Shawwāl 475/March 1082, the Ashᶜarī theologian al-Bakrī, who had previously accused the Ḥanbalīs of heresy, was prevented (probably with the consent of the political authorities) from preaching in the congregational mosque of al-Manṣūr, the stronghold of the Ḥanbalīs in Baghdad.[39]

It was probably also out of concern of turmoil in the public sphere that while visiting Baghdad in 484/1091 Niẓām al-Mulk convened a group of Ḥanbalīs to inquire about the theological debate between the *ahl al-ḥadīth* and *ahl al-raʾy* regarding the attributes of God. Having heard that the Ḥanbalīs had been accused by Ashʿarī-Shāfiʿīs of holding the extreme doctrine of anthropomorphising God (*tashbīh*), the vizier granted them the opportunity to justify and defend their theological postures. The query signifies an attempt of the central government to strengthen its rule by reducing potential tensions in the public sphere and harmonising between the religiously defined factions. 'We reject both the allegorical interpretation of the Koran (*taʾwīl*) and the anthropomorphizing of God,' the Ḥanbalīs responded. 'How can you criticize us while all we abstain from is the deep inquiry [into the scripture] that diverts from the method (*ṭarīqa*) of the forefathers (*al-salaf*)?' And they added, 'those who associate with rulers and seek worldly benefits have no right to defame us.'[40]

By the late 6th/12th century, moderate Ḥanbalism, in alliance with the other traditionalist currents that composed the mainstream Sunni camp, gained prominence in the public sphere of Baghdad. Men of piety and religious learning, who saw themselves as arbiters of 'true' Islamic faith and conduct, joined together to instil public morals and uproot deviations from the prophetic Sunna and violations of orthodoxy, even turned against members of their own circles. Shiʿis, so-called *zindīq*s (heretics), radical Ḥanbalī theologians, philosophers or freethinkers, ecstatic or antinomian Sufis and popular preachers who drew inspiration from Sufi mysticism – all were doomed to marginalisation, if not severe persecution. By that time, the madrasas of Baghdad no longer served as centres for religiously defined factions, and the city's *ribāṭ*s lost their character as arenas of factionalism, turning instead into centres of public devotion and distribution of charity as well as of pilgrimage to seek divine blessing. The flourishing of Ḥanbalī madrasas in the 6th/12th century is but one indication of the perception of the institution as a centre of orthodoxy and, as such, its foundation for the instruction of the legal and traditional sciences to the exclusion of the rationalist sciences.[41]

Significantly, in Baghdad it was the Abbasid caliph, rather than the Seljuq sultan, who, through his agents, eventually took up the role of suppressing deviations from the Sunna. Powerful *muḥtasib*s, who were appointed by the caliphs and seem to have worked for them in Baghdad, combated against violation of orthodoxy of all shades throughout the Seljuq period and, in particular, in the last decades of the caliphate's existence.[42] It is in light of the ascendancy of the mainstream Sunni camp in the public sphere and its alliance with the caliph that I seek to explain the efforts on behalf of the Seljuqs to acquire authority or at least legitimacy in the public sphere of the caliphal city.

RULERS AND THE 'PEOPLE OF THE SUNNA'

During the period of Sunni revivalism, notwithstanding the declining authority of the caliphate, the Sunnis of Baghdad sought refuge in Dār al-Khilāfa in times of turmoil and upheaval. At the time of the Basāsīrī revolt (in 450/1058), after the attack launched by the Shiᶜis of al-Karkh quarter (west Baghdad) against the Sunni population of the quarter of al-Baṣra Gate (west Baghdad), many crossed the Tigris fleeing to Dār al-Khilāfa.[43] In the same year, when news arrived that the caliph al-Qāᵓim and his grandson had fallen ill, the people were filled with much distress and fear. 'This was because no one was left from among the dignitaries who could provide them with shelter. When cured due to God's blessing, the people gathered for prayer and thanksgiving.'[44] Over a decade later, in 462/1069, a *fitna* broke out in al-Manṣūr Mosque as a result of attempts to free a woman from a Turk who had embraced her at the mosque's door. The Turkish soldiers fired arrows at the crowd praying in the mosque, killing a man and wounding a considerable number of people. Fearing the armed Turks present at the mosque, the crowd sought help at the caliph's palace, demanding that revenge be taken against the assassin and that the criminals be punished. To pacify the mass of the population, the caliph's vizier and others distributed garments and provisions among them.[45]

These and similar accounts signify that in the eyes of contemporary Baghdadians the caliphs were still perceived as the protectors of 'the people of the Sunna' in the face of its enemies and as symbol of the sole Sunni legitimate government. Ever since the conquest of the city by the Shiᶜi Buyids in the mid-4th/10th century, inhabitants of Baghdad were directly and forcefully affected by the all-embracing, radical changes produced by the disintegration of the Abbasid caliphate. This would explain the emergence of popular movements in Baghdad – the *ᶜayyarūn* (youth gangs or gallants), the *ᶜāmma-* (commoners-) led movements, and the Ḥanbalīs – partly as a reaction to these changes. By attacking the foreign Buyid and Seljuq regimes, all three movements struggled to defend the caliphate and to restore its authority. The *ᶜāmma* defended the caliphs and their power and the *ᶜayyarūn* opposed all foreign regimes of occupation. As for the Ḥanbalīs, though not hesitating to act against individual caliphs, they aspired to revive Islam's glorious past by insisting on morality and individual action to combat religious and social unwarranted innovations, and by strengthening the caliphate at the expense of the sultanate.[46]

However, with the passage of time, underneath the aura of fear and resentment, other factors made their imprint on the relations between society and its effective rulers. A ruler's upholding of the sacred law, his public deference to revered legal scholars who determined the norms of the public sphere, endowments by him, and measures that were taken to maintain or restore public order certainly contributed to his public legitimisation. No matter how limited and indirect the encounters or contacts between rulers and the 'people of the Sunna' of Baghdad, they must have also played a role in instilling sentiments of recognition of legitimate rule on the part of society and in rendering the barriers between the official and public spheres at least bridgeable.

Public sessions of Qur᾿ān and *ḥadīth* recital, inauguration of a madrasa, religious festivals and royal ceremonies that took place in a public space and were open to the participation of all, brought together rulers, local dignitaries, and other segments of society. The general public we have seen was invited to celebrate the inauguration of the Baghdad Niẓāmiyya, and the endowment deed of the madrasa was read publicly by the Seljuq official. There is no description of the ceremony that was held at the time, but accounts of inauguration ceremonies of other madrasas show them to be a great delight for the public. Such ceremonies usually included an inaugural lecture or lesson by the appointee to the office of the *mudarris*, and were attended by a large crowd, including noted legal scholars of the *madhhab*s, government and other dignitaries. Sweetmeats were prepared for the guests and robes of honour were bestowed on the new appointee.[47]

Two anecdotes in particular are illustrative of encounters between rulers and society in the public sphere. Ibn al-Jawzī reports that in the month of the *ḥajj* (the annual pilgrimage to Mecca) of the year 484/1091, Malikshāh performed the ceremonial rite of *sadhak* (lighting candles and torches during the whole night) in the Tigris. He ordered the building of large boats, each carrying wax candles, wood and a huge red tent. Niẓām al-Mulk and other men of the regime (*arbāb al-dawla*) displayed their ornaments, set the wood on fire, and sailed along the river, making their way to Dār al-Mamlaka. The Tigris was lightened with torches, and the people of Baghdad gathered on the river bank in order to view the spectacular sight, and spent the whole night there. The inhabitants of the western side of the city came along holding wax candles, and torches were placed in the courtyard of Dār al-Mamlaka beforehand.[48] Interestingly enough, notwithstanding the Zoroastrian origins of *sadhak*, the rulers displayed their power in ways that were at least familiar, if not acceptable, to the people of Baghdad. A ritual of extravagant illumination, called *laylat al-waqūd*, was gaining popularity among the general public and eventually became Sunna.[49] There are no accounts of the performance of *laylat al-waqūd* in Baghdad of the time, but sources from 6th/12th and 7th/13th Syria report that crowds gathered in congregational mosques for ceremonious prayers five nights a year: the blessed night of mid-Shaʿbān, 27 Ramaḍān, the night of 1 Muḥarram, and the nights of the two festivals. They lightened candles and kindling oil all night long.[50] The second account concerns a ceremony surrounding the rulers and attracting the public. Ibn al-Jawzī describes the excitement of the people of Baghdad when Khātūn, daughter of Malikshāh, was brought to the city in order to marry the caliph al-Mustaẓhir. She arrived on 28 Rajab 504/9 February 1111, and was housed in Dār al-Mamlaka, where her brother Sultan Muḥammad was dwelling. The bride dower was brought from the East and publicly displayed in Baghdad in the month of Ramaḍān, and the city was decorated for the occasion. All of its markets were locked, large red tents were set up for the dignitaries, and the people were filled with much delight.[51]

Victories in the name of Islam must have also affected the attitude of the 'people of the Sunna' toward the Seljuqs and instilled recognition of their legitimate rule. A story about the caliph's vizier Abū Shujāʿ may illustrate this last point. On 9 Ramaḍān 484/25 October 1091, following the Seljuq conquest of Samarqand, Niẓām al-Mulk issued a decree ordering the dismissal of the vizier from his office on the grounds of his criticism of the conquest of a land inhabited by Muslims, as well as his general ingratitude toward the army and central government. The caliph, who in any event was unsatisfied with his vizier's service, granted his consent and collaboration. On the next day, Abū Shujāʿ, escorted by a group of local supporters, addressed his steps as a matter of course to a mosque in his place of residence in Bāb al-Marātib (east Baghdad) to perform the congregational prayer there. His arrogant appearance in public aroused furious reaction among the common people. They rebuked him and forced him to leave the mosque and return to his home. Soon thereafter he was forced by the political authorities to leave the city itself.[52]

CONCLUSION

Grounded in the context of Seljuq Baghdad, this chapter advances a new approach to the relationship between the official and public spheres during the crucial period of Sunni revivalism. Its findings challenge the conventional view of an alien elite of military lords separated and estranged from the society under its rule by highlighting the dynamic and interactive, rather than detached and conflicting, relationships between rulers and the local forces at work. The mainstream Sunni camp, I find, emerged during this period of great significance out of internal dynamics and its construction occurred independently of the sphere of governmental authority – even though the Seljuq rulers, collaborating with this camp, contributed or at least facilitated the process of forming the Sunna and consolidating its forms of organisation.

Endowments made by a member of the ruling elite for the benefit of Sunni legal scholars, guardians of faith, the measures he took to safeguard public order, and his contacts with the 'people of the Sunna' in a public space – be it a chamber in a madrasa, the palace courtyard or the Tigris bank – generated a continuous discourse based on common religious norms and practices between rulers and society, and rendered the barriers between the official and public spheres bridgeable. The pattern of participation and involvement in the public sphere that was introduced by the Seljuqs in accommodation with the distinctive characteristics of government, religion and society in the caliphal city, may have been replicated and elaborated by the successor military regimes in the late medieval Near East. Further study of its various aspects and nuances may generate a fuller picture of the status and role of the rulers in the Sunni revival and their insertion into the new social order that was taking form in the wake of the Abbasid caliphate's disintegration.

NOTES

1. For studies that interpret the 'Sunni revival' as an outcome of developments within Sunni Islam itself, namely the triumph of traditionalism, see especially George Makdisi, *Ibn ᶜAqīl et la resurgence de l'Islam traditionaliste au XIe siècle (Ve siècle de l'Hégire)* (Damascus, 1963); George Makdisi, 'The Sunni revival', in *Islamic Civilization 950–1150*, ed. D. S. Richards (Oxford, 1973), pp. 155–68. Richard W. Bulliet, *Islam: the View from the Edge* (New York, 1994), pp. 101, 126–7, 146–8, has proposed that the notion of Sunni 'recasting' is a more accurate description of the process than the terms revival or renaissance. Traditionalism, in his view, was one aspect of a broader process of homogenising Sunni religious life during this period. Most recently, this interpretation has been elaborated upon by Jonathan P. Berkey in *The Formation of Islam: Religion and Society in the Near East 600–1800* (Cambridge, 2003), pp. 189–202.
2. Several historians of medieval Muslim societies have undertaken to study the period AD 950–1150 and the 'transformation' of Islamic civilisation at the close of the 6th/12th century. For their interpretation, see Richards, *Islamic Civilization*. See also Bulliet, *The View from the Edge*, for a social historian who abandons the view of Islamic history 'from the centre', focusing instead on changes in the social structure of the vast majority of Muslims who lived on the periphery, primarily eastern Iran. The literature on the origins and development of the madrasa is vast. The most important contribution is still that of George Makdisi, and especially 'Muslim institutions of learning in eleventh-century Baghdad', *BSOAS* 24 (1961), pp. 1–58; idem, *The Rise of Colleges: Institutions of Learning in Islam and the West* (Edinburgh, 1981), esp. pp. 29–30.
3. The public sphere is broadly defined as a space distinct from both the official sphere (i.e. the sphere of governmental authority) and the space of household and kin. On the notion of the public sphere as a key concept developed by social theorists and applied in historical studies – including the study of pre-modern Muslim societies – see S. N. Eisenstadt

and W. Schluchter, 'Path to early modernities – a comparative view', *Daedalus* 127 (1998), pp. 1–18.

4. Al-Fatḥ Ibn ᶜAlī Ibn Muḥammad al-Iṣfahānī al-Bundārī, *Zubdat al-nuṣra* [abridgment of ᶜImād al-Dīn al-Iṣfahānī's *Nuṣrat al-fatra*], in *Recueil de Textes Relatifs à l'Histoire des Seldjoucides* II, *Histoire des Seldjoucides de l'Iraq*, ed. M. T. Houtsma (Leiden, 1889), p. 32.
5. For the architectural history of the shrine, see Oleg Grabar, 'The earliest Islamic commemorative structures, notes and documents', *Ars Orientalis* 6 (1967), p. 25. Combining the tomb and the madrasa, this complex was one of the earliest of its kind in Islam. The sources at our disposal do not provide details that may show how the two buildings functioned together, what legal justification (if any) was proposed, and how the idea was received generally.
6. Abū l-Faraj ᶜAbd al-Raḥman Ibn al-Jawzī (d. 597/1200), *al-Muntaẓam fī taʾrīkh al-mulūk wa-umam*, ed. M. ᶜA. ᶜAṭāʾ (Beirut, 1412/1992), XVI, p. 100. Cited also by ᶜIzz al-Dīn Abū l-Ḥasan ᶜAlī Ibn al-Athīr (d. 630/1233), *al-Kāmil fī l-taʾrīkh*, ed. Tornberg (Beirut, 1385–/1965–), X, p. 54
7. This development is well attested in Ibn Jubayr's account of the madrasas in the eastern part of Baghdad (following his visit to the city in 580/1184): Ibn Jubayr (d. 614/1217), *Riḥla*, ed. W. Wright and M. J. De Goeje (Leiden, 1907), pp. 220–7.
8. Makdisi, *The Rise of Colleges*, esp. pp. 35–74.
9. Montgomery Watt, *Islamic Political Thought* (Edinburgh, 1968), pp. 75–6, was the first to point out that education in the Niẓāmiyya madrasa was designed to create an 'orthodox bureaucracy'. See also Bulliet's remark in *The Patricians of Nishapur: a Study in Medieval Islamic Social History* (Cambridge, MA, 1972), pp. 73–5, that the Niẓāmiyya madrasa became a vital instrument in Niẓām al-Mulk's policy of controlling of what he labels the 'patriciate' of Nishapur.
10. Omid Safi, *The Politics of Knowledge in Premodern Islam: Negotiating Ideology and Religious Inquiry* (Chapel Hill, NC, 2006), esp. pp. xxv, xxix, xxx, 96–7, 100.
11. The most telling example of such close relationships is that between Niẓām al-Mulk and the celebrated al-Ghazālī as depicted in the biography of the former by Tāj al-Dīn al-Subki (d. 771/1370), *Ṭabaqāt al-Shāfiᶜiyya al-kubrā*, 6 vols (Cairo, 1966–67), IV, pp. 101–20.
12. For details, see Daphna Ephrat, *A Learned Society in a Period of Transition: the Sunni ᶜUlamaʾ of Eleventh-Century Baghdad* (Albany, NY, 2000), pp. 118–24.
13. For an extensive exposition of this argument with regard to the endowed and patronised madrasas of Seljuq Baghdad, see Ephrat, 'Religious leadership and associations in the public sphere of Seljuk Baghdad', in *The Public Sphere in Muslim Societies*, eds Miriam Hoexter, Shmuel N. Eisenstadt and Nehemia Levtzion (Albany, NY, 2002), pp. 32–7. For a later period in Syria, see also in the same volume the well-documented and well-argued discussion by Daniella Talmon-Heller about the commitment of Nūr al-Dīn, Saladin and their successors to defending Sunni Islam against anything opposed to it and strengthening its mainstream camp: Talmon-Heller, 'Religion in the public sphere', in *The Public Sphere*, eds Hoexter, Eisenstadt, Levtzion, pp. 49–63. For a different interpretation, see Michael Chamberlain's argument that by founding madrasas powerful Ayyubid and Mamluk warrior households could insert themselves into the cultural, political and social life of the city and turn existing practices and relationships to their own benefits. Established out of control motives, charitable foundations became, in his

view, instruments of politics that served the ruling households. Michael Chamberlain, *Knowledge and Social Practice in Medieval Damascus, 1190–1350* (Cambridge, 1994), pp. 52–4.

14. For the use of endowments as an instrument of public policy, see S. A. Arjomand, 'Philanthropy, the law, and public policy in the Islamic world before the Modern Era', in *Philanthropy in the World's Traditions*, eds W. F. Ilchman, S. N. Katz and E. L. Queen II (Bloomington, IL, 1998), pp. 109–32.
15. Miriam Hoexter makes this thoughtful observation in 'The *waqf* and the public sphere', in *The Public Sphere*, eds Hoexter, Eisenstadt, Levtzion, p. 130ff. Following Hodgson (*The Venture of Islam*, II, p. 119), Hoexter describes the *waqf* as a major tool through which the Islamic idea of social order proper to the *umma* was implemented.
16. Compare with Omid Safi's central argument that in order to legitimise their political power, Seljuq rulers spread the message of religious orthodoxy that was constructed by religious scholars in state-sponsored arenas such as madrasas and *khānqāhs*: Safi, *The Politics of Knowledge*, XXV, pp. 4–5.
17. For the basic rules governing the *waqf*, see *EI2*, s.v. 'Waḳf', XI, pp. 60–3 (R. Peters).
18. Sibṭ Ibn al-Jawzī (d. 654/1256), *Mirʾāt al-zamān fī taʾrīkh al-ʿayān*, ms. British Museum, Or. 4619 (years: 282–460/895–1067), fol. 110b–111a. For a full quotation of this report, see Makdisi, 'Muslim institutions of learning', pp. 31–2.
19. Ibn al-Jawzī, *Muntaẓam*, XVI, p. 267.
20. ʿAlī al-Harawī (d. 611/1215), *Kitāb al-Ishārāt ilā mʿarifat al-ziyārāt*, ed. J. Sourdel-Thomine (Damascus, 1953), p. 74, where this place of pilgrimage is referred to as the Cemetery of al-Khayzurān.
21. For data on religious officials according to the legal school affiliation, see Ephrat, *A Learned Society*, figure 6.1.
22. One such was Qāḍī Abū Yaʿlā, who served as the *qāḍī* of Dār al-Khilāfa. See Abū l-Ḥusayn Muḥammad Ibn Abī Yaʿlā (d. 526/1131), *Ṭabaqāt al-ḥanābila*, ed. M. Ḥ. al-Fiqī (Cairo, 1952), pp. 380–1.
23. One of the most evident rivalries of this kind was that between the Dāmaghānī family of chief judges and judges, and the Zaynābīs, a native Ḥanafī-Hāshimī family that took over the chief judgeship in Baghdad (in 513/1119), along with that of the vizierate and the *niqāba*. On these families, see Ephrat, *A Learned Society*, appendix A.
24. See data in ibid. figure 2.4.
25. See al-Shīrāzī's biography in Subkī, *Ṭabaqāt al-Shāfiʿiyya*, VI, p. 149.
26. For examples, see Ephrat, *A Learned Society*, pp. 120–1.
27. See ibid. figure 2.7.
28. For the Ḥanbalīs of Baghdad during the Sunni revival, see especially Makdisi, *Ibn ʿAqīl*; Makdisi, 'The Sunni revival'; Makdisi, 'Hanbalite Islam', in *Studies on Islam*, ed. M. L. Swartz (New York, 1981), pp. 216–74.
29. See, for example, the descriptions of public demonstrations led by the Ḥanbalī scholar Ibn al-Wafāʾ in Ibn Rajab (d. 796/1393), *al-Dhayl ʿalā ṭabaqāt al-ḥanābila*, ed. M. H. al-Fiqī (Cairo, 1952–3), I, p. 52.
30. Ibn al-Jawzī, *Muntaẓam*, XVIII, p. 110.
31. Ibn al-Athīr, *al-Kāmil*, XVII, p. 210.
32. Jacqueline Chabbi, 'La fonction du ribāṭ à Baghdad du Ve siècle au début du VIIe siècle', *Revue des études islamiques* 42 (1974), pp. 107–9.
33. On the foundation of *ribāṭs* in Baghdad during this period, see esp. Mustafa Jawad,

'Al-Rubūṭ al-baghdādiyya', *Sumer* 10 (1954), pp. 218–49; Chabbi, 'La fonction du ribāṭ à Baghdad', pp. 101–7.

34. Cf. the persecution of hundreds of Ashʿarī (and by extension Shāfiʿī) scholars in Khurasan by the vizier ʿAmīd al-Mulk al-Kundurī in 453/1048, and the dramatic change in their fate after Niẓām al-Mulk brought about their rehabilitation. Omid Safi finds this episode to be a clear indication of the direct link between the rise of the various schools of thought and the political upheavals. See Safi, *The Politics of Knowledge*, pp. 52–60. For a detailed account of this episode, see also Bulliet, 'The political-religious history of Nishapur in the eleventh century', in *Islamic Civilization*, ed. Richards, pp. 80–5.
35. Makdisi was the first to dispute this view in 'The Sunni revival', in *Islamic Civilization*, ed. Richards, pp. 155–68, where he argues that the renewed activity of Sunni Islam was independent of the Seljuqs and Ashʿarism.
36. Sibṭ Ibn al-Jawzī, *Mirʾāt*, part. ed. A. Sevim (Ankara, 1968), p. 187. Ibn al-Jawzī, *Muntaẓam*, XVI, p. 181.
37. Ibid. p. 181.
38. Sibṭ Ibn al-Jawzī, *Mirʾāt*, ed. Sevim, p. 188; Ibn al-Jawzī, *Muntaẓam*, XVI, p. 182.
39. Sibṭ Ibn al-Jawzī, *Mirʾāt*, ed. Sevim, pp. 217–8; Ibn al-Jawzī, *Muntaẓam*, XVI, pp. 224–5.
40. Ibn al-Jawzī, *Muntaẓam*, XVI, p. 295.
41. Makdisi stresses this point in 'Muslim institutions', pp. 47–8.
42. See Christian Lange's contribution to this volume. See also the accounts collected by the same author on caliphal *muḥtasib*s' role in the purging of 'wrong' doctrines from Baghdad's madrasas in the late 6th/12th century, in Christian Lange, *Justice, Punishment, and the Medieval Muslim Imagination* (Cambridge, 2008), pp. 77, 82–3, 242.
43. Ibn al-Jawzī, al-Muntaẓam, XVI, p. 94.
44. Ibid. XVI, p. 295.
45. Abū ʿAlī Ibn al-Bannāʾ (d. 471/1078), *Taʾrīkh*, ed. and trans. George Makdisi as 'An autograph diary of an eleventh-century historian of Baghdad', *BSOAS* 19 (1957), p. 40 (Makdisi's translation).
46. See especially, Simha Sabri, *Mouvements Populaires à Baghdad à l'Epoque ʿAbbaside, IXe–XIe Siècles* (Paris, 1981), pp. 121–6.
47. A typical example is the inauguration of the Iqbāliyya that was founded in Baghdad in the early 7th/13th century. See the description in ʿImād al-Dīn Ibn Kathīr (d. 774/1374), *al-Bidāya wa-l-nihāya fī l-taʾrīkh*, 14 vols (Cairo, 1932), XIII, p. 129.
48. Ibn al-Jawzī, *Muntaẓam*, XVII, p. 294.
49. See Reinhart Dozy, *Supplement aux dictionnaires arabes* (Leiden, 1927), under *sadhaq* and *laylat al-waqūd*.
50. On this and other popular rituals, such as superogatory public prayers and saint worship, which became Sunna in medieval Syria, see Daniella Talmon-Heller, *Islamic Piety in Medieval Syria. Mosques, Cemeteries and Sermons under the Zangids and Ayyubids (1146–1260)* (Leiden, 2007), esp. pp. 61–3.
51. Ibn al-Jawzī, *Muntaẓam*, XVII, p. 120.
52. Ibid. XVI, pp. 292–3.

CHAPTER

9

CHANGES IN THE OFFICE OF *ḤISBA* UNDER THE SELJUQS

*Christian Lange**

The market inspector (*muḥtasib*), as censor of morals and prosecutor of offences perpetrated in the bazaars and streets of the Muslim city, has been called the 'guardian of the public space' in medieval Islam.[1] His primary sphere of influence, the market-place, was adjoined, on one side, by the Muslim city-dwellers' households, into which his authority could at times extend. On the other side, it bordered on the awe-inspiring citadel of the prince, conspicuous reminder of the ruler's dominion over the urban landscape; it was from here that the *muḥtasib*'s power ultimately derived.[2] The *muḥtasib* thus negotiated between the claims to the inviolability of Muslim households on the one hand, and the dictates of government on the other. Whoever defined the rights and duties of the *muḥtasib* had a share in drawing the line that separated the private from the public. As I suggest in this chapter, while the Seljuqs adopted and continued features of Abbasid, Buyid and Ghaznavid state organisation, the office of *ḥisba* underwent developments which gave it a new and distinctly Seljuq profile. The changes in *ḥisba* introduced under the Seljuqs reflect a new type of relationship between state and society, particularly with regard to the configuration of public and private space, in the territories under Seljuq control.[3]

TWO PROTOTYPES OF *MUḤTASIBS*: THE SAINT AND THE SCATOLOGIST

Under the Umayyads and the early Abbasid caliphs, the market inspector (then called *ṣāḥib*, or *ʿāmil al-sūq*) was primarily responsible for checking the

* I would like to thank D. G. Tor for reading and commenting on an earlier draft of this paper.

accuracy of scales and measures, and the quality of foodstuff sold in the market.[4] In the course of the 3rd/9th century, the religious dimension of the market inspector's office, as censor of public morals performing the Qurʾānic injunction (3:104) of *al-amr bi-l-maᶜrūf wa-l-nahy ᶜan al-munkar* ('commanding right and forbidding wrong'), became more prominent, and it is from this time onwards that he is no longer called *ṣāḥib* or *ᶜāmil al-sūq*, but *muḥtasib*.[5] At least in theory, it was now established that the *muḥtasib* should be a man of piety and, preferably, also of religious learning. *Ḥisba* came to be considered a religious office, a *waẓīfa dīniyya*, as it continued to be known in later centuries.[6] When in 318/930, the caliph al-Muqtadir wanted to appoint a police chief (*ṣāḥib al-shurṭa*) to the position of *muḥtasib* in Baghdad, the powerful general Muʾnis al-Muẓaffar insisted on the man's dismissal because he was neither a judge nor in any other way affiliated with the religious establishment.[7]

In the collective memory of later generations, the *muḥtasib* of the 4th/10th century who epitomised the ideal of the pious and learned *muḥtasib* was Abū Saᶜīd al-Ḥasan b. Aḥmad al-Iṣṭakhrī (d. 328/940), who served both as *muḥtasib* in Baghdad and as judge in Qum.[8] Ibn al-Nadīm (*fl.* 377/987) refers to al-Iṣṭakhrī as a chief (*raʾs*) in the *madhhab* of al-Shāfiᶜī.[9] He is credited with the opinion that *muḥtasib*s should be allowed to exercise their own free reasoning (*ijtihād*) in legal matters, which de facto requires them to be trained jurists.[10] His hagiographers praise his practice as *muḥtasib* of publicly burning musical instruments; he is also said to have ridden around on his mule through the markets of Baghdad, simultaneously praying and performing acts of *ḥisba*.[11]

However, under the Buyids, from the second half of the 4th/10th century and up until the arrival of the Seljuqs, the nature of *ḥisba* changed.[12] *Muḥtasib*s were no longer appointed on the authority of the caliph or his vizier but on that of the Chief Emir (*amīr al-umarāʾ*),[13] thus largely divesting the office of its sacral character. The administrative manual entitled *Siyar al-mulūk*, written by an experienced but rather low ranking clerk soon after the Buyid ascent to power,[14] states, in rather vague terms, that the *muḥtasib* should 'think well about jurisprudence' (*yakūnu qad naẓara fī l-fiqh naẓaran ḥasanan*), and that he should associate (*ṣaḥiba*) with judges, *maẓālim* officials and jurists.[15] A few decades later, a diploma of investiture for the *muḥtasib* penned by the celebrated Buyid vizier al-Ṣāḥib Ibn ᶜAbbād (d. 385/995) makes no mention of any religious qualifications whatsoever of the office holder.[16]

What is more, for all we know, *muḥtasib*s of the Buyid period, unlike the saintly figure of al-Iṣṭakhrī, were not exactly paragons of religious learning or, for that matter, of virtue. The example that comes most readily to mind is that of the *muḥtasib* Ibn al-Ḥajjāj (c. 330–91/941–1001), who is better known as the author of a large *oeuvre* of obscene and often scatological poetry (*sukhf*). Ibn al-Ḥajjāj, a Shiᶜi, enjoyed the tutelage and protection of a prominent member of the Persian administrative elite, the Director of the Royal Chancery (*ṣāḥib dīwān al-inshā*ʾ) Abū Isḥāq al-Ṣābiʾ (d. 384/994). He became *muḥtasib* in Baghdad during the vizierate of Ibn Baqiyya (r. 362–7/972–8), by appointment of the Chief Emir ᶜIzz al-Dawla Bakhtiyār (r. 356–67/967–78).[17] There was some tension, to say the least, between Ibn al-Ḥajjāj's claim to censorship of public morals and the kind of poetry he produced. His poems offer, for example, descriptions of his visits to prostitutes in the market of al-Karkh.[18] Ibn al-Ḥajjāj's poetic imagination, the delight he takes in wallowing in dirt, in painting images of grotesquely inflated, deformed and ugly bodies, appears to reflect the chaos of urban life under the Buyids, and it has indeed been suggested that, despite the cultural flowering of the period, there was a general erosion of the structures that held society together.[19] Few other *muḥtasib*s from the Buyid period are known,[20] most likely because they tended to be neither religious scholars nor judges and therefore did not make it into the later biographical literature.

Before the arrival of the Buyids, in early 4th/10th-century Iraq, *ḥisba* was considered the third-highest rank among the government officials (*aṣḥāb al-dawāwīn*), after the provincial governors (*ᶜummāl*) and the judges (*quḍāt*).[21] However, no such taxonomies seem to have applied under the Buyids. As for Western scholarship on the Buyid period, neither Heribert Busse nor John Donohue, in their surveys of Buyid state organisation, discuss the *muḥtasib*'s office, or bother to mention it at all.[22] Not even Adam Mez, the indefatigable collector of stories of Muslim social life in the 4th/10th and 5th/11th centuries, reports anything about *ḥisba* other than that Ibn al-Ḥajjāj occupied the post.[23] This would indeed seem to suggest that the office was not very highly regarded under the Buyids.[24] The Shāfiᶜī al-Māwardī (d. 450/1058), writing toward the end of the Buyid period, devotes the last chapter of his *al-Aḥkām al-sulṭāniyya* to *ḥisba*, detailing the considerable power enjoyed by the *muḥtasib* vis-à-vis other state officials. However, his account reflects an ideal rather than providing an accurate description of *ḥisba* in his day. As al-Māwardī himself admits, *ḥisba* had fallen into disrepute because it had been given to people whose only objective it was 'to profit and get bribes'.[25]

In other words, when the Seljuqs took over the task of governing from the Buyids, the office of *ḥisba* was in some need of revitalisation. Two prototypes of *ḥisba* were known to the newly arrived rulers and their administrative advisers: that of the pious and learned jurist al-Iṣṭakhrī, and that of Ibn al-Ḥajjāj, the corrupt libertine.[26] The Seljuqs, however, decided to channel *ḥisba* in a new direction altogether. This change came about gradually, but it can plausibly be argued that by the end of the Seljuq period, that is, toward the end of the 6th/12th century, a novel type of *muḥtasib* had emerged in the lands under Seljuq control.

MUḤTASIBS AND THE RELIGIOUS ELITE UNDER THE SELJUQS

It is worth noting that past scholarship has doubted that *ḥisba* under the Seljuqs changed at all. According to Willem Floor, author of a study dedicated to the history of the office in the lands of Iran, Seljuq *muḥtasib*s were not in the least different from Buyid ones.[27] According to Floor, *muḥtasib*s in Seljuq times continued to be greatly disliked by the populace; like their Buyid predecessors, they did little to prevent public nuisances such as begging and prostitution, and eating and sleeping in mosques.[28] A more nuanced view shall be proffered here, namely, that the Seljuqs made *ḥisba* undergo some significant developments, not only giving the office back some of its former reputation, but also by adding to its importance and authority. The Seljuq administration connected *ḥisba* to new functions and gave it new, previously unknown powers.

The first question one must ask to test this hypothesis concerns the relationship between *muḥtasib*s and the religious scholars (*ᶜulamāᵓ*) in the time of the so-called 'Sunni revival'. Prosopographical works would appear to promise an indication as to whether *ḥisba* under the Seljuqs was predominantly occupied by those connected to the (Sunni) religious elite or by people without affiliation to religious learning.[29] For *muḥtasib*s in the Seljuq period, however, prosopographical information is not easy to come by. Three monumental 8th/14th-century works containing biographical materials, al-Dhahabī's (d. 748/1348) *Tārīkh al-Islām*, al-Ṣafadī's (d. 764/1363) *al-Wāfī bi-l-wafayāt* and Tāj al-Dīn al-Subkī's (d. c. 771/1370) *Ṭabaqāt al-Shāfiᶜiyya al-kubrā* mention a mere eighteen *muḥtasib*s of the Seljuq period.[30] From these eighteen *muḥtasib*s, four held the position of Islamic judge (*qāḍī*) at one point in their career, another seven were trained jurists (*faqīh*s), and one was a popular preacher. Six are listed with no obvious religious qualification.[31] On the basis of this ratio (12:6), one could indeed infer that most Seljuq *muḥtasib*s were men of religion, or even that the office was gradually (re-)islamised under the Seljuqs. Other evidence would also seem to support this. The first Seljuq-period *muḥtasib* mentioned in the biographical dictionaries is one Muḥammad Ibn al-Dajājī ('the son of the man from [Nahr] al-Dajāj'), who died at Baghdad in 463/1071. His name suggests that he issued from a rather low (Shiᶜi?) merchant stratum with no direct connections to the *ᶜulamāᵓ*.[32] According to al-Ṣafadī, he was 'not praised' (*lam yumḥad*) and therefore deposed from his office.[33] Contrast this with how al-Ṣafadī praises the conduct of a *muḥtasib* in Baghdad some fifty years later, a Shāfiᶜī *faqīh* and *muḥaddith*.[34]

However, one obvious problem of the biographical sources is that they focus almost exclusively on the class of people who produced them, that is, the *ᶜulamāᵓ* themselves.[35] It can be assumed, therefore, that the proportion of *muḥtasib*s with credentials as *ᶜulamāᵓ* to those without was more balanced than is indicated by the two-to-one ratio one gleans from al-Dhahabī, al-Ṣafadī and al-Subkī. A further problem is that the biographical dictionaries relevant for the study of Seljuq history are almost entirely centred on Baghdad. The Abbasid caliphs, who continued to reside in the city throughout the Seljuq period, appointed their own *muḥtasib*s. They were generally keen to strike a posture of conformity with *sharīᶜa*, not least in order to differentiate themselves from the Seljuq sultans and atabegs, who lacked in religious legitimacy despite their efforts to portray themselves as the champions of Sunnism. The caliphs may therefore have been more inclined than the sultans to appoint religious scholars to the office of *ḥisba*, a tendency which can be said to have culminated in the *muḥtasib*-like powers enjoyed by the celebrated Ibn al-Jawzī (d. 597/1200), and the appointment of his son Muḥyī al-Dīn (d. 656/1258) and his grandson ᶜAbd al-Raḥmān (d. 656/1258) to the office of *ḥisba* in Baghdad.[36]

Other genres of literature, however, offer a different picture. The *Siyāsatnāma*[37] declares that *ḥisba* should be given to 'one of the nobility or else to a eunuch or an old Turk, who, having no respect for anybody, would be feared by nobles and commoners alike'.[38] This passage bluntly demands that *muḥtasib*s must *not* be recruited from among the *ᶜulamāᵓ*. Appointment deeds for *muḥtasib*s in the Seljuq and post-Seljuq periods point in the same direction. The *ᶜAtabat al-kataba*, a collection of thirty-eight chancery documents in Persian written between 528/1134 and 548/1153 at the court of the Great Seljuq Sanjar (r. 490–552/1097–1157) at Merv, contains one such appointment deed, concerning the office of *ḥisba* in Mazandaran province. It is dedicated to a certain Awḥad al-Dīn, who is praised for his knowledge of the 'ways of *sharīᶜa* (*rusūm-i sharīᶜat*)' and for his piety; but he does not seem to be a *faqīh*.[39] None of the existent chancery documents dealing with *ḥisba* from the Seljuq apanage kingdom of Kirman or from the Khwarizmshah, Rum Seljuq and Ayyubid periods suggest that *muḥtasib*s (while always enjoined to protect *sharīᶜa* and be pious) were trained jurists or religious scholars.

In consequence, it is safe to assume that the practice of appointing 'old Turks' and men without a madrasa rubberstamp to the office of *ḥisba* continued into the second half of the Seljuq period.[40] Let us note, also, that poets from the Seljuq period were rather acerbic in their assessment of *muḥtasib*s' commitment to the precepts of religion. Sūzanī-yi Samarqandī (d. 569/1173), a worthy successor to Ibn al-Ḥajjāj as an obscene poet, revels in accusing *muḥtasib*s of sexual depravity, especially sodomy (*liwāṭ*).[41] Al-Zamakhsharī (d. 538/1144) seems to be complaining against the excesses of the *muḥtasib*s of his time when he bitterly exlaims: 'If you do not command right, can't you at least refrain from destroying it? And if you do not forbid wrong, can't you at least refrain from committing it?'[42] Jamāl al-Dīn al-Iṣfahānī (d. 588/1192 or 3), who also worked as a goldsmith in the bazaar of Isfahan, likens a crow to a *muḥtasib*, vainly puffed up in a black robe (*ṭaylasān*) and cawing *ᶜamr-i maᶜrūf*.[43] In later Persian literature, the moral corruption of *muḥtasib*s became a trope. Niẓāmī, in the late 6th/12th century, warns his readers not to get entangled with *muḥtasib*s, lest they feel the whip of a satan (*dirra-yi Iblīs-vār*);[44] a century later, Saᶜdī (d. 691/1292) castigates the bigotry of *muḥtasib*s, who drink wine but punish others for it, or walk around 'bare-assed' (*kūn-birahna*) while telling prostitutes to veil their faces.[45] Needless to say, such accusations of deviance do not prove our point; to infer from them that *muḥtasib*s in Seljuq and post-Seljuq Iraq and Iran were not clerics would be naive. However, when Seljuq poets *do* have something positive to say about *muḥtasib*s it is usually not on account of their piety but of their efficiency as a state-appointed police force. For example, Sanāʾī (d. 525/1131), in a piece of panegyric poetry, praises *muḥtasib*s for offering a degree of security in times when 'the city is filled with thieves, and streets are filled with riffraff'.[46]

In sum, while a certain number of *muḥtasib*s under the Seljuqs, and especially in Baghdad under the Abbasid caliphs, appear to have been close to *ᶜulamāʾ* circles, it would be hasty to infer from this that the office was (re-)islamised. Not only is the biographical literature, as has been noted, tendentiously selective, but chancery documents do not support this idea. The existence of a number of *faqīh*s and judges among the *muḥtasib*s of the Seljuq period may also result from the Seljuq administration's attempt to draft *ᶜulamāʾ* into government service – a process which remains disputed among historians – so that *muḥtasib*s may have had a religious background without, however, representing the interests of the *ᶜulamāʾ* networks. The Seljuqs's 'politics of knowledge' are a contentious topic in Seljuq studies, with some scholars leaning toward the view that the *ᶜulamāʾ* largely caved in to government manipulation,[47] while others hold that they managed to uphold a certain autonomy vis-à-vis the state authorities and that government and religious elite formed largely separate networks of authority.[48] The sources consulted for this article, while not providing a clear-cut answer to this vexed question, give more support to the latter view; what they do reveal quite clearly, however, is that the nature and functions of *ḥisba* changed, as it became more closely attached to the higher echelons of government.

That the office acquired a more prominent place in the Seljuq administrative apparatus is already announced in the *Siyāsatnāma*, which stresses the close relationship between the king and *muḥtasib* and urges the ruler to lend the *muḥtasib* full support (*dast-i ū qavī dārad*).[49] It is recommended that the ruler appoint a *muḥtasib* to every town of the empire because *ḥisba* is 'one of the foundations of the kingdom'.[50] Even if this statement is hyperbolic, it would be difficult to argue that *ḥisba* had enjoyed a similarly high regard under the Buyids.[51] As is suggested here, Seljuq rule transformed the office of *ḥisba* into a key tool in the government's effort to widen its sphere of influence, and to achieve comprehensive physical control over the cities under its sway. It was no doubt a welcome side effect that by investing in the religious duty of *al-amr bi-l-maᶜrūf* the Seljuqs also buttressed their claim to being legitimate Islamic rulers.

In addition to the *Siyāsatnāma*'s statement to this effect, the elevated political rank of the *muḥtasib* can be seen in Seljuq panegyrics. It is striking that Seljuq poets such as Anvarī (d. c. 560/1164) and Khāqanī (d. 595/1199) do not hesitate to describe the ruler himself as 'the *muḥtasib* of the kingdom'.[52] *Mutatis mutandis*, the *muḥtasib* is seen as having a share in the power of the sultan. By meting out justice he instils comfort (and indeed fear) in the hearts of the subjects, pacifying the realm by his use of coercive force. In this context the link with the concept of *siyāsa* ('good government', but also '[capital] punishment', as in Persian *siyāsat kardan*, 'to execute') is significant. Under the Seljuqs, the royal ideology of *siyāsa* proposed that severe punishment by the king was a vital ingredient of good government.[53] This idea claimed the noblest of all pedigrees: ᶜUmar b. al-Khaṭṭāb was often portrayed as a kind of proto-*muḥtasib*, carrying around with him the *muḥtasib*'s tool *par excellence*, the switch (*dirra*).[54] Sanāᵓī thus could beg his patron to 'put the world right like ᶜUmar with his *dirra* (*yā chun ᶜUmar bi-dirra jahān-rā qarār dih*)'.[55] Such comparisons suggest that in Seljuq times, the authority of the sultan was extended to the *muḥtasib*, who came to be more closely tied to the ruler than perhaps ever before. In fact, absolute state power and *ḥisba* became synonyms. Some may still have felt that they were entitled to perform *ḥisba*, vigilante-like and based simply on the authority of their virtuousness and learning. But such challenges to government were quickly suppressed. Around 506/1112, the Ḥanafī jurist Muḥammad b. Yaḥyā al-Zabīdī (d. 555/1160) was banished by the governor of Damascus because he had behaved like a *muḥtasib* in public, commanding right and forbidding wrong.[56]

THE *MUḤTASIB* AND PUNISHMENT UNDER THE SELJUQS

The Seljuq *muḥtasib*, given his important share in the ruler's claim to lawful violence, was a crucial state agent, instrumental in ensuring the smooth running of the regime's repressive state apparatus. It is worth recalling that Seljuq rulers and their troops retained much of the old nomadic lifestyle, often pitching their tents in front of the city gates rather than seeking residence inside the city walls. *Ḥisba*, the most characteristically urban administrative function in medieval Islamic society, served them as a prosthesis to reach *intra muros*, and thus to stamp their authority on the cities in their domain.[57] This appropriation of the office by the new military overlords is reflected in the fact that the Seljuq *muḥtasib* became increasingly involved in the administration of punishment, whether by way of 'statutory punishment' (*ḥadd*, pl. *ḥudūd*) or 'discretionary punishment' (*taᶜzīr*), as the literature on the subject produced by government officials suggests.[58]

Limited power to punish offenders had been given to Buyid *muḥtasib*s. According to the Buyid *Siyar al-mulūk*, the *muḥtasib* could 'discipline' (*addaba*) fraudulent merchants.[59] The administration of corporal punishment, however, rested squarely with the chief of police (*ṣāḥib al-shurṭa*): he had to be familiar with all different kinds of penalties (*ᶜuqūbāt, ḥudūd*) and when to implement them, proactive in prosecuting crime (*jināyāt*), meticulous in his supervision of the local prisons, and careful to carry out punishment in public so that both commoners and the elite would witness it.[60]

Some decades later, in the *sijill* written by the Buyid vizier al-Ṣāḥib Ibn ᶜAbbād, the *muḥtasib* is enjoined to take care of 'the common good of all' (*maṣlaḥat al-kāffa*) by showing hardness (*ghilẓa*) toward the malefactors (*ahl al-fusūq*). He is explicitly encouraged to imprison offenders and discipline those who are misguided (*taᵓdību man taghurru nafsuhu*). However, Ibn ᶜAbbāds's diploma is very clear that the preferred method is to admonish people rather than to punish them physically.[61] No reference is made in the Buyid *inshāᵓ* documents to the *muḥtasib*'s power to mete out severe corporal punishments, whether as *taᶜzīr* or *ḥadd*.[62]

There is a marked difference, then, to a story told in approving fashion in the Seljuq *Siyāsatnāma*, in which the *muḥtasib* of Ghazna publicly flogs a powerful emir and army general for riding through the streets in a state of drunkenness.[63] While the *ḥisba* diploma in the *ᶜAtabat al-kataba* is a bit vague on the issue of the *muḥtasib*'s participation in the prosecution of crime – he is merely told to keep 'corrupt people' (*ahl-i fasād*) in check[64] – a Rum Seljuq *ḥisba* diploma (from Konya) instructs the *muḥtasib* to threaten criminals (*mujrimān*) with punishment according to their crimes.[65] In Waṭwāṭ's (d. c. 578/1182) appointment letter the preferred term for the *muḥtasib*'s punishment is still *taᵓdīb* ('disciplining') rather than *taᶜzīr*; but there is also an injunction to uphold the *ḥudūd* of God's law, as they are specified in revelation.[66] The *muḥtasib*'s share in *taᶜzīr* and in *ḥadd* punishment comes out very clearly in a *ḥisba* diploma written by ᶜImād al-Dīn al-Kātib al-Iṣfahānī (d. 597/1201), which instructs the *muḥtasib* to inflict both types of punishment, in addition to supervising the local prison.[67] Another couple of decades later, in an appointment letter for the *muḥtasib* written by Ḍiyāᵓ al-Dīn Ibn al-Athīr (d. 637/1239), the *muḥtasib* is instructed to publicly execute heretics or punish them with the *ḥadd* of flogging.[68] While these latter examples are taken from post-Seljuq (Ayyubid) sources, it is from Seljuq times onwards that the boundary separating the prerogatives and duties of the police forces (*shurṭa*) from that of the *muḥtasib* becomes blurred.[69] Overall, *ḥisba* under the Seljuqs claimed increasingly wide repressive and punitive powers.

This is also evinced by the chronicles of the Seljuq period, which give a plethora of examples of *muḥtasib*s, or their deputies, administering public punishments for a variety of offences, including ones unconnected to fraudulent behaviour in the marketplace or simple transgression against the norms of public decency.[70] For example, in 547/1152, a helper (*ghulām*) of the *muḥtasib* of caliph al-Muqtafī publicly exposed the deposed and disgraced director of the Niẓāmiyya madrasa on a platform at the Bāb al-Nūbā and beat him five strokes with the *dirra*.[71] One punishment, however, which really comes into focus in the Seljuq period as belonging to the *muḥtasib* is ignominious parading (*tashhīr*). *Tashhīr* processions led by the *muḥtasib* may have been an innovation that happened under the Seljuqs, at least as far as the lands of Iraq and Persia are concerned.[72] Previously, the *shurṭa*, whether acting on behalf of the judge or not, appears to have been primarily responsible for carrying out such shaming punishments.[73]

The first *muḥtasib* who is reported to have carried out ignominious parades in Seljuq times is Muḥammad b. al-Mubārak al-Khiraqī (or al-Kharaqī) (d. 494/1101), a Shāfiʿī judge and *muḥtasib* of Baghdad who served for over twenty years under the caliphs al-Muqtadī (r. 467–87/1075–94) and al-Mustaẓhir (r. 487–512/1094–1118).[74] Al-Khiraqī can be regarded as the dominant *muḥtasib* in the history of Seljuq Baghdad. The vizier al-Rudhrāwarī (r. 476–84/1083–91) instructed him to discipline (*an yuʾaddiba*) the cloth merchants and others who opened their shops on Fridays and instead closed them on Saturdays because, as the vizier reasoned, this would have strengthened the position of the Jews, who, as one infers, were a force to be reckoned with in Baghdad's economic life at the time.[75] Al-Khiraqī was also ordered to prevent women from going out at night for amusement.[76] He is also remembered for telling off a Ḥanafī judge for holding court in a mosque, a practice which the Shāfiʿīs condemned.[77] Al-Khiraqī threatened the owners of Baghdad's bath-houses with ignominious parading should they neglect to see to that a loincloth (*miʾzar*) was always worn inside their establishments.[78]

Seljuq *muḥtasib*s paraded people in other instances as well. In 467/1074 or 5, prostitutes (? *mufsidāt*) were shown around by the *muḥtasib* on donkeys and then banished to the western shore of Baghdad.[79] The secretary Abū l-Dulaf b. Hibat Allāh was paraded in Baghdad in 513/1119, while simultaneously being flogged by a *ghulām* of the *muḥtasib*.[80] Cheating merchants, thieves, grave-robbers, tricksters, drunkards, perjurers and blasphemers suffered *tashhīr*. A cannibal was paraded at Damghan in 494/1101, and Ismaʿilis at Isfahan and elsewhere around the turn of the century.[81]

THE INTERVENTIONIST NATURE OF *ḤISBA* UNDER THE SELJUQS

Only in some of these instances of *tashhīr* are *muḥtasib*s explicitly mentioned as having organised and carried out the ignominious parade. However, that the *muhtasib* should have been entrusted with this particular punishment is only logical. *Tashhīr*, the act of 'making notorious', was a penalty aiming, inter alia, to destroy people's privacy, that is, their right to be protected from the public gaze.[82] As such, it had a natural affinity with the office of *ḥisba* as the Seljuq administration conceived it. As is suggested here, the Seljuq *muḥtasib* became increasingly occupied with probing, crossing and subverting the line that separated the private from the public sphere.

This is the second significant change in the *muḥtasib*'s office in the Seljuq period. *Ḥisba* became more interventionist, in the sense that Seljuq *muḥtasib*s acquired greater authority to transgress into the private sphere of Muslim households. This development coincided with, and may have been informed by, the Seljuq preoccupation with a comprehensive system of surveillance, initiated by Niẓām al-Mulk's systematic attempts to 'extend the penetrating gaze of the central authority' by deploying espionage agents (*jāsūsān*) to all the provinces of the realm.[83] The *muḥtasib* became an important player in this network of reconnaissance.

That the government should intrude into the privacy of ordinary Muslims' lives had been a common fear among the subjects of political rule since the early centuries of Islam, in particular since the inquisition (*miḥna*) of the early 3rd/9th century, when the caliphal state had famously attempted to impose its own brand of orthodoxy on society.[84] This had involved a great deal of prying into the private beliefs of Muslims.[85] In the course of the *miḥna*, Ibn Ḥanbal (d. 241/855), the leader of the traditionalist *ᶜulamāᵓ*, was imprisoned and tortured for refusing to acknowledge the new caliphal doctrine, and his home was raided and searched.[86] In memory of this traumatic event, theoreticians of *ḥisba* from the ranks of the *ᶜulamāᵓ* took great care to stress that *ḥisba* is 'the commanding of right when it is *openly* neglected (*idhā ẓahara tarkuhu*) and the forbidding of wrong when the action is *openly* committed (*idhā ẓahara fiᶜluhu*)'.[87] In other words, the characteristic realm of the *muḥtasib*, according to the normative literature produced by the *ᶜulamāᵓ*, was the realm of the 'apparent' (*ẓāhir*).[88] The *muḥtasib* must not, on the other hand, preoccupy himself with 'that which is concealed' (*maktūm*) or secret (*sirr*). As al-Ṣāḥib Ibn ᶜAbbād's investiture diploma puts it, the *muḥtasib* must prevent the commoners (*raᶜiyya*) from 'expressing *openly* that which is prohibited' (*al-mujāhara bi-mā yuḥzaru*).[89]

However, some fifty years later, still in the Buyid period, the border of the *muḥtasib*'s sphere of influence appears to have shifted closer toward 'that which is concealed', regardless of what the *ᶜulamāᵓ* held to be the correct position on the matter. Al-Wazīr al-Maghribī, writing at the Marwanid court in Mayafariqin in the first half of the 5th/11th century, points out that the jurisdiction of the chief of police extends only to conspicuous (*ẓāhir*) challenges to the order, such as sins that are publicly known (*al-fisq al-mujāhir bihi*). The *muḥtasib*'s concern, by contrast, is also with hidden (*maktūm*) offences, which may cause greater harm than transgressions committed openly.[90]

There are no explicit statements in Seljuq *ḥisba* appointment deeds encouraging the *muḥtasib* to transgress into the privacy of houses. However, a number of *inshāᵓ* documents from the period make room for exactly this kind of interventionist understanding of the office. The *ᶜAtabat al-kataba* sets an example, even if the office in question is not *ḥisba* but *riyāsa* (of Mazandaran). The *raᵓīs* of the region, who throughout the diploma is entrusted with a number of duties very similar to those of the *muḥtasib*, is enjoined to respect the inviolability (*ḥurma*) of Muslim households and not intrude into them unless there is a clear proof (*bayyina*) of a sin going on inside.[91] In a similar vein, a *shiḥna* in the Seljuq kingdom of Kirman, in another investiture letter, is warned 'not to expose the privacy of Muslims to public ignominy on mere suspicion or based on acts of slander' (*bi-mujarrad-i tuhmat va saᶜāyat rusvāyi-yi ᶜawrāt-i musulmānān nakunad*).[92] The implication is that if 'clear proof' in excess of 'mere suspicion' is at hand, the repressive state authorities *are* allowed to intrude into the private sphere. What counts as 'clear proof', however, is a grey area. With regard to the *muḥtasib*'s power to intrude into the privacy of homes, the most striking statement in 6th/12th-century *inshāᵓ* literature can be found in Waṭwāṭ's appointment letter. Right at the beginning of the list of instructions to the *muḥtasib* Waṭwāṭ states that

> he must not climb up enclosures or walls in the pursuit of his office, or lift veils, or break into closed doors, or give unworthy people (*awbāsh*) power over the houses of the Muslims and the harems of the believers . . . thereby making public what God has commanded to be kept veiled and secret, and forbidden to show openly and make known in public.[93]

The novelty of Waṭwāṭ's letter is that it turns from *pre*scriptions about the *muḥtasib*'s duties to explicit *pro*scriptions against abusing the office, especially in terms of the *muḥtasib*'s violation of the sanctity of houses.[94] This shift in emphasis is significant. What Waṭwāṭ's formulation reveals is that by the end of the 6th/12th century, *muḥtasib*s had become extremely intrusive: they had become capable of climbing onto walls and roofs to spy on people, of breaking into houses even when doors were locked, or even of employing ruffians to carry out raids into the living quarters of Muslim households. And such sweeping prerogatives appear to have remained within the *muḥtasib*'s power also in later times.[95] The proscription against spying and prying, coupled with the lip-service injunction to respect privacy unless 'clear proofs' are found, reappears in the Ayyubid investiture deed written by ᶜImād al-Dīn for the *muḥtasib* of Aleppo.[96]

*Muḥtasib*s intruded into people's privacy not only in the territorial sense of entering into houses. When subjecting offenders to shaming punishments, such as ignominious parades, *muḥtasib*s also transgressed against the inviolability of peoples' bodies, short of exposing their shame zones (*ᶜawrāt*). Those paraded in *tashhīr* processions were dressed in rags which barely covered them; sometimes hair and beards were shaved as well.[97] Even women were paraded, although the sources give little detail on how this was done.[98] The punishment of *tashhīr* was a transgression against the right to remain private in the sense that personal dignity was destroyed. A key element of *tashhīr* was in fact loudly to announce the offenders' crimes to the crowd (*iᶜlān, taᶜrīf*), thereby revealing their sins to the public.[99]

The Seljuq *muḥtasib* intruded into the private sphere in another non-territorial sense, in as much as he was occupied with prying into peoples' religious beliefs and allegiances. The religious policy of the Seljuqs, given the tensions between them and the Fatimids and Ismaᶜili Nīzārīs, brought this characteristic of *ḥisba* to the fore. In the 5th/11th and 6th/12th centuries, *muḥtasib*s in the Seljuq domain became increasingly involved in the surveillance and suppression of those considered heretics by the ruling authorities. Mention has already been made of *tashhīr* processions of Ismaᶜilis. Around 544/1150, a popular preacher in Baghdad by the name of Badīᶜ was arrested and his house searched on suspicion of his Shiᶜi partisanship. Clay tablets into which the names of the twelve Imāms were engraved were found. Badīᶜ was publicly beaten and paraded at Baghdad's Bāb al-Nūbā.[100] In 559/1163 or 4, the *muḥtasib* of Baghdad ignominiously paraded a group of artisans who had shown their Shiᶜi sympathies by weaving the names of the twelve Imams into the mats they were manufacturing.[101]

Sweeping powers of investigation against non-orthodox groups were enjoyed by post-Seljuq *muḥtasib*s in Baghdad as well, particularly as the local Ḥanbalīs underwent a gradual rapprochement with the caliphal government.[102] Ibn al-Jawzī – who seems to have been appointed a *muḥtasib* himself, although the degree of his official affiliation with the office is difficult to determine – acted as a kind of inquisitor in Baghdad, especially under the caliph al-Mustaḍīᵓ (r. 566–75/1170–80). In 571/1176, Ibn al-Jawzī was given power to organise a crackdown on extreme Shiᶜites (*rawāfiḍ*), including the right to imprison people and demolish their houses.[103] In 588/1192, he aligned himself with the Ḥanbalī vizier Ibn Yūnus (d. 593/1197) in the condemnation of the director of the Jīliyya madrasa, a grandson of the famous Ḥanbalī jurist and mystic ᶜAbd al-Qādir al-Jīlī (d. 561/1166), accusing him 'of harbouring in his madrasa suspect books of philosophy and of *zandaqa*, in particular the *Rasāᵓil* of the Ikhwān al-Ṣafāᵓ'.[104] Although it cannot be proven, it is tempting to imagine that Ibn al-Jawzī, to whom the Jīliyya was given after its director's dismissal, had searched the madrasa in his function as *muḥtasib*.[105] It is difficult not to think that Ibn al-Jawzī, whose despisal of speculative theology (*kalām*) is well-known, was also involved in the following incident. In 567/1171–2, the director of the Niẓāmiyya madrasa had publicly lectured on an arcane topic in metaphysics, the question whether God can be described as an 'existent' (*mawjūd*). He was reported to the authorities, brought before and chided by the vizier, made to sit on a donkey and paraded around the city.[106]

Thus, one of the legacies of the Seljuqs to other Sunni regimes in the Near East was an understanding of the role of *muḥtasib* as an inquisitor, probing and prying into people's beliefs, and censoring heretical teachings. In Syrian cities, when the Fatimids were chased out by the Zengid and Ayyubid heirs of the Seljuqs, *muḥtasib*s were in charge of making sure that no songs insulting the first three caliphs were sung in the streets.[107] Ḍiyāᵓ al-Dīn's appointment letter for the office of *ḥisba* betrays an almost obsessive concern that state power be subverted by the covert preaching of heresy. The *muḥtasib* is exhorted to protect the 'saved group' (*al-firqa al-nājiᵓa*) of orthodox Sunnism, that is the followers of the 'righteous forefathers' (*al-salaf al-ṣāliḥ*), by keeping a close eye on the preachers of heterodox persuasion. The letter goes on to state that those in whose houses heretical books are found – one presumes after a search by the *muḥtasib* – 'must be arrested and publicly denounced' and that they must be 'punished with ignominious parading to serve as an example'.[108]

THE SELJUQ *ᶜULAMĀᵓ* AND CHANGING CONCEPTIONS OF PUBLIC AND PRIVATE IN THE SELJUQ PERIOD

By the end of the Seljuq period, the *muḥtasib* had assumed, in the words of Waṭwāṭ, the power to 'make public what ought to be concealed'. The *ᶜulamāᵓ*, ever suspicious of the government's claims to authority over the lives of their subjects, were rightly worried, even if their attitude was often ambivalent. Take al-Ghazālī as an example. In the ethical chapters of *Iḥyāᵓ ᶜulūm al-dīn* and in the *Kimiyā-yi saᶜādat*, one of al-Ghazālī's main aims of moral instruction is to convey the idea that sins committed in private must not be divulged and dragged into the realm of 'what is apparent', that is, the arena of public knowledge. This concern is especially prominent in the chapter he devotes to the 'sins of the tongue', which is one long warning against the sin of slandering others on account of their sins, whether real or imagined.[109] Al-Ghazālī's stress on the duty to cover up (*satr*) could appear to border on paranoia, but one of the reasons behind his eagerness to keep sins secret might be his fear that open display of private matters would undermine the concept of privacy, which under a repressive regime such as the Seljuqs was in constant need of protection.

On the other hand, al-Ghazālī's position vis-à-vis the *muḥtasib*'s right to intrude into Muslim houses, though delineated with extreme caution, is relatively permissive. His Shāfiᶜī predecessor al-Māwardī had prohibited *muḥtasib*s from entering into houses even if 'sinful' noises could be heard in the street. In such cases, the *muḥtasib*, according to al-Māwardī, should merely remonstrate from the outside.[110] Al-Ghazālī, however, takes a different, more activist view, and in this he is followed by most other Sunni jurists after him, including Ibn al-Jawzī.[111] For him, the sound of music or the voices of drunkards, if they can be heard in the street, justify the *muḥtasib*'s intrusion into the house.[112] Al-Ghazālī's example illustrates the dilemma faced by the *ᶜulamāʾ* confronted with the Seljuqs' expansionist policy of surveillance and control: the state's increasingly intrusive attitude, as it translated into the behaviour of state-appointed *muḥtasib*s, upset the delicate balance the *ᶜulamāʾ* had devised to reconcile the right of every Muslim to remain concealed with the duty of each individual to carry out *al-amr bi-l-maᶜrūf wa-l-nahy ᶜan al-munkar*. A more activist interpretation of this duty was, generally speaking, in the interest of the Sunni *ᶜulamāʾ*, who under Seljuq patronage had seen their self-confidence renewed;[113] but as *ḥisba* became one of the key repressive institutions of the Seljuq state, enthusiasm for the office waned among those who saw themselves in latent opposition to the *raison d'état*.

In conclusion, let us raise the question whether the *muḥtasib*'s new status is echoed in Seljuq-period *fiqh* beyond discussions specifically devoted to *ḥisba*. The changes in *fiqh* definitions of the inviolability of Muslim households have recently been made the object of study by Eli Alshech.[114] Alshech has traced the development in Islamic law from a rigid occupancy-based conception to a broader and more flexible notion of privacy, defined as the inalienable right of the (free) Muslim individual to be free from intrusive monitoring by the state authorities. In the first two centuries of Islam, Alshech suggests, the right to domestic privacy was primarily conceived as a function of rightful ownership of a space. If, for example, a person built a house and discovered upon completion that his neighbours were able to peep into in his house from their roof or through a window, he could not legally force them to obstruct the window or stop using their roof, because his neighbours' right of usage preceded his own. It was the builder's responsibility to find ways to conceal himself and his family from any curious gazes from the outside.[115] In later centuries, however, jurists increasingly tended to argue that with regard to privacy, the question of who possessed the older and therefore superior right of usage was irrelevant. According to this later view, privacy, the right to remain unseen, was to be protected under all circumstances. From now on, people were forbidden to walk on their roofs unless they installed a screen to block the view onto lower roofs.[116]

The development in *fiqh* that Alshech traces spans a long period of six centuries. He points out that the early Ḥanbalīs of the 4th/10th century, under the impression of both the *miḥna* (which had prompted their suspicion of intrusion of all sorts) and the rabble-rousing activism of the Baghdadi street preacher Barbahārī (Ḥanbalī, d. 329/941), had developed the new, broader understanding of privacy. However, the evidence cited by Alshech seems to suggest that in fact the most significant changes, or at least the most eloquent elaborations on these early efforts, occurred in the 5th/11th and 6th/12th centuries.[117] This is particularly the case with the Ḥanafīs, the school of law that most Seljuq rulers followed. The Ḥanafīs had traditionally shown themselves to be less concerned with privacy than the other schools.[118] Abū Yūsuf (d. 182/798), for example, is said to have held the view that a *muḥtasib* was allowed to enter into houses without seeking permission; his mere suspicion that a sin was being committed inside was enough.[119] However, his fellow Ḥanafī Ibn Māza, also known as al-Ṣadr al-Shahīd (d. 536/1141), states that 'the Ḥanafī scholars say that such a raid violates the Muslim's right to be concealed (*sitr al-muslim*) . . . and thus it should not be performed'.[120] Ibn Māza, a judge in Bukhara hailing from Nishapur, was an influential figure in the second half of the Seljuq period.[121] An advisor of Sanjar, killed fighting at the sultan's side in the battle of Qatwan (whence his sobriquet 'al-Shahīd'), he must have been acutely aware of the intrusiveness of the Seljuq state officials such as the *muḥtasib*.[122] It appears then, that Ḥanafī jurists writing in the Seljuq period increasingly recognised the need to protect the privacy of houses from the reach of the state.

Ibn Māza is also one of the first Muslim jurists to posit a general human desire for solitude. He states that a person 'needs to be alone' (*yaḥtāju ilā l-khalwa*), even for common daily acts such as eating, drinking, or performing ritual ablutions, activities which could hardly claim to be especially sensitive in nature and therefore deserving of privacy.[123] It is the Seljuq jurists, according to Alshech, who were the first to offer a substantial definition of the 'right to concealment' which did not only hinge on the concept of *ᶜawra*, the 'legal nakedness' of the human body, but included every object regarded as worthy of protection by its owner. Al-Zamakhsharī, who, as mentioned above, was wary of the *muḥtasib*s of his time, points out that entering into houses without permission is prohibited not only because the intruder might witness *ᶜawra*, but because one has no right to see that which people *wish* to conceal.[124] Overall, although the notion that privacy is an intrinsic right of the individual may not have been the prevalent one among the classical jurists,[125] the fact that the idea appears on the horizon of *fiqh* in the Seljuq period is noteworthy. It makes sense to relate this shift in legal doctrine to changes in the socio-political order, that is, the increased militarisation of government under the Seljuqs,[126] which ordinary Muslims faced particularly when they interacted with the agents of *ḥisba*, who were among the most prominent 'go-betweens' between state and society.[127]

This increased attention given by jurists of the Seljuq period to the issue of privacy may well reflect a heightened awareness that the domestic sphere was under attack and therefore in need of protection. The Seljuqs were off to a bad start in this respect. In 448/1056, during Sultan Ṭughril's year-long stay in Baghdad, his troops were quartered in private houses, which resulted in much-resented transgressions against the Baghdadi residents, earning the sultan a stern rebuke from the caliph.[128] Once the chaotic days of conquest had ended and the violence of the Seljuq state been institutionalised, officials such as the *muḥtasib* became the prime suspects of 'tearing apart the veil of integrity spread over the Muslims' (*hatk al-sitr ᶜalā ᶜiffat al-muslimīn*), as al-Sarakhsī's phrase has it.[129] Had not the *muḥtasib* gained new punitive powers under the Seljuq government, had his office not become more interventionist, as has been suggested here, the described shifts in emphasis in legal doctrine might not have taken place; the ethos of keeping sins hidden, which one sees in such pronounced fashion in al-Ghazālī's writings, might not have taken such deep roots, shaping Islamic attitudes towards the issue of privacy for centuries to come. In conclusion, *ḥisba* under the Seljuqs was not completely transformed; rather, a recasting of the office took place, giving the *muḥtasib* greater punitive powers (thus blurring the line separating *ḥisba* from *shurṭa*) and making his office more interventionist. Seljuq rule brought into Islamic society a new way of conceiving the relationship between state and society, and a new configuration of the boundary between public and private, which now appeared more precarious than ever, and was therefore all the more avidly defended.

NOTES

1. Yaron Klein, 'Between public and private: an examination of *ḥisba* literature', *Harvard Middle Eastern and Islamic Review* 7 (2006), p. 42.
2. Cf. Christian Lange, '*Ḥisba* and the problem of overlapping jurisdictions: an introduction to, and translation of, *ḥisba* diplomas in Qalqashandī's *Ṣubḥ al-aᶜshā'*, *Harvard Middle Eastern and Islamic Review* 7 (2006), pp. 95–6.
3. For the purpose of this study, I'm operating with a minimal definition of the public sphere as the sphere of influence for governmental authority. See *Dictionary of the Social Sciences*, ed. Craig Calhoun (Oxford, 2002), p. 392. Since my focus here is on

the relationship between the Seljuq state and the private sphere of 'ordinary' Muslim individuals and families, I leave aside the notion that there existed, in addition to the sphere of governmental authority, a number of other competing public spheres formed, for example, by the networks of *ᶜulamāᵓ* and/or local nobles. For an exploration of this topic in the Seljuq context, see Daphna Ephrat's contribution to this volume (Chapter 8). For a general discussion of the applicability and potential usefulness of the categories of a private and a public sphere in the study of pre-modern Islamic societies, see also Christian Lange and Maribel Fierro, 'Spatial, ritual and representational aspects of public violence in Islamic societies (1st–19th centuries CE)', in *Public Violence in Islamic Societies: Power, Discipline, and the Construction of the Public Sphere, 7th–19th Centuries* CE, eds Christian Lange and Maribel Fierro (Edinburgh, 2009), pp. 1–23.

4. Ronald P. Buckley, 'The Muhtasib', *Arabica* 39 (1992), p. 62. Cf. Abū l-Faraj ᶜAbd al-Raḥmān Ibn al-Jawzī, *Ṣifat al-ṣafwa*, ed. M. Fākhūrī (Beirut, 1979/1399), III, p. 301, for the *qāḍī* and *muḥtasib* Abū ᶜAbd al-Raḥmān ᶜĀṣim b. Sulaymān al-Aḥwal (d. 141 or 2/758 or 9), a *mawlā* of the Banū Tamīm, who was 'in charge of the ḥisba over scales and weights in Kufa'.
5. The active participle *muḥtasib* is derived from the verb *iḥtasaba*, the meaning of which Lane renders as 'to seek a reward from God in the world to come'. See Edward William Lane, *An Arabic-English Lexicon* (London, 1863), s.v. *ḥ-s-b*. On the changing nature of the office, see further Ernst Klingmöller, 'Agoranomos and Mutasib: Zum Funktionswandel eines Amtes in islamischer Zeit', in *Fs. Erwin Seidl* (Cologne, 1975), pp. 88–98.
6. Aḥmad b. ᶜAlī al-Qalqashandī, *Ṣubḥ al-aᶜshā fī ṣināᶜat al-inshāᵓ* (Cairo, 1918–22), XI, p. 211, XI, pp. 212–3, XII, p. 63 (with examples from Fatimid, Ayyubid and Mamluk times); Muḥammad b. Muḥammad Ibn al-Ukhuwwa, *Maᶜālim al-qurba fī aḥkām al-ḥisba*, ed. R. Levy (Cambridge, 1938), p. 13.
7. Adam Mez, *The Renaissance of Islam*, trans. S. K. Bukhsh and D. S. Margoliouth (London, 1975), p. 416.
8. On al-Iṣṭakhrī, see Tāj al-Dīn al-Subkī, *Ṭabaqāt al-shāfiᶜiyya al-kubrā*, eds M. M. al-Ṭanāḥī and ᶜA. M. al-Ḥilw (Cairo, n.d.), I, p. 109, III, pp. 230–53. According to al-Subkī, al-Iṣṭakhrī was one of the luminaries of the Shāfiᶜī school and wrote a book on *adab al-qāḍī*, among other works. Al-Māwardī (d. 450/1058) mentions al-Iṣṭakhrī's opinion on *ḥisba*-related issues a number of times throughout his chapter on the office. See Al-Māwardī, *al-Aḥkām al-sulṭāniyya* (Cairo, 1380/1960), pp. 241, 243, 251. As a legal scholar, al-Iṣṭakhrī acquired fame for issuing a *fatwā* calling for the execution of the Sabean community on the grounds of their worship of stars. See Ṣalāḥ al-Dīn Khalīl b. Aybak al-Ṣafadī, *al-Wāfī bi-l-wafayāt*, eds A. al-Arnaᵓūṭ and T. Muḥammad (Beirut, 1420/2000), XI, p. 287. See also Christopher Melchert, *The Formation of the Sunni Schools of Law, 9th–10th Centuries* CE (Leiden, 1997), XVI, p. 91, note 103.
9. Ibn al-Nadīm, *Fihrist*, ed. Flügel (Leipzig, 1871), p. 213.
10. Māwardī, *al-Aḥkām al-sulṭāniyya*, p. 241. Al-Māwardī himself leaned toward the view that the *muḥtasib* should not exercise *ijtihād*. See ibid. p. 256, stating that the judge has a superior (*aḥaqq*) right to adjudicate cases which require *ijtihād*.
11. Abū l-Fidāᵓ Ismāᶜīl b. ᶜUmar Ibn Kathīr, *al-Bidāya wa-l-nihāya* (Beirut, 1966), XI, p. 218.
12. Al-Qāḍī al-Tanūkhī (d. 384/994) tells stories of a few vigorous and incorruptible men who worked during his lifetime as *muḥtasib*s in Basra and Ahwas. See the anecdotes in

al-Tanūkhī, *Nishwār al-muḥādara*, ed. Margoliouth (London, 1921–2), I, pp. 163–4. While it is possible that al-Tanūkhī means to obliquely criticise Baghdad by contrasting it with the other cities of Iraq, a more marked decline of the office may have set in in the second half of the Buyid reign.

13. Heribert Busse notes that under the Buyids, police authority passed from the vizier (who acted on behalf of the caliph), to the Chief Emir or, in the provinces, to the *ᶜāmil*. See Heribert Busse, *Chalif und Großkönig: Die Buyiden im Iraq* (Beirut, 1969), p. 321. See also Buckley, 'The Muhtasib', p. 69.
14. J. Sadan, 'A new source of the Būyid period', *Israel Oriental Studies* 9 (1979), pp. 361–3.
15. Ibid. p. 373.
16. Al-Ṣāḥib Ibn ᶜAbbād, *Rasāʾil*, ed. ᶜA. ᶜAzzām (Cairo, 1366/1946 or 7), pp. 39–41.
17. See Joel Kraemer, *Humanism in the Renaissance of Islam: the Cultural Revival during the Buyid Age* (Leiden, 1986), p. 199.
18. Sinan Antoon, 'The poetics of the obscene: Ibn al-Ḥajjāj and *Sukhf*' (PhD Harvard, 2006), pp. 207–11. Ironically, the Mamluk *ḥisba* manual of Ibn al-Ukhuwwa enjoins *muḥtasib*s to prevent the youth from reading Ibn al-Ḥajjāj's poems. In a poem dedicated to the desirability of unlawful sexual intercourse Ibn al-Ḥajjāj states: 'My friends and brethren I give you advice, / seeking no price from my advice to you. / Get up, let us pledge that you and I / never ever do something that is lawful.' The translation is by Antoon, 'The poetics of the obscene', p. 216.
19. For a trenchant analysis of the social logic of Ibn al-Ḥajjāj's poetry, see ibid. pp. 228–50.
20. No *muḥtasib* of the Buyid period is mentioned in al-Subkī's *Ṭabaqāt al-Shāfiᶜiyya al-kubrā*. Al-Ṣafadī's *al-Wāfī bi-l-wafayāt* contains nine biographies of *muḥtasib*s from the century before the rise of the Seljuqs, but Ibn al-Ḥajjāj is the only Buyid *muḥtasib* among them. Al-Ṣafadī also mentions one Abū l-Ḥasan ᶜAlī b. Aḥmad al-Jurjānī al-Muḥtasib (d. 366/976), a *ḥadīth* transmitter who lived in Nishapur, but it is not actually clear that his name 'al-Muḥtasib' refers to him having held the office of *ḥisba*. See Ṣafadī, *Wāfī*, XX, p. 86.
21. See the list of formal addresses (*mukhāṭabāt*) written by the vizier Ibn al-Furāt (d. 312/924), reported in Hilāl b. al-Muḥassin al-Ṣābiᶜ, *al-Wuzarāʾ*, ed. ᶜA. A. Furāj (Cairo, 1958), pp. 172–6. This list must have been written between 309/921 and 312/924, since it mentions the *muḥtasib* Ibrāhīm b. Baṭḥa, who was appointed in 309/921 and died three years later. On Ibn Baṭḥā, see Willem Floor, 'The office of muhtasib in Iran', *Iranian Studies* 18 (1985), p. 61.
22. Busse, *Chalif und Großkönig*; John Donohue, *The Buwayhid Dynasty in Iraq 334 H./945 to 403 H./1012: Shaping Institutions for the Future* (Leiden, 2003).
23. Mez, *Renaissance*, p. 269.
24. The situation may have been different in the West, although there is some variation in scholarly assessments of the importance of *ḥisba,* for example, under the Fatimids. Cf. below, note 51.
25. Floor, 'Office of muhtasib', p. 62. Ibn al-Ḥajjāj appears to have had his share in this. It is said that his fellow poets envied him more for his lucrative post as *muḥtasib* than for his poetry. See Mez, *Renaissance*, p. 269.
26. Note that al-Iṣṭakhrī and Ibn al-Ḥajjāj, in addition to the Medinese Nāfiᶜ b. ᶜAbd al-Raḥmān al-Muqriʾ (d. 59/678 or 9), are the only *muḥtasib*s to find mention in Ibn

Khallikān's *Wafayāt al-aᶜyān*, albeit not on account of their having occupied the post of *ḥisba*. See Ibn Khallikān, *Wafayāt al-aᶜyān*, trans. G. de Slane (New York, 1842–71), I, pp. 374–5 (al-Iṣṭakhrī), pp. 448–50 (Ibn al-Ḥajjāj).

27. Floor, 'Office of muhtasib', pp. 63–4.
28. Ibid. pp. 63–4. A similar, if more nuanced view is offered by John Donohue, who states that 'from a superficial point of view, it can be said that the Seljuks repeated the Buwayhid experience with only minor modifications of the institutions the Buwayhids had shaped'. See John Donohue, *The Buwayhid Dynasty*, xv. Note, however, that Donohue does not discuss *ḥisba* in his book.
29. Research on *ḥisba*, for example in the Mamluk era, has begun to make use of prosopography. See Kristen Stilt, 'Price setting and hoarding in Mamluk Egypt: the lessons of legal realism for Islamic legal studies', in *The Law Applied: Contextualizing the Islamic Shari'a*, eds P. Bearman, W. Heinrichs and B. G. Weiss (London, 2008), pp. 57–78.
30. Cf. Vanessa van Renterghem, 'Les élites baghdadiennes' (PhD Paris-Sorbonne, 2004), II, p. 214 (Table 14-2). Van Renterghem counts seventeen *muḥtasib*s in Seljuq Baghdad, but hers is a much more in-depth analysis of the sources than I can offer here. Her list of Seljuq *muḥtasib*s is based on the chronicles of Ibn al-Jawzī, Ibn al-Athīr, Ibn Kathīr, Ibn al-Najjār, Sibṭ Ibn al-Jawzī, Ibn al-Dubaythī, and al-Qurashī; but she misses al-Ṣafadī's *Wāfī*.
31. Shams al-Dīn Muḥammad b. Aḥmad al-Dhahabī, *Tārīkh al-Islām*, ed. ᶜU. ᶜA. Tadmurī (Beirut, 1404/1987), XXXII, p. 87, XXXIV, p. 302, XXXV, p. 216, XXXVII, pp. 61, 222, XL, p. 296; Ṣafadī, *Wāfī*, IV, p. 101, V, p. 105, VI, p. 244, VII, pp. 9, 172, VIII, pp. 78, 79, XVIII, pp. 9, 30, XXII, p. 85; Subkī, *Ṭabaqāt*, VII, p. 333.
32. Nahr al-Dajāj was a neighbourhood in al-Karkh in West Baghdad, named after the canal running through it, the banks of which used to be occupied by the poulterers. See Guy Le Strange, *Baghdad During the ᶜAbbasid Caliphate* (London, 1924), p. 53.
33. Ṣafadī, *Wāfī*, IV, p. 101. Muḥammad Ibn al-Dajājī seems to be identical with the *muḥtasib* Saᶜd al-ᶜAjamī mentioned in van Renterghem, 'Les élites', I, p. 471, II, p. 214, of whom she says that 'en 461/1071, une émeute populaire conduisit au *dīwān* un group de Ḥanbalites, qui exigèrent du calife qu'il démit le *muḥtasib* jugé injuste; le calife accéda à leur requête', citing Sibṭ b. al-Jawzī, *Mirʾāt al-zamān fī taʾrīkh al-aᶜyān*, ed. Ali Sevim, pp. 173–9.
34. Abū l-ᶜAbbās Aḥmad b. Muḥammad Ibn al-Naqīb al-Shahrastānī al-Baghdādī, born in Tikrit, studied and eventually taught Shāfiᶜī *fiqh* in Baghdad, and was then appointed to the position of *muḥtasib* in 537/1142. See Ṣafadī, *Wāfī*, VIII, p. 79.
35. Cf. Stephen Humphreys, *Islamic History: a Framework for Inquiry* (Minneapolis, MN, 1988), p. 187.
36. On Ibn al-Jawzī's connection with *ḥisba*, see below. Both Muḥyī al-Dīn and ᶜAbd al-Raḥmān Ibn al-Jawzī were killed in the Mongol sack of Baghdad. See Ṣafadī, *Wāfī*, XXIX, pp. 104–5 (for Muḥyī l-Dīn), XVIII, p. 187 (for ᶜAbd al-Raḥmān).
37. For contributions casting doubt on the attribution to Niẓām al-Mulk, see Erika Glassen, *Der mittlere Weg: Studien zur Religionspolitik und Religiosität der späteren Abbasiden-Zeit* (Wiesbaden, 1981), p. 122ff.; M. Simidchieva, '*Siyāsat-nāme* revisited: the question of authenticity', in *Proceedings of the Second European Conference on Iranian Studies*, ed. B. G. Fragner *et al.* (Rome, 1995), pp. 657–74; Alexey Khismatulin, 'The art of medieval counterfeiting: the *Siyar al-Mulūk* (the *Siyāsat-Nāma*) by Niẓām al-Mulk

and the "full" version of the *Naṣīḥat al-Mulūk* by al-Ghazālī', *Manuscripta Orientalia* 14, 1 (2008), pp. 3–31.

38. Niẓām al-Mulk, *Siyāsatnāma*, ed. H. Darke (Tehran, 1962), p. 56.
39. Mu'ayyad al-Dawla Badī' Juvaynī, *'Atabat al-kataba*, eds M. Qazwīnī and 'A. Iqbāl (Tehran, 1329sh./1950), pp. 82–3. Note, however, that another appointment deed for a *qāḍī* also bestows on the same man the prerogative to act as *muḥtasib*. See ibid. p. 52.
40. In the biographical literature, one occasionally reads of *muḥtasib*s of the post-Seljuq period who lacked religious training. A case in point is Fakhr al-Dīn Ibn Madūdā Muḥammad b. Abī Bakr b. 'Abbās al-Amīr (d. 669/1270–1), who was first the *muḥtasib* of 'al-Jazīra al-'Umariyya', then moved to Mārdīn and was *muḥtasib* there, but then left the office and became a travelling merchant. See Ṣafadī, *Wāfī*, II, pp. 190–1.
41. Quoted in 'Alī Akbar Dekhoda, *Lughatnāmeh* (Tehran, 1946–), s.v. *muḥtasib*: *dar-i dakhl-i har shiḥna ū muḥtasib-rā / gushāda-ast tā hast izārat-i gushāda.*
42. Maḥmūd b. 'Umar al-Zamakhsharī, *Aṭwāq al-dhahab*, ed. C. Barbier de Meynard (Paris, 1876), p. 180.
43. Jamāl al-Dīn Iṣfahānī, *Divān*, ed. W. Dastgerdi (Tehran, 1362sh./1983 or 4), p. 129: *zāgh bā ṭaylasān chū muḥtasibī ki amr-i ma'rūf āshkārā kard.* I owe this reference to David Durand-Guédy. On al-Iṣfahānī's life and career, cf. *EIr*, s.v. 'Jamāl al-Dīn Moḥammad b. 'Alī Eṣfahāni', XIV, pp. 436–8 (D. Durand-Guédy).
44. Quoted in Dekhoda, *Lughatnāmeh*, s.v. *zīnhār*.
45. Ibid. s.v. *muḥtasib, birahna.*
46. Ibid. s.v. *kūy.*
47. Omid Safi, *The Politics of Knowledge in Premodern Islam: Negotiating Ideology and Religious Inquiry* (Chapel Hill, NC, 2006), pp. 90–7.
48. Daphna Ephrat, *A Learned Society in a Period of Transition: the Sunni 'Ulama' of Eleventh-Century Baghdad* (Albany, NY, 2000), pp. 16, 126–36, 152–3.
49. Niẓām al-Mulk, *Siyāsatnāma*, p. 56.
50. Ibid. p. 56.
51. The rank of the *muḥtasib* in 5th/11th-century Egypt was likewise low. See Yaacov Lev, 'The suppression of crime, the supervision of markets, and urban society in the Egyptian capital during the tenth and eleventh centuries', *Mediterranean Historical Review* 3 (1988), p. 76, quoting an incident from 414/1024 reported in al-Musabbiḥī's chronicle, where a rather low-ranking *dīwān* official, the Chief of the Office of Salaries (*dīwān al-tartīb*), rejects the offer to become *muḥtasib* of Cairo because he considers this to be below his dignity. On the other hand Roland P. Buckley, *The Book of the Islamic Market Inspector:* Nihāyat al-Rutba fī Ṭalab al-Ḥisba (The Utmost Authority in the Pursuit of Ḥisba) *by 'Abd al-Raḥmān b. Naṣr al-Shayzarī* (Oxford, 1999), pp. 8–9, states that the *muḥtasib* under the Fatimids became a 'grand dignitary'. No doubt this was the case under the Mamluks, when the Egyptian *muḥtasib* was considered to be fifth in rank of all the judicial posts. See ibid. p. 10, referring to Qalqashandī, *Ṣubḥ*, IV, pp. 34–5.
52. Dekhoda, *Lughatnāmeh*, s.v. *muḥtasibī*: *inṣāf-i tū miṣr-īst ki dar rasta-yi ū dīw / naẓm az jihat-i muḥtasibī dāda dukān-rā* (Anvarī). Cf. ibid. s.v. *muḥtasib* (Khāqānī).
53. Kayka'ūs b. Iskandar b. Qābūs, *Qābūsnāmeh*, ed. R. Levy (London, 1951), pp. 10, 55. Cf. Ann K. S. Lambton, *State and Government in Medieval Islam* (Oxford, 1981), p. 124; Christian Lange, *Justice, Punishment and the Medieval Muslim Imagination* (Cambridge, 2008), pp. 42–4.
54. In the old days, according to (Pseudo-)Ghazālī, it was enough for a ruler like 'Umar to

carry a simple whip on his shoulder to deter people from evil actions. However, 'the sultans of today must rely on punishment (*siyāsat*) and awe (*haybat*)'. See (Pseudo-) Ghazālī, *Naṣīḥat al-mulūk*, ed. J. Humāʾī (Tehran, 1361/1982), p. 148.

55. Quoted in Dekhoda, *Lughatnāmeh*, s.v. *dirra*.
56. ᶜAbd al-Qādir b. Muḥammad Ibn Abī l-Wafāʾ, *al-Jawāhir al-muḍiyya fī ṭabaqāt al-Ḥanafiyya* (Hyderabad, 1332/1914), II, 142.13, quoted in Michael Cook, *Commanding Right and Forbidding Wrong in Islamic Thought* (Cambridge, 2000), p. 316.
57. Cf. David Durand-Guédy's comment in his contribution to this volume (Chapter 10) that early Seljuq rulers 'sought to bypass old local solidarities' by 'monopolizing local and imperial offices'. – It may be that *ḥisba*, shorn of its local links of solidarity, exacerbated the decline of Iranian urban culture that set in in the 5th/11th century, as described by Richard Bulliet. See Richard Bulliet, *Islam: the View from the Edge* (New York, 1994), pp. 129–44.
58. I exempt from the following analysis the normative *ḥisba* literature written by the *ᶜulamā*, who at times, though not always, occupied an oppositional stance vis-à-vis the state. It is not surprising to see that in the theoretical literature produced by the *ᶜulamāʾ*, the *muḥtasib* is given extensive powers of prosecution and punishment. This served to delineate the office against other offices of prosecution which had no grounding in religious concepts such as *iḥtisāb* and *al-amr bi-l-maᶜrūf*. The 3rd/9th-century *ḥisba* manual written by the Zaydī Imām al-Nāṣir li-l-Ḥaqq al-Ḥasan b. ᶜAlī al-Uṭrūsh (d. 304/917), for example, gives the *muḥtasib* the power to inflict *ḥadd* punishment on wine-drinkers, and to punish with *taᶜzīr* Muslim slanderers. See R. B. Serjeant, 'A Zaydī manual of Ḥisba of the 3rd century (H)', *RSO* 28 (1953), p. 29. In al-Shayzarī's (*fl.* late 6th/12th) *ḥisba* manual, the *muḥtasib* is instructed to punish offenders with *taᶜzīr*; the text even details the appropriate procedure for stoning fornicators. See ᶜAbd al-Raḥmān b. Naṣr al-Shayzarī, *Nihāyat al-rutba*, ed. S. B. al-ᶜArīnī (Cairo, 1365/1946), pp. 9, 108–9.
59. Sadan, 'New source', p. 373.
60. Ibid. pp. 367–8, 370–1.
61. Ibn ᶜAbbād, *Rasāʾil*, pp. 39–41.
62. Note, however, that *taᶜzīr* as a distinct legal category only emerged in the early Seljuq period. See my *Justice, Punishment and the Medieval Muslim Imagination*, pp. 215–24.
63. Niẓām al-Mulk, *Siyāsatnāma*, pp. 53–4. Flogging by the *muḥtasib* is explicitly mentioned in Ghaznavid sources. See Bayhaqī, *Tārīkh-i Bayhaqī*, quoted in Dehkhoda, *Lughatnāmeh*, s.v. *muḥtasib*.
64. Juvaynī, *ᶜAtabat al-kataba*, p. 83.
65. *Taqārīr al-manāṣīb*, in *Türkiye Selçukluları hakkında resmî vesikalar*, ed. O. Turan (Ankara, 1958), p. 44 (Persian text).
66. Rashīd al-Dīn Muḥammad b. Muḥammad Waṭwāṭ, *Majmūᶜat al-rasāʾil*, ed. M. Fahmī (Cairo, 1939), pp. 80–1. The *ḥudūd Allāh* could also refer, of course, simply to 'God's laws', but the meaning of 'statutory punishments' is not entirely implausible. For the purpose of this chapter, a certain continuity of administrative organisation from the Seljuqs to the Khwarazmshahs is assumed. Cf. C. Edmund Bosworth's comment that 'the Khwārazmshāhs in eastern Iran and the network of Atabeg dynasties in western Iran and the Arab lands must be regarded as a continuation of [the] process [of] ethnic and tribal movements of Turks into the Middle East'. See C. Edmund Bosworth, 'Barbarian incursions: the coming of the Turks in the Islamic world', in *Islamic Civilisation 950–1150*, ed. D. S. Richards (Oxford, 1973), p. 10.

67. ʿImād al-Dīn al-Kātib al-Iṣfahānī, *al-Barq al-shāmī*, ed. F. Ḥusayn (Amman, 1987), V, pp. 137–8.
68. Ḍiyāʾ al-Dīn Ibn al-Athīr, *Tawaṣṣul al-mulūk*, ms. Oxford, Pococke 322, fol. 95a:12, 96a:5.
69. At times, *shurṭa* even seems to have become subsumed under the *muḥtasib*'s authority. For example, al-Shayzarī states that the atabeg Tughtakīn (d. 552/1128), ruler of Damascus and founder of the Burid dynasty, appointed a *muḥtasib*, giving him power over *shurṭa*. See Buckley, *The Book of the Islamic Market Inspector*, p. 31. The Crusaders, who borrowed *ḥisba* from the Arabs, called it the office of the 'master sergeant' or 'chief of police'. See ibid. p. 32, note 11.
70. Fatimid *muḥtasib*s in the 5th/11th century also had the power to implement harsh punishments, especially flogging and *tashhīr*, but seem to have been restricted to prosecution of offences bearing upon the grain trade, that is, specifically market-related offences. Cf. Lev, 'The suppression of crime', pp. 84–7. For examples of severe floggings by *muḥtasib*s in al-Andalus in the 3rd/9th and 4th/10th centuries, see Abū l-Walīd ʿAbd Allāh b. Muḥammad Ibn al-Faraḍī (d. 403/1013), *Tārīkh ʿulamāʾ al-Andalus* (Madrid, 1890–92), I, pp. 98, 303.
71. Ibn al-Jawzī, *Muntaẓam*, XVIII, p. 84.
72. Fatimid *muḥtasib*s of the 4th/10th and 5th/11th centuries are repeatedly reported to have paraded offenders. See Lev, 'The suppression of crime', pp. 84–7. Fatimid *muḥtasib*s are also known to have administered floggings. See Ibn Taghrībirdi, *al-Nujūm al-ẓāhira* (Cairo, n.d.), IV, p. 236; Dhahabī, *Tārīkh al-Islām*, XXVIII, pp. 97–8.
73. The Buyid *Siyar al-mulūk* mentions that the *ṣāḥib al-shurṭa* must first flog and imprison the makers of musical instruments, male and female singers, and effeminate men, then shave their heads and parade them. See Sadan, 'A new source', p. 369. Everett Rowson discusses a few cases of *tashhīr* in Umayyad times in his 'Reveal and conceal: public humiliation and banishment as punishment in early Islamic times', in *Public Violence in Islamic Societies*, eds Christian Lange and Maribel Fierro (Edinburgh, 2009), pp. 119–21. However, no *muḥtasib* appears to have been involved in these early historical examples of *tashhīr*. There is currently no study of the practice of *tashhīr* in 3rd/9th- and 4th/10th-century Iraq and Persia, and it may still come to daylight that the *muḥtasib* was involved in *tashhīr* also in earlier centuries.
74. Ibn al-Jawzī, *Muntaẓam*, XVII, p. 73.
75. Ibid. XVII, p. 24.
76. Ibid. XVII, p. 66.
77. See Shayzarī, *Nihāyat al-rutba*, trans. Buckley, *The Book of the Islamic Market Inspector*, pp. 131–2. Cf. Emile Tyan, *Histoire de l'orgaisation judiciaire en pays d'Islam* (Leiden, 1960), p. 641.
78. Ibn al-Jawzī, *Muntaẓam*, XVII, p. 73.
79. Ibid. XVI, p. 166.
80. Ibid. XVII, p. 172. See also ʿAbbūd Shāljī, *Mawsūʿat al-ʿadhāb* (Beirut, 1980), III, p. 246, quoting Ibn Khallikān, *Wafayāt al-aʿyān*.
81. See the cases collected in my *Justice, Punishment and the Medieval Muslim Imagination*, pp. 79–85.
82. Cf. Eli Alshech, 'Out of sight and therefore out of mind: early Sunnī Islamic modesty regulations and the creation of spheres of privacy', *Journal of Near Eastern Studies* 66 (2007), p. 268.

83. Safi, *Politics of Knowledge*, pp. 83–4.
84. Cook, *Commanding Right*, pp. 80–2, 99.
85. See Basim Musallam, 'The ordering of Muslim societies', in *The Cambridge Illustrated History of the Islamic World*, ed. F. Robinson (Cambridge, 1996), pp. 182, 184. For an interpretation of the *mihna* as a struggle between the caliphate and various camps of *ᶜulamāʾ* over the public sphere, see Nimrod Hurvitz, 'The *mihna* (inquisition) and the public sphere', in *The Public Sphere in Muslim Societies*, eds M. Hoexter, S. Eisenstadt and N. Levtzion (Albany, NY, 2002), pp. 17–30.
86. Cook, *Commanding Right*, p. 112.
87. Māwardī, *al-Aḥkām al-sulṭāniyya*, p. 240.
88. Ibid. p. 252. Cf. Cook, *Commanding Right*, p. 480; Klein, 'Between public and private', pp. 44–5.
89. Ibn ᶜAbbād, *Rasāʾil*, p. 40.
90. Abū l-Qāsim al-Ḥusayn b. ᶜAlī al-Wazīr al-Maghribī, *Kitāb fī l-siyāsa*, ed. F. ᶜA. Aḥmad (Alexandria, n.d.), p. 53. On al-Maghribī, cf. *EI2*, s.v. 'al-Maghribī, Banū', V, pp. 1210–12 (P. Smoor).
91. Juvaynī, *ᶜAtabat al-kataba*, p. 25.
92. Muḥammad b. ᶜAbd al-Khāliq Mayhanī (*fl.* 575/1180), *Dastūr-i dabīrī*, ed. A. S. Erzi (Ankara, 1962), p. 114.
93. Waṭwāt, *Rasāʾil*, p. 81.
94. This is also noted by Richard Wittmann, 'The *muḥtasib* in Seljuq times: insights from four chancery manuals', *Harvard Middle Eastern and Islamic Review* 7 (2006), p. 121. Wittmann does not see this characteristic of Waṭwāṭ's letter as part of a larger development in the office, but rather, as a 'puzzling' idiosyncrasy of *ḥisba* under the Khwarazmshahs.
95. In 6th/12th-century Baghdad, the police of morals entered into the houses to search for musical instruments and wine, and if they were found, the offenders were ignominiously paraded. See Ibn al-Jawzī, *Muntaẓam*, XVIII, p. 9.
96. ᶜImād al-Dīn, *al-Barq al-shāmī*, V, p. 137: 'He [the *muḥtasib*] must not proceed against those whose situation is concealed (*man iltabasa ᶜalayhi amruhu*), unless he has clear proofs (*dūna ẓuhūr amāratihā wa-wuḍūḥ bayyinātihā bi-firāsatihā*).'
97. Ibn al-Jawzī, *Muntaẓam*, XVI, pp. 37–8, XVIII, pp. 9, 84. Al-Māwardī condemns the shaving of beards in *tashhīr* but allows the shaving of heads. See Māwardī, *al-Aḥkām al-sulṭāniyya*, p. 239.
98. Ibn al-Jawzī, *Muntaẓam*, XVI, p. 166, XVII, p. 323, XVIII, p. 160.
99. Māwardī, *al-Aḥkām al-sulṭāniyya*, p. 239; Muḥammad b. Aḥmad al-Sarakhsī (d. c. 483/1090), *Mabsūṭ* (Cairo, 1324–31/1906–13), XVI, p. 145; Abū Bakr b. Masᶜūd al-Kāsānī (d. 587/1189), *Badāʾiᶜ al-ṣanāʾiᶜ* (Cairo, 1910), VI, p. 289.
100. Ibn al-Jawzī, *Muntaẓam*, XVIII, p. 84.
101. Ibid. XVIII, p. 159.
102. Cook, *Commanding Right*, p. 125, note 85 refers to Ibn Rajab; *al-Dhayl ᶜalā ṭabaqāt al-Ḥanābila*, ed. Fiqī (Cairo, 1952–3), II, pp. 121, 213, 258, 261, 262, for Ḥanbalite *muḥtasib*s in Baghdad in the last decades of the caliphate, who included Ibn al-Jawzī's son and three of his grandsons. See also Angelika Hartmann, *An-Nāṣir li-Dīn Allāh (1180–1225): Politik, Religion, Kultur in der späten ᶜAbbāsidenzeit* (Berlin, 1975), pp. 190–2, 290. There had been a tradition of Ḥanbalī activism in Baghdad since the 4th/10th century, and Ḥanbalīs increasingly aligned themselves with the caliphate in the last decades of its existence. See Cook, *Commanding Right*, pp. 121–8.

103. Ibid. p. 127. On Ibn al-Jawzī's career as 'inquisitor' of Baghdad, see also Angelika Hartmann, 'Les ambivalences d'un sermonnaire ḥanbalite: Ibn al-Ǧawzī (m. en 597/1201), sa carrière et son ouvrage autographe, le *Kitāb al-Ḫawātīm*', *AI* 22 (1986), pp. 51–115. Hartmann speaks of 'plusieurs autodafés et razzias' that Ibn al-Jawzī and the vizier Ibn Yūnus would have staged. See ibid. p. 67.
104. Ibn Rajab, *Dhayl*, I, pp. 425–6, quoted in *EI2*, s.v. 'Ibn al-Djawzī' (H. Laoust).
105. See Hartmann, 'Les ambivalences d'sermonnaire ḥanbalite', pp. 62–70, for a discussion of the unfolding of events in the conflict between the members of the al-Jawzī and al-Jīlī families.
106. Ibn al-Jawzī, *Muntaẓam*, XVIII, p. 196.
107. Dominique Sourdel and Janine Sourdel-Thomine, *La civilisation de l'Islam classique* (Paris, 1968), p. 253.
108. Ibn al-Athīr, *Tawaṣṣul al-mulūk*, fol. 95b:4–5.
109. Abū Ḥāmid al-Ghazālī, *Kīmiyā-yi saᶜādat* (Tehran, 1333/1914 or 5), pp. 471–503.
110. Māwardī, *al-Aḥkām al-sulṭāniyya*, p. 253.
111. Cook, *Commanding Right*, pp. 139, 480. As Cook notes, however, Ibn al-Jawzī injects *ḥisba* with a more 'state-friendly tendency'.
112. Ghazālī, *Iḥyā*ᵓ *ᶜulūm al-dīn*, trans. Buckley, *Book of the Islamic Market Inspector*, p. 157. Cf. Klein, 'Public and private', p. 48; Cook, *Commanding Right*, p. 481.
113. The opposite development appears to have taken place in Shiᶜi discussions of *al-amr bi-l-maᶜrūf*, where one sees moves toward a less activist interpretation from Buyid to 'post-Ṭūsian' Seljuq times. See Robert Gleave's contribution to this volume (Chapter 11).
114. Eli Alshech, '"Do not enter houses other than your own": the evolution of the notion of a private domestic sphere in early Sunnī Islamic thought', *Islamic Law and Society* 11, 3 (2004), pp. 291–332.
115. Ibid. p. 303. Witnesses for this early position include Ibn Mājishūn (Mālikī, d. 214/829) and Saḥnūn (Mālikī, d. 240/853). Alshech admits, however, that the position of the early Ḥanafīs and Shāfiᶜīs is less easy to reconstruct. See ibid. pp. 298–9.
116. Ibid. pp. 313–4.
117. Alshech cites a number of witnesses for the 'broad definition'. For the Ḥanbalīs: Abū Yaᶜlā b. al-Farrāᵓ (d. 458/1066), Ibn Qudāma (d. 620/1223); for the Shāfiᶜīs: al-Shayzarī (d. 589/1193); and for the Ḥanafīs: ᶜAbd Allāh b. Aḥmad al-Nasafī (d. 710/1310). Māwardī, *al-Aḥkām al-sulṭāniyya*, p. 253, seems to hold a middle position. He states that while it is not necessary for the *muḥtasib* to force people to completely cover up their roofs he must make sure that they do not look onto their neighbours (*lā yulzimu man ᶜalā bināᵓuhu an yastura saṭḥahu wa-innamā yulzimu an lā yushrifa ᶜalā ghayrihi*).
118. As Michael Cook points out, Ḥanafī *fiqh* did not develop much of a tradition of thinking about the nature, and the limits, of *al-amr bi-l-maᶜruf wa-l-nahy ᶜan al-munkar*. See Cook, *Commanding Right*, pp. 309–10. The lines of development proposed here, therefore, must be regarded as merely tentative.
119. Ibid. p. 309, note 14. However, as late an authority as al-Kāsānī (d. 587/1189) agreed with this interventionist interpretation of *ḥisba*. See ibid. p. 309.
120. ᶜUmar b. ᶜAbd al-Azīz Ibn Māza al-Bukhārī al-Ṣadr al-Shahīd, *Sharḥ Adab al-qāḍī li-l-Khaṣṣāf* (Baghdad, 1977), II, pp. 341–2, quoted in Alshech, 'Do not enter houses', p. 299, note 21.
121. On the close personal relationship of the Seljuq sultans with the *ᶜulamāᵓ*, see D. G. Tor's contribution to this volume (Chapter 3).

122. See ᶜUmar Riḍā Kaḥḥāla, *Muᶜjam al-muᵓallafīn* (Beirut, 1414/1993), II, p. 562. Ibn Māza is credited by Madelung with teaching a legal doctrine that sought to minimise differences between the Shāfiᶜīs and Ḥanafīs, thus preserving the unity of the *umma*. See Wilferd Madelung, 'The spread of Māturīdism and the Turks', in *Actas do IV Congresso des Estudos Árabes e Islâmicos, Coimbra-Lisboa 1968* (Leiden, 1971), p. 125, note 39. This may also have facilitated his proximity to temporal power. Sanjar continued the early Seljuq sultans' attachment to the Ḥanafī *madhhab*, which included taking Ḥanafī *fuqahāᵓ* with him into battle. Alp Arslān, when giving battle to the Byzantines, was accompanied by the *faqīh* Abū Naṣr Muḥammad b. ᶜAbd al-Malik al-Bukhārī al-Ḥanafī. See Safi, *Politics of Knowledge*, p. 94. Under Malikshāh, the Ḥanafī scholar Abū l-Muẓaffar al-Mushaṭṭab b. Muḥammad b. Usāma (d. 486/1093) from Farghāna used to accompany the army. See Madelung, 'Spread of Māturidism and the Turks', p. 143.
123. Ibn Māza, *Sharḥ Adab al-qāḍī*, III, p. 69. This is echoed by al-Marghinānī, *Hidāya* (Beirut, 1990), III, pp. 280–1, who states that people must have a place in which they can seclude themselves (*mawḍiᶜ al-khalwa*). Cf. Alshech, 'Do not enter houses', p. 318.
124. Ibid. p. 306, note 46.
125. Alshech, 'Out of sight', pp. 268–9.
126. According to Ann K. S. Lambton, this was brought about particularly through Niẓām al-Mulk's restructuring of *iqṭāᶜ*, merging military and administrative fiefs into one. See Lambton, 'Reflections on the *Iqṭāᶜ*', in *Arabic and Islamic Studies in Honor of Hamilton A. R. Gibb*, ed. G. Makdisi (Leiden, 1965), pp. 369, 373.
127. On the concept of 'go-betweens', cf. Jürgen Paul, *Herrscher, Gemeinwesen, Vermittler: Ostiran und Transoxanien in vormongolischer Zeit* (Stuttgart, 1996), pp. 4, 316. Paul mentions the office of *raᵓīs* as a prime example of this and refers to the *muḥtasib* only in passing. A good instance of a *muḥtasib* fulfilling this function is found in the 22nd *maqāma* of Ḥamīd al-Dīn Abū Bakr ᶜUmar b. Maḥmūd al-Balkhī, *Maqāmāt-i Ḥamīdī*, ed. ᶜAlī Akbar Abarqūᵓī (Isfahan, 1339/1960), 200, where the hero of the story, set in Balkh, is unjustly imprisoned in the 'prison of the *shiḥna*'; his friends among the local populace successfully intervene with the city's *muḥtasib* in order to procure his release.
128. ᶜIzz al-Dīn Ibn al-Athīr, *al-Kāmil fī l-tārīkh*, ed. Tornberg (Beirut, 1968), s.a. 448.
129. Sarakhsī, *Mabsūṭ*, IX, p. 85, XVI, p. 126.

CHAPTER

10

AN EMBLEMATIC FAMILY OF SELJUQ IRAN: THE KHUJANDĪS OF ISFAHAN

*David Durand-Guédy**

The Khujandīs, a family of Shāfiʿī *ʿulamāʾ* (religious scholars) brought to Isfahan by Niẓām al-Mulk, were major actors in that city during the Seljuq period and up to the Mongol invasion. From the end of the 5th/11th century they headed the local Niẓāmiyya madrasa, and they were also hereditary holders of the city's main local office, the *riyāsa*. The duration of their influence, the extent of their network and their capacity for political action were arguably unequalled in Seljuq-controlled territory. As the leading family in the greatest city of western – soon of all – Iran, they appear frequently in the sources on the period. However, and this is fairly typical of the lack of research on urban societies in western Iran in the two crucial centuries previous to the Mongol invasion, they have been largely overlooked in Western historiography (in comparison with Khurasan or the Arab Near East). The studies devoted to them to date are incomplete and inaccurate.[1] None take into consideration the documents in the *inshāʾ* compilation *al-Mukhtārāt min al-rasāʾil*, which contains forty letters written by or for the Khujandīs, even though the opportunity of combining historiographical sources with documents tantamount to an archive is exceptional and, in the current state of our corpus, unavailable for any other family of pre-Mongol Iran.[2] The main problem, however, is that these studies treat the Khujandīs in isolation

---

* This chapter brings together and supplements some of the analyses in the present author's *Iranian Elites and Turkish Rulers: a History of Iṣfahān in the Saljūq Period* (London–New York, 2010). It has been discussed in the seminar 'The urban/local elite in pre-modern Middle Eastern societies' which Dr Kazuo Morimoto and I organised at the University of Tokyo in 2009. I am very grateful to Dr Morimoto for his valuable comments on my final draft. Naturally all remaining errors are mine.

from their context, thus depriving themselves of any way to explain either their power or their rise and fall. The aim of this chapter is not to make a prosopographical reconstruction or a chronological presentation, but to provide a general overview of how the history of the Khujandīs is emblematic of developments in Iranian society under Seljuq rule, whether in relation to Iran's cultural identity, the relationship between the Iranian elites and the Turkish lords, the increasing militarisation of society or the intensification of so-called religious struggles.[3]

EASTERN IRAN, WESTERN IRAN

The Khujandīs were not an indigenous Isfahani family. Their name (i.e. here their *nisba*) refers to a city in Transoxiana, some 250km west of Samarqand, in the heart of what was then the Qarakhanid dominions. The founder of the line, however, Abū Bakr Muḥammad b. Thābit al-Khujandī, is first seen in Merv, which was then the capital of the Seljuq Chaghrï Beg and Alp Arslān. The vizier Niẓām al-Mulk had apparently been impressed by his preaching and his religious stance and, at the end of the years 450/1058–67, he summoned him to the new capital, Isfahan, and entrusted him with the direction of the Shāfiʿī madrasa he had founded there.[4] That a ruler would install a foreign elite in a new local context is not in itself novel. Looking just at the Seljuq period, the settlement of the Banū Badīʿ (an Isfahani family) in Aleppo by the emir Āq-Sonqur, or that of the Burhānīs (from Merv) in Bukhara by Sanjar are further examples of how new rulers sought to strengthen their local influence by promoting elites to whom they felt closer, and whom they therefore thought more likely to defend their interests. Also in the 6th/12th century, the Turkish and Kurdish rulers of Damascus promoted the settlement of Iranian and Arab elites to tighten their grip over local society.[5] In Isfahan, however, the place taken by foreign elites was perhaps more visible than elsewhere. The appointment of Khujandī is emblematic of an often overlooked aspect of early Seljuq rule: the monopolisation of local and imperial offices by the Khurasanis. Immediately after the conquest of Isfahan, the office of *qāḍī* (judge) had been given to the Khaṭībīs, a Ḥanafī family from Bukhara; the office of *ʿamīd* (civil governor) was first held by a secretary of Nishapur, and then by Niẓām al-Mulk's own son; and during Niẓām al-Mulk's long vizierate, the heads of the divans all came from Khurasan.[6] In founding various well-endowed institutions, the most important of which was the madrasa, Niẓām al-Mulk sought to bypass old local solidarities and establish himself as the main notable of Isfahan. The promotion of Abū Bakr Muḥammad I al-Khujandī was not so much due to his experience (i.e. the familiarity Khurasani *faqīh*s, or legal scholars, had with this kind of institution) as his ideology (the vizier and he shared a sense of regional solidarity and a shared history as well as an identical conception of the true religion) and politics (as the Khujandīs had no connections of their own in Isfahan, their loyalty was guaranteed). It is a historical irony that the Khujandī family, who would come to symbolise the power of local elites in the face of the Turks, owed their fortune to an attempt to ensure that local elites were under control.

In Isfahan the simultaneous deaths of the powerful vizier Niẓām al-Mulk and the sultan Malikshāh, in 485/1092, created a power vacuum and unleashed long-restrained tensions. For fifteen years, civil war pitted the followers of the Ismaʿili *dāʿī* Aḥmad Ibn ʿAṭṭāsh (d. 500/1107) against the families who had benefited from Seljuq rule and desired its restoration. The ferocity of the struggle, unparalleled in any other Iranian city, was directly proportional to the intensity of the Turko-Khurasani rulers' efforts to reshape local society in the previous decades. The Khujandī family played the leading role in resisting the Ismaʿilis. The killing of their patron Niẓām al-Mulk and the succession struggle with which the Turks were occupied left the field open for them. The sources emphasise the action of the *qāḍī* ʿUbayd Allāh al-Khaṭībī (d. 502/1108). However, given that the Ḥanafī community was but a small minority in 5th/11th-century Isfahan, the *qāḍī* could not aspire to command a popular movement. By contrast, the Khujandīs, who had become Isfahan's leading family after the deaths of Niẓām al-Mulk and his most capable son Muʾayyid al-Mulk (d. 494/1101), had the ability to mobilise large numbers and did not hesitate to do so. The key figure was Abū l-Qāsim Masʿūd al-Khujandī: he it was who in 492/1099 rallied what I have termed the 'pro-Seljuq networks' behind Muḥammad b. Malikshāh in his bid for the sultanate; he it was who in 494/1101 mobilised the urban militias to massacre the Ismaʿilis inside the city walls; he, too, in 500/1107, along with the *qāḍī* ʿUbayd Allāh al-Khaṭībī, orchestrated the downfall of the vizier Saʿd al-Mulk so that no negotiated settlement with Ibn ʿAṭṭāsh could take place. Such involvement had a price, and the brother of Abū l-Qāsim, Abū Muẓaffar, paid for it with his life in 496/1102–3 when he was killed in Rayy.[7]

The Khujandīs were not the only Khurasani family to have settled in Isfahan; however, they were the one whose fortune was the most enduring. Niẓām al-Mulk's family moved back to Khurasan, the Khaṭībīs lost their influence at the beginning of the 6th/12th century, and the Ṣāʿids (a family from Bukhara who replaced the Khaṭībīs as *qāḍī*s), only became major actors in Isfahan towards the end of the Seljuq rule. The Khujandīs on the other hand played the leading role for over a century, and remained important actors up to the Mongol onslaught. The price of this durability was integration into local society and loss of the family's Khurasani character. The turning-point in this evolution was the civil war of 485–500/1092–1107. The Khujandīs then became the champions of all those who rejected Ismaʿili rule: the 'Khurasanis', of course, but also, in far greater number, native Isfahanis of all social backgrounds. Their ample financial means enabled them to help those in need; their determination in fighting Ibn ᶜAṭṭāsh convinced the population that they were not going to turn tail; and their victories (especially the massacre of 494/1101) proved that a military solution was possible. As is often the case, in Iran as elsewhere, a war following a revolution accelerated the pace of social change. During these fifteen years, the Khujandīs had the opportunity to render services, and thus to build up to their advantage (and not to Niẓām al-Mulk's) loyalties within all layers of local society. Their bitter resistance, and the price they paid for it, also earned them the local legitimacy and prestige that they had previously lacked. Before 485/1092, the Khujandīs were only one element in Niẓām al-Mulk's network and were clearly identified as Khurasanis (the elder son of Abū Bakr Muḥammad I was born in Khurasan, and so perhaps were his brothers). After 500/1107, they had become Isfahanis. Thanks to the civil war, they became 'naturalized', to quote Cahen.[8] The change is particularly clear in the light of what happened immediately after the victorious assault against Ibn ᶜAṭṭāsh's stronghold and his ignominious death. ᶜUbayd Allāh al-Khaṭībī, the Ḥanafī *qāḍī*, then launched a witch-hunt against the secretaries and the notables from western Iran on the pretext that they did not qualify for serving the Seljuqs (the move was conveniently helped by the 'discovery' of Niẓām al-Mulk's political testament). According to Anūshirwān b. Khālid's very detailed account of this period, the Khujandīs stayed out of this.[9] The reason, I believe, is that Khaṭībī, who represented a *madhhab* (school of law) that was a very small minority in Isfahan, had everything to gain by forcing the sultan's hand and overturning the existing balance of power. The Khujandīs, by contrast, were already in a pre-eminent position and had everything to lose by reopening the Khurasani/non-Khurasani divide from which they had initially benefited but which now would undermine their local leadership.[10]

The Khujandīs' abandonment of their Khurasani identity is manifest by the 6th/12th century. Before 500/1107, the only persons explicitly linked to the Khujandīs were all Khurasanis (Niẓām al-Mulk, Khaṭībī, Siminjānī). In the next century, the documents of the *Mukhtārāt* show that they had built up a vast network including members of the old Isfahani elite: the Kūshidhis (whose ancestors were Zoroastrian priests, or *mobed*s), the Māshādhas, the Nājiyyas (who took their name from an Arab clan that had gained fame in the early years of Islam) and the family of ᶜImād al-Dīn al-Iṣfahānī. Nothing in their letters or in their many poems betrays any particular attachment to Khurasan. On the contrary, they made use of western Iranian points of reference, such as Ṣāḥib Ibn ᶜAbbād, the great Buyid vizier of Isfahani origin (for example, in a letter written by ᶜUbayd Allāh al-Khujandī: 'By God, I will never be able to succeed by coming after the vizier Ibn ᶜAbbād b. ᶜAbbās').[11] Outside Isfahan, the

Khujandīs' network was deliberately centred in the west. Its main points were in Rayy (where several of Abū Bakr Muḥammad I's pupils lived, including the *raʾīs* – see Table 10.1), Hamadan (the capital of the Seljuqs of Iraq from the years 520/1126–36 onward), Mosul (where their friend Jamāl al-Dīn al-Iṣfahānī served as the powerful vizier of the Zangids) and last but not least Baghdad (the seat of the caliphate, with which they had maintained close links since al-Mustarshid). The careers of Abū Bakr Muḥammad I's pupils confirm this western pattern (see Table 10.1). During the same period, Niẓām al-Mulk's family had ceased to play a significant role in Isfahan, and at the end of the 6th/12th century they had lost their influence to such an extent that the *raʾīs* Muḥammad IV al-Khujandī even confirmed a judgement against the great grandson of Niẓām (the latter was opposed to a group of women for the revenues of a *waqf* (endowment) established for the vizier's tomb).[12] To the question of whether the Seljuq conquest helped to reunite the different parts of the Iranian territory, the career of the Khujandīs gives a clearly negative answer. The various Iranian lands were briefly unified by reason of their conquest by the Seljuqs but this did not, in the longer term, bridge the deep division embodied by the great central deserts.

KNOWLEDGE AND POWER

The Khujandīs provide a textbook example of an alliance between knowledge and power. Their links with the rulers of the Seljuq state were long-standing and constant. Abū Bakr Muḥammad I was given an institutional position (as head of the madrasa) by Niẓām al-Mulk. His son Abū l-Qāsim Masʿūd, alias *malik al-ʿulamāʾ*, probably gained the *riyāsat al-balad*, a position which formalised his status as intermediary between the populace and the prince (the holder of this position was the *raʾīs*).[13] Abū l-Qāsim Masʿūd's close alliance with Sultan Muḥammad b. Malikshāh strengthened the family's hold in Isfahan. ʿAbd al-Laṭīf I was confirmed as *raʾīs* on his brother's death, which probably occurred during the reign of Maḥmūd (511–25/1118–31). Meanwhile, many of Abū Bakr Muḥammad I's students were appointed to important positions: among his fifteen known students, there were six *qāḍī*s, one of whom was also tutor to the caliph's children, and one *raʾīs* (see Table 10.1).[14] In the following generation, Abū Bakr Muḥammad II was closely linked to Sultan Masʿūd (d. 547/1152). He preached in the palace mosque (*jāmiʿ al-qaṣr*) in Baghdad,[15] and his fellow-countryman ʿImād al-Dīn al-Iṣfahānī reports that Masʿūd 'showed him great familiarity, was pleased with him, shared his food and drink with him, and due to his liking for him, treated him with kindness'.[16] In 551/1156–7, he was solicited by Sultan Muḥammad b. Maḥmūd (d. 554/1159) to help him persuade the caliph to accept the peaceful restoration of Seljuq authority in Baghdad;[17] two years earlier, his brother Maḥmūd

Table 10.1 Origin and career of the students of Abū Bakr Muḥammad I Khujandī

Name	Origin	Career	Source
ᶜAbd al-Karīm b. ᶜAbd al-Razzāq al-Ḥasanābādī (d. 522/1128)	Isfahan	*Faqīh* (legal scholar)	Subkī, *Ṭabaqāt*, VII, p. 178
Abū al-ᶜAbbās b. al-Ruṭabī (460–526/1068–1132)	Baghdad	*Qāḍī*, *muḥtasib* in Baghdad; tutor to the caliph's children	Subkī, *Ṭabaqāt*, VI, p. 19 and IV, p. 124; Ibn Kathīr, *Bidāya*, ed. ᶜA. al-Turkī (n.p., 1997), s.a. 527, XVI, p. 296
Abū ᶜAlī al-Iṣfahānī, al-Ḥasan b. Salmān (d. 525/1131)	Isfahan (?)	*Qāḍī* of Khūzistān; head of the Baghdad Niẓāmiyya	Subkī, *Ṭabaqāt*, VII, p. 62 and IV, p. 124
Abū Jaᶜfar b. al-Mashshāt (d. 498/1004–9)	Rayy	Taught *fiqh* in Rayy	Ibn al-Athīr, *Kāmil*, s.a. 498, X, p. 393
Abū Jaᶜfar Muḥammad al-Ṭabarī	Āmul	Deputy of the *qāḍī* in Āmul	Samᶜānī, *Taḥbir*, ed. al-Manṣūr (Beirut, 1418/1997), II, p. 66
Abū l-Qāsim ᶜAbd Allāh b. al-Muẓaffar al-Ṣāᶜighī	Rayy	*Qāḍī* of Rayy	Silafī, *Muᶜjam al-safar*, ed. al-Bārūdī (repr. Beirut, 1414/1993), p. 127, note 221
Abū l-Qāsim ᶜAbd al-Wāḥid b. Aḥmad al-Baṣrī (b. 458/1065–6)	?	*Qāḍī* of Nahr al-Dayr	Silafī, *Safar*, 185, note 302
Abū l-Qāsim al-Zāhid, ᶜAbd al-Jabbār b. Aḥmad b. Yusūf al-Rāzī (d. 497/1103–4)	Rayy	Unknown, died fighting the Franks	Subkī, *Ṭabaqāt*, V, p. 97
Abū l-Maᶜālī Ḥasan b. Muḥammad, Fakhr al-Dīn al-Warkānī (d. 559/1163–4)	Isfahan	*Mudarris* (professor of law at a madrasa) of the Isfahan Niẓāmiyya	Subkī, *Ṭabaqāt*, VII, p. 66
Abū Manṣūr Ibn Māshādha, Maḥmūd b. Aḥmad (d. 536/1141)	Isfahan	*ᶜĀlim* (specialist of Islamic law)	Subkī, *Ṭabaqāt*, VII, p. 285
Abū Saᶜd al-Baladī, al-Kāfī al-Karkhī, Sulaymān b. Muḥammad b. Ḥusayn b. Muḥammad (c. 460/1067–8 to 532/1138)	Baghdad	*Qāḍī* of al-Karkh in Baghdad	Subkī, *Ṭabaqāt*, VII, p. 95

Table 10.1 continued

Name	Origin	Career	Source
Abū Saᶜd al-Rāzī, ᶜAbd al-Raḥmān b. ᶜAbd Allāh b. ᶜAbd al-Raḥman al-Ḥaṣīrī (461/1068–9 to 546/1152)	Rayy	*Faqīh* in Rayy	Samᶜānī, *Taḥbīr*, I, 166; Subkī, *Ṭabaqāt*, VII, p. 150
Abū Saᶜd al-Karajī (c. 460/1067–8 to 538/1144)	Karaj	*Qāḍī* of Karaj	Samᶜānī, *Taḥbīr*, I, p. 123
Abū Ṭālib al-Rāzī, ᶜAbd al-Karīm b. ᶜAlī b. Abī Ṭālib (d. 522/1128)	Rayy (?)	Unknown, prob. in Fārs	Subkī, *Ṭabaqāt*, VII, p. 179
Muḥammad b. ᶜAbd al-Karīm b. Aḥmad, Ibn Wazzān (d. c. 525/1130–1)	Rayy	*Ra'īs* of Rayy	Subkī, *Ṭabaqāt*, VI, pp. 127–8

had been sent as ambassador to the court of the Seljuqs of Kirman to arrange a matrimonial alliance between the two branches of the family.[18]

In such conditions, one may wonder to what extent the Khujandīs were still considered to be *faqīh*s. There is no doubt that Abū Bakr Muḥammad I, the founder of the Isfahani branch of the family, was a genuine scholar, if not the greatest of his time (the Shāfiᶜī school of Iran was then at its zenith, with such illustrious figures as Abū Isḥāq al-Shīrāzī, Abū Ḥāmid al-Ghazālī and Abū l-Maᶜālī al-Juwaynī). Educated by the great professors of Khurasan, Abū Bakr Muḥammad I was not only the member of the Khujandī family who had most students (listed in Table 10.1), but also the only one whom we know for sure wrote at least two works of *fiqh* (Muslim jurisprudence).[19] The education of the later generations was by no means as expansive as that of the family's founder. As far as we know, it was confined to studying *fiqh* with their father and spending time with some Isfahani and Baghdadi traditionists. They do not seem to have written any books, and they soon delegated some of their teaching duties in the madrasa in order to concentrate on the *riyāsa* of Isfahan.[20] This retrenchment became more pronounced over time (the last Khujandī known to have had a pupil was ᶜAbd al-Laṭīf II)[21] and must be seen in the context of the ever younger age at which the Khujandīs found themselves loaded with political responsibilities. Abū Bakr Muḥammad II died before the age of fifty.[22] ᶜAbd al-Laṭīf II succeeded his father when seventeen years old, 'before having attained strength of years'.[23] His son Muḥammad IV died before having reached 'the age to transmit *ḥadīth* (*sinn al-riwāya*)'.[24] The great grandson of Muḥammad IV, Shihāb al-Dīn, was probably a child when his father's death propelled him to the post of *ra'īs* (he is

Table 10.2 Main phases of the history of the Khujandīs

Generation (G) of Khujandī	
G1 the settlement	Before 460/1067: nomination of Abū Bakr Muḥammad I at the head of the Niẓāmiyya madrasa
G2 the 'naturalisation'	489/1096: Abū l-Qāsim Masᶜūd (probably) becomes *raᵓīs* 492/1099: the Khujandīs form an alliance with Muḥammad b. Malik-Shāh against Sultan Barkyāruq 494/1101: Abū l-Qāsim Masᶜūd organises the massacre of the Ismaᶜilis 500/1107: Abū l-Qāsim Masᶜūd, allied with the *qāḍī*, brings about the downfall of the vizier Saᶜd al-Mulk, and hastens the reconquest of Shāhdiz fortress
G3 the emancipation from the Seljuqs	527/1133: Abū Bakr Muḥammad II causes the downfall of vizier Darguzīnī 542/1147–8: Abū Bakr Muḥammad II allies with rebel emir Boz-Aba; *fitna*; exile of the Khujandīs who are later reinstalled by the sultan 551/1156–7: Abū Bakr Muḥammad II refuses to help the Seljuqs during the siege of Baghdad
G4 the climax of the Khujandīs' power	560/1164–5: *fitna* c. 575/1179: ᶜAbd al-Laṭīf I II Khujandī kept prisoner by the Atabeg Pahlawān
G5 the marginalisation	From 581/1186: *fitna*s become endemic 583/1187: Muḥammad IV allies with Ṭoghrïl b. Arslān; he is given the position of *qāḍī* 588/1192: exile of Muḥammad IV to Bagdad c. 590/1194: the *riyāsa* of Iṣfahān is given to the Ṣāᶜid family 592/1196: execution of Muḥammad IV
G6–8 the attempts at a comeback	618/1221–2: ᶜUmar allies with the Khwārazmian prince Ghūr-Sanjī and plunders the Ḥanafī quarters 621/1224 to c. 630/1232–3: truce with the Ḥanafīs 633/1235–6: Shihāb al-Dīn probably allies with the Mongols; destruction of the Khujandī family in Iṣfahān

described as a 'lion cub' in the elegy composed for the occasion by Kamāl al-Dīn Ismāᶜīl).[25] This trend towards an ever lower age can be compared to that in the Seljuq family itself, who were being drawn on to the political stage ever earlier as the succession crisis became aggravated.

In the sources, even those favourable to the Khujandīs, it is their power more than their learning that is emphasised. Of Abū Bakr Muḥammad II, *raᵓīs* of Isfahan under the sultans Masᶜūd and Muḥammad b. Maḥmūd, Ibn al-Jawzī says that 'he had the highest rank with the sultans (*taqaddama ᶜinda l-salāṭīn*)' and that he 'inspired respect mixed with fear (*mahīb*)'.[26] Samᶜānī, who had spent much time in his company, explicitly says that 'he was more like the viziers than the *ᶜulamā* (*kāna bi l-wuzarāʾ ashbaha min al-ᶜulamāʾ*)'.[27] In Samᶜānī's writing, this was no compliment.[28] Speaking of ᶜAbd al-Laṭīf II, Subkī says nothing about his qualities as a *faqīh* but immediately notes that 'he managed the *riyāsa* like his ancestors and had great power over the sultans (*kānat lahu al-makāna ᶜinda l-salāṭīn*)'.[29] Ibn Jubayr, who met him in Medina, was struck by his 'royal bearing' (*mulūkiyya*).[30] Muḥammad IV, for his part, is described by Asnawī as a 'great *raʾīs* versed in the arts and in government (*arīf fī l-faḍl wa l-riʾāsa*)'.[31] Significantly, the Khujandīs excelled at delivering sermons, an activity that could bring them close to the rulers (and could also help them strengthen their bonds with the people of Isfahan). According to Ibn al-Athīr, Abū l-Muẓaffar was assassinated as he came down from the *minbar*, having just completed his sermon.[32] The sermons of Abū Muḥammad II and his son ᶜAbd al-Laṭīf II impressed those who attended them, whether noted preachers such as Ibn al-Jawzī, foreign pilgrims such as Ibn Jubayr or local rulers such as the Atabeg Pahlawān (d. 581/1186).[33] It is clear from the various descriptions that the taste the Khujandīs had for poetry (and their talent at composing it) served them well for their sermons.

Was this evolution inevitable? Many Shāfiᶜī *ᶜulamāʾ* in Isfahan had no particular contact with the rulers, one such example being Abū l-Futūḥ al-ᶜIjlī (d. 600/1230) who devoted himself to a commentary on Ghazālī (the very *faqīh* who most clearly raised the question of links between the *ᶜulamāʾ* and the rulers, and in the end called for complete separation).[34] The Khujandīs' political destiny was decided in the second generation. Samᶜānī tells us that 'Abū Saᶜd Aḥmad [one of the four sons of Abū Bakr Muḥammad I] learned *fiqh* from his father and excelled therein, and collected and transmitted *ḥadīth*s'. He then adds: 'when his father died [in 483/1090–1], instruction in the madrasa was entrusted to another, and he then remained at home until his death'.[35] The only way of interpreting this last phrase is to suppose that Abū Saᶜd, Abū Bakr Muḥammad I's designated successor and probably his eldest son, was put aside in favour of Abū l-Qāsim Masᶜūd, whom we find at the head of the family over the following decades. What is certain is that two years later, the Seljuq state was a shadow of its former self, the Turks were fighting among themselves, and the Ismaᶜilis had free reign to take on the Khurasani networks in Isfahan. In a situation such as this, where the family's future was at stake, Abū Saᶜd Aḥmad's 'legitimacy' and scholarship lost importance. The political crisis that was sapping Seljuq power permitted, and indeed obliged, local elites to play an ever more important political role. The

Table 10.3 Genealogical tree of the Khujandī family

- Abū Bakr Muḥammad I b. Thābit (d. 483/1090–1)
  - Abū Saᶜd Aḥmad (443/1051–2 – 531/1137)
  - Abū l-Qāsim Masᶜūd (d. after 500/1107)
  - ᶜAbd al-Laṭīf I (Ṣadr al-Dīn) (d. 523/1128–9)
    - Abū Bakr Muḥammad II (Ṣadr al-Dīn) (d. 552/1157–8)
      - ᶜAbd al-Laṭīf II (Ṣadr al-Dīn) (535/1141 – 580/1184)
        - Muḥammad IV (Ṣadr al-Dīn) (d. 592/1196)
          - ᶜAbd al-Ṣamad
            - ᶜUmar (Ṣadr al-Dīn) (d. before 635/1237–8)
              - Shihāb al-Dīn
            - Ḥasan (ᶜImād al-Dīn)
            - Thābit Abū Muḥammad (ᶜAḍud al-Dīn) (d. 637/1239)
      - ᶜUbayd Allāh (Kamāl al-Islām) (d. after 581/1185–6)
    - Maḥmūd (Jamāl al-Dīn) (d. after 549/1157–8)
      - Masᶜūd (Jamāl al-Dīn)
      - Muḥammad III (Kamāl al-Islām)
        - Aḥmad (Kamāl al-Dīn)
  - Abū l-Muẓaffar (d. 496/1102–3)

Khujandīs, as heirs of the Isfahan Niẓāmiyya, were naturally led to take up the place of their late protector in their dealings with the central authorities.

FORCED COLLABORATION

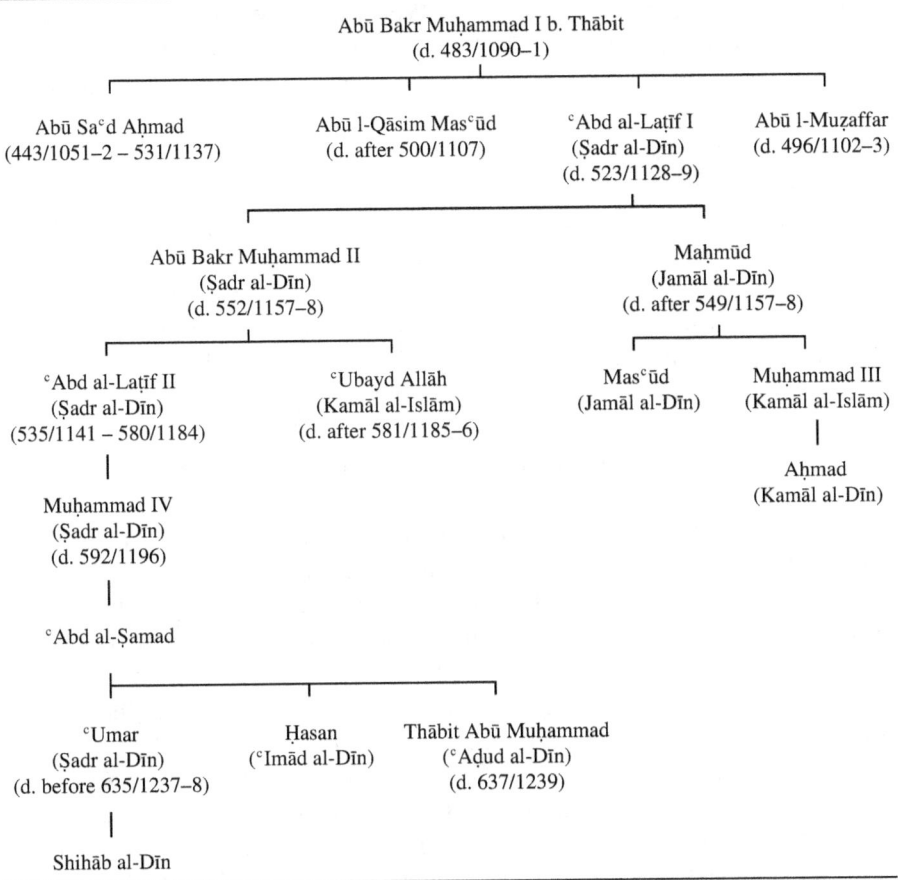

The basis of the Khujandīs' relationship with the Seljuq sultans was contractual: the former were guaranteed the preservation of the social status quo, the latter control of tax revenues. It could be expressed as follows: 'I recognise your role in the city by appointing you to the *riyāsa*, thereby making you my main interlocutor; in exchange for which you recognise my authority and you will ensure that the taxes are raised'. This type of relationship between local elites and the central authorities was classic in the Islamic East. It can be explained by the structural weakness of the pre-modern state (in the Weberian sense) in general, and of the Seljuq state in particular. Jürgen Paul speaks in this respect of the limited 'reach of the state'.[36] In other words, the state did not have the capacity to gain the manpower and funds it needed to survive without the collaboration of local elites. In the 6th/12th century, this 'reach' was even more reduced than usual. Not only had the succession crisis considerably reduced the authority of the sultans, but the context of endemic warfare had forced them (and their protectors the Atabegs of Ādharbaījān) to choose the more strategically located Hamadan over Isfahan as their capital. Since the latter remained the largest, and therefore richest, city of all western Iran (indeed, of all Iran after the ruin of Nishapur), it was essential to control it. As uncontested leaders of the majority *madhhab*, the Khujandīs were inevitable interlocutors for the Seljuqs, and indeed could not be got rid of as was shown by the events of 542–3/1147–8: in that year, the Khujandīs were exiled by the sultan for having opened the gates of Isfahan to a rebel emir. Barely a year later, they were pardoned, reinstated in their positions and invited to the court. 'So many kindnesses transformed Isfahan into a Paradise', wrote ᶜImād al-Dīn, who had been an enthusiastic witness to this restoration.[37]

At the same time that the Seljuqs were forced to accept the hereditary nature of Khujandī *riyāsa* (and thereby the limited nature of their own authority), they sought to undermine the bases of the Khujandī power the better to free themselves from it. 'It was their enmity towards the Shāfiᶜīs that united [the Turkish emirs] (*wa hum ᶜuṣbatun fīhim ᶜaṣabiyyatun ᶜalā l-shāfiᶜiyya*)', writes the Shāfiᶜī ᶜImād al-Dīn.[38] In concrete terms, the Seljuqs deliberately encouraged the development of a, hopefully loyal, Ḥanafī community by establishing richly endowed madrasas and making ever more open shows of support. This began in the reign of Muḥammad b. Malikshāh, when the power of the Khujandīs had become plain to all, and continued under the Seljuqs of Iraq (Muḥammad's successors) and the Atabegs of Ādharbaījān. These initiatives, which stand in contrast to the relative indifference of the first sultans to religious affairs, reveal the integration of the Turks into the Iranian political game. The Khujandīs reacted, of course, and in turn sought alliances that could counterbalance this increasing hostility. They thus developed direct relations with the caliphate, the source of superior authority as well as a temporal power. From the second generation on, we find Khujandīs teaching in the Baghdad Niẓāmiyya (starting with Abū Saᶜd Aḥmad),[39] but the relationship developed fully under the Seljuqs of Iraq (Kamāl al-Dīn Masᶜūd, in a letter to al-Muqtafī's divan, even speaks of the assistance his family provided to the Abbasids).[40] The alliance reached its high point in the years 580/1184–93, when the caliph al-Nāṣir first entrusted management of the Baghdad Niẓāmiyya's *waqf*s to Muḥammad IV al-Khujandī, and later offered him direct military assistance. In addition to the caliph, the Khujandīs also formed alliances with the Turks, although these were more conjectural and dependent on political developments. Thus, during the crisis that followed the death of Malikshāh, they backed Muḥammad against his brother Barkyāruq; in 527/1133, they backed Masᶜūd against his brother Ṭoghrïl; in 542/1147–8, Boz-Aba against Masᶜūd; and 556/1161, probably Saṭmāz against Eldigüz. They naturally paid the price for their involvement whenever Isfahan fell under the control of the rival prince (like Barkyāruq in 497/1104, Masᶜūd in 542/1147, Eldigüz in 556/1161).[41]

On one hand, therefore, the Seljuqs and the Khujandīs were obliged to compact with each other; on the other, each sought by all available means to gain their 'independence' from the other party. It is clear that these transverse alliances undermined the contract between the two parties, leading on occasion to farcical situations. Thus, in the years 580/1184–93, we see ᶜUbayd Allāh al-Khujandī asking the Atabeg Qïzïl Arslān (d. 587/1191) to send his soldiers to put down a peasant revolt that had shaken the environs of Isfahan, while simultaneously the Khujandīs supported Ṭoghrïl b. Arslān's efforts to emancipate himself from the Atabegs.[42] Unlike many members of the local elite, the Khujandīs never left Iran for the Arab world (like their friends Anūshirwān b. Khālid and ᶜImād al-Dīn al-Iṣfahānī),[43] nor yet did they retreat from politics to a more contemplative life. ᶜUbayd Allāh al-Khujandī reproaches the Atabeg Qïzïl Arslān with his lack of attention and presents himself as a Sufi: 'I do not know what can calm my grief. The vow of the Sufis is to bear injustice and accept difficult tasks out of loyalty'.[44] While it cannot be denied that Sufism made decisive advances in 6th/12th-century Iran, thanks to the particularly disturbed and depressing context, nothing in the conduct of ᶜUbayd Allāh or his relatives suggests that this phrase was anything other than a literary posture, and comparable as such to the attitude of the contemporary poet Jamāl al-Dīn al-Iṣfahānī, who sings the praises of ascetism but never actually goes so far as to become an ascetic himself. Despite their reverses, the Khujandīs never ceased to be what they had been since the beginning of the crisis of the Seljuq state: political leaders.

THE LOCAL INFLUENCE AND ITS LIMITS

The basis of the Khujandīs' power, the factor that allowed them play a political role in Seljuq Iran, was the local influence they enjoyed in Isfahan. This influence was first and foremost in the economic sphere. In Isfahan as elsewhere, we have very little knowledge of the sources of the local elites' wealth. Their income was mainly from landed property, as is indicated by the disproportionate number of disputes that concern land taxes in the requests written by Isfahani notables and preserved in *Mukhtārāt* (as against one single document mentioning long-distance trade). Similarly, one of the few pieces of information concerning the economic aspect of Ismaʿili activity in Isfahan concerns the taxes levied on 'the private holdings of the notables (*amlāk al-nās*) . . . so that the notables (*al-nās*) could no longer derive any income from their property'.[45] The dominance of the Khujandīs in landowning in Isfahan probably goes back to the time of Niẓām al-Mulk. The vizier was not shy of generously parcelling out lands (either as *iqṭāʿ* – temporary land grants – or as full property) in order to extend and reinforce his local network.[46] The Khujandīs, who were among the vizier's first clients in Isfahan, naturally stood to receive the most land (probably the proceeds of previous confiscations) in the very fertile valley of the Zāyanda-rūd. In addition, the Khujandīs controlled the income of the Niẓāmiyya madrasa's *waqf*s. The *waqf*s could in principle remain the property of an individual and his descendants, and it was clearly in order to enjoy that right of ownership that Niẓām al-Mulk had established them in most of the cities under Seljuq rule. But in the 6th/12th century, just as the Niẓāmiyya madrasa of Baghdad fell under the caliph's de facto control, that of Isfahan fell under Khujandī control. The details of this takeover are not given in the sources, but the key to it no doubt lies again in the period of civil war. The Ismaʿilis had seized the income of the *waqf*s funding the madrasa, which had then been recovered largely thanks to the Khujandīs. The official handing over of control of the madrasa to the family may therefore have been one of the results of the alliance between the Khujandīs and Muḥammad b. Malikshāh, once the latter had finally returned to his capital. (The diminishing interest of Niẓām al-Mulk's family in western Iran also helped their withdrawal from the Niẓāmiyya madrasas in Isfahan and Baghdad.)

While the wealth of the Khujandīs is never explicitly mentioned in the sources, it can be discerned through the aid that they were able to give to the population. The Khujandīs were clearly the principle patrons in the city.[47] Their action took multiple forms. These could include direct assistance for families in difficulty who requested 'the assistance of that lord's zeal and generosity'.[48] Jamāl al-Dīn Masʿūd al-Khujandī, probably the cousin of the *raʾīs* of Isfahan, is thus famous for having aided 'all the old women of the city (*ʿajāyiz-i shahr*)', apparently by providing them with cotton.[49] Their control of local institutions made them the arbitrators of their community. We see them in this capacity when Maḥmūd, brother of the *raʾīs* Abū Bakr Muḥammad II, restored the rights of a reader of the Qurʾān, which had been infringed by the heirs to a *waqf* from which he benefited.[50] But the Khujandīs were above all appealed to for intercession with the authorities. Many of the documents in *al-Mukhtārāt min al-rasāʾil* are requests imploring them to use their influence with the Isfahan tax administration to ensure the payment of pensions and, especially, to reduce the fiscal burden on lands.

The Khujandīs also used their wealth to finance cultural works from which they themselves benefited indirectly. After Isfahan lost its role as capital in the years 520–30/1126–35, the Khujandīs replaced the Seljuqs as the city's principle patrons of culture. In Seljuq Iran, poetry (especially in the form of the panegyric *qaṣīda*) was by far the mode in which the powerful preferred to be celebrated, and the Khujandīs, like other powerful men, were greatly praised by the poets. ᶜImād al-Dīn, in his *Kharīda*, preserves several Arabic panegyrics to the glory of the Khujandī family,[51] and Khāqānī and Ẓahīr al-Dīn Fāryābī frequented their court.[52] The Khujandīs were themselves poets of renown, and in fact it is as poets that ᶜImād al-Dīn and later ᶜAwfī and Shirwānī included them in their anthologies of poetry.[53] After Nishapur was laid waste, the library of the Niẓāmiyya madrasa in Isfahan was probably the greatest remaining in Iran (with the exception of those in the Ismaᶜili fortresses, which were inaccessible). ᶜImād al-Dīn al-Iṣfahānī speaks of it several times;[54] Warāwīnī possibly wrote part of his *Marzubān-nāma* there;[55] Jarbādhaqānī, the translator of *Taʾrīkh al-Yamīnī*, there discovered a precious commentary of the Qurʾān compiled under the aegis of the Saffarid ruler Khalaf b. Aḥmad and originating from Nishapur;[56] and Shihāb al-Dīn Suhrawardī, the philosopher of illumination, completed his education there between 577/1181–2 and 580/1184–5, no doubt familiarising himself with the thought of Avicenna.[57]

All these actions, in the social and cultural spheres, served to construct and maintain a vast network linked by these relationships of obligation which Mottahedeh has well described for the Buyid period. This network was the family's greatest asset. The *raʾīs* was its natural leader, but it must be noted that unlike the Seljuqs who tore themselves apart with fratricidal wars, the Khujandīs remained remarkably united. There is not the slightest trace in our sources of any tension inside the family (apart, perhaps, from the succession to Abū Bakr Muḥammad I). If from the time of ᶜAbd al-Laṭīf I the *riyāsa* was transmitted hereditarily from father to son that does not mean that the other members of the family were 'sidelined'. The letters in *Mukhtārāt* show that at the time of the powerful *raʾīs* ᶜAbd al-Laṭīf II, his brother ᶜUbayd Allāh and cousin Masᶜūd were among the main actors defending the family's interests (the former apparently as one of the principle architects of the alliance between the Khujandīs and the caliphate, and the latter managed as well as possible their turbulent relations with the Atabegs of Ādharbaījān). Basing himself on Mamluk cities, Lapidus concludes that 'where associational ties were strong in Muslim cities, they were apolitical'.[58] In the present case, it would appear to me that on the contrary, it was the strength of these same ties that made political action possible.

The Khujandīs' influence found itself limited by the existence of competing networks. While the phenomenon of rival *ᶜaṣabiyya*s (factions united by their *esprit de corps*) was a constant in the cities of the Muslim East, it took on a particular intensity in Isfahan: Ḥanbalīs vs Muᶜtazilīs in the Buyid period; Ismaᶜilis vs Khurasanis in the last third of the 5th/11th century. After the successful integration of the great Khurasani families into local society, a new cleavage divided Shāfiᶜīs from Ḥanafīs, with the latter enjoying the constant support of Turkish rulers (first the Seljuqs, then the Atabegs of Ādharbaījān, and then the Khwarazmshahs). For the 6th/12th century, Ibn al-Athīr no longer speaks of anything but the 'head of the Shāfiᶜīs' ('*raʾīs al-shāfiᶜiyya*').[59] No diploma of nomination for the Khujandīs has come down to us and it is not clear whether they had first gained the *riyāsat al-balad* or only the *riyāsat al-shāfiᶜiyya*. In any case, given the strong Shāfiᶜī majority in Isfahan,[60] it is plain that the Khujandīs represented the majority, but the nuance is important as it can be interpreted as a sign that their authority did not extend to the Ḥanafīs.[61] As the century progressed, the Ḥanafī community grew to the point of being able to mount a successful challenge to the Khujandīs' leadership. Thus when Ibn al-Athīr says that in 591/1195, the *raʾīs* Muḥammad IV was 'the leader of the city's population in its entirety (*ḥākim bi-Iṣfahān ᶜalā jamīᶜ ahlihā*)' and that 'the population hated' the Khwarazmshah's troops who were stationed in the city, it is a two-fold exaggeration, as on the one hand the Khujandīs' authority went no further than their own community, and the Ḥanafīs, led by the Ṣāᶜid family, were allies of the Khwarazmshah.[62] The *riyāsa* of Muḥammad IV proved the turning point for the family: he allied himself in turn with the sultan Ṭoghrïl b. Arslān, then the caliph al-Nāṣir, but twice lost his position in Isfahan, and was finally executed in 592/1196 by an emir in the service of the Abbasids. This execution is symptomatic of the new level of violence reached in western Iran after the end of the Seljuq dynasty (590/1194); it also reflects the shift in the local balance of power in favour of the Ḥanafīs.

The struggle between the Khujandīs and the Ṣāᶜids was reflected in polarisation of the urban space. Just as in the early 6th/12th century, with the construction of its four *īwāns*, the Friday mosque had been compartmentalised to allow the various *madhhab*s to pray in relative peace,[63] so too did the east of the city become a Ḥanafī zone, and the west Shāfiᶜī. The Khujandīs ruled from Dardasht, the Ṣāᶜids from Jūbāra. The two quarters were maybe physically separated, in line with the arrangements in other cities of the Muslim East in the pre-Mongol period (in 4th/10th-century Baghdad there were already walls separating Shiᶜa from Sunnis). We probably should not, therefore, imagine that tasks were divided between the *raʾīs* and the *qāḍī*: it is more likely that they were duplicated. Given the implacable nature of the Khujandī-Ṣāᶜid struggle, it is hard to imagine the Shāfiᶜīs having recourse to the Ḥanafī *qāḍī* to resolve their problems. The Khujandīs, who could take advantage of their special relationship with the caliph, maybe had the necessary authority to take charge, in their zone, of some of the functions delegated to the *qāḍī*.[64]

The growing tension spilled over into violent clashes. These clashes, termed *fitnas* in our sources, were made possible and indeed encouraged by the weakness and remoteness of the Seljuq sultan. The Khujandīs, and in the opposite camp the Ṣāᶜids, became military leaders, commanding not only their personal guard, but also battalions of supporters (and clients) armed for the occasion.[65] The first reference to an attack against the Khujandī positions in Isfahan dates to 542/1147–8. After the death of the Atabeg Pahlawān in 581/1186, internal strife became endemic, and the de facto submission of Jibāl to the far-away Khwarazmshahs could not put an end to it. Only the re-establishment of the Khwarazmshah state by Jalāl al-Dīn Mingburnu in western Iran in 621/1224, combined with the threat posed by the arrival of the Mongols, was reflected on the local stage by an – imposed – truce between the Khujandīs and their rivals the Ṣāᶜids. But for the Iranian elites, it was already too late. With or without the complicity of the Khujandīs (the question remains open since our main source, Ibn Abī l-Ḥadīd, speaks only of 'a group of Shāfiᶜī leaders'),[66] the Mongols captured the city in 633/1235–6 and massacred its population, bringing to naught the influence of both parties. The 'dynasty' founded by Abū Bakr Muḥammad I in Isfahan thus came to an abrupt end after a reign of some 175 years.

CONCLUSION

The Khujandīs of Isfahan are both atypical in the brilliance of their rise, and typical in their trajectory. They are emblematic of the Khurasani elites whom the new rulers installed in western Iran and who rapidly became integrated there thanks to the crisis of the years 485–500/1092–1107. They are also emblematic of the great influence that the urban elites had on the local political scene in the Seljuq period – an influence that was facilitated by the structural weakness of the Seljuq state and the distance that the Turks maintained from the cities. Thus, the same troubled situation that impelled ᶜImād al-Dīn al-Iṣfahānī to go into exile in the Arab world made the fortune of his friends the Khujandīs (as, in Sabzawar, it made the fortune of the family of *sayyids*). Finally, the Khujandīs are emblematic of the way that the religious elites succeeded in using their prestige to gain an institutional position, and then made use of the income provided by that position to create a vast network operating throughout the local society. In this sense, the Khujandīs proved themselves the best pupils of the man who had made their fortune, that master of networks Niẓām al-Mulk. Contemporary writers who longed for the Seljuq golden age, foremost among them ᶜImād al-Dīn al-Iṣfahānī, were not disappointed in them, and if they preferred not to remain at their side, they nevertheless celebrated their stance. At another level, the study of the rise and fall of this family of *ᶜulamāᵓ* confirms that in conflicts categorised as religious, there were not just doctrinal oppositions in play, but also concrete questions such as the relationship with power and control of wealth.

NOTES

1. In western studies the Khujandīs are mentioned by Ashtor and Cahen in their essential articles on the urban elites, but only marginally. See Eliyahu Ashtor, 'L'administration urbaine en Syrie médiévale', in *RSO* 31, 1–3 (1956), pp. 113–4; Claude Cahen 'Mouvements populaires et autonomisme urbain dans l'Asie musulmane du Moyen-Age', *Arabica*, 5–6 (1958–9), p. 57. Heinz Halm's treatment of them in his survey on the Shāfiᶜīs is too incomplete to be of any use. See Halm, *Die Ausbreitung der šāfiᶜitischen Rechtsschule von den Anfängen bis zum 8./14. Jahrhundert* (Wiesbaden, 1974), pp. 146–50. In his bio-bibliographical survey of poets, De Blois devotes a detailed entry to them which remains quite incomplete. (Oddly, de Blois does refer to *al-Mukhtārāt min al-rasāᵓil* but makes no use of ᶜImād al-Dīn's *Kharīdat al-qaṣr* despite the importance of this poetic anthology.) See de Blois, *Persian Literature: a Bio-Biographic Survey, vol. V, part 2* (*Poetry ca.* A.D. *1100 to 1225*) (London, 1994), pp. 401–5, entry no. 227. So far, the most complete notice on the Khujandīs, although strictly prosopographical and not devoid of factual mistakes, is S. A. Āl-i Dāwūd, 'Āl-i Khujand,' in *Dāyirat al-maᶜārif-i buzurg-i islāmī* (Tehran, 1989), I, pp. 694–8. The Persian bibliography for the Khujandīs is exhaustively set out in my forthcoming contribution to *EIr*, s.v. 'Ḫojandis of Isfahan'.
2. *Al-Mukhtārāt min al-rasāᵓil*, ed. Īraj Afshār and Ghulām-Riḍā Ṭāhir (Tehran, 1378sh./1999–2000).
3. For an up-to-date prosopographical account of the Khujandī family, see Durand-Guédy, 'Ḫojandis'. For a synthesized chronological outline, refer to Table 10.2 which lists the main events of the Khujandīs's history in Isfahan.
4. See Ibn al-Athīr, *al-Kāmil fī l-taᵓrīkh*, ed. Tornberg (Beirut 1968) sub anno [s.a.] 496, X, p. 366; Subkī, *Ṭabaqāt al-shāfiᶜiyya al-kubrā*, ed. Maḥmūd Ṭanāḥī and ᶜAbd al-Fattāḥ al-Ḥilw (Cairo, 1964–76), IV, p. 124; ᶜImād al-Dīn al-Iṣfahānī, *Kharīdat al-qaṣr*, ed. ᶜAdnān Āl Ṭuᶜma (Tehran, 1378sh./1999), I, p. 241. On the Khujandīs' settlement in Isfahan, see Durand-Guédy, *Iranian Elites*, pp. 125–6.
5. See Cahen, 'Mouvement populaires', p. 18; Omeljan Pristak, 'Āl-i Burhān', *Der Islam* 30, 1 (1952), pp. 81–96; Jean-Michel Mouton, *Damas et sa principauté sous les Saldjoukides et les Bourides, 468–549/1076–1154* (Cairo, 1994).
6. See Durand-Guédy, *Iranian Elites*, ch. 4.
7. All these events are presented and analysed in detail in Durand-Guédy, *Iranian Elites*, ch. 6.
8. Cahen, 'Mouvements populaires', p. 24.
9. See Bundārī, *Zubdat al-nuṣra*, ed. T. Houtsma, *Histoire des Seljoucides de l'Irâq* (*Recueil de textes relatifs à l'histoire des Seljoucides*, vol. II) (Leiden, 1889), pp. 91–100 (references to ᶜImād al-Dīn's *Nuṣrat al-fatra* are given in Bundārī's abridgment when the two versions are identical).
10. This conclusion seems to me more correct than my previous hypothesis, according to which 'There is . . . every reason to believe that the Khujandīs, in their own way, sought to perpetuate the anti-Ismaᶜili dynamic' (Durand-Guédy, *Iranian Elites*, p. 194). Although

the issue deserves a separate investigation, this interpretation is confirmed by the good relations the Khujandīs maintained with the Shiᶜis (like Anūshirwān b. Khālid, Najm al-Dīn Qumī, the Abbasid vizier Ibn al-Qaṣṣāb) during the 6th/12th century.

11. *Mukhtārāt*, p. 97.
12. See *Mukhtārāt*, pp. 423–4, no. 470 (report of the trial, dated 585/1189); p. 449, no. 444 (attestation of the *raᵓīs*). The first document has in part been analysed in Īraj Afshār, 'Turbat-i Niẓām wa Turbat-i Bahāᵓī dar Iṣfahān', *Yaghmā* 11 (1355sh./1977), pp. 670–4.
13. Even when diplomas exist (as they do for Khurasan), the duties of the *raᵓīs* remain vague. See Cahen, 'Mouvements populaires', pp. 54–6. On the position of *raᵓīs* in pre-Mongol Iran, see also Richard Bulliet, *The Patricians of Nishapur: a Study in Medieval Islamic Social History* (Cambridge, MA, 1972), p. 108; Jürgen Paul, *Herrscher, Gemeinwesen, Vermittler: Ostiran und Transoxanien in vormongolischer Zeit* (Stuttgart, 1996), passim; *EI2*, s.v. 'Raᵓīs', VIII, pp. 402–3 (C. E. Bosworth); and my *Iranian Elites*, pp. 197–9 and passim. No source specifies when and how the Khujandīs received the *riyāsa* of Isfahan. The first Khujandī to be explicitly mentioned as *raᵓīs* is ᶜAbd al-Laṭīf I. See Ibn al-Athīr, *Kāmil* s.a. 523, X, p. 659. However, it is highly probable that he was preceded in this post by his brother Abū l-Qāsim Masᶜūd. The mobilisation of the urban militias – as those which seem to take part in the anti-Ismaᶜili massacre of 494/1101 – was the prerogative of the *raᵓīs* in Syria, but also in Iran. See Cahen, 'Mouvements populaires' and my article 'Iranians at war under Turkish domination: the example of pre-Mongol Isfahan', *Iranian Studies* 38, 4 (2005), pp. 587–606. Abū l-Qāsim Masᶜūd would have become *raᵓīs* in 489/1096, after the death of the old *raᵓīs* al-Qāsim b. al-Faḍl al-Thaqafī. The Ḥanafī *qāḍī* ᶜUbayd Allāh al-Khaṭībī (d. 502/1108) is called '*raᵓīs* of Isfahan' by Bundārī, but we have already noted that this was a mistake; see Durand-Guédy, 'Un fragment inédit de la chronique des Salǧūqides de ᶜImād al-Dīn al-Iṣfahānī: le chapitre sur Tāǧ al-Mulk', *AI* 39 (2005), p. 208, note 20.
14. This result makes it possible to take an overall view of the different interpretations of the establishment of madrasas in the Seljuq period. The Niẓāmiyya madrasa in Isfahan was obviously founded to support the establishment of Niẓām al-Mulk in the city (by creating a new network at his service), which accords perfectly with the 'pragmatic' analyses of Makdisi (followed by Bulliet) who view the madrasa as a political instrument for the control of local societies. See Georges Makdisi, *Ibn ᶜAqīl et la résurgence de l'Islam traditionaliste au XIe siècle* (Damas, 1963), p. 226. It remains nonetheless true that the institution *also* trained individuals to serve in official positions in territories controlled by the Seljuqs.
15. See Ibn al-Jawzī, *Muntaẓam*, ed. Krenkow (Hyderabad, 1938–41), X, p. 179:15–9. (Here as well as in the following footnotes, the numbers behind the colon refer to the lines on the cited page.)
16. Bundārī, *Zubda*, p. 243:6–8.
17. Ibid. p. 252:3–10.
18. Ibid. p. 244:13–5.
19. See Subkī, *Ṭabaqāt*, IV, pp.123–4.
20. Abū l-Maᶜālī Ḥasan b. Muḥammad al-Warkānī (d. 559/1163–4), a local Isfahani, is described by Samᶜānī as the 'delegate of al-Khujandī's children for the teaching in the madrasa (*nāᵓib al-tadrīs fī l-Niẓāmiyya min jihat awlād al-Khujandī*)'. See Samᶜānī, *al-Taḥbīr fī muᶜjam al-kabīr*, ed. K. al-Manṣūr (Beirut, 1418/1997), I, p. 63, no. 111.

21. See Ibn Ṣābūnī, *Takmīlat ikmāl al-ikmāl*, ed. Muṣtafā Jawād (Baghdad, 1388/1957), p. 184.
22. See ᶜImād al-Dīn, *Kharīda*, p. 242.
23. Ibid. p. 245.
24. See Subkī, *Ṭabaqāt*, VI, p. 135.
25. Kamāl al-Dīn Ismāᶜīl, *Dīwān*, ed. Ḥusayn Baḥr al-ᶜUlūmī (Tehran, 1348sh./1970), p. 435, verse 7335.
26. Subkī, *Ṭabaqāt*, X, p. 179.
27. Ibid. VI, p. 133.
28. Samᶜānī does not include the Khujandīs of Isfahan in his *Ansāb* dictionary although he visited Isfahan twice (in 529/1134–5 and 538/1143–4). This silence is all the more surprising given that he devotes a laudatory entry to Abū l-Maᶜālī al-Warkānī, a pupil of Abū Bakr Muḥammad I and the family's delegate in the madrasa. Subkī does however mention 'Ibn Samᶜānī' as his authority on two members of the Khujandī family. See Subkī, *Ṭabaqāt*, IV, p. 123 and IV, p. 44 (concerning Abū Bakr Muḥammad I); VI, p. 133 (concerning Abū Bakr Muḥammad II). It is possible that Subkī is quoting from Samᶜānī's lost works (three have been preserved, but several dozen are attributed to him). See ibid. VII, pp. 180–5. The reason may also be that Samᶜānī was working on the *Ansāb* up until his death (in 552/1157, the same year in which Abū Bakr Muḥammad II died), and that in his eyes, the political career of the Khujandīs rendered them unworthy of inclusion in his dictionary. Significantly, Subkī (*Ṭabaqāṭ*, V, p. 51) indicates that Samᶜānī was taught by Abū Saᶜd Aḥmad (d. 531/1137), the oldest of Abū Bakr Muḥammad I's sons, who had been passed over in favour of his brother. This may be the key to the mystery.
29. Ibid. VII, p. 186.
30. Ibn Jubayr, *Riḥla*, ed. William Wright, rev. by de Goeje (Leiden and London, 1907), p. 201; trans. Ronald Broadhurst, *The Travels of Ibn Jubayr* (London, 1952), p. 209.
31. Asnawī, *Ṭabaqāt al-Shāfiᶜiyya*, ed. ᶜAbd Allāh al-Jubūrī (Baghdad, 1390/1970), I, p. 491.
32. See Ibn al-Athīr, *Kāmil*, s.a. 496, X, p. 366 (Ibn al-Jawzī and Sibṭ Ibn al-Jawzī give a different version).
33. Ibn al-Jawzī (*Muntaẓam*, X, p. 179:18), a Ḥanbalī who had no sympathy for the *ᶜulamāᵓ* associated with the Seljuqs, nevertheless remarks that Abū Muḥammad II 'had no like as a preacher (*mā kāna yandāra fī l-waᶜẓ*)'. Ibn Jubayr (*Riḥla*, p. 200:8; trans. p. 208), who attended a sermon given by ᶜAbd al-Laṭīf II in Medina, speaks of his 'bewitching eloquence' and provides a colourful description of the extreme emotions he aroused. Zakariyyā Qazwīnī says that the Atabeg Pahlawān was moved to tears by a sermon of ᶜAbd al-Laṭīf II, no doubt one along the same lines as the one that Ibn Jubayr had attended. See Qazwīnī, *K. Āthār al-bilād*, ed. Ferdinand Wüstenfeld (Göttingen, 1848), p. 198. The 'beauty' of Kamāl al-Islām Masᶜūd's sermons (I think this person is identical to the Jamāl al-Dīn Masᶜūd mentioned in the *Mukhtārāt* documents) is also noted by Ibn Fuwaṭī, *Majmaᶜ al-ādāb fī muᶜjam al-alqāb*, ed. Muḥammad Kaẓīm (Tehran, 1374sh./1995), IV, p. 260, no. 3805.
34. On Abū l-Futūḥ al-ᶜIjlī, see the notice in *Dāyirat al-maᶜārif-i buzurg-i islāmī* (Tehran, 1994), VI, pp. 114–15 (ᶜAbd al-Amīr Salīm).
35. Samᶜānī, quoted by Asnawī, *Ṭabaqāt*, I, p. 478.
36. Paul, *Herrscher*, p. 315.

37. ᶜImād al-Dīn, *Nuṣrat al-fatra*, ms. arabe no. 2145 (Bibliothèque Nationale Paris), fol. 246 (this passage is omitted by Bundārī). On these events, see Durand-Guédy, *Iranian Elites*, pp. 259–63.
38. Bundārī, *Zubdat*, p. 194:3–4.
39. See Ibn al-Jawzī, *Muntaẓam*, X, p. 68.
40. See *Mukhtārāt*, p. 54, no. 7.
41. Fully detailed in Durand-Guédy, *Iranian Elites*, pp. 173, 261–2, 270.
42. See *Mukhtārāt*, pp. 147–8, no. 52, translated in Durand-Guédy, *Iranian Elites*, p. 253.
43. See Durand-Guédy, 'Mémoires d'exilés. Lecture de la chronique des Salğūqides de ᶜImād al-Dīn al-Iṣfahānī', *Studia Iranica* 35 (2006), pp. 181–202.
44. See *Mukhtārāt*, pp. 147–8, no. 52, translated in Durand-Guédy, *Iranian Elites*, p. 253.
45. Ibn al-Athīr, *Kāmil*, s.a. 500, X, p. 431.
46. See Māfarrūkhī, *Maḥāsin Iṣfahān*, ed. Jalāl al-Dīn al-Ḥusayn al-Ṭihrāni (Tehran, 1933), p. 104, translated and commented on in Durand-Guédy, *Iranian Elites*, pp. 127–8.
47. A vast range of documents from *Mukhtārāt*, illustrating the different kinds of assistance that the Khujandīs provided to the people of Isfahan, has been translated and commented on in Durand-Guédy, *Iranian Elites*, pp. 246–53. The problems of identification posed by the *Mukhtārāt* documents will be the subject of a further publication in preparation.
48. *Mukhtārāt*, p. 85, no. 30.
49. Ibid. p. 111, no. 38.
50. Ibid. p. 448, no. 440 (dated 541/1146–7).
51. See ᶜImād al-Dīn, *Kharīda*, e.g. pp. 178, 259, 265, 266.
52. See Ẓahīr al-Dīn Fāryābī, *Dīwān*, ed. Amīr Ḥasan Yazdgirdī (Tehran, 1381sh./2002–3), p. 280.
53. See ᶜAwfī, *Lubāb al-albāb*, ed. Edward Browne and Mohammad Qazwini (London and Leiden, 1903–6), I, pp. 266–8; Shirwānī, J.-K., *Nuzhat al-majālis*, ed. A. Riyāḥī (Tehran, 1366sh./1987–8), passim.
54. See ᶜImād al-Dīn, *Kharīda*, e.g. p. 155.
55. See Warāwīnī, *Marzubān-nāma*, ed. Muḥammad Qazwīnī (Leiden and London, 1909), p. 9:9–14.
56. Jarbādhaqānī, *Tarjuma-yi Tārīkh-i Yamīnī*, ed. Jaᶜfar Shuᶜār (2nd edn, Tehran, 2537sh./1978), p. 253.
57. It is interesting to note that the scope of the Khujandīs' networks, and their role as patrons of the arts, placed them at the heart of the process of historiographical composition which is the foundation of much of what we know of the Seljuq state in western Iran. The three principal sources on the political and administrative history of the Seljuq state, Anūshirwān b. Khālid's *Nafthat al-masdūr*, Najm al-Dīn Qumī's *Taʾrīkh al-wuzarāʾ* and ᶜImād al-Dīn al-Iṣfahānī's *Nuṣrat al-fatra* were all the work of men very close to the Khujandīs (the two first-mentioned were under obligations to them, the third was their friend). The Shāfiᶜī Ibn al-Athīr was close to the son of the powerful Zangid vizier Jamāl al-Dīn al-Iṣfahānī, who had been a friend (if not a client) of the Khujandīs. The Shiᶜi authors, such as Qazwīnī Rāzī and Murtaḍā Rāzī, were openly favourable to them. The Khujandīs are not the target in any of the satirist Ibn Habbāriya's verse, which otherwise lays into the entire Seljuq elite. Even the ultra-Ḥanafī Rāvandī, for all his hostility in principle to the Shāfiᶜīs, spares the Khujandīs whom he knew to desire an alliance with his protector Ṭoghrïl b. Arslān. Thus, in the immense corpus of sources on western Iran in the 6th/12th century, it has not been possible to find a single author openly hostile to the

Khujandīs. As we have seen (see above note 20) Sam[c]ānī may have preferred conveying his disapproval by silence rather than criticising them.

58. Ira Lapidus, 'Muslim urban society in Mamlūk Syria', in *The Islamic City: Papers on Islamic History I*, eds Albert Hourani and Samuel Stern (Carbondale, IL, 1970), pp. 202–3.
59. Ibn al-Athīr systematically employs the expression '*ra*ʾ*īs al-shāfi*ʿ*iyya*' for all the Khujandīs whom he identifies as *ra*ʾ*īs*. See Ibn al-Athīr, *Kāmil*, s.a. 523, X, p. 659 (for ʿAbd al-Laṭīf I); s.a. 531, XI, p. 54 (for Abū Saʿd Aḥmad); s.a. 552, XI, p. 228 (for Abū Bakr Muḥammad II); and s.a. 592, XII, p. 124 (for Muḥammad IV). The expression is also used by Ibn Jubayr (*Riḥla*, p. 199:22; trans. p. 208), the Shāfiʿī traditionist Ibn Baṭīsh of Mosul (d. 655/1257) (quoted by Subkī, *Ṭabaqāt*, VI, p. 134) and in later compilations, e.g. Ibn al-ʿImād, *Shadharāt al-dhahab*, reprint Cairo edn (Beirut, 1966), s.a. 552, IV, p. 164 (for Abū Bakr Muḥammad II). We may note that ʿImād al-Dīn is content to speak of the '*riyāsa*' of Isfahan (see Bundārī, *Zubdat*, p. 221:4, for Abū Muḥammad II), but ʿImād al-Dīn was both a friend of the Khujandīs and a resolute enemy of the Ḥanafīs. His partisanship when speaking of the Khujandīs comes out most clearly in the chapter he devotes to them in his *Kharīda*, where he refers to their control of the *riyāsa* with some hyperbole. See e.g. ʿImād al-Dīn, *Kharīda*, p. 241: the children of Abū Bakr Muḥammad I 'were at the head of the *ʿulamā*ʾ (*ri*ʾ*āsat al-ʿulamā*ʾ) in the East and in the West'. Many later writers, basing themselves on ʿImād al-Dīn, also simply speak of the '*riyāsa* of Isfahan' in relation to the Khujandīs. See, e.g., Abū Shāma, *Dhayl ʿalā l-rawḍatayn*, ed. Ibrāhīm Shams al-Dīn (Beirut, 1422ah/2002), p. 12; Ibn Fuwaṭī, *Majma*ʿ, p. 493; Subkī, *Ṭabaqāt*, VI, p. 133 (for Abū Muḥammad II), VII, p. 186 (for ʿAbd al-Laṭīf II).
60. See the 6th/12th-century author Qazwīnī Rāzī, *K. al-Naqḍ*, ed. Jalāl al-Dīn Muḥaddith (Tehran, 1378sh./1980), p. 459 ('*Iṣfahān . . . hama shāfiʿī-madhhab bāshand*').
61. Such a *riyāsa* confined to one *madhhab* is attested at the same period in other places, such as Damascus and Merv. See Ashtor, 'Administration urbaine', p. 89, note 3; Muntajab al-Dīn Juwaynī, *'Atabat al-kataba*, ed. Muḥammad Qazwīnī and ʿAbbās Iqbāl (Tehran, 1950), pp. 85–8, no. 34.
62. Ibn al-Athīr, *Kāmil*, s.a. 591, XII, p. 117.
63. See Oleg Grabar, *The Great Mosque of Isfahan* (New York, 1990), p. 58; Durand-Guédy, *Iranian Elites*, p. 203.
64. We do not know to what extent the Khujandīs may have been able to monopolise other local positions (they are not quoted in the sources – except an allusion to the *muḥtasib* in a *qaṣīda* by Jamāl al-Dīn ʿAbd al-Razzāq Iṣfahānī, *Dīwān*, ed. Ḥasan Waḥīd-Dastgirdī (Tehran, 1320sh./1941–2), p. 129, verses 7–8).
65. See Durand-Guédy, 'Iranians at war', p. 594.
66. Ibn Abī l-Ḥadīd, *Sharḥ Nahj al-balāgha*, ed. M. A. Ibrāhīm (Beirut, 1963–4), III, p. 81; trans. John Woods, 'A note on the Mongol capture of Isfahan', *Journal of Near Eastern Studies* 36, 1 (1977), p. 50.

PART III

. . .

CULTURE

CHAPTER

11

SHIᶜI JURISPRUDENCE DURING THE SELJUQ PERIOD: REBELLION AND PUBLIC ORDER IN AN ILLEGITIMATE STATE

Robert Gleave

INTRODUCTION

The Seljuqs are characterised as fanatical promoters of Sunnism in almost all the primary sources and secondary literature. Ṭughril Beg's capture of Baghdad in 447/1055 brought Buyid power, at least in the capital, to an end. With the demise of the Buyids, an environment sympathetic to Shiᶜi expressions of Islam disappeared. When Ṭughril Beg quashed the almost immediate Fatimid-inspired coup attempt and recaptured the city, public expression of Shiᶜism inevitably faded within the caliphal capital. The Shiᶜi community, both in Baghdad and elsewhere in the Seljuq empire, faced considerable restrictions in this new context. The damage to the intellectual infrastructure of Shiᶜism was also significant. Amongst the attacks on Shiᶜi institutions of learning was Ṭughril Beg's reported order of the burning of libraries of scientific works, such as the Dār al-ᶜIlm in al-Karkh. This had been founded by the Buyid vizier Ṣābūr b. Ardashīr (Shapur Ibn Ardeshir, d. 416/1025–6) in 381/991 (or according to another report, in 383/993), and whilst not exclusively Shiᶜi in its contents or personnel, it was located in the Shiᶜi quarter of Baghdad.[1] Yāqūt (d. 626/1229) records laconically:

> In [al-Karkh] there was a book treasury which the vizier Abū Nasr Ṣābūr b. Ardashīr, the vizier to Bahāᵓ al-Dawla b. ᶜAduḍ al-Dawla had left as a bequest. There were no finer books in the world, all of them in the hands of, and recording the thoughts of, the past masters. They were burnt in a fire in the area of al-Karkh when Ṭughril Beg, the first of the Seljuq kings, entered Baghdad in 447.[2]

Shaykh al-Ṭāʾifa Muḥammad b. Ḥasan al-Ṭūsī (d. 460/1067), the leading scholar of the Shiʿites in Baghdad, witnessed the Seljuq arrival, experiencing the reassertion of Sunni Islam, and the suppression of Shiʿism. Ibn al-Jawzī (d. 597/1201) records that al-Ṭūsī's house was also looted and that he fled in 448/1056–7. Again, Ibn al-Jawzī records a year later:

> In Ṣafar of this year [449/1057–8], the house of Abū Jaʿfar al-Ṭūsī, the theologian of the Shiʿites, in al-Karkh was captured. Whatever was found [there] was taken, including his papers/books (*dafātīr*) and a chair on which he used to sit to teach. They took it out to al-Karkh, with three banners which, in the past, pilgrims from al-Karkh use to carry with them when they set out to visit Kufa. The whole lot was burned.[3]

Ibn al-Athīr (d. 630/1233) records that 'in the year of 449, the house of Abū Jaʿfar al-Ṭūsī in al-Karkh was raided. He was the *faqīh* of the Imamiyya, but he had already abandoned it [the house] for al-Mashhad al-Gharbī [the Western Mashhad, i.e. al-Najaf]'.[4] Other reports indicate that his books were burned regularly. Ibn Ḥajar al-ʿAskalānī (d. 852/1449), reporting from Ibn Najjār, writes: 'His books were burned on numerous occasions, in front of the people in the public square of the Naṣr congregational mosque. He had to hide himself away because of the criticisms of him which had been publicly aired.'[5] Whether he had fled after the first attack, or after the second (perhaps following a period in hiding) is not clear, though it is certain that within a couple of years of the Seljuq's arrival, al-Ṭūsī had left the capital and moved to the city of al-Najaf. His arrival in Najaf is celebrated within the Shiʿi tradition: from that point onwards, Najaf together with its neighbouring town, al-Hilla, became the major Shiʿi intellectual centre, and the Ḥawza (the name given to the independent Shiʿi seminary system which survives to this day) was born.

Whilst the genesis myth of the Ḥawza is linked to the Shiʿi withdrawal from Seljuq Baghdad and the establishment of Najaf, Shiʿi learning immediately following these events is viewed as entering a very lean period. The next century and a half, both within and outside of the Seljuq domains, is viewed as a period of (at worst) stagnation and (at best) unoriginality amongst the Shiʿi intelligentsia generally, and the jurists (*fuqahāʾ*) in particular. Modern scholars also view the period immediately following al-Ṭūsī as a period when little original work was either needed or carried out in the development of Shiʿi law.[6] According to Modarressi, 'None of the Shīʿī scholars of this period produced any major novel ideas'.[7] Jawād al-Shahristānī writes,

> The rest of the *ʿulamāʾ* of the Shīʿa, for a long time, did not go beyond recording the opinions of al-Shaykh [al-Ṭūsī], and commenting on them. For this reason,

> they are called 'imitators' (*muqallida*), because they did nothing more than imitate (*taqlīd*) the Shaykh . . . In this period, there was no independent jurist who was not a follower of the school of al-Shaykh al-Ṭūsī.[8]

Calder also states that all 'branches of Shīᶜī intellectual activity entered a period of stagnation, designated by Imāmī writers as a period of *taqlīd* (imitation) by which they mean *taqlīd* of Ṭūsī'.[9]

The negative portrayal of Shiᶜi scholarship during this period is not surprising. Even within the tradition, there is little positive comment. Ibn Ṭāwūs (d. 664/1266) records a statement of Sadīd al-Dīn al-Ḥimmaṣī (d. early 7th/13th century):

> There is no true mufti left amongst the Imamiyya. All of them have gone. In days gone by, there was a group of such scholars, but now, in our time, there is not one who could come close to them in these matters. I beg, for their sake, that the Occultation is extended . . . so they may, by the mercy of God, spend their time in study, learning and scholarship.[10]

Al-Ḥimmaṣī's ironic plea that the Occultation be extended (Shiᶜis normally pray for the hastened arrival of the Mahdi – 'Messiah') was to give the current generation a chance to apply themselves and force Shiᶜi jurisprudence to develop beyond the confines of *taqlīd*, and perhaps, thereby, to avoid censure when the Mahdi does eventually return. The critical view of Shiᶜi scholarship in the period immediately following al-Shaykh al-Ṭūsī does not, of course, appear in a purely neutral context. Al-Ḥimmaṣī was known to be critical of both al-Ṭūsī and his disciples, and his declaration that the Imāmīs had lost their muftis (and hence their intellectual drive) is probably an exaggeration based on the common theme of *fasād al-zamān*. Modarressi identifies him as part of a 'tendency' which rejected the legacy of al-Ṭūsī, and criticised those who did unthinking *taqlīd* to him.[11] As with the earlier scholar, Ibn Idrīs al-Ḥillī (d. 598/1202), it appears he had a vested interest in portraying al-Ṭūsī and his followers as intellectually impoverished. However, his negative assessment seems to have coloured subsequent assessments of the quality of Shiᶜi learning generally, and Shiᶜi legal scholarship in particular in the early years after the Seljuq capture of Baghdad. In this chapter, I demonstrate that this characterisation is, to an extent, unfair. Such a depiction is, I suspect, promulgated in Shiᶜi legal histories in order to establish al-Ṭūsī as the undisputed progenitor of the Shiᶜi legal tradition.

Both al-Ṭūsī's pupils and his opponents within the Imamiyya produced a number of *fiqh* works which are rarely cited in the subsequent tradition, but which nonetheless represent an impressive corpus of material. Of the works which have survived, there are a number of *fiqh* works which are rarely studied in modern Shiᶜi seminaries, but which clearly formed part of the legal literary canon of later scholars, including al-ᶜAllāma al-Ḥillī (d. 726/1325), as he cites them regularly.

The works form an excellent base from which to examine whether the post-Ṭūsī tradition was as moribund as some writers suspect. Examples of originality and development, I argue below, can be located in the jurisprudence of the disputed subject of legitimate and illegitimate violence within the Imāmī Shiᶜi tradition. The legal justification for violent acts in Islamic law generally is normally located in a handful of chapters in works of *fiqh*. The most famous is, of course, the *kitāb al-jihād*, but the disciplining of wives (in the *kitāb al-nikāḥ*) and of children is also, occasionally, explored in some detail. And analogously, there is some discussion of a master's rights over his or her slave, and whether disciplinary acts with violent elements can be justified in such contexts. Legitimate (violent) punishment for crime can be found in the chapters on *qiṣāṣ* (encompassing retaliatory justice) and *ḥudūd* (punishment for 'crimes against God'). Further questions relate to when and how a leader (*imām*) might put down a rebellion, and how the rebels might subsequently be punished afterwards. The qualifications and functions of a judge in the state system and the persistently debated issue of the implementation of the court's decision (the operation of the state police force) also touch on the legitimation of violence. One can also include the general duty of Muslims to 'command the good and forbid the evil' (*al-amr bi-l-maᶜruf wa'l-nahy ᶜan al-munkar*), and the possible validation of vigilante action contained therein, and the linked notion of *ḥisba* (the market police, charged with ensuring public order). Finally, there is the disputed concept of *al-siyāsa al-sharᶜiyya* (politically appropriate, but not necessarily textually supported legal activity), where the *imām* may have permission to act 'extra-judicially' (and when necessary, with violence), in order to preserve society's order. In nearly all these areas of (potentially) legitimate violence, the Imāmī legal tradition had a more acute problem than most of the Sunni legal traditions: nearly all forms of legitimate violence, a sanctioning (usually, state) power is necessary, and the Imāmī jurists were bound by the theological notion that the only legitimate religious and political leader was the Imam. Since 260/874, when the Twelfth Imam went into hiding (*ghayba*), there has been no accessible Imam, and therefore, it is quite possible that any legitimate state-sanctioned violence (not only the *jihād*, but also punishments for crimes, and even controlled retaliatory justice) is unattainable before the return of the hidden Imam. The dynamic of these distinctly Imāmī discussions illustrates the development of Shiᶜi legal thought under the Seljuqs.

ORIGINALITY AND DISAGREEMENT IN THE POST-ṬŪSĪ PERIOD

It would be possible to present a statistical analysis of where post-Ṭūsī scholars agree and disagree with al-Ṭūsī and this, it could be argued, would reveal the extent of their *taqlīd*. Of course, there would be a much greater level of agreement than disagreement: the scholars are, after all, working within the same legal tradition.[12] To make this meaningful, we would need a control whereby we could estimate 'normal' levels of intra-*madhhab* agreement. With this we could compare post-Ṭūsī jurisprudence with previous periods to discover whether the period of the Seljuqs was unusually slavish. The utility of such an ambitious enterprise would be impaired by the disagreement within and between al-Ṭūsī's own writings, which happens with some frequency. More revealing, in my view, than a simple quantitative account, is an analysis of selected areas of legal dispute (*khilāf*) with an assessment of whether significant differences in the outlook and methods of legal argumentation come to light. It is, after all, these rather minor details of legal doctrine which are supposed to characterise the differences between al-Ṭūsī's school and that of his opponents. The most commonly cited controversy is the authority of 'isolated' reports from the Prophet or Imams (*akhbār al-āḥād*),[13] though the differences between al-Ṭūsī and the small band of opponents which emerged after him were not limited to this dispute. Whilst not comprehensive, examining particular areas of dispute should enable us to enumerate where post-Ṭūsī scholars, most of whom are described as 'mere' *muqallida* of the Shaykh, demonstrate independence of thought and originality. I have selected two such issues for examination: commanding right/forbidding wrong and the law of rebellion.

COMMANDING RIGHT AND FORBIDDING WRONG

Amongst the so-called followers of al-Ṭūsī was Muḥammad b. ᶜAlī b. Ḥamza al-Ṭūsī, known within the tradition as Ibn Ḥamza (d. after 566/1171). His best known legal work is *al-Wasīla ilā nayl al-faḍīla*. He is sometimes referred to as Abū Jaᶜfar the second (the first Abū Jaᶜfar being al-Shaykh al-Ṭūsī himself), and according to some reports was a pupil of al-Ṭūsī,[14] and if not al-Ṭūsī himself, then a pupil of al-Ṭūsī's son Abū ᶜAlī (d. after 515/1121).[15] His dates would seem to suggest the latter being more likely, though the former is more commonly proclaimed within the tradition.

In the section on 'commanding right and forbidding wrong' in *al-Wasīla*, he writes:

> Commanding right follows the right in terms of obligation and recommendation; and forbidding wrong follows the wrong. If the wrong thing is prohibited, then

> forbidding is obligatory. If [the wrong thing] is discouraged, then forbidding it is recommended.[16]

This doctrine (to be explained in more detail below) was accepted Shiʿi doctrine in later years, but at the time of Ibn Ḥamza, it was more than a little controversial. It is worth noting at the outset that on this issue, this 'follower' of al-Ṭūsī disagrees with his master. In his *al-Iqtiṣād*, al-Ṭūsī wrote:

> Right is of two sorts – obligatory and recommended. The commanding of an obligation is itself obligatory, and [the commanding of] a recommended thing is itself recommended. This is because the command cannot, itself, exceed the commanded thing. The prohibited is not so divided; rather all of it is evil, and so prohibiting it, in its entirety, is obligatory.[17]

Interestingly, the members of the 'anti-Ṭūsī' tendency, including Ibn Idrīs, agree with al-Ṭūsī on this point, whilst two uncontroversial scholars (the contemporary Abū al-Ṣalāh al-Ḥalabī, d. 447/1055–6 and Ibn Ḥamza) are the only ones disagreeing with al-Ṭūsī. Clearly being a follower of al-Ṭūsī did not entail entire slavish agreement, and being a critic did not require constant dismissal of al-Ṭūsī's position.

The dispute itself revolves around the classification of the duty to 'command right and forbid wrong'. It is well-known that every Muslim has a duty to command right and forbid wrong for their fellow Muslims, and perhaps for society more widely. The actions involved in commanding/forbidding are not limited to simply speaking out, but there is placed on the individual an obligation to command and forbid with the 'hand, tongue and heart' (it should be noted that the order of priority between these three is disputed). The imposition of this duty presupposes knowledge of what is right and what is wrong (a ponderous task in itself), but, leaving this aside, the duty has been established and accepted in various formulations by Muslim jurists in both the classical and modern periods, and forms an item in the list of duties incumbent upon the ruler (*imām*) in Muslim society, as well as a general duty for individuals charged with obedience to the divine law (*mukallafūn*).

Locating the dispute between al-Ṭūsī and Ibn Ḥamza within the discussions of 'commanding right and forbidden wrong' relies on keeping in mind an important distinction. There is a difference between the moral classifications of 'right' (*maʿruf*) and 'wrong' (*munkar*) on the one hand, and the five established legal (*sharʿī*) classifications of actions on the other. The five classifications are, of course, obligatory (*wājib/farḍ*), recommended (*mandūb/mustaḥabb*), permitted (*mubāḥ*), discouraged (*makrūh*) and forbidden (*ḥarām/maḥẓūr*). The term *ma^cruf* is generally viewed as covering both obligatory and recommended actions under the Sharī^ca. Jurists viewed commanding a fellow Muslim to perform an obligatory action (such as daily prayer) to be itself obligatory. But what of commanding a fellow Muslim to perform a recommended action (such as performing a full body wash before Friday prayers irrespective of purity status)? It is surely a meritorious deed to encourage a Muslim not only to perform the obligatory duties but also to gain additional religious rewards by performing superogatory deeds. But is it obligatory (*wājib*) for Muslims to command other Muslims to perform recommended actions, in the same way as they are obligated to command Muslims to perform obligatory actions? The general Imāmī answer at al-Ṭūsī's time was in the negative. Since the action being commanded (*al-ma^ɔmūr bihi*) itself is superogatory, the duty to command others to do it was also superogatory. There is a divisibility (*inqisām*) within the duty to command right, and for this reason Cook labels it the 'doctrine of divisibility'.[18] The logical reason for the mirroring of the classification of the thing commanded and the command itself is, as al-Ṭūsī puts it, that 'the command cannot, itself, exceed the commanded thing'. Or to fill out this explanation further: the aim of a command is to bring into existence the thing commanded. If the thing commanded is an obligatory action which, if neglected, will put the individual in religious peril, then it follows that attempting to bring about the performance of this obligatory act is itself also an obligatory action for the Muslim capable of influencing the situation. If, however, the thing commanded is merely a preferred and/or recommended action, the neglect of which will not, in itself, endanger the individual's religious standing, then it cannot be obligatory for a Muslim to try to bring this state of affairs into existence.

The thinking here, I surmise, is that individual Muslims are charged by God with attempting to establish a society in which the (Muslim) members fulfil the obligatory duties. Not attempting to establish such a society is, in itself, considered a moral failure: the duty to command good and forbid wrong establishes, in turn, a duty to adopt a policy of 'active citizenship'. Members of society are encouraged to fulfil the divine law, and are (or should be) constantly reminded of their duties under it. However, for al-Ṭūsī, the obligations of active citizenship do not extend to moral improvement of one's fellows beyond the performance of the obligatory duties. One is not required by the divine law to attempt to improve the religious/moral standing of one's fellows beyond the benefits they will receive from performing obligatory duties. It is not illegal to so attempt; indeed it is encouraged and 'recommended' that one does attempt to improve one's fellows in this way, and one receives religious benefits for this effort. However, it is not a requirement of being an observant Muslim that one command ('with hand, tongue and heart') one's fellow Muslims to perform superogatory acts. It is a good deed, but it is not essential to one's personal duty. In this, the Imāmī jurists agreed.

The dispute, however, appeared when considering the duty to 'forbid wrong'. The term *munkar* is often taken to refer to both the legally prohibited (*ḥarām*) and the legally discouraged (*makrūh*). In the same way, it is obligatory to forbid ('with hand, tongue and heart') one's fellows from performing a prohibited action since the performance of this act places them in religious peril. But what of acts which are not prohibited but merely discouraged? Is it, analogously, merely recommended that one forbid one's fellows from performing discouraged acts? Al-Ṭūsī argued that it is more than recommended to forbid one's fellow Muslims from committing discouraged actions, and that there is no analogy. It is obligatory to forbid both the *ḥarām* and the *makrūh*. There is a 'divisibility' for commanding right which is absent for forbidding wrong. For al-Ṭūsī, the patterns on either side of the 'permitted' point can be distinguished: it is *wājib* to command the *wājib*, and it is *mustaḥabb* to command the *mustaḥabb*, but it is *wājib* to forbid both the *ḥarām* and the *makrūh*. Cook points out that this is a clear example of the Imāmīs incorporating Basran Muᶜtazilī doctrine.[19] Ibn Ḥamza's view, contrary to al-Ṭūsī, is that there is mirroring here, and later Shiᶜi tradition agreed with him: they found his position so convincing they were even willing to ditch a view attributed to the majority of the early luminaries (including al-Ṭūsī) in favour of Ibn Ḥamza's minority view.[20]

Al-Ṭūsī's reasoning is not spelled out in his legal texts, but would seem to derive from a particular view of the nature of the duty to command right and forbid wrong. Both discouraged and forbidden actions are evil (*qabīḥ*). They are recognised as such through reason and/or revelation (which was disputed but it is not central to the argument here for us to know the answer): it is uncontroversial that it is obligatory for a Muslim to forbid a prohibited action. Al-Ṭūsī, and those who argued with him, also argued that it was obligatory for a Muslim to forbid (in the sense of *al-nahy*) discouraged things because they were also evil. They argued that it cannot, rationally speaking, be merely recommended that a Muslim forbid another from performing an 'evil' action. Al-Ṭūsī clearly envisages the prevention of evil within society to be of greater concern than the promotion of good. Muslims, under his scheme, have an obligation to forbid evil actions (whether they are classified legally as discouraged or forbidden), but the duty to command the right is divided between being obligatory (when the good is obligatory) and recommended (when the good is recommended). Al-Ṭūsī, along with those who took the same position, sees Muslims as having an obligation to attempt to prevent not only prohibited actions, but discouraged ones also. Given that it is clearly obligatory to command obligatory acts and forbid prohibited ones, the controversial aspects of al-Ṭūsī's view can be formulated under two additional regulations:

1. Muslims are recommended (but not obligated) to attempt to morally improve their fellows' behaviour through the promotion of the performance of supererogatory acts
2. Muslims are obligated to attempt to prevent the moral decay of their fellows through the attempted prevention of discouraged acts.

In this sense, al-Ṭūsī's position makes the community as a whole responsible not only for the maintenance of the obligatory boundaries, but also the prevention of personal moral decay by persistent individual performances of discouraged acts. He is, in a sense, promoting a sort of ethical interventionism.

Ibn Ḥamza's view is that it cannot be the duty of Muslims to forbid, with their hands, tongues and hearts, the performance of discouraged acts. The community has an obligation to try and ensure individuals perform obligatory actions and do not perform prohibited ones. But the performance of recommended actions (and the non-performance of discouraged actions, *makrūhāt*) are matters which affect an individual's personal religious standing and not public morality as such. The duty to correct these is less compelling than preventing the commission of *ḥarām* acts and promoting good. There cannot, in Ibn Ḥamza's view, be an obligation placed on the community (collectively or individually, whether through the *imām* or through vigilante action) to forbid discouraged actions, the avoidance of which is perhaps morally improving, but is not legally required. Now, I do not want to portray Ibn Ḥamza as arguing coherently for what might anachronistically be called a classical liberal view of the state. He does not argue that Muslims should not command the recommended and forbid the discouraged. Rather, he argues that these are superogatory acts, for which one receives a reward in heaven; however, failure to command and forbid them does not entail a transgression of the divine law, just as performing them is not forbidden. We return to the point that they are good things for the community to do, but they are not essential to ensure community compliance with the obligation to command right and prohibit wrong.

It could be argued that the two positions, represented here by the views of al-Ṭūsī and Ibn Ḥamza, have, at their root, two distinct conceptions of the moral responsibility of an individual Muslim towards the moral wellbeing of his neighbour and society more generally. Al-Ṭūsī has a more proactive view, effectively branding as failures and legal transgressors all who do not forbid their neighbours from performing the *makrūhāt*. Ibn Ḥamza places a slightly less exacting requirement on the believers: they can intervene and forbid the *makrūhāt* – but not doing so is neither a sin nor a crime. The difference is subtle, but significant in that it reveals different values placed on the policing of society's morals. It is possible that Ibn Ḥamza saw this as the result of pure theological and legal reasoning – though the different circumstances in which the two scholars were operating might have a bearing on the adoption of these contrasting views. Al-Ṭūsī's theological formation took place in the later Buyid Baghdad, where the Shiʿi community held a high level of state and community importance. The bold notion that a Shiʿi was obligated to forbid not only the prohibited but also the discouraged reveals (perhaps) a certain level of confidence that the community was internally strong and sufficiently unified to survive such a policy of public moral enforcement. Ibn Ḥamza does not abandon this completely. Biographical sources place him (at different times) in Mashhad, Hamadan and Najaf (he was buried in Karbala, but he was not necessarily resident there). His doctrine represents a withdrawal from al-Ṭūsī's command for proactive public moral policing. This might be attributed to the less favourable position in which the Shiʿi community found itself under Seljuq rule. Aside from this speculative explanation, the important point revealed here is that the so-called followers of al-Ṭūsī did not always share his outlook, and were not simply *muqallida*. Their differences may be due to a more thorough recognition, reflected in incremental shifts in their *fiqh* positions, that the high standing of the Shiʿa and the confidence that accompanied it, had been lost with the Seljuq arrival.

THE LAW OF REBELLION

Rebellion (*baghy*) is usually covered under a dedicated heading in the chapter on *jihād* in *fiqh* works, and it is often defined as 'the setting out' (*khurūj*) against the Muslim ruler (*imām*) from within the Muslim territory by those who claim to be Muslims. Rebellions of the 'People of the Book' (*ahl al-kitāb*, namely Jews, Christians and, for most, Zoroastrians also) form a different category, as this constitutes a violation of the covenant of protection (*al-dhimma*) under which they live within Muslim territory. The complex set of regulations found in Sunni works of *fiqh*, and the differing conceptions of the state and its legitimacy embedded within these discussions are replicated within Imāmī *fiqh* with the added issue of the well-rehearsed question of state legitimacy during the absence of the Imam.

In the only extended study in English of rebellion in Islamic law, Abou El Fadl makes much of a supposed shift in usage from 'the just *imām*' to 'a just *imām*' (*al-imām al-ʿādil* to *imām ʿādil* – i.e. from definite to indefinite) in Imāmī *fiqh* at around the time of al-Shaykh al-Ṭūsī (and perhaps a little earlier).[21] Abou El Fadl claims that the new indefinite term is almost intentionally vague in order to leave available the possibility of a ruler other than the usurped and absent Imam being a just ruler. That is, by this time in development of Shiʿi *fiqh*, jurists were making a distinction between the legitimate ruler (*al-imām, sulṭān al-haqq* and other cognate terms) and a (indefinite) just ruler (*imām ᶜādil*). It had been thought that it was impossible to be the latter without also being the former, with the result that no ruler other than the sinless Imam (currently in hiding) could be just, and the right to rule was preserved for him alone. For Abou El Fadl, the shift in terminology from definite to indefinite signifies the acceptance of the possibility than an *imām* may be illegitimate but also just, and through having the quality of justice, the legal attitude towards rebellion against him changes. The possibility was not fully exploited at the time, but the jurists introduced the grammatical change in order to signal a legal development. The current ruler, previously irredeemably illegitimate and unjust (*jāʾir/ẓālim*), could have a potentially legitimate claim on the support of the Shiᶜa during the Occultation. Now, the fact that the indefinite locution *imām ᶜādil* can be found in texts earlier than al-Ṭūsī would seem to indicate that the shift either happened earlier or is loaded with excessive significance by Abou El Fadl. Imam Jaᶜfar al-Ṣādiq (d. 148/765) is reported using the locution regularly, as in his statement that God is too great and glorious to leave the earth without 'a just *imām*'.[22] One could not argue in such a context that he means anyone other than the Imams designated by God, and yet he refers to an indefinite 'just *imām*'. The term is found in other *ḥadīth*s from the Imams also: Ibn Bābūya al-Shaykh al-Ṣadūq (d. 381/991), writing a century before al-Ṭūsī, says that *jihād* is obligatory with 'a just *imām*'.[23] Whilst the term *al-imām al-ᶜādil* is also used, it does not appear that there was a shift here. A simpler explanation is that we have an indefinite noun being used to signify a general category (a perfectly acceptable Arabic usage) rather than any deliberate imprecision on the jurists' part.

Nevertheless, it is worth exploring whether there was a development in the Imāmī Shiᶜi law of rebellion in the period immediately following al-Ṭūsī. The idea that the *fiqh* changed as a result of the shift in Shiᶜi fortunes from dominant party (under the Buyids) to the margins of power and possible suppression (under the Seljuqs) is possible. Abou El Fadl, however, seems to think not, for reasons which (to me at least) are not entirely clear.[24] A more detailed analysis is necessary before any definitive conclusion can be drawn. The argument has to take account of the context in which jurists were writing (not all were living under Seljuq control), offset, to an extent, by the fact that most Imāmī Shiᶜi legal discourse (and, for that matter, most *fiqh* discourse generally) is primarily interested in reacting to previous writings on the subject (namely a juristic tradition) and less to social reality. It is of course possible that the Shiᶜi *fiqh* writers are deliberately ambiguous – speaking of 'a just *imām*' or simply referring to 'the *imām*' and not explicitly mentioning that they were talking here about the Sinless Imam, the last in the line of twelve, who is currently in occultation. I prefer, however, to see this as a stylistic requirement of legal writings. That is, the Imam fulfils many different functions in Imāmī Shiᶜism, from the cosmic to the mundane, but when there is a reference to the *imām* in works of *fiqh*, the writers are talking about him as leader of the Muslim community, outlining the role he performs. With this restricted brief, their discussions of the Imam's role and function may appear general and non-specific (i.e. the *imām* referred to in these works does not seem the exalted figure of Imāmī theology), but this is a generic requirement rather than any indication that the position of *imām* within the system outlined here is generally available.

As has been recognised by recent commentators, the Shiᶜi juristic position on rebellion and the treatment of rebels and brigands was not left unaffected by the fact that the Shiᶜa themselves were, from their inception, a rebellious group. A blanket condemnation of any and all rebellion was, therefore, out of the question. There was, however, an extended discussion on where rebellion began and simple brigandage ended. The crucial difference between the two actions (technically termed *baghy* and *ḥirāba* respectively) lay in the existence of a plausible *taʾwīl* (interpretation, i.e. ideology or message) that had inspired the perpetrators. Rebels were involved in a campaign for ideological reasons. Brigands were simply common thieves with a high level of organisation: they were, with indulgence, rebels without a cause. The legal difference was akin to the modern distinction between a political prisoner and a criminal. Within Shiᶜi *fiqh* works, there was some discussion about how to recognise a *taʾwīl*. However, it is not only this broader discussion of rebellion which can illuminate Imāmī juristic developments in the period of early Seljuq rule. The minutiae of the rules concerning rebels (*aḥkām al-bughāt*, or often more bluntly *qitāl ahl al-baghy* – 'fighting the people of rebellion') can reveal differences in ethical and political outlook amongst the Shiᶜi *fuqahāʾ*.

Generally speaking, the Shiᶜa were forced to argue that rebellion against an illegitimate ruler (i.e. one who has usurped the position of the true Imam) was not, in itself, a justified action against that individual. Neither was it a prompt for condemnation from a legal perspective. There was, of course, the record of the early history of the Muslim community (and the Shiᶜa in particular), bursting with accounts of Shiᶜi rebellions. This record required accommodation with a legal structure developed after (and to an extent, in response to) the events described therein. In general, rebellion was obligatory when led by the true (infallible) Imam against the usurper; but was invalid when led by another, whether against the true Imam or against a usurper. The Imāmī position was basically quietist, but at the same time it ceded little or no legitimacy to the existing power structures. Suppression of internal rebels was one of the forms of *jihād* within the Shiᶜi framework, and as early Shiᶜi law was markedly cautious on the legitimation of *jihād* during the Occultation of the Imam, it followed, *mutatis mutandis*, that they would be similarly cautious about permitting participation in the suppression of rebels in the absence of the Imam. Within this framework, however, there was ample room for disagreement and juristic debate.

For example, there was a dispute around what to do with the war booty following the suppression of an uprising against the Imam by a group claiming to be Muslim. In a *jihād*, the war booty of the defeated enemy is given the term *ghanīma* and is distributed amongst the Imam and the fighters (*mujāhidīn*). Should the same rules apply in the case of rebels (*bughāt*)? As al-Sayyid al-Murtaḍā (a classmate and probably teacher of al-Ṭūsī, d. 436/1044) had argued, 'It is not permitted to treat as war booty and divide up the rebel's property in the manner one might divide up the property of the people of the abode of war.'[25] Al-Ṭūsī would appear to have agreed when he stated in his *Mabsūṭ*:

> [Following the battle] if a person finds another in possession of [the first person's] wealth, then [the first person] has ownership rights over it, whether this person was of the people of Justice or the rebels . . . ᶜAlī was asked [after the Battle of the Camel] 'are you not going to take their possessions?' He replied, 'No. For they are protected by the protection of Islam, and their possessions are not permitted in the land of the Hijra.'[26]

The opposing view, that is, that their property is classed as normal war booty, is attributed to the controversial figure of Ibn Junayd al-Iskāfī (d. 381/991), though his writing are not extant to confirm this.[27] And furthermore, in other writings, al-Ṭūsī is recorded as holding an opposing view. For example, in his *Nihāya* he writes:

> It is permitted for the Imam to take their property found amongst the troops and divide it amongst the fighters in the manner we have already described. However, he is not permitted [to do this with] what was not [found] amongst the troops.[28]

How might the subsequent generation of al-Ṭūsī 'followers' select an opinion to adopt when al-Ṭūsī contradicts himself? Whilst it is not clear how such a decision is made, the verdict of the subsequent generation is almost unanimous. All, as far as I can ascertain, decided to adopt the second of al-Ṭūsī's views listed above, rather than the first – for later Imāmī *fiqh*, the property of the rebel found amongst the defeated army is treated in the same way as the property of an unbeliever: it is war booty. First, the contemporary classmate and supposed pupil of al-Ṭūsī, the *qāḍī* Ibn al-Barrāj (d. 481/1088) opts for the view that the property is subject to division: 'The only element of their wealth which is divided as booty is what they had with them on the battlefield – not anything else, such as what they did not have with them.'[29] Ibn Ḥamza al-Ṭūsī, mentioned above, also opts for the view that their property is booty,[30] as does the author of the work entitled *Iṣbāḥ al-Shīᶜa bi-miṣbāḥ al-Sharīᶜa*, attributed within the tradition to Niẓām al-Dīn Sulaymān al-Ṣahrashtī, a pupil of al-Ṭūsī living in Najaf.[31] Even Ibn Zuhra al-Ḥalabī (d. 585/1189–90), a supposed dissenter who criticised al-Ṭūsī, agrees that the rebels' property is available as booty.[32] The first to argue for the opposite view is, predictably, Ibn Idrīs al-Ḥillī, who declares himself for al-Ṭūsī's *Mabsūṭ* position (and hence al-Sayyid al-Murtaḍā's view also), and disagrees with al-Ṭūsī's *Nihāya* position. He adds that al-Ṭūsī's self contradiction itself indicates how the quality of al-Ṭūsī's scholarship has been exaggerated – though this sort of open criticism is quite normal in Ibn Idrīs's work which seems to have as its *raison d'être* the refutation of al-Ṭūsī's opinions in most areas of *fiqh*.[33]

Now, the choice of which of al-Ṭūsī's opinions to favour is initially puzzling. This is particularly the case when the rejected opinion had the backing of another giant in the field, al-Ṭūsī's own teacher, al-Sayyid al-Murtaḍā. Furthermore, the *ḥadīth* evidence (including a bundle of sayings attributed to Imam ᶜAlī himself) would seem to give much greater support to the view the later tradition rejected. A possible reason might lie in the implications of the belief status of the rebels which follow from the adoption of one or other of the options. Put simply, if the property of the rebels is exempt from distribution following defeat (as per the opinion of al-Ṭūsī, al-Sayyid al-Murtaḍā and Ibn Idrīs), then they are Muslims whose property is sacrosanct, even if they have rebelled against the Imam. So, the various groups who rebelled against ᶜAlī's caliphate (the opponents in the Battle of the Camel including ᶜĀʾisha, Muᶜāwiya and the subsequent Umayyads) are Muslims and their property is protected. The problem can be extended further to those who rejected the authority of the Imams after ᶜAlī, and hence could apply to the Sunnis generally. They are Muslims, and they are accorded, in Shiᶜi *fiqh,* certain rights as such, even when they rebel against the Imam's political rule (and hence refuse to recognise his authority). It was this opinion which was rejected in favour of a more 'sectarian' view. If al-Ṭūsī's *Nihāya* position is taken as the *madhhab* opinion (as it was by his supporters and even by some of his dissenters like Ibn Zuhra), then the rebels' property becomes booty, meaning they have lost their property rights by rebelling (and hence they no longer have the protection afforded to Muslims). The result is a quite different legal position for those who reject the Imam's authority, and a more exclusive legal attitude predominates. It is, of course, not a total rejection. Those who refuse to recognise the Imam (the rebels, *al-bughāt*) are not identical with the defeated unbelievers (*kuffār*) in a *jihād.* The differences are technical, but nonetheless important. For the *kuffār*, not only the property on the battlefield, but all their property is booty; their women and children become slaves. For the *bughāt*, their property elsewhere is preserved for their descendents, and their women and children are not captured and enslaved. The *bughāt*, then, are portrayed here as similar but not identical to the *kuffār*.

The different positions attributed to al-Ṭūsī are followed through into other areas of the law. For example, is it permitted to wash and pray over the corpses of the rebels in the manner in which one might for a non-rebellious Muslim? Just as al-Ṭūsī has two answers over whether the property of the rebels is counted as war booty, similarly he states in one place that one must not perform the ritual washing and prayer,[34] and in other places that one should.[35] The later scholar al-ᶜAllāma al-Ḥillī, when discussing this difference within al-Ṭūsī makes the debate explicit:

> The reason for the difference here is whether [the rebel] is an unbeliever or not. If we rule that he is an unbeliever, then we should not wash or pray over him. If [we rule] conversely, then both [washing and praying] are obligatory.[36]

Incidentally, al-Ḥillī himself tends towards the view that the rebel is an unbeliever, but he accepts that this is an issue on which there can be legitimate difference of opinion between the *fuqahā*ᵓ. He sidesteps the eschatological question, focusing instead on the practical legal questions of whether the Imam can and should (legally speaking) fight the rebels, and how the conduct of such a campaign should be regulated. If, following this, some *fuqahā*ᵓ wash and pray over the corpses and others do not, this does not affect the more important questions of how rebellions should be quashed.

Another example of an area of dispute and innovation in the period immediately following al-Ṭūsī concerns the subdivision of the rebels. Al-Ṭūsī himself had distinguished between rebels who had reinforcements (*fi*ᵓ*a*) and those who did not. For al-Ṭūsī, different regulations apply to each category. Those who do not have reinforcements are treated more leniently by the forces of the Imam. The injured and the slaves of rebels with reinforcements can be killed by the Imam (he has a choice here; he is not compelled), and the fugitives can be pursued and (presumably) killed. In contrast, the injured, the slaves and the rebel fugitives without reinforcements must not be harmed.[37] The thinking here is presumably that rebels with reinforcements represent a more organised opposition force, and therefore are a more potent challenge to the Imam (who embodies not only legitimate rule, but also theological righteousness). Consequently, there is a need to eliminate them completely (by killing their wounded, slaves and fugitives) in order to prevent any future challenge to the Imam's religious authority and political rule. Their threat is not simply political, but religious also. Unlike unbelievers, however, the relatives of the rebels are exempt from harm, as they were Muslims before the rebellion, and the assumption is they remain so and cannot be held responsible for their relatives' actions. It is in this detail that the legal consequences of rebellion differ from a *jihād* with the unbelievers.

This two-fold division of the *ahl al-baghy* into those with and those without reinforcements is parroted by al-Ṭūsī's immediate successors. Ibn Ḥamza al-Ṭūsī makes the same division with the same responsibilities to each party.[38] The *Iṣbāḥ al-Shīᶜa* (al-Kaydarī) makes the same distinction, as does Ibn Zuhra al-Ḥalabī in his *Ghunyat al-nuzūᶜ*, interestingly using identical wording:

> Anyone who opposes Islam is an unbeliever whose frontline troops and fugitives are to be killed, as are their prisoners, and their wounded can be finished off. This applies to the rebels against the Imam also, if they have reinforcements on which they call. If they do not have reinforcements, then he does not pursue their fugitives, nor finish off their wounded, nor kill their slaves.[39]

The presentation here obviously owes much to al-Ṭūsī (who, in turn, probably acquired the categorisation from the Ḥanafī school);[40] but the imitators here include those who are normally portrayed as opponents of al-Ṭūsī's method (such as Ibn Zuhra). Furthermore, there are attempts to refine and improve on al-Ṭūsī's presentation. The work of Ibn Abī al-Majd al-Ḥalabī (d. late 6th/12th century) entitled *Ishārat al-Sabq*, does not have a separate section of its *kitāb al-jihād* devoted to rebels (as had become the standard organising principle), but instead counts them with the '*ḥarbiyyūn*' against whom the Imam must wage a *jihād*. Ibn Abī al-Majd, then, takes al-Ṭūsī's position (i.e. that rebels are unbelievers) to its logical conclusion, and structures his work of *fiqh* accordingly. It is more appropriate, in his view, to treat rebels along with the other militant unbelievers (or *ḥarbīs*) rather than as a special class on their own. However, the tradition of al-Ṭūsī (perhaps introduced to the Imāmī school before him) is too strong; Ibn Abī al-Majd cannot evade its influence completely. He is forced to make untidy caveats for the *bughāt* at various points, one of which relates to this distinction between rebels with and without reinforcements:

> The *ḥarbiyyūn* are to be fought, both the front line and the fugitives such that the fugitives can be pursued, and their defeated can be killed, as can their slaves. Their injured can be finished off, whether they are unbelievers of a *milla* [non-Muslim religious communities] or are apostates who have reinforcements to whom they might turn. But this should not be done to the people who rebel out of apostasy but who have no reinforcements. Rather, with these one may only fight them, and not pursue [their fugitives], and not finish off [their wounded] or kill [their slaves].[41]

The legal information is the same, but it is organised and presented differently. It should be noted here that the rebels are treated as apostates (*bughāt ahl al-ridda*), thereby extending al-Ṭūsī's tying of commitment to the Imam's rule as a measure of faith. Ibn Zuhra and the author of *Iṣbāḥ al-Shīᶜa* also explicitly link rebellion against the Imam to rejection of Islam. Ibn Abī al-Majd, however, is distracted into discussing those who are apostates but who do not rebel, and the procedure for prosecuting apostasy (all of which are not, in truth, relevant to the subject matter of a *kitāb al-jihād*). The result here, as in the passage cited above, is far from satisfactory in organisational terms, and the presentation lacks the neatness and finesse so prized in the *fiqh* tradition. The Shiᶜi tradition appears to have agreed with my assessment here: Ibn Abī al-Majd's structure was not imitated by subsequent authors, whilst that of al-Ṭūsī became the generic norm.

There were additional interesting developments from al-Ṭūsī's presentation of the two-fold division of rebels and the rules appertaining to them in the period under consideration. The first is that of Ibn al-Barrāj, a contemporary of al-Ṭūsī. ᶜAbd al-Azīz Ibn al-Barrāj was a *qāḍī* in Tripoli under the Shiᶜi rulers of the Banū ᶜAmmār. The Banū ᶜAmmār declared independence from the Fatimids in 462/1070.[42] He had trained with al-Ṭūsī in al-Sayyid al-Murtaḍā's class, where he was certainly second in prestige to al-Ṭūsī (Ṭūsī received twelve dinars allowance to Ibn al-Barrāj's eight). Some even report that he was a pupil of al-Ṭūsī after al-Murtaḍā's death in 436/1044. Ibn al-Barrāj was, supposedly, sent to Syria by al-Ṭūsī to be his representative there. For at least the last twenty years of his life (and possibly from as early as 438/1046–7), he was *qāḍī* in Tripoli. He did not, it seems, witness the Seljuq arrival in Baghdad first hand, having left before then for Syria, and he probably never lived under the Seljuqs.[43] It is possible that this biographical information aids us in our understanding of Ibn al-Barrāj's discussion of *ahl al-baghy* (rebels), though it remains speculative. Whilst Ibn al-Barrāj does utilise al-Ṭūsī's two-fold division, he also considers the situation of a civil war:

> If two parties fight each other with words . . . and do not draw their weapons, then [you should] reconcile them . . . If one of them rises up against the other, and the aggressors draw their swords against the oppressed, then it is obligatory to fight this rebellious group until they return to the order of God. This is obligatory for the Muslims, if the Imam, seeking their aid and assistance, calls them to do this – [they must] rise up with him in a war against them. No one may tarry in this task. There is, here, no difference between a group who rise up against another group of believers and those who rise up against the Imam.[44]

Ibn al-Barrāj, perhaps uniquely in Shiᶜi *fiqh*, widens the category of rebel (*bughāt*) to include those who foment internal strife between groups within the community of believers (*al-bāghiyya ᶜalā ṭāʾifa min al-muʾminīn*) and not only rebels against the Imam. This innovation is, in itself, interesting, as it places a community's internal peace on a par with the authority of the Imam's rule. Ibn al-Barrāj's whole passage is, unsurprisingly, written with the ambivalence which characterises Shiᶜi discussions of such matters: it is never entirely clear whether these rules can be activated by, or apply to, a current ruler, or whether these are theoretical discussions outlining how the absent Imam would run things were he here. A current ruler, or perhaps a member of the *fuqahāʾ*, might stake a claim to be the unidentified 'one whom the Imam has designated' (*man naṣabahu al-imām*) referred to regularly in Imāmī discussions of these issues. That is, they may be employing the notion of *niyāba* (designation), which became increasingly common in *fiqh* discussions from al-ᶜAllāma al-Ḥillī (d. 726/1325) onwards and later formed a mainstay of juristic argumentation. The ambiguity gives rise to debate both within the tradition and amongst secondary commentators. Whether or not a reference to current rulers is intended here (perhaps Ibn al-Barrāj was turning to his patrons, the Banū ᶜAmmār), raising the importance of internal community strife to a level of rebellion against the Imam is significant. Possibly it emerges from Ibn al-Barrāj's position as a *qāḍī* (he would be constantly attempting to achieve community reconciliation). Perhaps, his innovative presentation of rebellion, both in form and in content, can be traced to his position of relative confidence (Shiᶜi *qāḍī* in a supposedly Shiᶜi state) where internal concord is essential to the establishment and preservation of political stability.

A second innovatory approach is less surprising, in that Ibn Idrīs, as we have already seen, spent much of his *fiqh* work, *al-Sarāʾir*, criticising al-Ṭūsī's approach. His section on 'fighting the rebels' is, in structural terms, not so dissimilar to those that immediately preceded him. However, his examination of the two categories contains a significant variation on the usual wording:

> The people of rebellion are of two types according to our colleagues: a section who fight, but they do not have a leader (*raʾīs*) to whom they refer, and another type who have an *amīr* and a leader to whom they turn in their affairs . . . When they do not have a leader to whom they refer, then their wounded are not finished off, and their fugitives are not pursued, and their relatives not imprisoned, and their slaves are not killed. But when they have a leader to whom they refer in their affairs, then the Imam can finish off their injured and chase down their fugitives and kill their slaves – though it is never permitted to imprison their offspring.[45]

In the other post-Ṭūsī works, it is the presence of reinforcements (*fiʾa*) which acts as the trigger for the harsh treatment of rebels in the post-conflict situation. Above I speculated that this was on the basis of the relevant level of threat represented by the different categories of rebels. With Ibn Idrīs, the activating factor shifts to the presence of a leader (*raʾīs, amīr*) to whom the rebels refer. One sees here a reference not to the numerical power of the rebels, but to their ideological challenge to the Imam. A group which stands up and attempts to acclaim someone as the Imam who is clearly not the Imam deserves (relatively speaking) harsher treatment than those who have no leader with whom to make this claim. The threat to the Imam's power is both military and ideological, though it is the ideological which is more significant for Ibn Idrīs. In subsequent Imāmī *fiqh*, writers oscillated between the two positions (i.e. between reinforcements and leader being the greater threat and therefore worthy of mention). Some, like al-ᶜAllāma al-Ḥillī, attempted to merge the two elements into a single category. He phrases this category as 'those who have no reinforcements on which they might call, nor a leader around whom they have gathered'.[46]

From his writings, it is not clear what Ibn Idrīs's attitude towards Seljuq rule might have been – he lived south of Baghdad, outside of the orbit of rigorously enforced Seljuq power. However, it is clear that he viewed the Imam as the ideal ruler, whose governorship was not simply politically effective, but also religiously mandated. Any who challenge this (i.e. any who might claim the Imam's rightful place) were subject to the harshest treatment possible under the laws of rebellion. However, it is also important to note that although the rebels against the Imam are, for Ibn Idrīs, dangerous, and hence legitimate targets, they hold a different (and marginally more acceptable) legal status than the *harbī* unbelievers. Nonetheless, the general trend, following al-Ṭūsī, is for the *bughāt-ḥarbī-kuffār* equation to become the underlying presumption in the Imāmī discussions of rebellion. Interestingly, then, in the period following the collapse of Shiᶜi influence at the centre of power, and the rise of the Seljuqs, the Imāmī *fuqahāʾ* select a legal position which views the (now dominant) Sunnis as, by implication, on the edge of (and perhaps excluded from) the category of Muslims. Such a development could be explained by this loss of influence, not in the sense of petulance, but more as a recognition that the future of Imāmī scholarship lay in the development of a separate legal identity. In this sense, the admittedly limited evidence presented here would seem to support Stewart's carefully worded conclusion concerning early Seljuq Shiᶜi intellectual activity:

> [A] period of intellectual activity and exchange crucial for the development of the Shiite legal tradition came to a close. Yet by then, the Twelvers had acquired the major practical and theoretical foundations necessary to maintain a legal *madhhab* parallel to those of the Sunnis. The tradition was carried on in Najaf and in other cities in Syria and Iran, where Sunni opposition was less severe. It was this historical combination of situations during the Buwayid period, the high

profile of Shiᶜism in the social and political arena coupled with a conservative Sunni traditionalist reaction against religious pluralism, that set the stage for the formation of the Twelver Shiite *madhhab*.[47]

CONCLUSIONS

The above discussion indicates, I hope, that the portrayal of Shiᶜi jurisprudence in the early Seljuq period as consisting of mere reproductions of al-Ṭūsī's positions is not entirely fair. This is not to underestimate al-Ṭūsī's influence on the structures of Shiᶜi legal thought, as well as his role in the establishment of a new Shiᶜi intellectual centre in al-Najaf/al-Ḥilla following the Seljuq capture of Baghdad. A more accurate characterisation, at least on the evidence examined here, is that there was considerable dispute and difference amongst the Imāmī *fuqahāʾ* of the period, and these disputes were not confined to the usual suspects (such as Ibn Zuhra and Ibn Idrīs). Other so-called followers of al-Ṭūsī's approach, including on occasions those who were pupils of the Shaykh himself, differed from him in significant ways. Of course, Ibn Idrīs and his rejection of al-Ṭūsī's reliance on isolated traditions does create a 'two-school' dynamic, but on some issues Ibn Idrīs shares an opinion with al-Ṭūsī which his followers refused to adopt. In the details of *furūᶜ* (substantive law), the dispute amongst al-Ṭūsī's pupils was oftentimes as great as between al-Ṭūsī's school and the anti-Ṭūsī tendency headed by Ibn Idrīs. What is clear is that this was not a period of moribund imitation. Debate may have happened within strictly patrolled parameters, and major intellectual advance may have been restricted by the fact that the Shiᶜi juristic community was scattered, living under Seljuq rule, on its margins and outside of it. Yet despite this geographical and political dispersal, the Imāmī *fuqahāʾ* viewed themselves increasingly as participants in a juristic tradition with its own internal dynamic, and not merely as poor cousins of their better known, and more numerous, Sunni counterparts.

NOTES

1. Ruth Stellhorn Mackensen 'Four great libraries of Medieval Baghdad', *The Library Quarterly* 2, 3 (1932), pp. 288–93; George Makdisi, 'Muslim institutions of learning in eleventh-century Baghdad', *BSOAS* 24, 1 (1961), pp. 7–8.
2. Yāqūt b. ᶜAbd Allāh al-Ḥamawī (d. 626/1229), *Muᶜjam al-buldān* (Beirut, 1979), II, p. 534. See also ᶜIzz al-Dīn Abū al-Ḥasan ᶜAlī Ibn al-Athīr (d. 630/1233), *al-Kāmil fī l-tārīkh*, ed. Tornberg (Beirut, 1385–/1965–), IX, p. 350.
3. ᶜAbd al-Raḥmān b. ᶜAlī Ibn al-Jawzī (d. 597/1201), *al-Muntaẓam fī taʾrīkh al-mulūk wa'l-umam*, eds Muḥammad ᶜAṭā and Muṣṭafā ᶜAṭā (Beirut, 1992), VI, pp. 173, 179.
4. Ibn al-Athīr, *Kāmil*, IX, pp. 637–8.

5. Aḥmad b. ᶜAlī Ibn Ḥajar al-ᶜAsqalānī (d. 852/1449), *Lisān al-mīzān* (Beirut, 1971), V, p. 135.
6. Abdulaziz Sachedina, *Islamic Messianism: the Idea of the Mahdi in Twelver Shi'ism* (Albany, NY, 1981), p. 33, speaks of the period following al-Ṭūsī's death as a time when 'Imamite scholars went into hiding'. Subsequent scholars were 'explicitly following' al-Ṭūsī, as 'very little elaboration' was needed, and by implication, was received in the years to follow.
7. Hossein Modarressi Tabātabāʾi, *An Introduction to Shīᶜī Law: a Bibliographical Study* (London, 1984), p. 45.
8. Jawad al-Shahrastānī, 'Introduction' to ᶜAlī b. al-Ḥusayn al-Karakī (d. 940/1533–4), *Jāmiᶜ al-maqāṣid* (Qum, 1408/1987), I, p. 18 (editor's introduction). It has to be said that the phrasing of al-Shahrastānī's remarks is remarkably close to that of Modarressi.
9. Norman Calder, 'Doubt and Prerogative: the emergence of an Imāmī Shīᶜī theory of *ijtihād*', *Studia Islamica* 70 (1989), p. 64: 'With the advent of the Saljuqs, the removal of Ṭūsī to Najaf and the gradual cessation of meaningful polemical debate between sects, it became impossible to sustain the hard edge of sophisticated argument . . . Problems of continuity, flexibility and *ikhtilāf* were obscured by a general uncritical submission in legal affairs to the views propounded by him.'
10. Abū al-Qāsim ᶜAlī b. Mūsā Ibn Ṭāwūs (d. 664/ 1266), *Kashf al-mahajja*, ed. al-Ḥassūn (Qum, 1412/1992), p. 127f. (and found cited regularly in subsequent writings – see for example, al-Ḥasan b. al-Shahīd al-Thānī (d. 1011/1602), *Maᶜālim al-uṣūl*, ed. Muḥammadī (Qum, 1374/1954), pp. 244–5.
11. Modarressi, *Introduction*, p. 46.
12. The same could be said of a comparison of the doctrines of al-Ṭūsī and his Sunni counterparts. There will always be more agreement than disagreement, but this does not mean that there are not distinctive schools of law presented here. See, for example, Muḥammad b. al-Ḥasan al-Ṭūsī (d. 460/1067), *al-Khilāf* (Qum, 1408/1988).
13. Calder, 'Doubt and Prerogative', pp. 64–5.
14. ᶜAbd Allāh b. ᶜĪsā al-Afandī (d. c. 1130/1718), *Riyāḍ al-ᶜulamāʾ wa-ḥiyāḍ al-fuḍalāʾ*, ed. Ḥusaynī (Qum, 1403/1983), VI, pp. 16–17. He relates from the Shaykh with or without an intermediary (*bi-lā al-wāsiṭa aw bi-wāsiṭa*). In particular he relates the Shaykh's opinion on the prohibition on convening congregational prayer (*ṣalāt al-jumᶜa*).
15. Ibid. VI, p. 17. A detailed biography can be found in Muḥammad Bāqir al-Khwānsārī, *Rawḍāt al-Jannāt,* ed. Kashfī (Beirut, 1411/1991), VI, pp. 243–54.
16. Abū Jaᶜfar Muḥammad b. ᶜAlī Ibn Ḥamza al-Ṭūsī (d. after 566/1171), *al-Wasīla ilā nayl al-faḍīla* (found in the lithograph collection published by the Library of Ayatallāh al-Sayyid al-Marᶜashī entitled *al-Jawāmiᶜ al-fiqhiyya*) (Qum, n.d.), p. 733.
17. Muḥammad b. al-Ḥasan al-Ṭūsī, *al-Iqtiṣād al-hādī ilā ṭarīq al-rashād* (Qum, 1400/1980), p. 148.
18. Michael Cook, *Commanding Right and Forbidding Wrong in Islamic Thought* (Cambridge, 2000), pp. 288–90.
19. Ibid. p. 202.
20. Ibid. p. 288–90.
21. Khaled Abou El Fadl, *Rebellion and Violence in Islamic Law* (Cambridge, 2001), pp. 218–19.
22. Abū Jaᶜfar Muḥammad b. Yaᶜqūb al-Kulaynī (d. 329/941), *al-Kāfī*, ed. al-Ghaffārī (Qum,

1388/1968), I, p. 178. Anyone who makes a pilgrimage to the grave of al-Ḥusayn received benefits in the next life as if he has performed 20 *ḥajjs*, 20 *ᶜumras* and 20 raids (*ghazwa*) with 'a prophet who has been sent or a just Imam'. See ibid. IV, p. 580.

23. Ibn Bābūya al-Shaykh al-Ṣadūq (d. 381/991), *al-Khiṣāl,* ed. al-Ghaffārī (Qum, 1403/1981), p. 607.
24. See Abou El Fadl, *Rebellion and Violence*, p. 217: 'It is possible that the Shīᶜī jurists responded to the Seljuq challenge by systematizing their discourses on rebellion. Nonetheless, this is unlikely because most of the Shīᶜī discourses, at this stage, were concerned with responding to the Sunni arguments about the religious status of those who rebelled against ᶜAlī. Furthermore the majority of Shīᶜī discourses in the fifth/eleventh century focussed on addressing the status of those who rebel against the true and infallible *imām.*' There is a lack of precision here, and Abou El-Fadl seems to contradict his later assertion that the shift to using 'a just ruler' by 'a large number of Imāmī jurists' (in the 5th/11th century) is significant. See ibid. p. 298.
25. ᶜAlī b. al-Ḥusayn al-Sayyid al-Murtaḍā (d. 436/1044), *Masāᵓil al-nāṣiriyyāt* (Beirut, 1417/1997), p. 444.
26. See Ṭūsī, *al-Mabsūṭ*, ed. Kashfi (Qum, n.d.), VI, pp. 266–7.
27. Al-ᶜAllāma al-Ḥillī al-Ḥasan b. Yūsuf (d. 726/1325), *Mukhtalaf al-Shīᶜa* (Qum, 1412/1992), IV, p. 450. Ibn Junayd's notoriety is linked to his promotion of *qiyās* as an acceptable juristic mechanism (a position which was rejected by Imāmī legal theory). See Modarressi, 'Rationalism and traditionalism in Shīᶜī jurisprudence', *Studia Islamica* 59 (1984), p. 153; Robert Gleave, 'Imāmī Shīᶜī refutation of *qiyās*', in *Studies in Islamic Legal Theory*, ed. B. Weiss (Leiden, 2002), pp. 267–91.
28. Ṭūsī, *Nihāya*, ed al-Ṭihrānī (Qum, n.d.), II, p. 12.
29. Al-Qāḍī ᶜAbd al-ᶜAzīz Ibn al-Barrāj (d. 481/1088), *al-Muhadhdhab*, ed. Subḥānī (Qum, 1406/1986), I, pp. 325–6.
30. Ibn Ḥamza, *Wasīla*, p. 732.
31. Niẓām al-Dīn Sulaymān b. Ḥasan al-Ṣahrashtī (attrib., d. 6th/12th century), *Iṣbāḥ al-Shīᶜa bi-misbāh al-sharīᶜa*, ed. Bahādurī (Qum, 1416/1995), p. 190. On the authorship of this text, and a persuasive argument that it is actually the work of Quṭb al-Dīn Muḥammad al-Kaydarī (d. 6th/12th century), see the introduction to this edition by Jaᶜfar al-Subḥānī (pp. 10–18).
32. ᶜIzz al-Dīn Ḥamza b. ᶜAlī Ibn Zuhra al-Ḥalabī (d. 585/1189–90), *Ghunyat al-nuzūᶜ* (in *al-Jawāmiᶜ al-fiqhiyya*), p. 522.
33. For more on Ibn Idrīs's criticism of al-Ṭūsī, see the editor's introduction to Muḥammad b. Manṣūr Ibn Idrīs al-Ḥillī (d. 598/1202), *K. al-Sarāᵓir al-ḥāwī li-taḥrīr al-fatāwī* (Qum, 1410/1989), I, pp. 11–16.
34. Ṭūsī, *Mabsūṭ*, I, p. 182.
35. Ṭūsī, *Khilāf*, III, p. 168.
36. ᶜAllāma, *Mukhtalaf*, IV, p. 456.
37. Ṭūsī, *Nihāya*, p. 297.
38. Ibn Ḥamza, *Wasīla*, p. 733.
39. Ṣahrashtī (attrib.), *Iṣbāḥ al-Shīᶜa*, p. 189; Ibn Zuhra, *Ghunyat al-nuzūᶜ*, p. 522.
40. Abou El Fadl, *Rebellion and Violence*, p. 221.
41. ᶜAlī b. al-Hasan Ibn Abī al-Majd al-Ḥalabī, *Ishārat al-sabq*, ed. al-Bahādurī (Qum, 1414/1993), p. 144.
42. *EI2*, s.v. ᶜAmmār, Banū, I, p. 448.

43. Khwānsārī, *Rawḍāt*, IV, pp. 198–202, and the references therein.
44. Ibn al-Barrāj, *Muhadhdhab*, I, p. 325.
45. Ibn Idrīs, *Sarāʾir*, II, p. 16.
46. ᶜAllāma, *Taḥrīr al-aḥkām*, ed. al-Bahādurī (Qum, 1420/1999), II, p. 233.
47. D. Stewart, *Islamic Legal Orthodoxy: Twelver Shi'i Responses to the Sunni Legal System* (Salt Lake City, UT, 1998), p. 128.

CHAPTER

12

IN DEFENCE OF SUNNISM: AL-GHAZĀLĪ AND THE SELJUQS

*Massimo Campanini**

In this chapter I shall attempt to place al-Ghazālī's political thought in the context of the Seljuq sultanate and the late Abbasid caliphate, starting from two premises: firstly, that al-Ghazālī's political thought is as significant as his mystical or theological thought; and secondly, that it is understandable only in the light of the political developments of his time.

I should like to begin to formulate an answer to the question raised in the title of the conference whose proceedings are collected in this volume: did the Seljuqs revitalise Islam? Probably they did or at least they brought a measure of order to a Muslim world in turmoil, but in so doing they sacrificed the prestige and the very role of the caliphate. There has been a wide debate about whether the Seljuqs were the defenders or the enemies of the caliphate. In a sense, they defended the caliphate insofar as they allowed it to endure a few centuries longer. But from another point of view, they were enemies of the caliphate in that they imposed a secular image of power against the religious legitimisation of the caliphal power. In other words, while, on the one hand, the Seljuqs protected the institution of the caliphate against its many adversaries, like the Isma^{c}ilis, on the other hand they made it evident that the management of power in Islam was no longer a question of the Islamic state but rather of an Islamic model of the state.[1] Let us examine these contentions more closely.

When the Seljuqs took power in 447/1055, the caliphate was going through a period of deep crisis. The efforts of caliphs like al-Qādir to revitalise Abbasid authority were doomed to failure because of the progressive decline in

---

* I thank Caroline Higgitt, who helped me to improve my English.

significance of the very notion of the caliphate. A universal *umma* (community of the believers) embodied in a universal empire no longer existed: the fragmentation of the Islamic world brought about the end of the idea of the caliphate as universal political organism. Al-Māwardī (d. 450/1058) tried to inject new blood into the dying institution, developing for the first time in the history of Islamic political thought a systematic theory of the caliphate. He was aware that the caliphate was no longer an Islamic state, however. As an Islamic state, the caliphate would bring together the religious and the political dimensions of power. This had occurred – at least in Islamic political mythology – at the time of the Prophet's rule over Medina and of the four *rāshidūn* (right-guided caliphs). But already from the Omayyad period, it was no longer the case. It is true that some of the first Abbasid caliphs claimed to be 'caliphs of God', but, as Patricia Crone points out, it was not long – when the *asḥāb al-ḥadīth* (traditionists) fixed the number and the hierarchy of the *rāshidūn* caliphs, a couple of centuries after Muḥammad's death (and it is worth recalling the role of Ibn Ḥanbal in this process) – before 'mainstream Muslims laid down that religious guidance could never be concentrated in the head of state again'.[2] The 'multi-purpose polity [that is, the *umma*]', as Crone calls it, was moving rapidly towards a separation of powers. The ideal situation of Muḥammad's Medina, where, in accordance with God's will, political power and religious guidance were strictly intertwined, was definitely over. Especially under the Abbasid caliphs, the unity of the *umma* was broken and the political and the religious functions were no longer united in the head of the state.[3]

Al-Māwardī knew perfectly that the two functions – the political and the religious – were irretrievably separated; the first was practically in the sultans' hands; the second formally in the caliphs'. It goes without saying that he tried to subject the secular and political power of the sultans to the religious power of the caliphs. But he was well aware that the secular and political power of the sultans was independent of the religious power of the caliphs. Thus, he acknowledged the reality of the Buyid-Abbasid relationship. The Buyids were sultans and the Abbasids caliphs; officially the Buyids were legitimised by the Abbasids; but in practice the Buyids controlled the caliphal nomination and moreover they managed the substantial power of the state through the administration and the army. In this way, the dual system of sultanate-caliphate was no longer an Islamic state but an Islamic model of the state: a *siyāsa* (politics) in agreement with *sharīʿa* (religious law) at best; a secular *siyāsa* governing in the name of *sharīʿa*, but in reality doing without it in practice. The Seljuqs, successors of the Buyids, definitively deprived the caliphs of their authority: they allowed the caliphate to survive, but they ruled without any caliphal supervision and reproduced the situation of a secular *siyāsa* governing in the name of *sharīʿa*, but doing without it.

Meanwhile, the Sunni world was threatened by Isma^c^ilism, both in the form of the Fatimid caliphate in Cairo and later of the 'heretic' Alamut state in Persia. Isma^c^ilism had been from the outset a revolutionary movement. As Bernard Lewis put it:

> To the discontented, [the Isma^c^ilis] offered the attraction of a well-organized, widespread and powerful opposition movement, which seemed to provide a real possibility of overthrowing the existing order and establishing in its place a new and just society, headed by the Imam – the heir of the Prophet, the chosen of God, and the sole rightful leader of mankind.[4]

The Alamut state of Ḥasan-i Ṣabbāḥ, founded in 483/1090, had a subversive programme. The Seljuqs opposed the Niẓārī Isma^c^ilis of Alamut, the 'Assassins', in the name of the caliphate in a struggle that was more political than religious. This is clear at least in the stance of the great vizier Niẓām al-Mulk. As William M. Watt put it,

> the second part he [Niẓām al-Mulk] added shortly before his death [to the *Siyāsat-nāma*] is evidence of increasing anxiety over the Bāṭinite movement . . . The interesting point about Niẓām al-Mulk's account is that he regards as Bāṭinite or approximately Bāṭinite a number of revolts in various parts of the East between 133/750 and 364/975 . . . All these movements were revolts against established authority in the interests of a different kind of authority.[5]

Thus, Niẓām al-Mulk's concern was for the social peace and stability of the Seljuqs' authority – an authority challenged by the Bāṭinite new kingdom in Alamut.

In the summer of 485/1092 the sultan Malikshāh dispatched an expedition against Alamut which was repelled. In Ramaḍān 485/October 1092, an Assassin murdered the vizier Niẓām al-Mulk, the first murder by a *fidāʾī* (literally 'one who sacrifices himself'). It was the first of a long series of attacks. But a little later Barkyāruq, Malikshāh's successor, 'had little attention and few forces to spare for the Ismā^c^īlīs; at worst, he or some of his lieutenants were ready to tolerate Ismā^c^īlī action against his enemies and even perhaps, on occasion, discretely to seek their help'.[6] In time, the Niẓārī state became an undisputed reality.

From at least one point of view the Seljuqs contributed to religious revival. It is well known how their great vizier, Niẓām al-Mulk, masterminded the revival of Sunni Islam through the foundation of Niẓāmiyya madrasas, the spreading of Shāfi^c^ism and Ash^c^arism and the dispute over the religious ideology of Isma^c^ilism.[7] This was undoubtedly a characteristic of the Seljuqs' rule. In this historical and intellectual context, Abū Ḥāmid al-Ghazālī's political contribution was no less original than his contributions in other fields. I should like to suggest immediately the main points of my argumentation:

1. Al-Ghazālī was a reformist Muslim intellectual whose intellectual, philosophical and theological skills were directed at a revitalisation of Sunni Islam.
2. Hence, he directly challenged Isma^cilism in order to defend Sunnism and at the same time the role of Sunni *ᶜulamāᵓ* in religion and politics. In this sense, he put forward a theological interpretation of Niẓām al-Mulk's political project.
3. To pursue this aim, he defended the legitimacy of the caliphate and the sultanate alike. He was completely aware of the twofold reality of power in the Muslim world. While al-Māwardī asserted the supremacy of the caliphate over the sultanate, al-Ghazālī put them on a par with the same level of importance and legitimacy. Once again, he theorised an Islamic model of the state and not an Islamic state.
4. Al-Ghazālī considered himself more a servant of the caliphs than of the Seljuqs, however. He deemed the secular power to be corrupting; necessary but corrupting. From this point of view he distinguished himself from Niẓām al-Mulk. While the latter's political theory was deeply imbued with the Iranian tradition of the 'mirrors for princes', al-Ghazālī's political theory was heavily influenced by the Islamic tradition of juridical treatises.

The starting point must be al-Ghazālī's biography itself. His role as a Muslim intellectual consisted of three main phases. The first corresponds to the time when he was teaching in Baghdad's Niẓāmiyya madrasa (484–8/1091–5); the second corresponds to his period of concealment in pursuit of the mystic path (488–99/1095–1106); the third corresponds to his return to teaching and political engagement (499–503/1106–9). In the first phase al-Ghazālī was involved in Niẓām al-Mulk's politics. He was summoned by the vizier to teach in the Niẓāmiyya and it is likely that the vizier was sure that he was a faithful supporter of the existing Seljuq power, or at least that he was not interested in creating political trouble. The second mystical phase does not concern us here. In the third phase of al-Ghazālī's life, he resumed teaching on the invitation of Fakhr al-Mulk, vizier of the Seljuq sultan Sanjār and Niẓām al-Mulk's son, confirming his closeness to power.

On the whole, however, al-Ghazālī lived far from the political centres of the Seljuq empire. In Baghdad he acted in accordance with Niẓām al-Mulk's political and religious plans. But perhaps it is significant that he began his period of concealment when Barkyāruq ascended to power and only ended it after Barkyāruq's death. The bad relations with the Seljuq sultan were probably one of the reasons why he left Baghdad in 488/1095. Al-Ghazālī's uncompromising stance against Isma^{c}ilism was in contradiction with Barkyāruq's appeasement of the radical Shī^{c}ite sect. It does not mean that al-Ghazālī was an enemy of the sultanate though, as I will argue below.

Al-Ghazālī showed a continuous interest in politics and ethics throughout his life. He dealt with ethical and political issues in both the *Iqtiṣād fī l-i^{c}tiqād* and the *Mīzān al-^{c}amal*, for example, but he assumed a political stance even in the mystical work *al-Munqidh min al-ḍalāl*, written at the very end of his life. The *Munqidh min al-ḍalāl*'s content makes it possible to date it beyond any doubt to around 499/1106 – very probably to 500/1107 and certainly not later than 503/1109. It consists mainly of the intellectual autobiography of the author, describing his psychological crisis, his doubts about the foundation of truth, the new intellectual and spiritual certainties acquired in Sufism after long studying and painful suffering, his return to teaching in Nishapur and the motives that convinced him to reappear on the public scene after his years in concealment. He was convinced that God had predestined him to be the *mujaddid* or renewer of religion and of Muslim intellectual morality (al-Ghazālī's return to teaching in Nishapur in 1106 corresponded exactly to the Hegira year 499, on the eve of the 6th century of the Islamic era/12th century of the Christian era). His project was both cultural and political, although the full content and limits of that project escape us, at least from the political point of view. In any case, as Fazlur Rahman put it,

> there was [in al-Ghazālī] an acute need to return to law and theology at that critical juncture. The Ismā^{c}īlī revolt was in full swing and their assassinations so rampant that they had become extremely dangerous to Sunnī Islam. The situation desperately required the restoration of the social order and hence a reassertion of the authority and supremacy of the *sharī^{c}a*. The political authority itself had become very weak and the Seljuq princes recurrently and quickly succeeded each other as rulers and were recognized as such by the shadowy caliphate authority. Perhaps this is also what al-Ghazālī means by the words [contained in the *Munqidh*] 'then divine decree drove me to return to public teaching', for external circumstances freed him to accept Fakhr al-Mulk's invitation to head the Niẓāmiyya at Nishapur.[8]

It is only natural that a political stance is so overwhelmingly evident in the *Mustaẓhirī*, where roughly the same imperatives as can be found in the *Munqidh* are detectable. In the *Mustaẓhirī* the author defends both Sunnism against

Ismaᶜilism and the role of just and righteous *ᶜulamāᵓ* against corruption and moral laxity. Let us take a closer look at this work.

Al-Ghazālī was commissioned to write the *Faḍāᵓiḥ al-Bāṭiniyya wa faḍāᵓil al-Mustaẓhiriyya* by the caliph al-Mustaẓhir (ascended to the throne in 487/1094) who wished to have at his disposal a forceful treatise devoted to disputing the Ismaᶜili demands. Al-Ghazālī outlines his most complete analysis of the Ismaᶜili danger (referring explicitly to the Alamut state) claiming to reassert the religious and political centrality of the Prophet Muḥammad. Actually, the unreasonableness of the infallible *imām*'s conception – a judgment useful to al-Ghazālī in order to stress that the only true infallible *imām* is the Prophet Muḥammad – is not considered only as the outcome of a theological-juridical absurdity, but also as the negative outcome of an intellectual contradiction. The logical inconsistencies of the Ismaᶜili discourse are very clear to al-Ghazālī: either when it tries to demonstrate the unreliability of human reasoning through the same reasoning, or when it claims to integrate the sound prescriptions of the religious Law with the debatable opinions of the *imām*. Al-Ghazālī is absolutely positive: the Ismaᶜilis invalidate logic,[9] and he is safely able to demonstrate this in many places. For instance:

> But if you needed reflection, then was that reflection known [recognized] by the intellect or not? And one [of the Ismaᶜilis] must answer: By the intellect. Then we say: And if, upon reflection, the intellect decided something, was it veracious or not? If they say it was not – then why did they give it credence? And if they say it was veracious – then they have indeed invalidated the principle [basis] of their doctrine, vis. their assertion that there is no way to give credence to the intellects [but make recourse to the *imām*].[10]

A short book by Faruk Mitha discusses the *Mustaẓhirī* in depth. His general thesis is not particularly new. The *Mustaẓhirī* is a treatise of *siyāsa sharᶜiyya*, that is, in Mitha's words, a juridical-political work.[11] Although it is clear that by *siyāsa sharᶜiyya* al-Ghazālī did not mean the same as Ibn Taymiyya, the *Mustaẓhirī* is surely a work in which al-Ghazālī aimed to give politics an interpretation from the point of view of religious Law. Moreover, as Mitha argues, the book has been written to challenge the Ismaᶜili doctrine of *taᶜlīm* (authoritative teaching) and, on the other hand, to defend the Sunni order represented by the Abbasid caliphate on the level of religious and moral legitimacy and by the Seljuq sultanate on the level of political and military legitimacy. The defence of the Sunni order against Ismaᶜili deviations 'is articulated in terms of al-Ghazālī's recurrent emphasis on the centrality of the Law as the *raison d'être* of the Muslim Community and . . . [in terms of] al-Ghazālī's conviction that the Law is preserved and obeyed only through the life of the community'.[12]

Mitha argues that al-Ghazālī – underlining the validity of reason and claiming for himself a rationality that was lacking in Isma^cili thinking – had as his goal a revaluation of the *ta^clīm* of the Sunni *^culamā^ᵓ*. For al-Ghazālī,

> the entire Shī^cī Ismā^cīlī enterprise of the Fatimids represented the 'wholly other', with whom no compromise was possible. Epistemologically and politically, it was the same worry of Niẓām al-Mulk. The Shī^cī Imām's claim to infallible authority challenges the very premises of the Sunni legal tradition, and hence also the *raison d'être* of the Sunnī *^culamā^ᵓ*.[13]

In other words, al-Ghazālī was the spokesman of well-defined corporate interests – the defence of the caste, that of the *^culamā^ᵓ*, he belonged to – while naturally seeking to uphold religion and defend 'orthodoxy'.

Mitha argues that 'one of the central concerns of the text [the *Mustaẓhirī*] has been to demonstrate the instrumental interdependence of law and theology in constructing a conception of orthodoxy in Islam', and he suggests that 'the disciplines of law and theology are systems of interpretation and hence orthodoxy is ultimately not a given postulate but represents a problem of interpretation'.[14] Unfortunately, Mitha does not elaborate on this intriguing observation.

Al-Ghazālī's theory of the caliphate in the *Mustaẓhirī* is on the whole what could be described as traditional and functional. It is functional in the sense that the author wished to contrast the legitimacy of the Abbasid caliph with the illegitimacy of the Isma^cili *imām*. It is traditional insofar as it is based on the classical concepts of *ikhtiyār* (free choice), *bay^ca* (homage) and *ijmā^c* (consensus) and on the recognition of the specific qualities of the caliph as an honest and just man, proficient in religious studies and duties and able to face the necessities of war. Moreover, al-Ghazālī seems to single out the caliph's figure without any reference to the Seljuq sultan. How to interpret this silence? While Ann Lambton spoke of the author's 'idealism',[15] and Carole Hillenbrand argued for an implicit acceptance of the Turks' power,[16] Mitha maintains that the point was to affirm the symbolic status of al-Mustaẓhir, whose competition with the Isma^cili *imām* could be compromised by a too obvious tribute to the sultans.[17]

What is needed is a global reflection on al-Ghazālī's political thought. The problem of the caliphate assumes a particular shape in consideration of the historical context in which the author lived. At the risk of over-generalising, it is possible to say that on one side of the coin is the necessity of the caliphate, while on other is the obligation of the subjects to obey the king without conditions. The presupposition of this contention is the idea of a necessary relation – a relation of connection and not of integration however – between religion and politics. The contention that religion and politics are twins is repeated many times in al-Ghazālī's works: in the *Iqtiṣād fī l-iᶜtiqād*, in the *Naṣīḥat al-mulūk* and in the *Mīzān al-ᶜamal* as well. In the *Iqtiṣād* we read a clear explanation of the connection between religion and politics:

> Mundane life and the security of people and property are guaranteed by a power whose authority is respected. The experiences of bloody struggles and of murders of sultans and caliphs [in this our time] is a clear demonstration of this . . . Religion and power are in complete agreement: religion is that sound basis of which the power must be the guardian. Everything with no basis breaks down; and everything with no guardian risks to get lost. Being stated the differences of classes and opinions [among the people] nobody will deny that the people will perish without a powerful and obeyed authority able to assert itself over different and contrasting tendencies. To sum up, political authority is inescapable for the order of social life, and social life is inescapable to guarantee religion, and religion is necessary to earn the future life.[18]

A sound political authority, able to control any centrifugal thrust, protects the security of the religious life.[19]

In the *Naṣīḥat al-mulūk* partially attributed to al-Ghazālī, we read that God sent kings to preserve people from destroying each other, entrusting them with the duty to defend the institutions of faith.[20] The concept of political power, either of the caliphs or of the sultans, is universal like the power of the prophets. It is limited to secular issues – in the sense that it cannot interfere with religious matters – but claims to a religious charisma. For the caliphate is not a rationally justified system, but is prescribed by *sharīᶜa*; it is a religious duty. All the good qualities of the caliph al-Mustaẓhir are justified in the light of the religious Law, and al-Ghazālī recommends the caliph to act in agreement with the religious Law.[21]

As for the sultan, the just king has to act along with the good operating for the prosperity of his subjects. The latter, however, have the duty to obey him – a duty that is both religious and civil. The believers must love and obey the kings, acknowledging that their sovereignty is willed by God.[22] A common idea of the *Mustaẓhirī* is that the necessity of obedience derives from the fact that the political power is instituted by God. To oppose it means to oppose God himself.

Al-Ghazālī was constantly concerned about social peace.[23] In this perspective, we are able to understand his doctrine about the caliphate and the sultanate. At odds with al-Māwardī who supported the idea that the sultan must be subordinate to the caliph who gives the sultan his legitimacy to rule, al-Ghazālī maintains that the supreme religious authority pertains to the caliphs, but maintains also that the sultans draw absolute legitimacy to rule from their use of force. Political authority pertains wholly to the sultans without any mediation.

The sultans are the defenders of the caliphs and of the *umma* and their recourse to force and the army is perfectly legitimate. Thus, al-Ghazālī discovered a position of equidistance between the Abbasid caliph and the Seljuq sultan: the former exerts a spiritual influence on the religious life of the people; the latter has the ability and capacity to guarantee social security and universal peace through *shakwa*, 'strength'.

This is the theory. In reality, from the point of view of the actual management of power, the caliphs were disempowered by the sultans and they had almost lost even their religious appeal. Al-Ghazālī was completely aware of this. As Jules Janssens put it:

> The imamate clearly mattered enormously to al-Ghazālī, but only because he regarded a legitimate caliph as necessary for the validity of the law in its entirety, not because he saw the caliph as an ideal ruler, or indeed as a ruler at all. Real politics was the domain of sultans.[24]

Al-Ghazālī was supremely realistic: the caliph is no more than a mark of legitimation whereas the sultan manages the real power. He was convinced that the classical caliphate could not be restored and consequently that the reconstruction of the *Islamic state* was no more on the agenda. The sultanate is the Islamic model of state most fitted for the contemporary situation. It is true, as Mitha put it, that 'al-Ghazālī was forced to negotiate a *modus vivendi* between the *de facto* power of the Seljuq sultan and the *de iure* authority of the Abbasid caliph'.[25] But this is not enough. The *modus vivendi* was de facto unbalanced in favour of the sultans whose specific aim was to defend religion, while the caliphs were no longer able to do so in a practical way.

Discussing al-Ghazālī's political thought, I believe I have shown that a religious dimension is at work. The religious dimension of al-Ghazālī's political thought is partially at odds with Niẓām al-Mulk's 'mirror for princes' *Siyāsat-nāma*.[26] Niẓām al-Mulk was, as Michele Bernardini put it, 'the best representative of a typically Iranian sophisticated and deep art of government'.[27] One of the meaningful sentences opening the *Siyāsat-nāma* is that a kingdom can stand without faith but not without justice and order. Secular governance was the main characteristic of Seljuq rule. Al-Ghazālī's *Naṣīḥat al-mulūk* does not constitute a proof *au contraire*. For the treatise is undoubtedly partially apocryphal and it is characteristic that the apocryphal parts are those inspired by Iranian political tradition. The original parts of *Naṣīḥat al-mulūk* are those concerned with the Islamic moral and religious presuppositions of the discourse.

To sum up, al-Ghazālī was interested in the sultanate – and in particular in the Seljuq sultanate – only insofar as it was useful to defend Sunnism. Mustafa

Hogga suggested that al-Ghazālī was compliant with the religious politics of the Seljuqs. We can summarise his view in the following quotation:

> Al-Ghazālī's attitudes are for the most part an outcome of the Seljuqs' social and religious policy; his thought was never so inconsistent and contradictory as it was presumed; on the contrary, it had a remarkable inner logic . . . Showing how the Seljuqs succeeded in militarizing society, in constructing a hegemonic power and in imposing a dogmatic religious policy will be useful to explain al-Ghazālī's performance as their 'official' thinker . . . We shall see everywhere the spiritual submitted to the political . . . The political pattern of al-Ghazālī's ethical doctrine – strict social stratification, rigidity and verticality of relations, links of constriction and domination – coupled with repression (the condemnation of Ḥallājian sufism) produces the deep consistency of ethics with politics and religion.[28]

Now, it is perfectly true that the Seljuqs promoted a *doctrine officielle*. Niẓām al-Mulk was the main defender and organiser of this 'officiality' and Niẓām al-Mulk summoned al-Ghazālī to the Niẓāmiyya college in Baghdad. But there is no proof that al-Ghazālī was an 'official thinker'. His attitude of quietism, defence of political order, condemnation of the Isma^cilis and endorsement of the use of force for managing power can be easily understood as a reaction to the troubled situation of his time. Al-Ghazālī's intentions were first of all religious although he was aware that only a strong political power could support religion. He did not consider the Seljuqs as the only or the best gerents of power. They just happened to be the present rulers of the Islamic empire.[29] Al-Ghazālī's analysis is simply a picture of the actual situation: the situation of a state constructed according to Islamic models without being an Islamic state. As for the future, he did not foresee any important change of the status quo. From the point of view of theory, the caliphate remains the best way to rule the state. But al-Ghazālī is realistic: the duality of power is a de facto reality in the Muslim world of his time and there is no way of returning to the pristine perfection of old.

His position is not heuristic and the unbreakable continuity of the duality between caliphal and sultanic power is correctly identified by Muḥammad ᶜĀbid al-Jābrī as one of the main faults in Arab and Islamic political thought:

> In the field of politics, Islamic thought knew only the mythology of the imamate and the ideology of the sultanate. If the Sunnis have been engaged in disputing the former in order to sanctify the *status quo*, nobody later tried to dispute the latter, neither in its ancient nor in its modern forms. The critique of the Arab political intellect needs to begin with the critique of the mythology [of the imamate] and of the *status quo* [of the sultanate].[30]

Accordingly, we can fully understand why al-Ghazālī, who was very far from being a revolutionary, believed that forty years of tyranny are better than a week of turmoil and why he recommended to the wise men and the Sufis to keep away from caliphs and sultans. Political power is necessary, willed by God, but not blessed by Him.

NOTES

1. I have discussed this concept elsewhere. See Massimo Campanini, 'Islam e politica: il problema dello stato islamico', *Il Pensiero Politico* 37, 3 (2004), pp. 456–66; Massimo Campanini, 'A dialéctica utopia-antiutopia no pensamento politico islâmico medieval', in *Busca do conhecimento: Ensaios de filosofia medieval no Islã*, ed. Rosalie de Souza Pereira (São Paulo, 2007), pp. 125–44; Massimo Campanini, *Ideologia e politica nell'Islam* (Bologna, 2008).
2. Patricia Crone, *Medieval Islamic Political Thought* (Edinburgh, 2004), p. 31.
3. Ibid. pp. 31–2.
4. Bernard Lewis, *The Assassins: a Radical Sect in Islam* (London, 1985), p. 27. The reference book on Isma[c]ilism is Farhad Daftary, *The Ismā[c]īlīs: Their History and Doctrines* (Cambridge, 1990).
5. William M. Watt, *Muslim Intellectual: a Study of al-Ghazālī* (Edinburgh, 1963), p. 74.
6. Lewis, *Assassins*, p. 51.
7. See the works of George Makdisi, in particular 'The Sunnī revival', in *Islamic Civilization 950–1150*, ed. D. S. Richards (Oxford, 1973); George Makdisi, *The Rise of Colleges: Institutions of Learning in Islam and the West* (Edinburgh, 1981); and many others.
8. Fazlur Rahman, *Revival and Reform in Islam* (Oxford, 2003), p. 128.
9. *Mustaẓhirī*, translated by Richard McCarthy, in *Freedom and Fulfillment* (Boston, MA, 1980), p. 207.
10. Ibid. p. 249. (Square brackets contain McCarthy's additions.)
11. Faruk Mitha, *Al-Ghazālī and the Ismailis: a Debate on Reason and Authority in Medieval Islam* (London, 2001), pp. 13, 17.
12. Ibid. p. 100.
13. Ibid. p. 21.
14. Ibid. p. 89.
15. Ann Lambton, *State and Government in Medieval Islam* (Oxford, 1981).
16. Carole Hillenbrand, 'Islamic orthodoxy or realpolitk? Al-Ghazālī's views on government', *Iran: Journal of the British Institute for Persian Studies* 26 (1988), pp. 81–94.
17. Mitha, *Al-Ghazālī and the Ismailis*, p. 76.
18. Al-Ghazālī, *al-Iqtiṣād fī l-i[c]tiqād*, ed. M. M. Abū l-[c]Alā (Cairo, 1972), p. 191.
19. Ibid. p. 195.
20. Al-Ghazālī, *Naṣīḥat al-mulūk*, trans. F. R. C. Bagley, *Counsel for Kings* (London, 1964), especially p. 45.
21. *Mustaẓhirī*, trans. McCarthy, p. 274, but see all of chapter IX.
22. See al-Ghazālī, *Naṣīḥat al-mulūk*, trans. Bagley, p. 46.
23. See Henri Laoust, *La politique de Ġazālī* (Paris, 1970), p. 75.

24. Jules Janssens, 'Al-Ghazzālī's political thought', *Mélanges de l'Université Saint Joseph* 57 (2004) (special issue on *The Greek Strand in Islamic Political Thought*), p. 403.
25. Mitha, *Al-Ghazālī and the Ismailis*, p. 12.
26. W. Montgomery Watt wrote that 'Al-Ghazālī's outlook was close to that of Niẓām al-Mulk. This may be presumed from his association with the statesman, but it is also shown by passages in his writings, such as his repetition of the dictum that 'religion and government are twin-brothers'. He must also have shared the older man's concern about the growth of Ismāᶜīlism'. See W. Montgomery Watt, *Muslim Intellectual*, p. 82.
27. Michele Bernardini, *Storia del mondo islamico (VII–XVI secolo): Il mondo iranico e turco* (Torino, 2003), p. 95.
28. Mustafa Hogga, *Orthodoxie, subversion et réforme en Islam: Al-Ghazālī et les Seljūqides* (Paris, 1993), passim.
29. If it is true that 'Niẓām al-Mulk put forward the picture of the sultan as a sovereign monarch, the goal of the Seljuq sultan [being] to close, once and for all, whatever gap existed between the sources of power as distinct from those of authority' (Mitha, *Al-Ghazālī and the Ismailis*, pp. 15–16, passim), it is obvious that al-Ghazālī went further than Niẓām al-Mulk.
30. Muḥammad ᶜĀbid al-Jābrī, *Al-ᶜAql al-siyāsī al-ᶜarabī* (Beirut, 1992), p. 362.

CHAPTER

13

ARABIC AND PERSIAN INTERTEXTUALITY IN THE SELJUQ PERIOD: ḤAMĪDĪ'S *MAQĀMĀT* AS A CASE STUDY

Vahid Behmardi

The relationship between Arabic literature, on the one hand, and Persian literature, on the other, falls under two major topics: the general impact of Arabic literature on Persian literature, and the transmission and adaptation of Arabic literary texts into Persian. This chapter seeks to examine the development of Persian literature in the Seljuq period by investigating the organic relationship that exists between this development and previous Arabic literary works. This approach relies on the concept of 'intertextuality' in literary studies which denies 'an ultimate referent that would make possible the self-presence and meaning of a text' and instead proposes to see texts as 'fragments in open and endless relations with all other texts'.[1] It is common knowledge that all universal traditions of literature constitute one progressive stage in a sequence of literary accomplishments that are established on former ones and contribute to the formation of others in the future, regardless of quality or merit. Classical Arabic and Persian literatures are no exceptions in this regard.

This chapter is concerned with a specific period and a particular region in the Middle East. The period under consideration is named by historians after the major ruling dynasty at the time, that is, the Seljuqs, and the region is the historic land of the Persians (*bilād fāris*) which covers the territories whose native citizens had Persian as their mother tongue. This would include, according to modern political borders, Iran with some territorial extensions on the periphery. Though it lasted effectively just more than one century, the Seljuq period determined the future destiny of Persian literature. As this chapter intends to show, from the invasions of Chagri Beg and Ṭughril Beg in 431/1040 until the death of Sanjar in 552/1157, Iran underwent a major transition from literary Arabism to literary performance in Persian.

The Seljuq rule over Persia followed that of the Samanids (261–390/874–999), Buyids (321–447/934–1055) and other minor dynasties. The century which preceded the rise of the Seljuqs in the 5th/11th century witnessed a significant upsurge of Arabic literature in Iran. To understand Persian/Arabic intertextuality in the Seljuq era, it is imperative to investigate the evolution of Arabic literature in Iran in the centuries that followed the Arab invasion, that is, before Persian literature gradually started to replace its Arabic counterpart parallel to the rise of the Seljuqs.

The boom of Persian literature at the dusk of the Buyid age, in both poetry and prose, is arguably an extension of the already existing modes and genres of Arabic literature but with an Iranian twist typical of Persian stylistics. Of course, Iranian writers and poets introduced novel themes and imagery uncommon in earlier Arabic literature, but it can be suggested that Persian literature remained highly indebted to the existing tradition of Arabic literature. An intertextual study of some of the Persian works which emerged in the Seljuq period may verify or falsify the above theory. In this chapter the Persian *Maqāmāt* by Abū Bakr Ḥamīd al-Dīn ᶜUmar b. Maḥmūd al-Balkhī 'al-Ḥamīdī' (d. 556/1164) shall be examined to illustrate this.

THE PRETEXT TO INTERTEXTUALITY IN THE SELJUQ PERIOD

The infiltration of Arabic into Iran can be traced back to the early decades of the Islamic era when 'groups of Arab colonists settled in eastern Iran because of the proximity of the Holy War at the [eastern] frontiers'.[2] The geographer al-Muqaddasī (d. 380/990), who visited Khurasan almost four centuries later, noticed that the inhabitants of that region were similar to the Arabs and that both shared common customs.[3] The direct result of this cultural and social assimilation between Arabs and Iranians was that, ultimately, 'Khurasan became a stronghold of Islamic studies and therefore of Arabic literature'.[4]

It should be noted, however, that the Arabic literature which gradually evolved in Iran differed in many respects from the Arabic literature which was cultivated by native Arabs who were nurtured in Arab lands.[5] The former was the outcome of a cultural struggle in Iran following the invasion of the Arabs which resulted in the dominance of Arabic language, on the one hand, and of Iranian culture, on the other. This affiliation between Arabic language and Iranian culture was illustrated in literary and other artistic forms.

At the time when Persian literature was beginning to revive, writers and their literary products were frequently classified and identified according to the Arab/Iranian and Arabic/Persian distinction. This is evident, for example, in Badīᶜ al-Zamān al-Hamadhānī's (d. 398/1007) account in one of his letters of his debate with Abū Bakr al-Khwārizmī (d. 383/993). When Hamadhānī supported the value of some verses he had composed by comparing them to similar ones composed by Arab poets, Khwārizmī complained by saying: 'What is permissible for Arab [poets] is not permissible for you'[6] – indicating that he regarded both himself and his fellow *littérateur* as eminent men of Arabic letters in their time. Another such example is found in one of Khwārizmī's letters where he compares himself to his addressee, an Arab, by identifying himself as being a man with 'Khwārizmī tongue, Ṭabarī brain and non-Arab (*a*ᶜ*jamī*) thought', whereas he identifies his Arab addressee as someone being endowed with 'Arabic tongue, Qurayshī brain, Meccan upbringing and Makhzūmī wittiness'.[7] In one of his poems, al-Mutanabbī (d. 354/965) describes the Buyid vizier and writer Abū al-Faḍl Ibn al-ᶜAmīd (d. 360/970), who was considered to be 'the second Jāḥiẓ' (*al-Jāḥiẓ al-thānī*)[8] or 'the last Jāḥiẓ' (*al-Jāḥiẓ al-akhīr*),[9] as a man whose 'tongue is Arabic, his thought philosophical and his feasts Persian'.[10] These examples, which belong to the 4th/10th century, demonstrate how writers and poets in Iran began to distinguish between Arabian and Iranian cultures at the dawn of the Seljuq age.

Danner presents a brief and interesting analysis of the literary situation in Iran at that transitional period in its literary history. He states that

> one feels that in Iran the masters just mentioned [i.e. Khwārizmī and Hamadhānī] had finally, after several centuries, reached the point where they had exhausted the belles-lettrist possibilities of Arabic and were now very busily burning up its resources . . . That could not be the start of a new age of Arabic belles-lettres in Iran. Rather, it is the last movement of a literary current begun in the 1st/7th century, a sort of galvanized prestidigitation before the curtain falls. It is surely not by accident that the New Persian letters, with their fresh untapped sources, were coming upon the scene precisely at that moment. True, in the 4th/10th century, Arabic would be the main vehicle for the Persian man of culture. But the rise of Persian letters would soon change the situation.[11]

It is true that, by the end of the 4th/10th century, though Arabic literature in Iran was about to relinquish its own arena to the emerging Persian literature, it reached an unprecedented climax which marked the peak of one distinctive epoch in the literary history of Iran. It goes without saying that this climax in excellence in Arabic literature in Iran, especially in the domain of prose, constituted a solid ground on which Persian literature would establish its edifice in the following centuries.

As it happens, not infrequently, with prevalent languages, independent regions allege superior mastery of that language. In the light of this, the high standard of Arabic literature in Iran, in the period under consideration, made al-Muqaddasī testify that the Arabic language, which was used in Khurasan, was the most genuine Arabic he had ever heard during his travels throughout the Muslim world.[12] Such excellence in the use of Arabic in Iran, where the majority of the population was non-Arab, can be attributed, according to Frye, to the fact that 'Arabic dialects [in the Arab world] soon began to widen the gap between themselves and Quranic Arabic. Iranians, however, maintained their tradition of Quranic Arabic since it was the only kind of Arabic taught to them'.[13]

Of course, Persian never ceased to be the spoken language of Iranians at a popular level, despite the fact that the intelligentsia, up to the 4th/10th century, made use of Arabic as the major language in the composition of poetry and prose, as well as works representing other branches of learning. However, there is plenty of evidence which confirms that even the intelligentsia used Persian as their spoken language in their daily life. For instance, sources mention that the eminent philologist of Arabic in Iran during the Buyid age, Aḥmad Ibn Fāris (d. 395/1004), used to speak Persian with the accent of the people of Qazwīn in his daily communications.[14] On both scholarly and popular levels, bilingualism in Iran in the first five centuries of its Islamic history had two outcomes: the first was the preservation of Iranian identity with its main distinctive characteristics; the second was the introduction of new elements into Arabic literature which were developed later in the emerging Persian literature.

Frye remarks that 'the Bedouins of the Arabian desert brought their language as well as their religion to the entire Near East . . . Only Iran, together with Anatolia,[15] escaped from becoming an Arabic speaking land'.[16] It can be concluded that the Arabs successfully introduced to the Persians their newly born religion and the language of the Qurān as an inseparable element of that religion. On the other hand, the Iranians succeeded in preserving their culture within the context of Islam. This led to the emergence of what is often called 'Iranian Islamic culture' which varies, in many respects, from the Islamic culture of the Arabs.

The literature of the 4th/10th century, which was cultivated in Iran, can be regarded as the climax of this unity between the Islamic faith and language, on the one hand, and Iranian culture and mentality, on the other. The use of Arabic as a medium for literary performance by the Persians supplied Arabic literature with much novelty and resulted in the evolution of new literary forms and themes in Arabic that were unknown to the majority of the native Arabs. For example, the sophisticated ornamentation of prose by al-Ṣāḥib Ibn ᶜAbbād (d. 385/995), Khwārizmī and Hamadhānī are new developments in literature that Iranian writers introduced into Arabic during the closing decades of the 4th/10th century.

One aspect that distinguished these poets and writers from their contemporaries in Arabia, as well as from both their Iranian and Arab predecessors, was their progressive approach to Arabic literature which, later on, contributed to the process of Persianising literature in Iran. In a letter written by Ibn Fāris and related by Abū Manṣūr al-Thaᶜālibī (d. 429/1038), the former criticises the conservative and unprogressive scholars who oppose any renewal in the established traditional literature of the Arabs and instead claim that what was brought forth by their predecessors was perfect enough and did not require any kind of development. Ibn Fāris refuses this dogmatic approach to literature and argues that, as long as time progresses and people and circumstances change, innovations in literature remain inevitable. He even asserts that much of what is brought about by the 'latter ones' (that is, his contemporaries) can be, in many respects, greater than what has been inherited from their predecessors.[17] This approach to literature by Ibn Fāris, in the 4th/10th century, continued in the Seljuq age. It is evident, for example, in Niẓāmī-yi ᶜArūḍī's (*fl.* 504–51/1110–55) list of poets and writers whom he considered to be perfect models for anyone who intends to become a perfect scribe.[18] Such a critical approach to literature, as a progressive aspect of human culture, eventually led to literary works in Iran which were unique and novel in their time.

One of the significant changes that occurred during this transitional period, in regard to prose, was that it began to gain the same prestige that poetry possessed as an effective and esteemed instrument for praise and satire. In other words, during the Umayyad and the early Abbasid ages, praise and satire were normally expressed in verse. In the 4th/10th century, however, the current of praise and satire began to evolve in prose writing. A figure no less than Hamadhānī now composed his praise and satire in the form of *maqāma*s and letters, and, in return, received gifts from his patrons, or the wrath of his enemies. Like many contemporary writers, Khwārizmī also praised his friends and satirised his foes in epistles and other prosaic forms. It is noteworthy that all the above-mentioned men of letters, al-Ṣāḥib Ibn ᶜAbbād, Khwārizmī and Hamadhānī, were accomplished poets, and each produced a *dīwān* containing his Arabic poems. However, their eminence and status is due to their achievements in the field of prose while their poetry is barely tackled by scholars.

FROM LITERARY ARABISM TO PERSIAN LITERATURE

While Arabic literature had flourished under the patronage of the Iranian Buyids, Persian literature was swiftly emerging in the eastern provinces of Iran under the patronage and care of the Turkic Ghaznavids (351–582/962–1186). Figures like Abū al-Qāsim Firdawsī (d. 411/1020), ᶜAlī b. Jūlūgh Farrukhī-yi Sīstānī

(d. 429/1037), Abū al-Qāsim Ḥasan-i ᶜUnsurī-yi Balkhī (d. 431/1040) and Abū al-Faḍl Bayhaqī (d. 470/1077) are just a few among many prominent poets and men of letters who received encouragement and patronage from the Ghaznavids and established the solid foundations of Islamic Persian literature.

Similarly, the Seljuqs, who were ethnically Turks like the Ghaznavids, were closer to Persian culture and language than to Arabic, unlike the Buyids who were patrons of Arabic-speaking poets and writers in Iran. This fact contributed significantly to the gradual dominance of Persian literature over Arabic in Iran under the Seljuqs. In other words, the Persian literature which flourished in Iran during the Seljuq period was, to a large extent, a natural replacement of the Arabic literary heritage which had flourished in Iran under the Buyids. At the same time, however, Arabic literature continued to be seen as the basis of Persian literature, and literacy in Arabic literature remained essential for anyone claiming excellence in Persian literature. There was thus a strong bond between Arabic literature and the evolution of Persian literature. This resulted in an assimilative development of literature based on textual interaction between Arabic and Persian literary products of that age and contributed to the emergence of Arabic-Persian intertextuality.

A good example of this cohesive interaction between Arabic and Persian literature in the Seljuq age is found in one of the 'Four Discourses' (*Chahār maqāla*) of Niẓāmī-yi ᶜArūḍī. In the discourse entitled 'on the essence of the secretarial function and the nature of the perfect scribe' (*dar māhiyyat-i dabirī va-kayfiyyat-i dabīr-i kāmil*), ᶜArūḍī recommends that, in order to achieve the level of excellence, scribes must be accustomed to 'peruse the Scripture of the Lord of Glory [the Qurᵓān], the Traditions of Muḥammad . . . the Memoirs of the Companions, the proverbial sayings of the Arabs, and the wise words of the Persians'.[19] After mentioning these prerequisites, ᶜArūḍī proceeds to enumerate the books of the ancients (*kutub-i salaf*) and the writings of their successors (*ṣuḥuf-i khalaf*), referring to the literary works of those authors and poets who lived in pre-Seljuq times and those who followed them and were contemporaries of the author. This is an approach similar to that of Ibn Fāris mentioned earlier.

ᶜArūḍī divides the literary works which he recommends into eight categories, naming for each one three writers or poets: (1) correspondence (*tarassul*): Ṣāḥib, Ṣābī and Qābūs; (2) compositions (*alfāẓ*): Ḥammādī, Imāmī and Qudāma b. Jaᶜfar; (3) gests[20] (*maqāmāt*): Badīᶜ [al-Zamān al-Hamadhānī], Ḥarīrī and Ḥamīd [al-Dīn Balkhī, i.e. Ḥamīdī]; (4) rescripts (*tawqīᶜāt*): Balᶜamī, Aḥmad-i Ḥasan and Abū Naṣr Kundurī; (5) letters (*nāmhā*): Muḥammad ᶜAbduh, ᶜAbd al-Ḥamīd and Sayyid al-Ruᵓasāᵓ; (6) séances (*majālis*): Muḥammad-i Manṣūr, Ibn ᶜAbbādī and Ibn al-Nassaba al-ᶜAlawī; (7) poetical works of the Arabs (*dawāwīn-i ᶜarab*): Mutanabbī, Abīwardī and Ghazzī; (8) poetry of the

Persians (*shi*ᶜ*r-i* ᶜ*ajam*): the poems of Rūdakī, the *Mathnavī* of Firdawsi [i.e. the *Shāhnāma*] and the panegyrics of ᶜUnṣurī. ᶜArūḍī states that each of the works he has listed is an 'incomparable and unique product of its time', and asserts that 'every scribe who hath these books, and stimulates his mind, polishes his wit, and enkindles his fancy by their perusal, will ever raise the level of his diction, whereby a scribe becomes famous'.[21]

A simple statistical analysis of this list, written by a prominent author of the Seljuq period and more precisely, a contemporary of Sultan Sanjar (511–52/1085–1157), demonstrates a strong correlation between Arabic and Persian literatures in Iran in that particular age. It is obvious that ᶜArūḍī was addressing Persian-speaking scribes for two reasons: one is the fact that his work is in Persian, the other that he includes the 'poetry of the Persians' as one of the sources for obtaining literary excellence, something that an Arab scribe was not normally required to know.

To the Qurʾān, *ḥadīth*, memoirs of the Companions and proverbial sayings of the Arabs (*amthāl*), which are all in Arabic, ᶜArūḍī adds 'the wise words of the Persians'. Writings in this last category could have been known in both Persian and Arabic but probably were transmitted mostly in the latter, since the majority of the narratives about pre-Islamic Iran were recorded in Arabic during the Abbasid era, or translated into Arabic from Pahlavi. Certainly, ᶜArūḍī cannot mean the Pahlavi original sources here, because these were either unavailable or, if available, incomprehensible to Iranians living in the Seljuq period. Of course, this does not exclude some works in Persian which were emerging at the time, and which introduced to Iranians their ancient pre-Islamic heritage. Such works, however, relied on earlier Arabic primary sources to a large extent. This transmission of the ancient Iranian heritage to Persian through the medium of Arabic is one aspect of the intertextuality that can be observed in the Ghaznavid and Seljuq periods.

As for ᶜArūḍī's actual list, what is more significant in relation to the purpose of this study is that he lists eight categories of literature, as noted above, and names three authors or particular works by specific authors as pinnacle achievements in each category. The twenty-four literary works and authors may be considered a 'literary sketch' for men of letters that reflects the literary perspective in Iran at the time of the Seljuqs. It is noteworthy that only four out of the twenty-four names mentioned in ᶜArūḍī's 'sketch' refer to literary works in Persian: one is Ḥamīdī's *Maqāmāt*, and the remaining three are works of poetry, namely the *Shāhnāma* by Firdawsī and the poems of Rūdakī (d. c. 325/937) and ᶜUnṣurī. Out of the four, only Ḥamīdī belongs to the Seljuq period whereas the other three died shortly before the Seljuqs came to power. It is remarkable also that only one out of the list's four works in Persian is in prose. Further, in the classification which ᶜArūḍī applies, he is systematic in including either three Arabic or three Persian works under each category. The only exception is found in the third category, the *maqāmāt*, where he includes two *maqāma* works in Arabic (Hamadhānī and Ḥarīrī) and one in Persian (Ḥamīdī).

It is clear that each category includes three works of the same literary genre with common features. For example, when he presents the three models of correspondence (*tarassul*), he refers to the letters which were composed by al-Ṣāḥib Ibn ᶜAbbād, the letters of Hilāl al-Ṣābiᵓ (d. 448/1056) collected in one volume by the author himself under the title *Ghurar al-balāgha*, and finally the letters of Qābūs b. Vushmgīr (d. 356/967), the Ziyarid king whose letters were compiled by ᶜAbd al-Raḥmān al-Yazdādī under the title *Kamāl al-balāgha*.[22] The three collections of letters belong to the same school of artistic Arabic prose which was established by Ibn al-ᶜAmīd, and which was distinguished by verbal over-ornamentation with emphasis on rhyme in prose (*sajᶜ*). The criterion of relative uniformity of language and style is applicable to a large extent to all the categories in ᶜArūḍī's 'sketch', except in the case of the *maqāma* where this kind of uniformity is not maintained.

It may be suggested that ᶜArūḍī considered Ḥamīdī's *Maqāmāt* as a Persian extension of the former Arabic *Maqāmāt* of Hamadhānī and Ḥarīrī. In other words, Ḥamīdī's literary performance, in relation to his predecessors, is an outstanding example of intertextuality. Therefore, putting the Arabic works by Hamadhānī and Ḥarīrī in the same category as the Persian work by Ḥamīdī would not affect the homogeneous and systematic categorisation which ᶜArūḍī is so careful to maintain.

ḤAMĪDĪ'S *MAQĀMĀT*

The above analysis, based on ᶜArūḍī's 'literary sketch', leads to the assumption that Ḥamīdī's *Maqāmāt*, in spite of being written in Persian, are simply the *Maqāmāt* of Hamadhānī and Ḥarīrī, transformed from the Arabic realm to the Persian domain without losing their essential original Arabic identity. Ḥamīdī himself does not deny the fact that his work was a Persian version of the former Arabic ones, which he had composed for his countrymen.[23]

E. G. Browne, in his account of Persian prose works that were composed during Sanjar's reign, lists six works that he identifies as being among 'the most important Persian prose works of this period'.[24] These are *Ḥadāᵓiq al-siḥr fī daqāᵓiq al-shiᶜr* by Rashīd al-Dīn Waṭwāṭ (d. 567/1172), *Kīmiyā-yi saᶜādat* by Abū Ḥāmid al-Ghazzālī (d. 505/1111), *Dhakhīra-yi Khwārizmshāhī* by Ismāᶜīl al-Jurjānī (d. 531/1137), Ḥamīdī's *Maqāmāt*, and *Kalīla wa-Dimna* by Naṣrullah Munshiᵓ (d. c. 554/1159). All six works are, in one way or another, Persian adaptations of former works in Arabic. This again demonstrates the Arabic and Persian intertextuality which was at work in the time of the Seljuqs.[25]

The author of the Persian *Maqāmāt* listed in ᶜArūḍī's 'sketch' is Ḥamīd al-Dīn Abū Bakr ᶜUmar b. Maḥmūd al-Balkhī, who is better known by his title 'Ḥamīdī'. A jurist in the city of Balkh in the Iranian province of Khurasan, his fame lies, primarily, in his composition of a collection of *maqāmas* following the pattern of Hamadhānī and Ḥarīrī. He was a well-known writer and poet in Khurasan who died in Balkh in 556/1164 when the Seljuqs were losing control over Khurasan to the Oghuz following the death of Sanjar.[26] Sources list several literary works by him out of which only one is in verse.[27] Upon Ḥamīdī's completion of his *Maqāmāt*, his contemporary poet ᶜAlī b. Muḥammad Anvarī (d. 565/1170), who was affiliated with the court of Sanjar and eulogised several Seljuq sultans, praised him with the following verses:

> Every discourse which is not the *Qurᵓan* or the Traditions of Mustafa
> Hath now, by the *Maqāmāt* of Hamidu'd-Din, become as vain words.
> Regard as blind men's tears the *Maqāmāt* of Hariri and Badiᶜ
> Compared with the Ocean fulfilled out of the Water of Life . . .[28]

In his introduction to the *Maqāmāt*, which were completed in 551/1156,[29] Ḥamīdī explains that while he was engaged in reading books day and night, he came across the *Maqāmāt* of Hamadhānī and Ḥarīrī. He was told by an anonymous individual whom, as he states, he could not disobey, that since both books were in Arabic, and the Iranian rank and file (*ᶜawāmm*) were unable to benefit from them, he would be doing a great favour to his countrymen if the two books were made a trilogy by composing another one in Persian. Ḥamīdī quotes this anonymous person as saying that Iranians were incapable of understanding the Arabic language of the *Maqāmāt* of Hamadhānī and Ḥarīrī, and consequently unable to appreciate the quaint conceits (*nukat*) in these two books, highlighting the connotative content of both works.[30] In describing the style which he upheld in composing his *Maqāmāt*, Ḥamīdī says that he has mixed Arabic with Persian in order to demonstrate his mastery of both languages.[31]

Several points can be deduced from Ḥamīdī's introductory remarks. First, Ḥamīdī composed his *Maqāmāt* 153 years after the death of Hamadhānī and 35 years after the death of Ḥarīrī. It is obvious, from what he says, that Ḥarīrī's *Maqāmāt* were already highly celebrated in Khurasan. Second, the Iranian population in Khurasan was no longer able to comprehend Arabic literature and, therefore, could not appreciate its eloquence. This shows that the social literary tendencies in Khurasan, towards the end of the Seljuq period, had completely changed compared to what they were before the Seljuqs, especially given that Hamadhānī's *Maqāmāt* were composed in Khurasan and received by Khurasanians. Third, Ḥamīdī's *Maqāmāt* were meant to be an elaboration on, or a disclosure of, what is hidden in the *Maqāmāt* of Hamadhānī and Ḥarīrī; Ḥamīdī thought of the earlier two *Maqāmāt* not merely as eloquent and ornamented narratives, but rather as depositories of *nukat* that required explanation and elaboration in Persian for Iranians. Fourth, the ideal of literary supremacy imposed on authors the necessity of being able to express themselves eloquently in both Arabic and Persian, one of ᶜArūḍī's prerequisites for writers. Fifth, Ḥamīdī transferred into Persian the literary and rhetoric elements that distinguish the Arabic *maqāma* from other Arabic literary genres. In other words, Ḥamīdī's *Maqāmāt* were intended to be a Persian identical twin of the Arabic *Maqāmāt*.

In his conclusion to the *Maqāmāt*, Ḥamīdī makes two significant remarks. He says that upon completing the twenty-third *maqāma*, the conditions that surrounded him have become contrary to what they were when he embarked on writing the first *maqāma*. Therefore, he admits, he has lost all the enthusiasm for writing which he enjoyed earlier. It is very likely that his original intention was to compose fifty *maqāma*s to balance his work with that of Ḥarīrī. However, something must have happened which prevented him from accomplishing his original objective. The other significant point in the conclusion is that his work was a Persian 'translation' that 'followed' Arabic poetry and prose (*man dar īn maktūb dar tarjuma-yi pārsī bar pā-yi naẓm va nathr-i tāzī rafta-am*). Ḥamīdī clearly states here that his work is based on an Arabic text, and that he merely transformed a specific Arabic text, not a genre as such, into Persian. That is why he adds that, because of the strictures of translation, some of his poems appeared to be loose in some instances.[32]

The question that should be raised here is the following: since Ḥamīdī's intention behind the composition of the *Maqāmāt* was to compensate for the shortcomings of Iranian laymen's understanding of the Arabic *Maqāmāt* literature, how could they possibly understand the sophisticated Persian of Ḥamīdī and the relatively large amount of Arabic passages and verses of poetry that he incorporated in his work? A careful examination of the text of Ḥamīdī's *Maqāmāt* shows that he did not succeed in fulfilling his goal of rendering service to his Persian-speaking constituency. However, he was successful in transforming the essence of two Arabic works into a Persian framework in a manner that demonstrates the degree of Arabic-Persian intertextuality in the Seljuq period. It is clear that all the rhetorical sophistication that an Arab reader would find in Ḥarīrī's *Maqāmāt* is encountered, at the same level and intensity, by an Iranian reader of Ḥamīdī's *Maqāmāt*.

A comparative analysis of the *Maqāmāt* trilogy shows that each one of the three, although belonging to the same genre, has its own internal and external aspects which reflect the character of each author, the milieu in which it was composed, and perhaps the different objectives. For example, Hamadhānī's *Maqāmāt* is a collection of fifty narratives which were composed in a scattered manner and not as a cohesive single work, despite the fact that the narrator, ᶜĪsā b. Hishām, and the hero, Abū al-Fatḥ al-Iskandarī, whenever he appears in a *maqāma*, are consistently the same throughout the whole text. The fact that Hamadhānī's *Maqāmāt* do not have an introduction, unlike the *Maqāmāt* of Ḥarīrī[33] and Ḥamīdī, is due to the fact that they were not composed by the author in the form of a complete book.[34] In addition to this, Hamadhānī's *maqāma*s are much shorter than those of the other two authors.

The structure of Ḥamīdī's work is identical to that of Ḥarīrī except for the different number of *maqāma*s in each one. Both start with an introduction and end with a concluding statement. The manner in which Ḥarīrī praises his predecessor, Hamadhānī, in his introduction is not much different from the way Ḥamīdī praises his twin forerunners. The humble tone of Ḥarīrī's conclusion is also similar to the tone Ḥamīdī uses for ending his work with the twenty-third *maqāma* (instead of the fiftieth, as in the case of Ḥarīrī). Finally, Ḥamīdī's *maqāma*s are, like those of Ḥarīrī, longer than the ones composed by Hamadhānī. The conclusion to be drawn from this may be that, structurally speaking, Ḥamīdī transferred Ḥarīrī's *Maqāmāt* into Persian. As for the content, however, both works were taken into consideration by Ḥamīdī. This becomes clear when the titles and content of the *maqāma*s in the three works are compared. Stylistically speaking, Ḥamīdī's Persian reflects the Arabic sophistication of Ḥarīrī more than that of Hamadhānī.

Perhaps the most outstanding example of intertextuality in the three works is Hamadhānī's *Maḍīriyya*,[35] Ḥarīrī's *Sinjariyya*[36] and Ḥamīdī's *Sikbājiyya*.[37] The *Maḍīriyya* is the longest *maqāma* composed by Hamadhānī. The *Sikbājiyya* is also the longest in Ḥamīdī's. Although the structure of both *maqāma*s is almost identical, Ḥamīdī's *maqāma* is more elaborate and more eventful. The points of similarity and contrast between the two *maqāmas* clearly illustrate the nature of the intertexuality in Ḥamīdī's *Maqāmāt*. In other words, it shows that Ḥamīdī did not translate the *maqāma*, in the narrow sense of translation, but developed it away from Hamadhānī to the extent that it approached the spirit of Sufi literature, which flourished extensively under the Seljuqs.[38]

The presence of a narrator is a major ingredient of the *maqāma* genre. It should be mentioned here that both Hamadhānī and Ḥarīrī identify such a narrator, ᶜĪsā b. Hishām and al-Ḥārith b. Hammām respectively, whereas Ḥamīdī's narrator is an anonymous 'friend' (*dūst*) who is described throughout as loving, caring, faithful, sincere and the like. Contrary to this, the two narrators in Hamadhānī and Ḥarīrī's *Maqāmāt* are often involved in swindle and mendacity. The same applies to the heroes of the two Arabic *Maqāmāt*, Abū al-Fatḥ al-Iskandarī in Hamadhānī and Abū Zayd al-Sarūjī in Ḥarīrī, who are presented as witty imposters. In Ḥamīdī's take, however, the main characters remain as anonymous as the narrator. In other words, anonymity is a major feature of Ḥamīdī's Persian *Maqāmāt*, while appellation is a major aspect in the other two Arabic *Maqāmāt*.

The ambiguity of characters in the Persian *Maqāmāt*, contrary to its two Arabic counterparts, shows that Ḥamīdī was not a blind follower of his predecessors. His purpose in composing the *Maqāmāt* seems to go far beyond the goals pursued by Hamadhānī and Ḥarīrī. The anonymity in Ḥamīdī's work creates a mystical atmosphere; this is intensified by the extensive use of Sufi terminology throughout the work. This distinctive phenomenon shows that intertextuality in the Seljuq period was an evolutionary process: Arabic texts were transferred into Persian by incorporating new rhetorical and terminological ingredients, ingredients which were unavailable to those former authors writing in Arabic due to the social and cultural differences which characterised the successive epochs in the history of the Persian and Arab Orient.

The notion of space in the three *Maqāmāt* is another distinctive aspect that requires attention. The scene of events in almost all of Hamadhānī's *maqāmas* is specified by naming the city or the area in which the events take place, such as Baghdad, Kufa or Armenia. The same applies to Ḥarīrī. In Ḥamīdī's *Maqāmāt*, the situation is completely different; the scene of events rarely carries a proper name or a geographic location. It is always a marketplace, a mosque, a house, a court and the like, but names of cities are scarcely mentioned. In other words, space in the Persian *Maqāmāt* is a vague category compared to the Arabic *Maqāmāt*. This also reflects one of the major distinctive features of Arabic and Persian literature in general: the latter tends to more obscurity than the former.

To clarify the above point, let us note that Hamadhānī does not give titles to his *maqāmas*. These were numbered subsequently by the compiler and, in the course of time, became known (in some instances) by designated titles. Harīrī's fifty *maqāmas* were named by the author. Out of the fifty *maqāmas*, thirty-nine carry names of cities or specific geographic locations such as the Tigris River (*al-Furātiyya*).[39] The remaining eleven carry thematic titles. In Ḥamīdī's *Maqāmāt*, of the twenty-three *maqāmas*, only two carry names of cities, the eighteenth (Balkh) and the nineteenth (Samarqand). The remaining titles include themes such as grey hair and youth (second), invasion (third), springtime (fourth), mysticism (eighth), love (eleventh), and the lover and the beloved (fourteenth). This gives Ḥamīdī's *Maqāmāt* a thematic dimension different from those of his predecessors. One wonders if Ḥamīdī, by doing so, elaborated on the *nukat* which were enclosed in the *Maqāmāt* of Hamadhānī and Ḥarīrī – this, however, is a question that would require a separate investigation.

CONCLUSION

Intertextuality in the Islamic context can be traced back to Ibn al-Muqaffaᶜ (d. 142/759), the Arabicised Persian writer, who translated the Pahlavi version of *Kalīla wa-Dimna* into Arabic, adding some Islamic flavour. The reverse process was galvanised in the Seljuq age by the translation of Arabic literary works into Persian with an added Iranian aroma. It can be argued that when most of the Iranian provinces were under the control of the Seljuqs, the Persian *Kalīla wa-Dimna* by Naṣrullāh Munshiᵓ, which was translated into Persian from the Arabic version of Ibn al-Muqaffaᶜ for the Ghaznavid prince Bahrāmshāh (512–47/1118–52), paved the way for further translations of Arabic texts into Persian. A comparative analysis of Ibn al-Muqaffaᶜ's Arabic version of *Kalīla wa-Dimna*, on the one hand, and Munshiᵓ's Persian version of the same book, on the other, shows that the latter established the pattern for the translation of Arabic literature into Persian that was followed, to a large extent, by writers who came after him. There are many common intertextual features in the Arabic and Persian *Kalīla wa-Dimna* and the Arabic and Persian *Maqāmāt* of Hamadhānī, Ḥarīrī and Ḥamīdī.[40]

It is obvious that the literary arena in Seljuq Iran underwent a rapid transformation from one phase, stretching back to the Arab invasion, to another. This latter phase would lay out the road map for the future literary history of Iran with Persian as its instrument for expression. The 'two centuries of silence',[41] according to Zarrīnkūb, were already bygones. A new age was approaching.

It is significant that the Buyids, who were known for their Iranian prejudice, were, like the Barmakids before them, patrons of Arabic literature in Iran, whereas the Ghaznavis and the Seljuqs, who were Turks with Turkish as their native language, were patrons of the golden age of Persian letters and poetry. This paradoxical phenomenon, which characterised literature throughout the Abbasid age, can be seen as the result of a strategy to legitimise power, especially that of minorities who, when they came to rule, had to back their authority by embracing the culture of the majority under their rule. In as much as the Iranian Buyids had to appear to the public majority more Arab than the ruling Abbasid Arabs, the Seljuqs had to appear more Persian than the Iranian masses who came under their rule. Arabic and Persian literature in Iran have always been acclimated to the ruling dynasty or dynasties at the time.

Arabic and Persian literature have, throughout history, reflected the cultural, social and political aspects of every epoch in every part of the Muslim world, a fact which demonstrates the strong correlation between literary texts, on the one hand, and their external contexts, on the other. From what has been discussed above, it is evident that the evolutionary advance of literature in Iran under the

Buyids, Ghaznavids and the Seljuqs was, to a large extent, a cohesive process of mergence between Arabic literature and Persian language, the outcome of which was Persian literature.

NOTES

1. *The New Princeton Encyclopedia of Poetry and Poetics*, eds A. Preminger and T. Brogan (Princeton, NJ, 1993), s.v. 'Intertextuality', p. 620 (H. R. Elam).
2. Victor Danner, 'Arabic literature in Iran', in *The Cambridge History of Iran*, vol. 4: *The Period from the Arab Invasion to the Saljuqs*, ed. R. N. Frye (Cambridge, 1975), p. 568.
3. Muḥammad b. Aḥmad al-Muqaddasī, *Aḥsan al-taqāsīm fī maᶜrifat al-aqālīm*, ed. M. J. De Goeje (Leiden, 1876), p. 194.
4. Danner, 'Arabic literature', p. 569.
5. The author distinguishes between what is called 'Arabic literature' and 'the literature of the Arabs'. The former refers to the literary heritage which used Arabic language as a medium of expression and can also represent cultures and societies which differed from those of Arabs. The literature of the Arabs, however, refers to what was composed by Arabs and reflects the culture of the Arabs, not that of non-Arab nations and cultures.
6. Ibrāhīm al-Aḥdab al-Ṭarabulusī, *Kashf al-maᶜānī wa-l-bayān ᶜan rasāᵓil Badīᶜ al-Zamān* (Beirut, 1890), p. 47.
7. Abū Bakr al-Khwārizmī, *Rasāᵓil*, ed. M. al-Jabr (Damascus, 2006), p. 52.
8. Ḥannā Fākhūrī, *Tārīkh al-adab al-ᶜarabī* (7th edn, Beirut, n.d.), p. 716.
9. Abū Manṣūr al-Thaᶜālibī, *Yatīmat al-dahr fī maḥāsin ahl al-ᶜasr*, ed. M. M. Qumayḥa (Beirut, 1983), III, p. 183.
10. Arthur J. Arberry, *Poems of al-Mutanabbi* (London, 1967), p. 132.
11. Danner, 'Arabic literature', pp. 593–4.
12. Muqaddasī, *Aḥsan al-taqāsīm*, p. 32.
13. Richard N. Frye, *The Golden Age of Persia* (London, 1977), p. 170.
14. See ᶜAlī b. Yūsuf al-Qifṭī, *Inbāh al-ruwāt ᶜalā anbāh al-nuḥāt*, ed. M. Mu'in (Tehran, 1963), I, p. 94.
15. However, Anatolia, in this particular case, cannot be compared with Iran because when the Muslim Arabs invaded Iran, Anatolia was a part of the Byzantine empire. Several centuries later, the Ottoman Turks invaded that region, defeated the Byzantines and established their own Ottoman empire with its own Turkish language. Therefore, Turkish did not survive in Anatolia as Persian did in Iran, rather it was an alien language which was brought to that region by the invaders who came from the far Orient.
16. Frye, *Golden Age*, p. 2.
17. See Thaᶜālibī, *Yatīmat al-dahr*, III, pp. 463–8.
18. See following section 'From literary Arabism to Persian literature'.
19. Niẓāmī-yi ᶜArūḍī Samarqandī, *Chahār maqāla*, ed. M. Qazvīnī (2nd edn, Tehran, 1341/1962), p. 14. The translation is from E. G. Browne, *Chahár Maqála (The Four Discourses) of Nidhámí-I-ᶜArúḍí-I-Samarqandí* (London, 1921), p. 24.
20. 'Gest' is the translation E. G. Browne chooses for *maqāma* (ibid.). It is obvious that he took into consideration the content of the three *maqāma* collections mentioned above.
21. Browne, *Chahár Maqála*, p. 25.

22. E. G. Browne, in his translation of this section of ᶜArūḍī's list, refers to the *Qābūsnāma* which was composed by Kaykāvūs b. Iskandar b. Qābūs b. Vushmgīr. However, the *Qābūsnāma* cannot be categorised within *tarassul*. As stated above, what ᶜArūḍī must have meant here are the *rasāʾil* of Qābūs b. Vushmgīr, the grandfather of the author of the *Qābūsnāma*. See ᶜAbd al-Raḥmān al-Yazdādī, *Kamāl al-balāgha* (Cairo and Baghad, 1341/1922–3).
23. See Ḥamīd al-Dīn al-Balkhī [= Ḥamīdī], *Maqāmāt-i Ḥamīdī*, ed. R. Anzābī Nizhād (first publ. 1365/1986–7, 2nd edn Tehran, 1372 1993), pp. 21, 22, 214.
24. Edward G. Browne, *A Literary History of Persia* (Cambridge, 1929), II, p. 346.
25. It should be noted here that Persian poetry in the Seljuq period in relation to Arabic poetry is a complex topic that requires independent study, and falls outside the scope of this chapter.
26. For the biography of Ḥamīdī, see *EI2*, s.v. 'Ḥamīdī', III, p. 134 (H. Masse).
27. See ᶜAlī Akbar Dihkhudā, *Lughatnāma*, ed. M. Muᶜīn (Tehran, 1337/1958), XX, p. 808.
28. For the complete original eulogy, see ᶜAlī b. Muḥammad [sic] Anvarī, *Dīvān*, ed. M. Razavī (5th edn, Tehran, 1376/1997), II, p. 523. The translation is by Browne, *A Literary History*, II, p. 347.
29. Balkhī [Ḥamīdī], *Maqāmāt*, p. 20.
30. Ibid. pp. 21–2.
31. Steingass explains the meaning of Persian *nukta* as 'an impression made with the tip of the finger or with a stick on the ground; a point; a subtle or quaint conceit, nice or metaphysical distinction, mystical signification, quaint saying, pithy sentence'. See Francis Steingass, *A Comprehensive Persian-English Dictionary* ([1892] reprint London–New York, 1995), p. 1422.
32. Balkhī [Ḥamīdī], *Maqāmāt*, pp. 213–14.
33. The fifty *maqāmas* in Ḥarīrī's *Maqāmāt* do not follow the chronological sequence of their composition. For example, the forty-eighth *maqāma* (*al-Ḥarāmiyya*) is, chronologically speaking, the first *maqāma* composed by Ḥarīrī. See Abū Muḥammad al-Qāṣim al-Ḥarīrī, *al-Maqāmāt al-adabiyya* (Beirut, n.d.), p. 523, note 1.
34. It may be that the *maqāmas*, which Hamadhānī used to compose separately at different occasions, were complied, after his death, by Abū Saᶜīd ᶜAbd al-Raḥmān b. Dūst of Nishapur in Khurasan (see his brief biography in Thaᶜālibī, *Yatīmat al-dahr*, IV, pp. 491–4), who also compiled Hamadhānī's letters in one volume. In his introduction to Hamdhānī's letters, he says that he was commissioned to compile all the poetry and prose by Hamadhānī. See Ṭarabulusī, *Kashf al-maᶜānī*, p. 6. This could have included Hamadhānī's *Maqāmāt*.
35. Badīᶜ al-Zamān al-Hamadhānī, *Maqāmāt*, introduced by M. ᶜAbduh (8th edn, Beirut, 1973), pp. 104–17.
36. Ḥarīrī, *Maqāmāt*, pp. 176–89.
37. Balkhī [Ḥamīdī], *Maqāmāt*, pp. 63–74.
38. For a detailed study of the two *maqāmas*, see Vahid Behmardi, 'The Madira of Baghdad versus the Sikbaj of Nishapur: the migration of a maqāma from Arabic to Persian', in *Poetry's Voice – Society's Norms: Forms of Interaction between Middle Eastern Writers and Their Societies*, eds A. Pflitsch and B. Winckler (Wiesbaden, 2006), pp. 95–104.
39. Ḥarīrī, *Maqāmāt*, p. 213.
40. One of those common features is the excessive use of Arabic poetry quotations by both Munshiʾ and Ḥamīdī.

41. This is the title of a controversial book by the late Iranian Professor of Persian literature at Tehran University, ᶜAbd al-Ḥusayn Zarrīnkūb. Zarrīnkub elaborates, with evident anti-Arab sentiment, on the silence (*sukūt*) of the Persians in Iran during the two centuries that followed the Arab invasion. The book was first published in Tehran in 1951 and continues to be republished in thousands of copies until now.

CHAPTER

14

CITY BUILDING IN SELJUQ RUM

Scott Redford

After more than a century of instability, the Rum Seljuq state came into its own subsequent to the Third Crusade. In the period after the Fourth Crusade, starting after 1211, peace with the Laskarid state to the west allowed the Seljuqs to expand north, south and, especially, east. This chapter concerns this period of prosperity at the beginning of the 13th century, during which so much of Rum Seljuq building took place. In it, I would like to focus principally on the epigraphic programme of some of the cities that the Seljuqs rebuilt in the roughly twenty-year period between the mid-1210s and mid-1230s. Using the inscriptions on city walls, gates and citadels, this chapter aims to establish parameters for an examination of the Rum Seljuq building apparatus and the relationship between official and personal, state and military, patronage. In the end, it hopes to use building inscriptions as a means to shed light on the Rum Seljuq elite itself.[1]

In medieval Anatolia, building meant rebuilding, recasting and recycling. The Seljuqs of Rum may have learned architectural recycling from the Byzantines, who had long plundered the stone blocks of buildings from earlier eras for the stuff, and ornament, of their buildings. The quantity of building undertaken by the Rum Seljuqs during this period is unthinkable without this thrifty building principle in mind.

In discussing Rum Seljuq urbanism, it is important to remember four factors: existing urban fabric, walls, labour and patronage. First and most evident, all cities of the Rum Seljuq realm had most recently been Byzantine and long before that Roman: from these and other eras many standing buildings, streets, and other architectural and urban features remained. Second, when the Rum Seljuqs acquired them, all of these cities already possessed city walls and citadels: walls indeed strong enough to daunt the Rum Seljuq armies, which, of the cities under consideration here, were capable of taking only Antalya by military force (and that after previous failures); both Sinop and Alanya were acquired by negotiation.

Fortifications, especially, but not exclusively those of citadels, are directly related to the third and fourth factors: labour and patronage. Although we have no direct evidence of corvée or forced labour in Seljuq Anatolia, they need to be posited in order to understand the speed and extent of construction discussed above. The *fatḥnāma* inscription of Antalya boasts that the citadel and city walls were rebuilt in two months after the Ramaḍān 612/January 1216 conquest of the city. When one looks at the slapdash workmanship there, the towers with no internal vaulting and little architectural detailing, and in almost *all* Rum Seljuq fortifications, we can visualise the unskilled work gangs that must have existed in order to make this happen. Inscriptions record breakneck building speed, and basic building technique and materials support a picture of feverish construction activity. Even if the labour used for these walls was not always forced, most of those involved must have been unskilled.[2]

Fortifications, in turn, constitute the principal architectural space for the display of dynastic power in the city. They also constitute the principal epigraphic source for patronage of the Rum Seljuq dynasty, surpassing any one architectural type in their iteration of the names and titles of the reigning sultan and those emirs who paid for them. As was the case with their Byzantine predecessors, they also served as the major locus for the display of public art – often reused classical statuary and architectural ornament, but also purpose-made figural reliefs. But lest one think the Rum Seljuqs borrowed these practices exclusively from the Byzantines, we can point to inscriptions like those from the late 11th century of the Great Seljuq sultan Malikshāh on the walls and towers of Diyarbakır, with their purpose-made sculpture, and the contemporary Artuqid dynasty, among others in the Islamic world.[3]

Four Rum Seljuq cities: Sinop (Sīnūb), Konya (Qūnīya), Antalya (Anṭālīya), and Alanya (ᶜAlāʾiyya), allow us to examine relationships between city building and the construction of the Rum Seljuq state itself (Figure 14.1).

The walls of Konya were rebuilt by order of the new sultan ᶜAlāʾ al-Dīn Kay Qubādh beginning in 617/1221. The other three cities were newly conquered or re-conquered: Sinop in early Rajab 611/November 1214, Antalya in late Ramaḍān 612/January 1216, and Alanya in 617(?)/1221. Prosperity and relative stability coincided with a centralisation of administration, one whose workings are not clear at all from the sources. How can city building help us understand state building, in the multiple senses of the word?

After the Rum Seljuq sultan Kılıç Arslan II divided his realm amongst his ten sons in or about 583/1187, and after subsequent fraternal conflict and the

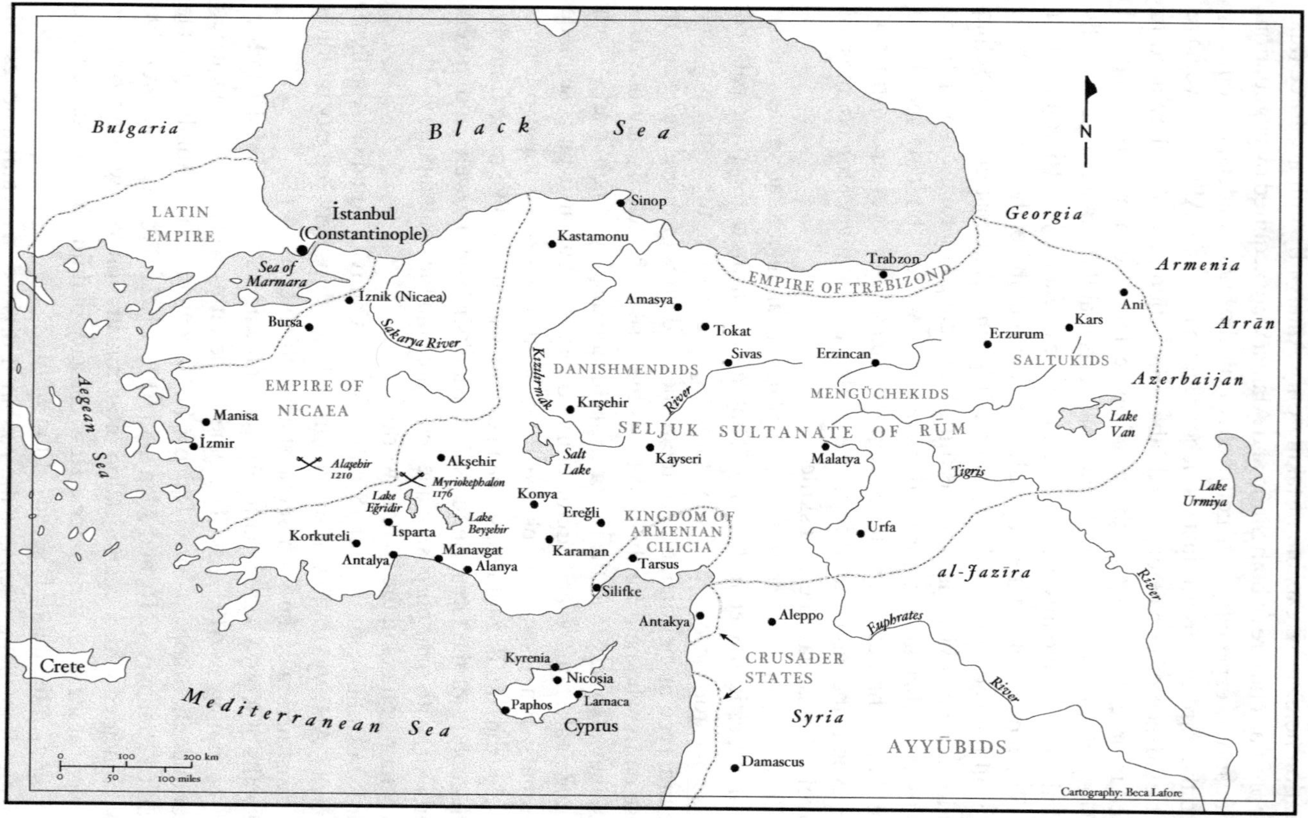

Anatolia in the early thirteenth century (modern Turkish place names)

Figure 14.1 Map of Anatolia in the early 7th/13th century (Redford and Leiser 2008, Figure 1)

disruption caused by the armies of Frederick Barbarossa on Crusade, beginning in 1205, with the return of Ghiyāth al-Dīn Kay Khusraw I to Konya, the Rum Seljuq state began a process of centralisation. It is true that the sons of the reigning sultan continued to be granted provincial cities where they ruled as *malik*s (princes), and no clear principle of dynastic succession was established. But Rum Seljuq sultans centralised the state by appointing military emirs to governorships, increasing their reliance on converted slave troops over Türkmen tribal forces, and by strengthening the administration. Part of that state bureaucracy must have had to do with building: it is in these years that we begin to see architects associated with Rum Seljuq building projects, in some cases over a span of many years. Even though the financing of these projects was personal (mostly paid for by emirs), the standardisation of building plans, types and decorative vocabulary at this time also bespeaks increasingly centralised planning and organisation.

Who were the emirs who functioned at the highest levels of the Rum Seljuq administration? Claude Cahen emphasises the old *mashriqī* (or eastern Islamic world) traditions of division between a Turkic military elite and Persian bureaucracy. However, he adds to that elite 'foreign turkicized military slaves'. The slave soldiers were 'often islamized prisoners, who were later freed. But while elsewhere it was a question mainly of Turkish slaves, in this case they were often Greek slaves obtained in frontier razzias . . .' He admits that there was no clear line between military and others emirs, something that seems to be contradicted by our main written source for Seljuk Rum, the historian Ibn Bībī, who on several occasions makes a distinction between emirs of the court, or *dargāh* (who in turn are called great or middling – *kibār* and *avsaṭ*), and military emirs, *umarā-ye ḥasham* or *lashkar*, or *sarvarān-e bargāh*.[4]

Bombaci underscores the costliness of Kipchaks – the backbone of the military slave elite in neighbouring Syria and Egypt – as militating against their incorporation into the Rum Seljuq army on a scale seen under the later Ayyubids and Mamluks. In a separate but related matter, Bombaci reminds us that the Seljuq army consisted of a standing force, *qadīmī*, probably largely of slave origin, and occasional troops, vassal or mercenary, engaged for particular campaigns, and argues for *iqṭā*ᶜ (land grants) as the major source or revenue for these slave troops.[5]

When we look at the inscriptional record on Rum Seljuq city walls, we often encounter the former: individuals who had risen through the ranks, often as personal slaves of the sultan, to become emirs. With the sultan trying to command and control greater power, what was the physical relationship between those who served as state emirs, with specific administrative and ceremonial duties relating to (to cite two examples from inscriptions discussed here) the royal wine cellars (*sharābsālār*) or the administration of justice (*amīr dād*), and provincial governors (with or without *iqṭāᶜ*s)? Did one graduate from the provinces to the court or get demoted from court to the provinces? If one was both provincial governor and court emir, from which position did one derive one's fortune, the one necessary, for instance, to pay for the building of multiple city walls and towers?

Even though the Rum Seljuq state was centralising, with specific bureaucratic offices located in the capital of Konya, the sultan and his court (together with emirs, of course) were peripatetic. The sultan and his emirs had palaces and garden complexes in or near all of the major cities, and passed parts of the year in the different climes of the realm. This process of constructing and reproducing an elite environment for the sultan and court runs in tandem with, and indeed informs, the city-building that is the focus of this chapter. As the reader will remark later, this process is most intertwined in the building of Alanya.[6]

Any discussion of the Rum Seljuq elite has to tackle the issue of the overlap between provincial, court and military offices at a time when the most common terms for army commander, *sūbāshī* and *isfahsālār*, seem to have superceded *ṣāḥib*, the common term for governor, in major cities. In other words, was there no real difference between emirs with military and non-military titles, as Cahen's statements would suggest? These questions are key to Rum Seljuq administrative history and urbanism alike, because several emirs, including ones mentioned below, plotted a revolt against Sultan ᶜAlāᵓ al-Dīn, a plot that was suppressed in 620/1223. What was the cause of discontentment? The expense of building – especially city walls![7]

SINOP, 612/1215

The Black Sea port of Sinop, a possession of the Komnenian empire of Trebizond, surrendered to the Rum Seljuq army on 28 Jumādā II 611/2 November 1214. Fifteen Rum Seljuq inscriptions on the walls of Sinop citadel date between April and September of 1215, in the year following the conquest; in other words, when the weather was good enough for building. Ibn Bībī reports that before Sultan ᶜIzz al-Dīn departed the city, he appointed a garrison commander (*kūtūvāl*) and garrison troops (*mustaḥfeẓān*) who repaired the walls, and also appointed a military commander (*az umarāᵓ-ye lashkar yeki sarlashkari mawsūm kardānīd*) and administrators (he only mentions religious personnel but there must have been many others). Those emirs, soldiers and other Seljuq personnel remaining in Sinop must have used the winter months profitably, because come spring a great spurt of building activity occurred.[8]

Rum Seljuq building inscriptions from this period at Sinop are found exclusively on the citadel walls (although similar inscriptions for buildings built or reconfigured – Ibn Bībī reports the conversion of a church into the Friday mosque – at that time also existed). There is only one later inscription, from the fore-wall of the citadel, dating three years later, that shows that construction continued under one Badr al-Dīn Abu Bakr, who seems to have been the emir appointed as that military governor: he calls himself *isfahsālār* in this inscription (although in his first inscription, from 612/1215, he is called *ṣāḥib* of a neighbouring city).[9]

The walls of Sinop provide us with a snapshot of the summer of 612/1215, revealing much about the nature of the group of emirs appointed by the sultan to continue work on the walls, and their activities. If Ibn Bībī, who wrote some eighty years after the event, is to be trusted, then all of them can be considered military emirs, although the inscriptions show considerable variation, as we shall see. At this time, at least twelve emirs, along with the notables, *umarā' wa akābir*, of at least nine provincial Rum Seljuq cities supervised the rebuilding of Sinop citadel. They employed four architects (*miᶜmār*), one a Muslim from the city of Kayseri (Qayṣariyya), one a Christian named Sebastos, and the third a Muslim perhaps from Ankara. The fourth architect was a Syrian Muslim best known for his construction, over ten years later, of the Red Tower and Tophane tower in Alanya. The name of a scribe, also from Kayseri, a slave of the ruling military governor there, is found on two of the inscriptions. The job of supervising (*naẓar, tawallī*) fell to two emirs. One, of sultanic slave origin, was in charge of three emirs from Sivas (Sīwās) and their section of walls. He also built the citadel mosque. The other supervisor, the only to sport a court title, was the *Amīr Dād*, or emir in charge of courts. Because of his high rank, and the placement of the inscription bearing his name above the main citadel gate from the city (the gate now called Lonca Kapısı), we can surmise that he was in charge of the entire project.[10]

The army chief who led the Sinop campaign was another emir of sultanic slave origin, Ḥusām al-Dīn Yūsuf, who was also the military governor, *isfahsālār*, of Malatya (Malaṭiya). His inscription stands in a prominent location near the main entrance to the citadel, and gives the longest list of titles of the sultan of any of the Sinop inscriptions. Another nearby inscription, unique in Rum Seljuq epigraphy, vaunts Ḥusām al-Dīn's accomplishments in Persian epic verse (Figure 14.2).

This last inscription also has a different format – it looks like an open book – and is written in *naskh*, different from the style of all the other inscriptions. The rhyme scheme is based on the name of the ruling sultan, Kay Kāwūs, but also mentions Ḥusām-e Dīn (sic) by name.[11]

Badr al-Dīn Abū Bakr, mentioned above as the governor of Sinop, placed his 612/1215 inscription on the adjacent tower, the tower housing the entrance to

Figure 14.2 Sinop citadel, 612/1215, Persian poetic inscription

the citadel. It also is unique in the annals of Seljuq epigraphy, as it is bilingual, giving not exactly, but approximately, the same information, first in Arabic and then in Greek. The fact that Badr al-Dīn was, at the time of the conquest, governor (*ṣāḥib*) of Sīmra, the town closest to Sinop of all cities listed, shows two things: first that local knowledge, and the local language, were important to the Seljuqs and, second, that at least this inscription was meant to be read by the inhabitants of the city.[12]

In Sinop, we can see a newly established system in flux, but one with some emerging order. Here we can observe two emirs with the military titles of *sūbāshī* and *isfahsālār* in the important eastern cities of Kayseri and Malatya. By contrast, five others, governors of other cities, are named *ṣāḥib*. Others are called simply emir, paired with a particular city only by their inscriptional association with (other) emirs or, in the case of Malatya, notables: *umarāʾ* or *umarāʾ wa akābir*, emirs, or emirs and notables. It is possible to posit a hierarchy here, with military governors serving in major cities and other emirs getting provincial *iqṭāʿ*s or other simple appointments without being called *sūbāshī* or *isfahsālār*. The cities governed by the military governors presumably belonged to the sultan directly. The fact that elsewhere the governors of the port cities of Antalya and Sinop were called *sūbāshī* or *isfahsālār* point to the importance of port towns, along with the major cities to the east of the Seljuq realm, as homes of military governors. A *waqfiyya*, or foundation document, of the *sūbāshī* of Antalya refers to that port as *dār al-thaghr* (capital of the (coastal) frontier), emphasising its military importance. In writing of Sinop, Ibn Bībī uses the same term.[13]

Despite the relocation of many of the inscriptions, it is possible to posit a two-level hierarchy of positioning that roughly reflects this pecking order. The largest inscriptional tablets, with the longest inscriptions, belonged to the military governors of the largest cities (Kayseri, Malatya) or large cities without military governors (like Sivas and Amasya), and were placed on the towers of the city facing east across the city and west facing the approaches to the city. The prominence of Kayseri – with a military governor, architect and scribe – in this ensemble can be attributed at least in part to its role as a base of support for the sultan during the recently concluded power struggles with his brother.[14]

The smaller inscriptions – both in size and length – of the governors, *ṣāḥib*, of other, presumably lesser or more secure cities seem to have been placed principally on those towers facing north and south, facing the entry into the city along the north through the Kum Kapı gate, and the harbour. A major exception to this rule is the smaller-sized, bilingual inscription of Badr al-Dīn mentioned above, but both its prominent location near the gate, and its bilingual format can be attributed to his status as incumbent governor of Sinop.[15]

All of the emirs listed in Sinop, whether of slave origin (a total of three) or not, bear similar names. The only emir with a *nisba*, the part of the name denoting place of origin, is the only one not to be associated directly or indirectly with a city. His name is 'Mubāriz al-Dīn ᶜAbdallāh b. ᶜAlī al-Mihrānī'. Mehran is a city on the western border of present-day Iran. This personage is not mentioned again in the Rum Seljuq historical or inscriptional record. Could it be that here, along with two emirs with supervisory roles, and the chief of the army, we have an upper level member of the Persianate bureaucracy, sent here to establish the local fiscal administration?[16]

In style and layout these inscription conform to general Seljuq practice deriving not from the Great Seljuqs, but from 6th/12th-century Syria; they are written on rectangular marble blocks not in angular Kufic, but in cursive: an elongated, monumentalised version of *tawqīᶜ*, with each line separated from the next by a heavy bar. There is considerable variation in quality, with finer inscriptions presumably written by the scribe from Kayseri, and others by lesser hands. However, the Arabic employed is Persianate, with several implied *iẓāfe*s, Persian possessive constructions not found in Arabic, and many grammatical errors. Two factors point to the emirial retinues as the source of these inscriptions – both in content, style, and execution. The first is the aforementioned scribe, Najm al-Dīn Yawāsh, who is styled as coming from Kayseri in one inscription, and as a slave of the governor of Kayseri in another. The second is the inscription of the emir

Figure 14.3 Sinop citadel, 612/1215, inscription of emirs and notables of Amasya (Sinop Museum, accession no. 4.29.71)

of Amasya (Amāsīya), Mubāriz al-Dawla wa'l-Dīn, and brother of Badr al-Dīn (Figure 14.3).

Here, obviously due to an objection to the content of the inscription, the scribes have added three words, expanding the description of the stretch of citadel (re)constructed from 'the two towers and (stretches of) curtain wall' by the addition of 'and three arches (*qanāṭira*)'. This modification gives a sense of immediacy and close contact between the patron, the scribe and the building project underway.[17]

The walls of Sinop give us an inscriptional portrait of a group of emirs and notables expressing not only their building accomplishments, but also the order of the Rum Seljuq state. A superficial sameness of style and format betray considerable variation, in order, title, language and chain of command. The variety expressed by the Sinop inscriptions also includes the emirs themselves, who were a combination of freeborn and slave, with only one obviously non-Anatolian Muslim, as well as the state building apparatus, with four architects, one scribe and two supervisors, one a freeborn state emir of justice, the other of slave origin.

How much this project was a centralised state operation and how much it was placed on the shoulders of individual emirs by the absent sultan, we do not know. In this jostling, competing portrait, the most notable absence is he who

Figure 14.4 Sinop citadel, 612/1215, inscription of Sultan ᶜIzz al-Dīn Kay Kāwūs flanked by lions

should have been the centre of the group portrait. Sultan ᶜIzz al-Dīn Kay Kāwūs himself is given one, small, four-line inscription, albeit the only Sinop inscription to be flanked by lions, the first dateable Seljuq works of figural sculpture (Figure 14.4).

In the lower left hand corner of this inscription, the slogan *al-ḥamdu lillāh al-mulk ᶜalā Allāh*, 'God be praised, sovereignty belongs to God (alone)', has been squeezed in in tiny letters. This phrase may be thought of as the *tawqīᶜ* or pious phrase used by medieval Islamic monarchs as a signature, and device. Here, its diminutive and squashed location is a far cry from the use of similar pious taglines by ᶜIzz al-Dīn's brother and successor ᶜAlāʾ al-Dīn.[18]

This sultanic inscription is much shorter than that of army commander Ḥusām al-Dīn Yūsuf, which contains many more titles of the sultan. It may be that it was supplemental to the main inscription over the entrance to the citadel, a large tablet that has long ago been mutilated beyond recognition, but that inscription is not flanked by any sculpture. Be that as it may, despite its flanking lions, its small size and indifferent execution make it look almost like an afterthought. The sultan is gone and, if not forgotten, has certainly been upstaged in this particular collective performance. Of all of the major cities of the Rum Seljuq realm, only Konya is not represented in these inscriptions, most obviously because it belonged to the sultan. Could it be an exaggeration to maintain that, with their insistent identification of person with place, the inscriptions of Sinop present the sultan as the ruler of the realm, certainly, but one whose implicit power base is a city/province too – that of Konya?

ANTALYA, 612/1216

After Sinop, Seljuq emirs never list their provincial governorships in their inscriptions. Never again, too, are anonymous provincial emirs and notables allowed to mark their presence. What is more, after Sinop, court offices are almost never given in inscriptions. However, military ranks continue to be mentioned, albeit more rarely. Antalya was captured in Ramaḍān 612/late January of 1216, just four months after the last dated inscription on Sinop. On the walls of Antalya citadel, we again encounter Ḥusām al-Dīn Yūsuf, the army commander from Malatya, in an inscription where he is named *sūbāshī*, and a grander, great (or state) emir, *amīr al-kabīr*, presumably because of his role in the successful siege of that city.[19]

In direct opposition to Sinop, in the inscriptional program of Antalya, thc sultan's presence is paramount. This presence is literal as well as figurative: Sultan ᶜIzz al-Dīn stayed in the city for a time after leading the successful siege of the city. With this sultanic presence came a variety of expressions of power hinted at in the lions flanking the puny inscription of ᶜIzz al-Dīn in Sinop. On the citadel walls of Antalya, sultanic presence is expressed principally by an Arabic language chancery document in stone laying claim to the conquest and the city. It is a *fatḥnāma*, an epistolatory document usually issued by sultanic chanceries after victories, and sent to friend and foe.[20]

In Antalya, unique in Seljuq epigraphy, this document was inscribed on cut sections of marble column and inserted into the curtain walls and towers of the citadel next to its principal gate into the city (Figure 14.5).

The *fatḥnāma* is written like a document – in un-monumentalised, un-barred scribal hand – and bears none of the Persianisms found at Sinop and elsewhere. All titles listed are caliphal or those current in Syria: Seljuq titles that did not pass into Zangid or Ayyubid usage are excluded, as are blatantly Persian language titles like *shāhānshāh,* King of Kings. This is a document stemming from the sultanic *dīwān al-inshāʾ*, or chancery, supplanting emirs as the principal expressors of state power. It can be seen as a sultanic, court version of the Persian verse celebrating the conquest of Sinop on the walls of the citadel there.[21]

The citadel walls of Sinop and Antalya shed light on the centralisation of the state, the hierarchy of military and non-military governors, and state emirs. Sinop especially tells us much about the organisation of the fledgling Seljuq

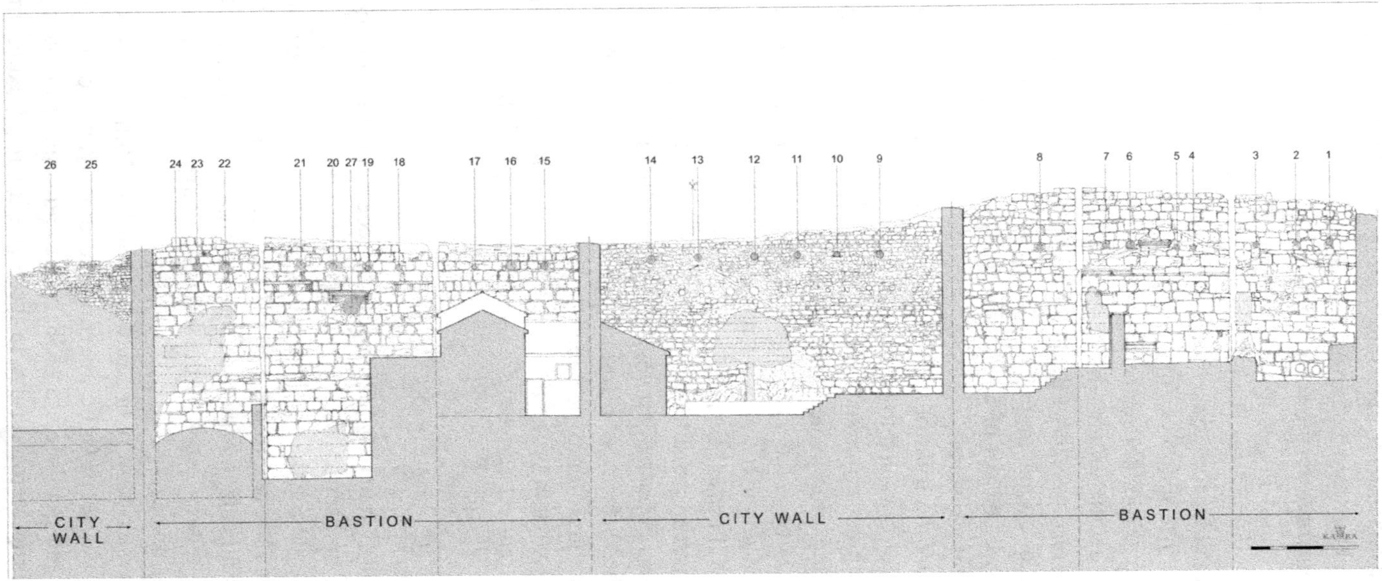

Figure 14.5 Antalya citadel, elevation of walls and towers showing location of 612/1216, *fatḥnāmā* inscription of Sultan ᶜIzz al-Dīn Kay Kāwūs (drawing by Zehra Tulunoğlu; Redford and Leiser 2008, Figure 3)

building apparatus that was to shift into high gear in the following decade. But neither citadel can be considered a visually successful expression of state power and ideology. Compared to the scale of the architecture, the writing is small, set high on walls, and, while reflecting internal state dynamics, does not aim to convince, let alone intimidate. The bilingual inscription of Sinop is the only one to make even a small gesture towards the native population.

The *fatḥnāma* inscription on the walls of Antalya also demonstrates that the sultan could, and did, undertake the building of fortifications himself. The *fatḥnāma* makes clear the sultan's direct role in ordering, and presumably paying for, the rebuilding of the walls of the citadel, as well as those of the city. At the most simple level, one could argue that the fact that the sultan stayed on after the conquest of Antalya, and not of Sinop, affected the inscriptional programme of the walls, and nothing further.

Without denying the truth of this statement, we should not be limited by it. For one thing, there continued to be delegation: the sultan did not sponsor *all* of the rebuilding, as the inscriptions of Ḥusām al-Dīn Yūsuf and at least one other emir show. And the prominence ᶜIzz al-Dīn chose for himself was unusual: the sultan did not *have* to have the *fatḥnāma* written and inserted in the citadel walls. The fact that this text was written and incised in a manner so totally different from the Syrian inscriptional format found at Sinop betrays the role of a native Arabic speaker in the sultan's retinue – presumably a member of the state chancery – who was not usually involved in composing foundation inscriptions. In my opinion, the difference in format and style of the *fatḥnāma* inscription constituted a conscious effort to differentiate and highlight the contribution of the sultan as opposed to that of his emirs. Other aspects of the state apparatus evident in Sinop, scribes, architects, supervisors, are all subsumed to his presence as well.

KONYA, 616/1221

The death of ᶜIzz al-Dīn in 616/1220 led to the accession of his brother ᶜAlāᵓ al-Dīn, one of whose first actions was to order the rebuilding of the walls of Konya. Ibn Bībī notes his ordering the payment for part of the job from the state treasury, while parcelling out the rest to the well-off state emirs. This passage also notes the presence of architects (*meᶜmārān*) and designers (*rassāmān*), at hand, who were commanded to begin work by the sultan – another indication of a standing bureaucracy in this respect.[22]

Although the walls were pulled down in the late 19th and early 20th centuries, we have what seem to be generally accurate views of them made by Leon de Laborde and published in 1838. Some elements of the wall sculptural and inscriptional programme survive in the İnce Minareli Medrese museum in

Konya. These walls are well-enough known to allow me to dwell on them only briefly. Suffice it to say that iconographically and calligraphically they redressed the inadequacies mentioned above. The extensive use of spoliated architectural members reflected Byzantine practice while assigning to the past contained therein an Islamicate pedigree by virtue of two factors: purpose-made relief sculpture, and inscriptions consisting of quotes from the Qurʾān, *ḥadīth* (sayings of the Prophet Muḥammad), wisdom literature, *aḥkām*, and the Persian epic, the *Shāhnāma*.

Epigraphically, in Konya, the tablet form seemed to have been reserved for lesser emirs, while the sultan and one select emir, Ioannes Maurozomes (Komnanūs Kālūyān Mafrozom – whose sister was one of the wives of ʿAlāʾ al-Dīn's father), had their names written monumentally, combining cursive style more popular in Syria with a band format more popular in Great Seljuq lands. Kaloyan can be identified with the 'Emir Komnenos Mafrozom' mentioned by Ibn Bībī as a military governor under ʿAlāʾ al-Dīn, and as his friend. From other sources, we know that this son of a high-ranking Byzantine general never converted to Islam.

The prominence of this inscription reflects the political situation at the time, after the fall of Constantinople to the armies of the Fourth Crusade in 1204, when three Byzantine successor states, based at Iznik (Nicaea), Trabzon (Trebizond) and Epiros, vied to take back the city. All three of these states highlighted their rulers' connection with the overthrown Komenenian dynasty. With this inscription on the walls of Konya, the Rum Seljuq state put forward its claim in this respect as well.[23]

Elsewhere, I have argued that the iconographic and inscriptional content of the walls of Konya reflect the *nasīḥatnāma*, or 'mirror for princes', genre that formed a significant part of the education of medieval Islamic princes. In the capital city, the new sultan's order placed him at the centre of a constellation of images and texts, recycled and new, expressing links to the past of Anatolia and of medieval Islamdom. Nevertheless, the rest of the state hierarchy is present. Kaloyan Maurozomes is given much greater prominence than lesser emirs like Ḥasan son of Yūsuf Qabāqulāq (Mumps Yūsuf), whose inscriptions are small and extremely short. Despite the overwhelming display of sultanic dominance in Konya, the expense of these walls, with their lavish sculptural and inscriptional programmes, helped spark an emirial plot to overthrow ʿAlāʾ al-Dīn in 620/1223.[24]

ANTALYA, 622/1225

Sultan ʿAlāʾ al-Dīn Kay Qubādh shored up the defences of Antalya in 622/1225 by rebuilding an internal city wall complete with twelve towers and a new gate. Here, each tower bore the name of an emir – much as before – but all of the emirs are new and must have been elevated following the 620/1223 purge, although their exact status is unclear. This is due to the fact that the names of many of them are restricted to one, without any mention of title or geneaology, a significant onomastic curtailment also found at Konya (although these are better carved, and have longer sections with names and titles of the sultan). In addition, all emirs are called *al-ᶜabd al-ḍaᶜīf*, 'the weak slave', a typical formula used to contrast the majesty of the monarch with the lowliness of his subjects. However, unlike the case in Sinop, none of the emirs in Antalya in 622/1225 was allowed to omit this formula: at Sinop and at Antalya, Ḥusām al-Dīn's higher status was indicated, in addition to his title, by the lack of this phrase.

The emir Ayāz must have supervised the work – he is called *mutawallī*, or supervisor, in three building inscriptions from the Alaeddin mosque in Konya and one from the walls of Konya. His inscription from Antalya was found in secondary reuse, but both Ayāz's Konya inscriptions, and the date here (also 622/1225), associate him with this building project in Antalya, even though he is not called *mutawallī*. Instead, his title is *sharābsālār*, or keeper of the royal wine cellars; surely a court title if ever there was one.

It is possible, also, to associate this building project with an architect from Kayseri (different from the Kayseri architects who worked on Sinop's walls). Although the inscription mentioning this architect, too, is without architectural context, it mentions the building of a blessed *qaṣr* and towers, *abrāj*, of the protected city (of Antalya). Although the word *qaṣr* can mean palace or pavilion in addition to fortification, the fact that it is called *mubārak*, or blessed, and is associated with the building of towers and the protection of the city, make me think that it refers to this project.[25]

ALANYA, 623/1226

The walls, towers, gates, arsenal, bathhouses, mosque and palaces of Alanya, built in the second half of the 616/1220s and early 627/1230s, also show the consequences of the 620/1223 plot. Despite the fact that this port town – called Kalonoros by the Byzantines – had been conquered in 617/1221, construction on it did not begin until 623/1226, so it was the largest building project by far of Sultan ᶜAlāᵓ al-Dīn's reign.

At Alanya, this dimunition of emirial presence continued. Besides the sultan, the only names mentioned inscriptionally are those of the Syrian architect Abu ᶜAlī, on the Red Tower, and three sultanic slaves, Qarāja, Yāqūt, and Benek, the latter two of which employ Persian and not Arabic. Yāqūt is listed as *Uṭāqbāshī*, Master of the Tent, a military title. These inscriptions come from the area of the main city gate (Kale Kapısı) and Ehmedek citadel. Tower inscriptions, normally the purview of emirs, contain only the name of the sultan. The one exception to this subsuming of emirial authority was an emir named Aqshe, who built a mosque and perhaps other constructions.[26]

At Alanya, there were two citadels, one palatial and one military, fitting a model found also in Konya and Sivas (but not Sinop and Antalya). Both of Alanya's citadels were high atop the castle rock and far from view. It is therefore significant to note that the greatest sculptural and epigraphic investment in Alanya is found not on the citadel walls, but on those walls facing the sea and port above the arsenal or *tersane*.

Contrary to scholarly consensus, in my opinion, the walls of Alanya descended to the sea well before the Rum Seljuq conquest, and indeed must have been re-fortified in the 6th/12th century by the Byzantines. Harbourside, Abū ᶜAlī built two towers: the Red Tower to guard the port, and the Tophane tower to watch over the arsenal. A new wall was added seaside, setting off a triangular area from the rest of the settlement. This area may be thought of as a kind of third citadel, combining military and palatial functions with the visibility demanded by the Rum Seljuqs for their inscriptional programmes. No inscriptions have been found in the Alanya citadel that housed the main palace (the İçkale) and relatively few from the Ehmedek citadel.

Here, harbourside, in plain view, in addition to spolia and purpose-carved lions, multiple inscriptions of the sultan and one inscription with a series of quotations from the Qurʾān are to be found. In contrast to Sinop, the phrase *al-mulk lillāh* ('sovereignty [alone] belongs to God'), which must have been ᶜAlāʾ al-Dīn's *tawqīᶜ* or device, is prominently featured here. A small bathhouse and ruined pavilion survive at the foot of the tower adjacent to the Red Tower, the main entrance of which is surmounted with a hitherto unremarked portrait bust (Figure 14.6).

All of these indications – architectural, sculptural and inscriptional – point to a palatial function to this area, and recall similarities with ᶜAlāʾ al-Dīn's lakeside palace of Qubādābād, built at this time.[27]

CONCLUSION

The inscriptional record on Rum Seljuq citadel walls reflects the growing centralisation of the state and the power of the sultan. Emirs who were provincial governors, and after them military emirs, are stripped, as it were, of their titles, and given permission to record their contribution only in terms of their names. The expression of sultanic power finds its outlet in complex combinations of device, quotation, reuse and figural invention that must be an expression of a

Figure 14.6 Carved profile bust on stone block above entrance to the Kızıl Kule, Alanya

close relationship between patrons, builders, scribes and other craftsmen. In the citadels of ʿAlāʾ al-Dīn Kay Qubādh, all of these are monumentalised. Contrary to the traditional picture of Seljuq Anatolia as a provincial backwater, these artistic and architectural experiments affected the iconographic and inscriptional programmes of citadels built in subsequent decades in cities like Aleppo and Damascus.

While the inscriptional programmes of these walls cannot reveal the structure of the Seljuq elite, they give insights into the tensions between that elite and the sultan himself. The sultan seems to have used these walls, among many other things, as a way to curb the power of the state emirs and military commanders: two groups that seemed to overlap. This group was partially of slave origin; although the origin of these 'slave' emirs is largely unknown, clues in Rum Seljuq history and inscriptions argue for their being at least partially, if not largely, of Anatolian Christian stock/background. In this way, the inscription of Kalūyān Mafrozom can be seen as not so much of an anomaly. Indeed, it can be seen as part of deliberate policy, in which emirs of slave origin (and therefore presumably Greek-speaking) are put in charge of armies attacking cities in the hands of Christians: Ḥusām al-Dīn Yūsuf in the case of Sinop and Antalya, and Mubāriz al-Dīn Ertoqush at Alanya. Maurozomes was not a slave soldier, but he was made army commander by Sultan ᶜAlāᵓ al-Dīn and sent to battle the Kingdom of Armenian Cilicia. If I am correct in my reading of Ibn Bībī, then the sultan's choice of emirs of slave origin to build the walls of Konya can be seen as a deliberate attempt to curb the growing power of these in particular.

Other members of the emirial class were not of slave origin, and probably belonged to the Turkic ruling military elite discussed by Cahen. The inscriptional record also gives hints of the Persianate administration. What is striking is the absence of the office of vizier, so prominent and powerful among the Great Seljuqs; present in Rum, but not important in the ongoing tug of war between emirs and the sultan himself in Seljuq Rum.

NOTES

1. This chapter is partially based on research in the Sinop Museum, and inscriptional survey at Sinop citadel that I undertook in the summer of 2008 with the permission of the Turkish Ministry of Culture and Tourism and funding from Georgetown University. Results presented here are preliminary. Unless modified by further research, they will form part of a larger work on Rum Seljuq urbanism.
2. J. M. Rogers examined many of the issues addressed in this chapter in a seminal article, 'Waqf and patronage in Seljuk Anatolia. The epigraphic evidence', *Anatolian Studies* 26 (1976), pp. 69–103. Although many of its conclusions are disputed here based on different readings of the inscriptional record, it is valuable as the only work that systematically addresses issues raised by Seljuq building inscriptions.
3. Albert Gabriel, *Voyages archéologiques dans la Turquie orientale* (Paris, 1940), I, pp. 164–7 for a presentation of the relief sculpture, pp. 318–19 for Jean Sauvaget's reading of the texts. The latest consideration of the epigraphic programme of the walls of Diyarbakır is found in Sheila Blair, 'Decoration of city walls in the Islamic world: the epigraphic message', in *City Walls: the Urban Enceinte in Global Perspective*, ed. James D. Tracy (Cambridge, 2000), pp. 488–529. In this article, Blair mainly connects the Great Seljuq inscriptions here to rivalry with the Fatimids. She limits her discussion of the sculpted imagery surmounting and surrounding two of these inscriptions to the following (p. 504): 'The pictures (sic) were presumably meant to reinforce the meaning of the text on the two towers . . .' These inscriptions are in bands, and are in floriated Kufic script.
4. Claude Cahen, *Pre-Ottoman Turkey* (London, 1968), pp. 224, 228, 231. On pp. 222–3 he makes the following statement: 'The sultan was surrounded by a certain number of persons holding office or dignities at court, some of whom may have been identical with those who also held office in the political and military hierarchy, which were always given to members of the caste which furnished it. Almost all bore partly Persian titles already known among the Seljukids of Iraq-Iran.' These words emphasise continuity, while the demographic situation – the 'turkicized' former Christian slaves found only in Anatolia – demands a degree of change he does not discuss. See Ibn Bībī, *El-Evāmirü'l-ᶜAlāᵓiyye fi'l-Umūri'l-ᶜAlāᵓiyye*, ed. A. S. Erzi (Ankara, 1956), p. 289 for middling emirs, pp. 215 and 264 (among other places) for grand ones (also called state emirs – *umarāᵓ-ye dawlat* in reference to the building of the walls of Konya, p. 253), p. 271 for *sarvarān-e bargāh*, p. 118 for *umarāᵓ-ye ḥasham*, and p. 74 for *umerā'-ye lashkar*. See the discussion of the

walls of Sinop below for more military titles and the walls of Antalya for the term *mamlūk* applied to these (former) slave emirs.

5. Alessio Bombaci, 'The army of the Saljuqs of Rūm', *Annali dell'Istituto Universitario Orientale di Napoli* 38 (1978), pp. 355, 365ff.
6. For the creation and duplication of elite environments in Alanya and elsewhere around the Rum Seljuq realm, see Chapter 2 of my *Landscape and the State in Medieval Anatolia: Seljuk Gardens and Pavilions of Alanya, Turkey* (Oxford, 2000).
7. Ibn Bībī, *El-Evāmirü'l-ᶜAlāᵓiyye*, p. 264; Anonymous, *Tārīkh-i Āl-i Saljūq* (Ankara, 1952), pp. 45–6.
8. Six of the Sinop citadel inscriptions bear Islamic dates giving the month as well as year. Of these, five date to a month more or less coterminous with August, and one with September. However, the Greek part of the bilingual inscription of Badr al-Dīn Abu Bakr mentions the months of April and September.
9. Mehmet Behçet, 'Sinop Kitabeleri', *Türk Tarih Encümeni Mecmuası* n.s. 1/2 (1929), p. 38. The inscription is dated 615/1218. It is currently housed in the storerooms of the Sinop Museum. A fragmentary inscription of an emir of Sultan ᶜIzz al-Dīn was noted on the citadel mosque before it fell into ruin and disappeared. Although its published reading was garbled, the publication indicates that the citadel mosque was constructed under this sultan by Ismāᶜīl Yūsuf. For this inscription, now lost, see Mehmet Behçet, 'Sinop Kitabeleri 3', *Türk Tarih Encümeni Mecmuası* n.s. 1/5 (1930–1), p. 56.
10. For the texts of these inscriptions, see *Répertoire chronologique d'épigraphie arabe* 10 (henceforth *RCEA*), eds É. Combe *et al.* (Cairo, 1939). For the Muslim architect Mubāriz al-Dīn Aqshā (corrected reading), see *RCEA* 3760; for the Christian architect Sifistūs (Sebastos) (corrected reading), see *RCEA* 3764. The Syrian architect Abū ᶜAlī al-Ḥalabī b. al-Kattānī is mentioned in two inscriptions at Sinop, both on the main citadel gate (Lonca Kapısı), see *RCEA* 3761 and 3774. The architect Nujām (?) al-Dīn Ankara(wī) (?) (new reading) is found at the end of the inscription of the governors of Aksaray (*RCEA* 3763). For the scribe Najm al-Dīn Yawāsh al-Bahāᵓī (corrected reading – meaning slave of Bahā' al-Dīn Kutlughja, governor of Kayseri) see *RCEA* 3760. For the inscription noting the supervision (*naẓar*) of Amīr Dād Sinān al-Dīn Ṭughril, see *RCEA* 3761. For the inscription noting the supervision (*tawallī*) of Ismāᶜīl b. Yūsuf al-sulṭānī (corrected reading, with the addition of al-sulṭānī, meaning of sultanic slave origin), see *RCEA* 3766. This emir also seems to have been in charge of building the citadel mosque; see note 8 above. I write 'at least' because we know of at least three inscriptions that give us no information about emirs and cities: the defaced inscription above the Lonca Kapısı, an empty slot for a large inscription on one of the eastern towers of the citadel that does not fit the dimensions of any surviving inscriptions, and a previously unrecorded emirial inscription on a north-facing tower of the citadel that has lost its critical last line.
11. This inscription, which is highly weathered, was partially published by M. Şükrü Ülkütaşır, 'Sinop'ta Selçukiler Zamanına Ait Tarihi Eserler', *Türk Tarih Arkeologya ve Etnoğrafya Dergisi* 5 (1949), pp. 123–4.
12. Sīmra/Sīmre has yet to be localised, although it may have been located in the area of the current towns of Vezirköprü and Havza. ᶜIzz al-Dīn and his father employed a similar strategy for the chief Seljuq Mediterranean port of Antalya, where its *sūbāshī*, Mubāriz al-Dīn Ertoqush, is twice described by Ibn Bībī as knowing the language and practices of the people of the Antalya region, indicating that he must have been originally a Christian

from this region; see Scott Redford and Gary Leiser, *Victory Inscribed. The Seljuk* Fetihname *on the Citadel Walls of Antalya, Turkey* (Istanbul, 2008), p. 92. Badr al-Dīn does not appear to have been of slave origin, but he brought local knowledge from Simre – and employed it in this inscription.

13. Redford and Leiser, *Victory Inscribed*, p. 98.
14. Kayseri continues to furnish architects to the Seljuqs: see note 25 below for another architect from Kayseri working later in Antalya.
15. Due to both extensive rebuilding and destruction, no general statement can be made about the ensemble of inscriptions on the west side of the citadel aside from the fact that the two that can be assigned to the western side of the citadel are both large. Mehmet Behçet, 'Sinop Kitabeleri', *Türk Tarih Encümeni Mecmuası* 1/4 (1930) notes the inscription of the emirs of Sivas (*RCEA* 3766) on the north face of the second tower from the north of this stretch of the walls. The only other inscription that can be thought of as once being located on the west facade is that of the governor and emirs of Amasya (*RCEA* 3771) mentioning three arches – and indeed there were three monumental arches here until the early 20th century. Both of these inscriptions are presently stored in the garden of the Sinop Museum. The inscription of the governor (*ṣāḥib*) of Tokat (*RCEA* 3768) does not fit the paradigm noted above: it is small and is located on a tower on the east of the citadel. However, it looks as if it is not in its original position.
16. *RCEA* 3772.
17. See note 14 above for probable placement of this inscription.
18. *RCEA* 3770 (corrected reading; pious motto added.)
19. Scott Redford, 'A newly read inscription on the walls of Antalya, Turkey', *Muqarnas* 25 (2008), pp. 177–83.
20. Redford and Leiser, *Victory Inscribed.*
21. Ibn Bībī, *El-Evāmirü'l-ᶜAlā'iyye*, p. 153, notes the scribes, whom he calls *nūṭārān*, who travelled with the sultan to Sinop, and prepared official documents there. Such scribes must have accompanied the sultan regularly.
22. Ibn Bībī, *El-Evāmirü'l-ᶜAlā'iyye*, pp. 253–4. At the same time, the sultan also orders that the princes (*mulūk*) and emirs of Sivas bear the cost of new walls there. Here a hierarchy is posited, with state emirs paying for the fortifications of the capital, while in Sivas, the local elite was held entirely responsible.
23. Scott Redford, 'The Seljuks of Rūm and the Antique', *Muqarnas* 10 (1993), pp. 148-56; Scott Redford, 'Maurozomes in Konya', *Proceedings of the First International Sevgi Gönül Byzantine Studies Symposium* (Istanbul: Vehbi Koç Foundation, 2010), pp. 48–50.
24. Ibn Bībī, *El-Evāmirü'l-ᶜAlā'iyye*, p. 264ff.; Remzi Duran, *Selçuklu Devri Konya Yapı Kitabeleri (İnşa ve Ta'mir)* (Ankara, 2001), nos. 51, and 53. Both of the surviving emirial inscriptions begin with 'al-sulṭānī', and there are also other inscriptional plaques from these walls that bear this word – meaning 'belonging to the sultan, or slave of the sultan' alone; see Duran, *Selçuklu*, nos. 23 and 48. In this respect, it is interesting to note that in the passage from Ibn Bībī, the emirs chosen by the sultan to build these walls are called *umarā'-ye mamālīk*, a phrase that has been taken to mean 'emirs of the realms'. However, in my opinion, the proper reading is 'slave emirs' – with the word in question being not the plural of realm, but of slave soldier, or *mamlūk*, despite the small orthographic difference between the two. This reading is given credence by the inscription of Ayāz from Antalya discussed below, which can only be understood when this orthographic difference is taken into account.

25. Ahmed Tevhid, 'Antalya Sur Kitabeleri', *Tarih-i Osmani Encümeni Mecmuasi* 16 (1926), pp. 173–6; Leyla Yılmaz, *Antalya. Bir Ortaçağ Türk Şehrinin Mimarlık Mirası ve Şehir Dokusunun Gelişimi (16. Yüzyılın Sonuna Kadar)* (Ankara, 2002), p. 136 no. 22 for the inscription of 'Mi^cmār . . . Jamāl al-Dīn Jastān [or Ḥastān] bin Ya^cqūb al-Qayṣarī . . .' For the inscription of Ayāz, see Yılmaz Önge, 'Antalya'daki Selçuklu Çeşmeleri Hakkında Bazı Görüşler', *Antalya IV Selçuklu Semineri Bildirileri* (Antalya, 1993), pp. 70–2. Here, I give corrected readings of his epithets and the date. Since this article was written, the following book has appeared: Leyla Yılmaz and Kemal Tuzcu, *Antalya'da Türk Dönemi Kitabeleri* (Haarlem, 2010).
26. Ali Yardım, *Alanya Kitabeleri* (İstanbul, 2002), p. 117 for Benek (Banāk) (corrected from Īnāl/Yınal); Seton Lloyd and D. S. Rice, *Alanya (ʿAlāʾiyya)* (London, 1958), nos. 13 and 27 for Qarāja and no. 15 for Yāqūt Utāqbāshī.
27. Lloyd and Rice, *Alanya*, nos. 4–13 for the inscriptions in this area; four of ten bear the motto *al-mulk lillāh*; Yardım, *Alanya Kitabeleri*, pp. 90–1, for the inscription with Qurʾānic quotations. For explanations for corrected readings of the names Aqshe and Benek, see my 'Some problems of Anatolian Seljuk inscriptions from Antalya and Alanya', in *Bizans ve Çevre Kültürler: Yıldız Ötüken'e Armağan*, eds S. Doğan *et al.* (Istanbul, 2010), pp. 304–10.

CHAPTER

15

THE SELJUQ MONUMENTS OF TURKMENISTAN*

Robert Hillenbrand

This chapter discusses a compact body of high-quality medieval monuments from Turkmenistan. In order to say something worthwhile in the limited space available, it seems sensible to deal swiftly with the geographical setting, the distribution of these monuments in time and space, and their political context. The bulk of this chapter will then focus on their structural features and on their place within the wider framework of architecture in the Iranian world in this period. In that context, the thrust of the argument will be that the 5th to 6th-/11th to 12th-century monuments in modern Turkmenistan constitute a distinct local school of Seljuq architecture,[1] with a recognisable repertoire of forms and style of decoration. The chapter will end with a brief assessment of the major building of the whole school, the building popularly known as the mausoleum of Sultan Sanjar.[2]

SETTING

First, then, the geographical and physical setting. A brief glance at a map is enough to show that the modern state of Turkmenistan possesses clear natural boundaries to the south, east and west. These are, respectively, the Köpet Dāgh

* I should particularly like to thank the Iran Heritage Foundation for providing the grant that made it possible for me to see these monuments in the context of the International Merv Project, as well as Dr Georgina Herrmann, the Co-Director of the Project, for making all of the necessary arrangements, which was a truly formidable administrative task and was impeccably accomplished. It is also a great pleasure to acknowledge the key roles played by Akmuhammad Agaev, David Gye, Kathy Judelson, Joe Rock and last – but absolutely not least – our driver, Ashir, who brought us safely there and back again.

range of mountains which separates it from Iran; the River Oxus, or Āmū Daryā, with modern Uzbekistan on its other bank; and the Caspian Sea. Only to the north, where lies Kazakhstan, is there no natural barrier. In contrast to Iran, which lies directly to the south, Turkmenistan is not a plateau but lies for the most part barely above sea level. Most of Turkmenistan, in fact, comprises deserts of notable severity, of which the Kara Kum is the most famous. Hence the lack of settlements, whether ancient, medieval or modern, in most of the centre and north of the country. It is true that man-made catastrophes have had their share in this bleakness; the medieval chronicles, for example, specifically describe the massive devastation wrought by the Mongols in 617–18/1220–1 on the extensive irrigation network which underpinned the prosperity of Urganj, now Kunya Urgench. More recently, in Soviet times, the dominance of the cotton-growing industry has altered the water table and the traditional operation of the canals. One result of this has been the increasing salinity of the soil, which has eroded the lower walls of many a medieval building and caused widespread collapse.

Next, the distribution of the monuments in time and space. The combination of natural deserts and man-made desertification just described helps to explain the rather modest tally of surviving monuments datable between, say, 390/1000 and 761/1360, that is, between the end of the Samanid and the beginning of the Timurid period, and their concentration in a few settlements along the southern fringe of the country. Some three dozen buildings from these three and a half centuries survived into the age of photography, and about a third of those have since disappeared. Some of those that have not technically vanished have been rebuilt in the past two decades virtually from scratch in a remarkably clumsy and ignorant way, presumably in a bid to attract tourists. This has been very much the fashion in post-Soviet Turkmenistan, and for that matter Uzbekistan too, and it is heartbreaking to see monuments that have suffered this treatment. Their evidential value is nil, as the ᶜAlambarda mausoleum shows.[3] Since this is happening repeatedly, and quietly, it is worth sounding the alarm before still more damage is done by local officials and their jobbing contractors. Nor are standing monuments exempt; the indiscriminate use of sanding machines to remove the patina of age has denatured the appearance of numerous medieval buildings (Figure 15.1), from the humblest mausoleum to the tomb of Sanjar. One is dealing, therefore, with a rapidly diminishing legacy.

The principal centre of these monuments is the extended oasis of Merv, which in pre-Mongol times was unquestionably the major city in what is now Turkmenistan;[4] next in importance, with half a dozen significant buildings each, come Kunya Urgench, the only major medieval settlement in the north of the country, and Dahistān or Mashhad-i Miṣriyān in the west, in the area of the oil-fields currently under exploitation. Nearly all the other major structures are, so

Figure 15.1 Mausoleum of Muḥammad b. Zayd, Merv, façade

to speak, singletons scattered all over the southern part of the country. This is a picture very different from that presented by, say, Isfahan or Yazd, with their rich heritage of medieval buildings and a hinterland with many more of them. But then, neither of those cities was sacked by the Mongols, and in Iran proper very little remains of the kind of city that was a metropolis in its region, like Nishapur[5] or Rayy, and that was indeed sacked by the Mongols. But Turkmenistan differs not only from most areas of comparable size in pre-Mongol Iran in that it has fewer 5th to 6th/11th to 12th-century buildings; it is also signally poor in monuments of the 8th to 9th/13th to 14th centuries. The most significant remains are in Kunya Urgench, among which, apart from several monuments of contested date for parts of which a 14th-century date has been proposed,[6] are two anonymous mausolea,[7] the mausoleum of ʿAlī al-Ramitānī al-Bukhārī,[8] the shrine complex of Ibn Ḥājib,[9] one of the 'little cities of God' so popular in the 14th century,[10] and a whole series of major monuments, including the almost entirely vanished Gulgerdān mausoleum, which rivalled that of Turābek Khānum in scale and splendour, and was notable for its furrowed external dome resting on a flanged drum, with an interior clearly related to that of the Turābek Khānum mausoleum;[11] the richly decorated portal of a major public building;[12] the shrine of Najm al-Dīn Kubrā;[13] the towering minaret of Qutlugh Tīmūr;[14] and of course the lofty, spectacular mausoleum of Turābek Khānum.[15] Here is the clearest indication that this area bore the brunt of the Mongol invasion, and that the damage inflicted was such as to inhibit recovery for almost two centuries.

What of the political context? It is worth remembering that the Seljuqs entered Iran by way of Turkmenistan, and indeed that the key battle which destroyed Ghaznavid power in the eastern Iranian world and thus gave the Seljuqs access to the plateau was fought in 431/1040 at Dandānqān,[16] not far from Merv. Moreover, the history of this particular region in the Seljuq period is one of constant political unrest and of hostilities not only between the settled agricultural population and the nomads or half-nomads who were making constant inroads into their lands, but also between the various nomadic clans themselves, for instance the Khalaj, Oghuz and Qarluq. They were often pagan, and were apt to execute the *ʿulamāʾ* (the Islamic clergy), burn libraries and to violate the sanctity of mosques.[17] Their centres of power were in northern Afghanistan,[18] especially Balkh, east Uzbekistan and southern Tajikistan. The Seljuq administration attempted to police the inroads of these tribes by deploying the Turkmen (often simply called Turks) of Khurasan to guard the frontiers.[19] But as Seljuq authority waned towards the middle of the 6th/12th century it became increasingly difficult to control these tribes from the east. During the Ghuzz rebellion of 548–51/1153–6,[20] which followed close on the heels of a massive migration of that tribe south of the Oxus into the area of Balkh,[21] the Seljuq ruler, Sultan

Sanjar himself, was captured and remained in the hands of the Ghuzz for three years. The evidence suggests that the presence of the Turkic nomads was more intrusive in Turkmenistan than in Iran proper, and this may help to explain the relative dearth of surviving religious monuments such as mosques and madrasas, especially as Agadžanov has interpreted the ill feeling between the settled population and the nomads as expressing itself under the mask of religion.[22] Be that as it may, the salient fact is that, from 490/1096 to 552/1157, the ruler of Turkmenistan and of neighbouring eastern Iran was Sanjar b. Malikshāh – first as governor and then, on the death of his brother Sultan Muḥammad, in 512/1118, as supreme sultan of the entire Seljuq empire. This meant that Khurasan, as his power base, enjoyed the privileged position formerly accorded under earlier Seljuq sultans to Iraq and western Iran. Despite the fact that Turkmenistan and north-eastern Iran are geographically distinct, in this period they were politically and culturally one, and were at the centre of events. The Seljuq monuments of Turkmenistan were thus produced directly within the orbit of the court. Hence one would be justified in expecting to find here the finest architecture that the age could produce. But that is not so, and the monuments of central and western Iran – at Marāgha,[23] Hamadan[24] and the Isfahan oasis[25] – are a reminder of that fact. Such a straight value-judgment of course requires justification, which will be forthcoming at the end of this chapter.

STRUCTURAL FEATURES

What is the structural interest of these monuments? It has everything to do with the actual material of construction, and so the cardinal fact to remember is that this is not rammed earth or mud brick, as in earlier local architecture, but baked brick. Much follows from this change of material – for the Seljuq architects did not choose simply to translate familiar forms from one material to the other. This suggests that the material itself had much to do with the development of the standard forms. To begin with, baked brick was very much more expensive – enough fuel had to be found, in a countryside where wood was scarce, to keep the brick-making kilns at the right temperature for the right length of time.[26] The very use of a kiln itself, with the concomitant need to stack bricks in tiers, made the production of baked bricks more time-consuming, as against the manufacture of mud bricks, which were simply spread out on the ground. Where the material of construction was so costly, in terms of time and money, it behoved builders to use it with extra care, and above all not to waste it. That meant, for example, planning in advance if bricks of other than standard size were needed, for whereas mud bricks could easily be chipped to the desired size if a smaller or uneven shape were required, the much harder material of baked brick made such

Figure 15.2 Kiz Bibi mausoleum, Merv, squinch zone

re-sizing difficult. But more generally it implied re-thinking many a premise of traditional vernacular architecture – for there is no evidence that there was a widespread tradition of using baked brick in Turkmenistan before the 5th/11th century. On the contrary, the surviving early Islamic buildings (Figure 15.2)[27] suggest that mud brick or rammed earth were the standard materials.

Figure 15.3 Greater Kiz Qal^ca, Merv, exterior from south-east

Local builders using baked brick therefore had to learn as they went along. They must soon have found that it demanded a greater degree of precision than did rammed earth and mud brick.

A whole series of changes followed, and it is worth mentioning some of them – though the changes were so radical and far-reaching that they deserve a much more profound and detailed study than can be attempted here. Thus the very thick and over-built walls that characterised the *köshk*s (palatial structures) of the Merv oasis (Figure 15.3) were replaced by much thinner walls.

The massive corrugations, while not entirely forgotten, as the case of Rabaṭ-i Malik shows,[28] largely gave way to much more complex forms of articulation: blind arches and panels, often of varying scale and filled with decorative brickwork, as at Miḥna[29] and Sarakhs.[30] The massive talus on which those corrugations typically rest shrinks to a modest foundation a few brick courses high and parallel to the wall above. Buildings were much more carefully planned, and with due regard for proportional relationships; as a result they acquire a new harmony and balance.[31] The work done by Soviet-era scholars on the mathematical calculation which underlies these buildings has tended to obscure the fact that the inter-relationship of the component parts of a monument was achieved by the simplest and most practical methods dependent ultimately on the squaring of the circle, for which a peg and a length of string sufficed.[32] Symptomatic of the new precision was the development of innovative arch forms. The elliptical arch profiles so popular in pre-Islamic times[33] disappear from the standard vocabulary of the architect, as do sequences of identical arches set one within and behind the other (Figure 15.4).[34]

Figure 15.4 Lesser Kiz Qal^ca, Merv, multiple recessed arches in stairway

Figure 15.5 Mausoleum of Imam Bāḥir, squinch zone

The area of transition between lower chamber and dome takes on a new crispness as the focus widens to take in not just the squinch itself but the entire zone of which it is part. Now, that transition zone is positively highlighted by decorative mouldings which define its upper and lower limits, and by a new emphasis on the intermediate area between the squinches, as at Imām Bāhir (Figure 15.5).[35]

A tentative move in this direction can already be seen at the little Kiz Kala (Figure 15.6),[36] though there the intermediate space between the squinches is not even an arch but simply a flat framed panel.

On the whole, mud brick proved to lack the sophistication and precision needed to devise such grace notes. But with the advent of baked brick the squinches begin to assert themselves visually, acquiring extra internal ornament in the form of herringbone patterns or decorative strips which serve to subdivide their volumes.[37] Vaults develop a much greater sophistication and variety, as can be seen at Dayā Khātūn with its array of half a dozen different systems of roofing: domes on squinches, as well as cloister, groin, domical, barrel, cradle and Balkhī or squinch vaults, are used side by side, and one particularly has to admire the consistently ingenious solutions which this architect devises for the intersection of vaulted spaces.[38] It is no accident that some of these vaults are unknown in mud brick. Baked brick clearly fostered far more playfulness and inventiveness. And it transformed decoration no less than structure, for its small

Figure 15.6 Lesser Kiz Qal^ca, Merv, upper storey, room 8

scale and precision lent themselves to more elaborate patterning than the simple play of vertical and horizontal courses which had generally been the limit of earlier experiments in mud brick. The so-called Tomb of the Samanids, datable before 943, has become an art-historical cliché, but the fact remains that here, *in nuce*, the range of the new material is on show.[39] This is truly an architectural heritage transformed and catapulted to a much higher level of sophistication.

The contrasts of material can best be appreciated when both are used in the same building, as at Khudāy Naẓar Awliyā᾿, where a baked-brick skin (Figure 15.7)[40] has been added to a mud-brick core[41] – and transforms it.

This structure is also interesting in that it shows that architects were not constrained to choose between mud brick and baked brick but could combine the two. But one may note here that the decision to construct the core of the monument in mud brick means that its walls are significantly thicker than those of comparable buildings erected entirely in baked brick.

Perhaps the key factor that made baked brick such an important agent of change was its combination of lightness and strength. In both of these respects it was very markedly superior to mud brick. Once again, the implications are legion. Given that the basic building unit was now light – the typical brick measures 25 cm square by 4–5 cm thick – it was easy to carry and to handle; it could be tossed from the ground to the mason by his apprentice. There was no need to

Figure 15.7 Mausoleum of Khudāy Naẓar Awliyāᵓ, exterior

toil repeatedly up a ladder or scaffolding with a heavy load and then descend for more building material. This alone made it a more flexible medium with which to work, and that opened new horizons. One thinks of how the flexibility and ductility of plasticine liberates the imagination of a child at play. Moreover, the greater strength of baked brick allowed supports to be more slender and vaults and domes to be thinner, as at Dayā Khātun.[42] And as so often happens, one innovation quickly generated another. In this case, the potential of baked brick was released by the development of a very hard and quick-setting lime mortar.[43] This allowed masons to experiment with new kinds of vaults and domes, and, by means of trial and error, rapidly to test the boundaries of this new combination of materials. The parallel with Justinianic architecture in the eastern Mediterranean in the early 6th century is compelling: there too, architecture was transformed by the widespread use of very light small bricks. In Seljuq architecture, in just the same way, speedy construction encouraged bold experiment. A vault comprising a single skin of baked bricks could obviously be erected much more quickly than a significantly thicker vault in mud brick. If it was too weak, the fatal flaw would probably announce itself in advance by lines of stress in the brick masonry, lines that could be interpreted by an experienced mason. Thus, as in Gothic architecture in the medieval west, the intelligent observation of failure moderated the urge to innovate.

That testing of the boundaries was not just a matter of structural tolerances but also of aesthetic possibilities. For, quite apart from its suitability for applied ornament, which is a separate issue, the use of baked brick created a new range of three-dimensional opportunities for architects. So vaults were built higher and spanned wider spaces than before, with a consequent transformation of interior space. Larger dome chambers became the norm, bringing with them greater volume, even a sense of majesty.[44] Their spaces are subdivided and can therefore be played off against each other – lower chamber versus squinch zone versus dome. Of course this was theoretically possible with the smaller spaces which were the norm in mud brick architecture. But since architecture is all about the third dimension, space, extra scale is crucial to its deployment: think of the different feel of low ceilings as against high ceilings in modern houses or offices. Nor was it a simple matter of increased absolute height. The so-called mosque of Talkhatān, probably a *muṣallā*, *namāzgāh* or *ᶜīdgāh* for supererogatory prayers, comprises a central dome chamber typologically akin to those of Iran proper: Gulpāygān, Ardistān and the Isfahan *jāmiᶜ*. But this dome chamber is not conceived like them, that is, as a free-standing structure which happens to be surrounded by lesser covered spaces. Instead, it is flanked by two low and narrow halls, each furnished with two openings into the main chamber and each consisting of two vaulted bays. Thanks to the use of baked brick, the supports of these vaults are sufficiently slender to encourage the free circulation of space and thus to make the whole interior a single continuous volumetric space (Figure 15.8).

At the same time, the openings of the halls, the lateral vaults and the central dome are all of different heights, and the interpenetration, the rise and fall, of these curvilinear volumes is integral to the whole design. The constant changes of height, breadth and depth at the caravansarai of Dayā Khātūn illustrate another aspect of these constantly changing volumes, for the differences there are to do with function and status.

A LOCAL SCHOOL VERSUS THE IRANIAN CONNECTION

It is now time to determine how far this is a local school. The matter is complicated by the lack of comparative studies. Until the fall of the Soviet Union these buildings were scarcely known to Western scholars, and conversely the buildings of Iran were scarcely known to Soviet specialists. Thus the Iron Curtain prevented the spread of information which could contextualise the architecture of either area properly. So the present decade is the first time that this question could be tackled on the basis of actual study of the buildings concerned rather

Figure 15.8 Mosque of Talkhatān Bābā, interior

than just a familiarity with the relevant publications on either side of the divide. What, then, gives these buildings their distinctive character? And conversely, do they lack any features that are commonly encountered in the Seljuq architecture of Iran proper? In other words, what are the significant features, both present and absent? This is the key question for determining how the architecture of Turkmenistan fits into a pan-Iranian context.

Let us begin with the absences. Perhaps the most surprising one, though it is not diagnostic for the identification of a local school, is that Seljuq Turkmenistan offers almost no examples of mosques, whereas this is the commonest building type in Iran proper in this period. To some extent this must be an accident of survival, but it may also suggest that there were simply fewer settlements, and also that the ravages of the Mongol invasion were more severe in Turkmenistan than in much of Iran. The prominent role of pagan or lightly Islamised nomads of Turkic stock in 6th/12th-century Turkmenistan may also be relevant here, and may help to explain the prevalence of shrines, with their traditional appeal to folk Islam, as at Astana Baba. Equally striking is the total absence of the standard Iranian minaret, a slender lofty tower of baked brick decorated with patterned brickwork and inscriptions. Yet this is a building type which spread throughout the rest of the Iranian world – modern Afghanistan, Uzbekistan, even Kyrgystan. There are no madrasas at all, which is not surprising given the relative rarity of surviving examples in Iran, and also no tomb towers, even though this was a popular building type in Seljuq Iran. Similar absences are noticeable in architectural decoration: thus one encounters very little terracotta ornament – the facade of the tomb of Fakhr al-Dīn Rāzī at Urgench, dated 605/1208, and otherwise known as the tomb of Īl-Arslan, is a rare exception – and virtually no carved stucco, the tomb of ᶜAbdallāh b. Burayda notwithstanding (Figure 15.9), though recent finds at Sulṭān Qalᶜa prove that at least incised stucco was part of the decorative repertory, while the *miḥrāb* of the Shīr Kabīr mausoleum at Dahistān proves that stucco carving in high relief *was* locally used in the pre-Seljuq period.

Glazed tilework appears – to judge by surviving examples – almost a century later than in Iran, and is monochrome (light blue) rather than employing two or three colours. On the other hand, the three examples known – at Dahistān and at Kunya Urgench – all illustrate different ways of using colour, which points to the likelihood that glazed tilework was well established. Indeed, the glazed epigraphic plaques in high relief used at the tomb of Tekesh may well be ahead of anything known in Iran c. 597/1200, just as – 160 years later – the tomb of Turābek Khānum, also in Kunya Urgench, uses tile mosaic on a scale exceeded only by the Yazd *jāmiᶜ* in Iran itself and of a variety that is in some respects ahead of anything in contemporary Iran. Finally, it is worth pointing out that there are relatively few inscriptions. Despite such notable exceptions as the

Figure 15.9 Mausoleum of ᶜAbdallāh b. Burayda, Vakīl Bāzār, stuccowork of interior

mausolea of Muḥammad b. Zayd (Figure 15.10), ᶜAbdallāh b. Burayda (Figure 15.11) and Sultan Sanjar[45] there is nothing in Turkmenistan to match the rich epigraphic programme of Ardistān, the mosques at Zavāra and Qazvīn and the mausolea at Damghān.

More than that, major buildings like Talkhatān, ᶜAlambarda, and Sarakhs lack all trace of contemporary inscriptions, while Dayā Khātūn, a highly ornamented building, also has no inscriptions apart from the names of the four Rightly Guided caliphs emblazoned on its façade[46] – and even this seems to be an echo of the contemporary Iranian caravansarai at Zaᶜfarūniya.[47] All these absences, or differences in emphasis, add up to a school of architecture that in many respects had little in common with the Seljuq buildings of Iran itself. In Iran proper only Ribāṭ-i Sharaf[48] and the tomb of Luqmān Bābā at Sarakhs[49] – and both of these are only just over the modern border – echo the style of Turkmenistani architecture, which suggests that there was indeed a difference even between eastern Iran and Turkmenistan in this period, for all that both were part of Khurasan. This finding tallies with the indications of geography and 6th/12th-century demography[50] that Turkmenistan did have its own character at this time.

It may sound rather carping to rehearse these many ways in which the Seljuq architecture of Turkmenistan differs from that of Iran proper, and in some ways to its detriment. But there is a purpose behind the process, namely to show that by degrees these two traditions, though very closely related in their initial stages,

Figure 15.10 Mausoleum of Muḥammad b. Zayd, Merv, inscription in dome chamber

Figure 15.11 Mausoleum of ᶜAbdallāh b. Burayda, Vakīl Bāzār, inscription on façade

Figure 15.12 Mausoleum of Sultan Sanjar, Merv, gallery, inscription

began to part company. Put simply, the Iranian taste for colour and for intricate ornament in terracotta, stucco and epigraphy found little echo in Turkmenistan. In Iran that taste comfortably complemented the so-called 'naked brick' style expressed in the great dome chambers of the Isfahan oasis. Nor do the Seljuq buildings of Turkmenistan offer sufficiently close parallels for the spatial complexities and the dynamic, restless energy of Iranian Seljuq transition zones[51] or the vaults of the Isfahan *jāmi*ᶜ.[52] They are staid in comparison. They have less to offer; there is some dimension missing.

There is no cause for surprise in any of this. It is entirely reasonable that the huge territories ruled by the Seljuqs should have generated various schools, or at any rate sub-sets, each of a recognisably distinct style of architecture. Setting aside the lands under Seljuq control in Syria and Anatolia, with their strong local tradition of using stone as the basic building material – the Euphrates marks the border between stone and brick – the brick architecture of Iraq and the Iranian world from the 5th/11th to the 7th/13th century has several well-defined local groupings of this kind. Broadly speaking, these were located respectively in Iraq, north-west Iran, central Iran, Central Asia[53] – especially Turkmenistan – and Afghanistan. These individual sub-schools have still to be defined by modern scholarship in the necessary detail. The present chapter is a limited attempt in that direction.

Enough, then, of what is not there in the Seljuq architecture of Turkmenistan. More to the point, what *is* there? What are the *positive* distinguishing features of this school? They are of various kinds. Some are frankly decorative and immediately recognisable: visual trademarks like doubled stretchers, terracotta stamps used as brick-end plugs, and long guard strips with motifs like bow ties, diamonds or trefoils used to mark off one space from another, particularly in the case of otherwise unarticulated flat panels.[54] In other words, this is a language of ornament largely driven by forms closely based on bricks, even if those bricks have been pre-cut before firing into quite varied shapes. But the emphasis is unmistakably on thick and rectilinear forms rather than, say, thin and curvilinear ones of the kind favoured in Iraq and Afghanistan. Other such distinguishing features have to do with bridging elements: corners spanned by corbelled blocks in stepped tiers, or by stepped recesses, and squinch hoods lightly articulated by ornamental strips or half-filled with decorative brickwork; these too occur often enough to rate as clichés, though quite elaborate trefoil squinches are also known, as at Yārtī Gunbad.[55] Yet other telltale signifiers have to do with arches: multifoil profiles, bricks used narrow edge on in order to outline the upper profile of an arch, rows of blind arches employed to articulate a facade, as at Talkhatān or the tomb of Muḥammad b. Zayd at Merv, and – a feature clearly related to the stepped recesses just mentioned – a preference for multiple recessed arches used in a variety of contexts.[56] All these diagnostic features serve to lend character to the wall itself (Figure 15.13), a trend foreshadowed in those *köshk*s which used alternately horizontal and vertical courses in an attempt to create a patterned wall surface.[57]

It was common for the *köshk*s to have plastered walls[58] and it is quite possible that this practice was widely followed in the Seljuq buildings too, even though very few examples survive. The case of Yārtī Gunbad shows how this use of plaster, painted and incised, could embellish the baked-brick core of a building,[59] just as a baked-brick skin embellished a mud or mud-brick core.

So much for the outward, as it were, measurable signs of this well-defined sub-set of Seljuq architecture. What of the more intangible indices of its character? It seems to be a profoundly conservative house style. When one studies it, words like sober, austere, even grim, come naturally to mind. These buildings, at least in their present state, rely for their impact almost exclusively on brick – chunky, angular brick, unmodulated by the supple, slender curvilinearity of carved terracotta,[60] let alone the softer, smoother, elastic quality of stucco-work, with its inbuilt leaning towards fantasy.[61] The virtues of brick are those of plain statement and muscularity, not of pliability and ambiguity. 'Seek rather to suggest than display', says the Chinese proverb; but this is an architecture of display, not suggestion. Its frankness, strength and monumentality are directly related to the unbroken focus on a single material. This extends even to the

Figure 15.13 Mosque of Talkhatān Bābā, row of blind arches on south-west façade

joint plugs between the bricks. In Iran these are of stucco, with a consequent texturing and differentiation of the wall surface.[62] But here the wall, even when richly ornamented, is all of a piece. There is no sense of multiple, contrasting levels, of plot and sub-plot. The urge to display helps to explain the strong patterns, often made stronger still, as at the tomb of Muḥammad b. Zayd,[63] by the contrast between recessed and outset fret designs. And when these designs are placed side by side, for example within a dome chamber[64] or along a stretch of exterior wall,[65] each one is enriched by its neighbour, and the end result is one of cumulative magnificence (Figure 15.15).

It is a little like visiting a picture gallery and strolling from one canvas to the next. But decoration is not an end in itself; it is always – even at Talkhatān, the most richly ornamented of these buildings – subordinated to severely architectural qualities. Form dominates. And that form is often as simple and direct as the wooden building blocks of a child's nursery – powerful cubes, squares, hemispheres. The innate capacity of baked brick to suggest content and mass is exploited to the full, as seen at Miḥna, the ᶜAlambardar mausoleum and the tomb of Abū l-Faḍl at Sarakhs.[66]

If there is a single structure which encapsulates the characteristic virtues of Seljuq architecture in Turkmenistan, it must be the tomb of Sanjar (Figure 15.16).[67]

Figure 15.14 Palace of Shāhriyār Arg, Merv, patterned brickwork

Figure 15.15 Mosque of Talkhatān Bābā, main façade

Figure 15.16 Mausoleum of Sultan Sanjar, Merv, aerial view

It is no accident to have left this monster building – a major monument at the heart of a major city – until last. It does not really belong with the others because it represents a quantum leap forward – in terms of ambition, scale, patronage, funding and sheer engineering. But it is also their apotheosis. Built by a local man, Muḥammad b. Atsız of Sarakhs,[68] perhaps around 534/1140, it possesses in fuller measure than any of them the key diagnostic features of the local school – that solemn, slightly dour majesty, that simplicity of form (overwhelming in this case), that reliance on plain brickwork as an index of strength, that indifference to spatial dynamism in the squinch zone, and, above all and controlling all, an innate conservatism. This last judgment does not, incidentally, apply to the method of dome construction, which is of absorbing interest, for it seems to be highly experimental and is unparalleled in the architecture of the period.

At first glance, the tomb projects the idea of crushing weight by virtue of its rather cumbersome design – the great double dome deposited so to speak baldly on a high cubical platform of much greater diameter. The gallery goes some way towards tempering this brusque contrast of forms, but not far enough – there is still a visually uncomfortable gap between the outer edge of gallery and dome respectively (Figure 15.17).

This is all the more serious a deficiency because the mausoleum was never intended to be free-standing, but was compassed around with subsidiary structures: mosque, palace, library, madrasa and other buildings.[69] Much of the interest of the building, incidentally, lies in this complex, which gives perhaps the fullest and most varied context known for any surviving mausoleum of this period in the Iranian world. Early archival photographs make the tomb look like a beached whale in a flat and featureless landscape (Figure 15.18).

They are thoroughly misleading. In fact it was the upper half of the building only that constituted its visible profile; *this* was the main landmark of the Seljuq city. And its huge high gallery was suitably monumental. But one has only to compare the treatment of this upper half with the solution adopted at Öljeitü's tomb at Sulṭāniya,[70] erected after 704/1305, which formally speaking is a lineal descendant of Sanjar's tomb, to recognise the difference between bluntness and elegance. Decoration on any substantial scale for the lower half of Sanjar's tomb would have been counter-productive, for the mausoleum was so compassed around by ancillary structures that such applied ornament would not have had enough room to make an impact. For the same reason, many minarets of the Seljuq period have plain exteriors below roof level; their decoration begins only above that level.[71]

The interior too has a slightly uncouth quality. It is an overpowering space, but an empty one. This is because there is no significant system of articulation for the lower walls. Moreover, the zone of transition can be described as another

Figure 15.17 Mausoleum of Sultan Sanjar, Merv, exterior, upper part

missed opportunity, for it consists simply of eight large arches, with no internal subdivisions at all (Figure 15.19).

That solution is fine for a small building, but it does not work for a structure of this size; the whole zone looks curiously incomplete. Not enough is going

Figure 15.18 Mausoleum of Sultan Sanjar, Merv, west façade

on. The tiers of cells in the spandrels take up the bridging theme so familiar in contemporary local buildings, though the distinctive trio of trilobed arches in the top tier is a new departure. That same trilobed theme is repeated at the base of the dome (Figure 15.20), but this is by no means a true sixteen-sided zone of the kind always found in other large Seljuq domes: it belongs rather with the patterned networks found on the underside of some of those domes.[72]

Figure 15.19 Mausoleum of Sultan Sanjar, Merv, interior, zone of transition

Figure 15.20 Mausoleum of Sultan Sanjar, Merv, interior, ribs of dome

The reason why the trilobed theme is imperfectly integrated with the network of ribs above may have to do with an unresolved confusion as to the role of this area around the collar of the dome – that is, whether it is intended as decoration or as structure made manifest. The ribs culminate in a little oculus whose symbolic associations are a study in themselves. No doubt the interior was not always as bare and echoing as it appears today; the upper part of the wall had a long Kufic inscription in painted plaster, and lesser painted cursive inscriptions can still be seen on the underside of the ribs in the dome, and these ribs also bore sinuous knotted vegetal decoration, with further vegetal scrolls painted in blue, red and white just below the zone of transition.[73] But none of this applied ornament could disguise the extreme plainness of this interior in architectural and architectonic terms. None of the large Iranian domes have so little happening inside. It is as if mere size were a sufficient end in itself.

What, finally, of the wider significance of this monument? Assuming that its traditional identification is correct – and the onus of disproof lies with the doubters – this is the only tomb of a Great Seljuq sultan which has survived, and so there is an obvious problem posed by the lack of comparable monuments in the contemporary Iranian world. Mahmud of Ghazna surely rivalled, indeed exceeded, Sanjar in prestige;[74] but his own tomb, for all the splendour of the cenotaph[75] and the wooden doors,[76] is intrinsically a modest building, even if the structure currently known by that name is essentially a 16th-century reconstruction. The tomb of Sanjar does not belong to the tradition of free-standing mausolea of which there are so many surviving examples from Seljuq Iran, though it could perhaps be interpreted as a very free variation on the familiar theme of the domed chamber of the Seljuq mosque. At the same time, the attempt to explain it as an import from the south quickly runs into difficulties, for some of the characteristic features of those monumental Seljuq mosques – their multiple openings, their rich applied ornament, their spectacularly complex zones of transition – find no echo in this building. Yet equally one must admit that it appears as a lusus naturae in the context of the architecture of Turkmenistan in the 6th/12th century. Nothing on a remotely similar scale survives from this area and period. Its importance in its own time and place is underlined by the report of the geographer Yāqūt, who commented that its blue dome could be seen from a day's journey away.[77] But its real importance transcends that time and place, and only emerges when this tomb is considered in the context of how the medieval Islamic mausoleum evolved. It is of course difficult to calculate trends on the basis of surviving buildings alone. But the quantity of later, more familiar mausolea of gigantic size – in Cairo,[78] Sulṭāniya, Multān,[79] Samarqand,[80] and of course those of northern India in the 10th/16th and 11th/17th centuries built for Sher Shāh,[81] Humāyūn[82] and Akbar[83] – has tended to obscure the place of Sanjar's tomb as a key forerunner of them all. It is also the earliest to survive. Here then, embedded in that Turkic Central Asian milieu which the Mughal emperors repeatedly claimed as their own, is a dry run for the Tāj Mahal.[84]

NOTES

1. For a very general overview of how these monuments fit into the wider context of medieval architecture in Central Asia, see *EIr*, s.v. 'Architecture IV. Central Asia', II, fasc. 3–4 (1986), cols 336a–337a (G. A. Pugachenkova), with a very useful bibliography at 338b–339a; for a more detailed general survey, see G. A. Pugachenkova, 'Khorasanskie Mavzolei', in *Khudozhestvennaya Kul'tura Srednei Azii IX-XIII veka*, ed. L. I. Rempel (Tashkent, 1983), pp. 14–29.
2. For good photographs of its condition before its restoration, see E. Cohn-Wiener, *Turan. Islamische Baukunst in Mittelasien* (Berlin, 1930), plates VII–VIII. For a wider selection of archival photos, reproduced at thumbnail scale and interspersed with modern photographs, see G. Herrmann, H. Coffey, S. Laidlaw and K. Kurbansakhatov, *The Monuments of Merv. A scanned archive of photographs and plans* (London, 2002), pp. 20, 22, 24–33.
3. For a good-quality large-scale photograph of how the building looked before its total demolition and subsequent rebuilding, see *Pamyatniki arkhitekturi Turkmenistana*, ed. V. Pilyavski (Leningrad, 1974), p. 236.
4. It was described in official documents as the *dār al-mulk* of the Seljuq state and, with some 150,000 inhabitants and ten major libraries plus an observatory, well deserved that title; see S. G. Agadshanow, *Der Staat der Seldschukiden und Mittelasien im 11.-12. Jahrhundert (Turkmenenforschung Band 17)*, trans. R. Schletzer (Berlin, 1994), pp. 210–11.
5. Though here the American excavations of the 1930s uncovered a rich store of architectural decoration; see C. K. Wilkinson, *Nishapur. Some Early Islamic Buildings and Their Decoration* (New York, 1986).
6. These are the mausoleum of Pīryār Vali: N. Khalimov, *Pamyatniki Urgencha* (Ashkhabad, 1991), pp. 66–8 and M. Mamedov and R. Muradov, *Gurgandzh. Arkhitekturnii Putevoditel'* (Istanbul, 2000), pp. 40–1, and the mausoleum of Sayyid Ahmad (Khalimov, *Pamyatniki Urgencha*, pp. 86–8; Mamedov and Muradov, *Gurgandzh*, p. 42); there are also two 8th/14th-century cenotaphs.
7. Mamedov and Muradov, *Gurgandzh*, pp. 23–4.
8. Khalimov, *Pamyatniki Urgencha*, pp. 83–5; Mamedov and Muradov, *Gurgandzh*, pp. 22–3.
9. Khalimov, *Pamyatniki Urgencha*, pp. 72–9; Mamedov and Muradov, *Gurgandzh*, pp. 26–8.
10. L. Golombek, 'The cult of saints and shrine architecture in the fourteenth century', in *Near Eastern Numismatics, Iconography, Epigraphy and History. Studies in Honor of George C. Miles*, ed. D. K. Kouymjian (Beirut, 1974), pp. 419–30.
11. Mamedov and Muradov, *Gurgandzh*, pp. 24–6.
12. The building has been variously identified as a palace of the Khwarizmshāhs or an 8th/14th-century caravansarai; see Khalimov, *Pamyatniki Urgencha*, pp. 50–1 and 8th un-numbered colour plate. For a colour plate of the tilework of this building see Pilyavski, *Pamyatniki*, p. 191 (see also p. 165), and Mamedov and Muradov, *Gurgandzh*, pp. 19–20.
13. See Khalimov, *Pamyatniki Urgencha*, pp. 52–64 and 9th and 10th un-numbered colour plates; Pilyavski, *Pamyatniki*, pp. 210–19; Mamedov and Muradov, *Gurgandzh*, pp. 33–9.
14. Pilyavski, *Pamyatniki*, pp. 191–4; Khalimov, *Pamyatniki Urgencha*, pp. 31–41, 135–7, 140, figs 19–21, 23 (excellent drawings of the very curious Kufic inscriptions); V.

V. Zotov, 'Novoye o minarete Kutlug Timura', *Vestnik Dobrovol'nogo Obshchestva Okhrani Pamyatnikov Istorii i Kul'turi Turkmenistana* 2, 50 (1990), pp. 13–15; Mamedov and Muradov, *Gurgandzh*, pp. 58–65.

15. Pilyavski, *Pamyatniki*, pp. 164, 194–209; Khalimov, *Pamyatniki Urgencha*, pp. 42–9; Mamedov and Muradov, *Gurgandzh*, pp. 51–8.
16. This was the site of yet another recently destroyed monument of high quality, a Seljuq mosque with sumptuous stucco ornament, fragments of which are displayed in the museum at Ashgabat. For a discussion of this monument and illustrations of a selection of this material, which includes a fragmentary *naskhī* inscription of astonishing virtuosity with lavish use of overlap, see O. Orazov, *Arkheologicheskie i Arkhitekturn'ie Pamyatniki Serakhskogo Oazisa* (Ashkhabad, 1973), pp. 88–91. See also G. A. Pugachenkova, *Puti razvitiya arkhitektury yuzhnogo Turkmenistana pory rabovladeniya i feodalizma* (Moscow, 1958), pp. 256–9 and S. Khmel'nitski, *Mezhdu Samanidami i Mongolami. Chast' I. Arkhitektura Srednei Azii XI-nachala XIII vv.* (Berlin and Riga, 1996), pp. 78–81.
17. C. E. Bosworth, 'The political and dynastic history of the Iranian world (A.D. 1000–1217)', in *CHI5*, pp. 153–4. They also murdered quantities of people in mosques (Agadžanov, *Selǧūkiden und Turkmenien im 11.-12. Jahrhundert. Turkmenenforschung Band 9*, trans. R. Schletzer (Hamburg, n.d., c. 1986), p. 124).
18. For Seljuq monuments in this area, see G. A. Pugachenkova, 'Little known monuments of the Balkh area', *Art and archaeology research papers* 13 (1978), pp. 31–3, 38.
19. Agadžanov, *Selǧūkiden und Turkmenien*, p. 92.
20. Agadžanov, *Selǧūkiden und Turkmenien*, pp. 122–7.
21. Agadžanov, *Selǧūkiden und Turkmenien*, p. 93.
22. Agadžanov, *Selǧūkiden und Turkmenien*, pp. 125–6.
23. A. Godard, *Les Monuments de Marāgha (Publications de la Société des Études iraniennes et de l'art persan 9)* (Paris, 1934); A. Godard, 'Notes complémentaires sur les tombeaux de Marāgha (Ādharbaidjān)', *Athār-é Irān* 1 (1936), pp. 125–60.
24. R. Shani, *A Monumental Manifestation of the Shī'ite Faith in Late Twelfth-Century Iran: the Case of the Gunbad-i ᶜAlawiyān, Hamadān (Oxford Studies in Islamic Art 11)* (Oxford, 1996).
25. A. Godard, 'Ardistān et Zawārè', *Athār-é Irān* 1 (1936), pp. 285–309; O. Grabar, *The Great Mosque of Isfahan* (New York, 1990); M. B. Smith, 'Material for a corpus of early Iranian Islamic architecture. II. Manār and Masdjid, Barsīān (Iṣfahān)', *Ars Islamica* 4 (1937), pp. 1–40; M. B. Smith, 'Two dated Seljuk monuments at Sīn (Iṣfahān)', *Ars Islamica* 6 (1939), pp. 1–10.
26. For a detailed account of the technicalities of producing baked brick in the Iranian world, see Hans E. Wulff, *The Traditional Crafts of Persia* (Cambridge, MA, 1966), pp. 115–7.
27. See G. Herrmann, *Monuments of Merv. Traditional Buildings of the Karakum* (London, 1999), pp. 47–67.
28. See *A Survey of Persian Art from Prehistoric Times to the Present*, eds A. U. Pope and P. Ackerman (London, 1939), plate 271 for a photograph which shows how the main façade looked before the current Bukhara-Samarqand highway was bulldozed through it.
29. G. A. Pugachenkova, *Iskusstvo Turkmenistana. Ocherk c drevneitikh vremen do 1917 g.* (Moscow, 1967), plate 91.
30. Pugachenkova, *Iskusstvo*, plates 92–3.

31. These issues are discussed at length in M. S. Bulatov, *Geometricheskaya Garmonizatsiya v Arkhitekture Srednei Azii* (Moscow, 1978).
32. The process is well described by Robert Irwin for a monument at the other end of the Muslim world, namely the Alhambra; see R. Irwin, *The Alhambra* (London, 2004), pp. 109–21. See also N. M. Gedal, 'The Great Mosque of Cordoba: geometric analysis', *Global Built Environment Review* 2,3 (2002), pp. 20–31, especially p. 30, fig. 1.
33. N. S. Baimatowa, *5000 Jahre Architektur in Mittelasien. Lehmziegelgewölbe vom 4./3. Jt. v. Chr. bis zum Ende des 8. Jhs. n. Chr. (Archäologie in Iran und Turan. Band 7)* (Mainz, 2008), pp. 177, 309, 328, 342; Herrmann, *Monuments*, p. 198, fig. 198.
34. Baimatowa, *Architektur*, pp. 370, 378, 412; Herrmann, *Monuments*, p. 198, fig. 195; Pilyavskii, *Pamyatniki*, p. 128. But in some monuments which may be as late as the Seljuq period a combination of the elliptical profile and a sequence of arches of diminishing size does occur; this deserves closer study in the context of the evolution of the squinch zone.
35. Herrmann *et al.*, *Archive*, p. 55 (images numbered 18036, 18037, 18042, 18045 and 18047).
36. Herrmann, *Monuments*, p. 199, fig. 201.
37. For a conspectus of the major types, see Pugachenkova, 'Mavzolei', drawings on pp. 15–17.
38. A. M. Pribytkova, *Pamyatniki Arkhitekturi XI Veka v Turkmenii* (Moscow, 1955), pp. 41–9.
39. L. I. Rempel, 'The Mausoleum of Isma[c]il the Samanid', *Bulletin of the American Institute for Persian Art and Archaeology* 5, 4 (1936), pp. 199–209; M. S. Bulatov, *Mavzolei Samanidov – Zhemchuzhina Arkhitekturi Srednei Azii* (Tashkent, 1976); G. Stock, 'Das Samanidenmausoleum in Bukhara II', *Archäologische Mitteilungen aus Iran* 23 (1990), pp. 231–60.
40. Best seen in its state c. 1950: Pugachenkova, *Puti*, pp. 311, 313.
41. Herrmann *et al.*, *Archive*, p. 60 (image HNO28) and p. 61 (image HNO35).
42. Pribytkova, *Pamyatniki*, pp. 41, 43, 46, and figs 41, 44, 48.
43. For a detailed description and analysis of mortar types in the Iranian world, see Wulff, *Crafts*, pp. 111, 113, 123, 125–8.
44. Even the acoustic changes.
45. Though most of the inscriptions from the latter building have now disappeared.
46. Pribytkova, *Pamyatniki*, pp. 50–1, 54–5, figs 53–4, 57–9.
47. E. Herzfeld, 'Damascus: studies in architecture – II', *Ars Islamica* 10 (1943), pp. 22–3; N. Khanikov, *Mémoire sur la partie méridionale de l'Asie centrale* (Paris, 1861), pp. 88–9.
48. A. Godard, 'Khorāsān', *Āthār-e Irān* 4,1 (1949), pp. 7–68; *Discoveries from Robat-e Sharaf*, ed. Y. Kiani (Tehran, 1981), pp. 15–39. The rich array of stucco decoration at this caravansarai, which brings to mind the similarly lavish decoration in the gallery of the tomb of Sanjar (Figure 15.12), might best be explained by the royal patronage of both buildings.
49. E. Diez, *Churasanische Baudenkmäler. Band I* (Berlin, 1918), pp. 62–6 and plates 20/1–22/2. A re-assessment of this mausoleum, which bears an inscription dated 757/1356 but whose basic form is unmistakably at least two centuries earlier, is long overdue.
50. Agadshanow, *Staat*, pp. 225–39.
51. R. Hillenbrand, 'Saljuq dome chambers in north-west Iran', *Iran* 14 (1976), pp. 97–8 and

plates IIa–IIId; R. Hillenbrand, 'The Ghurid tomb in Herat', in *Cairo to Kabul. Afghan and Islamic Studies presented to Ralph Pinder-Wilson*, eds W. Ball and L. Harrow (London, 2002), pp. 129–30, plates 12.8–12.12 and figs 12.2–12.5.

52. E. Schroeder, 'Islamic architecture. F. Seljūq period', *Survey*, pp. 1029–35, figs 365–6 (drawn by Ugo Monneret de Villard) and plates 294–300, 303B and D; see also S. P. Seherrr-Thoss, *Design and Color in Islamic Architecture. Afghanistan, Iran, Turkey* (Washington, DC, 1968), pp. 46–51 and colour plates 12–16.
53. Where such early monuments as the Tomb of the Samanids and the mausoleum at Tīm indicate that decorated brick architecture was fully in vogue as early as the 4th/10th century. For the latter building, see G. A. Pugachenkova, 'Mazar Arab-ata v Time', *Sovietskaia Arkheologia* 4 (1961), pp. 198–211; G. A. Pugachenkova, *Iskusstvo Zodchikh Uzbekistana. II. Mavzolei Arab-Ata* (Tashkent, 1963).
54. Pribytkova, *Pamyatniki*, pp. 101-3, figs 111–5.
55. Pilyavski, *Pamyatniki*, p. 88.
56. As on the tomb of Abū Sa^cīd at Miḥna (Pugachenkova, *Puty*, p. 284) and the tomb of Abū l-Faḍl at Sarakhs (Pilyavski, *Pamyatniki*, p. 83).
57. As in the façade of the Shahriyār Arg at Merv (Pugachenkova, *Puty*, p. 217). See Figure 15.14.
58. As at the tomb of Muḥammad b. Zayd, Merv (Pilyavski, *Pamyatniki*, pp. 134–5, 137).
59. Pilyavski, *Pamyatniki*, p. 78.
60. As at the Shāh-i Mashhad madrasa (R. Michaud *et al.*, *Colour and Symbolism in Islamic Architecture* [London, 1996], pp. 48–9).
61. This is well illustrated in the Gunbad-i ᶜAlawiyyān at Hamadan (Shani, *Manifestation*, p. 88, fig. 57). The imagination baulks at visualising how it looked when its original polychrome splendour was undimmed.
62. Schroeder, 'Architecture', p. 1042, fig. 376b.
63. Piliavski, *Pamyatniki*, pp. 134–5, 137.
64. As at Talkhatān; see A. M. Pribytkova, *Pamyatniki Arkhitekturi XI Veka v Turkmenii* (Moscow, 1955), pp. 94–5, figs 105–6 (drawings); cf. Pilyavski, *Pamyatniki*, p. 142.
65. Again, Talkhatān furnishes an excellent example: see Pribytkova, *Pamyatniki*, pp. 86–7, figs 97–8 (drawings of rear façade; cf. Pilyavski, *Pamyatniki*, p. 143).
66. Pilyavski, *Pamyatniki*, pp. 93–4, 236 and 84 respectively.
67. What follows is based on the pre-restoration form of the building. The identification is traditional and not supported by epigraphical evidence, and there is no remnant of the famous blue-tiled exterior covering of the dome mentioned by Yāqūt. For the mausoleum in its restored state, see M. Mamedov, *Soltan Sanjaryn Kümmeti. Mavzolei Sultana Sandzhara. Mausoleum of Sultan Sanjar* (Istanbul, 2004), p. 155.
68. For a detail of the inscription, showing only the first half of the text in an undamaged state, see Mamedov, *Mausoleum*, p. 211.
69. For a useful account of the building and its context, see S. Chmelnizkij, 'Das Mausoleum des Sultans Sandschar in Merw', *Architectura* 1 (1989), pp. 20–35.
70. A. Godard, 'The mausoleum of Öljeitü at Sulṭāniya', *Survey*, pp. 1103–18; and D. N. Wilber, *The Architecture of Islamic Iran. The Il-Khānid Period* (Princeton, NJ, 1955), pp. 139–41.
71. M. B. Smith, 'The manārs of Iṣfahān', *Athār- é Irān* 1 (1936), figs 207, 209, 213, 218 and 225, to cite only pre-Mongol examples.
72. The best example is the north dome of the Isfahan *jāmi*ᶜ (Seherr-Thoss, *Design and*

Color, colour plate 11), but there are other instances at Ardistān, which contains a grid of little stars (*Survey*, plate 320), Zavāra (Godard, 'Ardistān et Zawārè', p. 301), Barsiyān (Smith, 'Barsīān', fig. 16) and Gulpāyagān (*Survey*, plate 309). Even the tomb of Sanjar has something similar, this time in the form of ribs that stand proud of the inner dome surface rather than being flush with it (*Survey*, plate 310).

73. For colour plates of these details, see Mamedov, *Mausoleum*, p. 207; for further details, see I. F. Borodina, 'Stennie rospisi i tsvet v arkhitekture intererov Srednei Azii X–XII vv.', in *Kul'turnie Svyazi narodov Srednei Azii i Kavkaza. Drenost' i Srednevekov'e*, eds A. M. Leskov and B. Y. Staviskii (Moscow, 1990), p. 111 and figs 33–5.
74. C. E. Bosworth, 'Maḥmūd of Ghazna in contemporary eyes and in later Persian literature', *Iran* 4 (1966), pp. 85–92.
75. J. Sourdel-Thomine, 'À propos du Cénotaphe de Mahmūd à Ghazna (Afghanistan)', in *Essays in Islamic Art and Architecture in Honor of Katharina Otto-Dorn (Islamic Art and Architecture, Volume 1)*, ed. A. Daneshvari (Malibu, 1981), pp. 127–35 and plates 1–4. For colour plates, see *Islam. Art and Architecture*, eds M. Hattstein and P. Delius (Cologne, 2000), pp. 330–1.
76. *Survey*, plate 1462. See also S. Flury, 'Das Schriftband an der Türe des Maḥmūd von Ghazna (998–1030)', *Der Islam* 8 (1918), pp. 214–27 and plate 4; cf. J. M. Rogers, 'The 11th century. A turning point in the architecture of the Mashriq', in *Islamic Civilisation 950–1150*, ed. D. S. Richards (Oxford, 1973), pp. 238–41, 249.
77. Yāqūt al-Ḥamawī, *Muᶜjam al-buldān*, trans. C. Barbier de Meynard as *Dictionnaire géographique, historique et littéraire de la Perse et des contrées adjacentes* (Paris, 1861), p. 529.
78. For the tomb of al-Shāfiᶜī, see K. A. C. Creswell, *The Muslim Architecture of Egypt. Volume II. Ayyubids and Early Bahrite Mamluks* A.D. *1171–1326* (Oxford, 1959), pp. 64–76 and plates 22–6.
79. R. Hillenbrand, 'Turco-Iranian elements in the medieval architecture of Pakistan: the case of the Tomb of Rukn-i 'Alam at Multan', *Muqarnas* 9 (1992), pp. 148–74.
80. L. Golombek and D. N. Wilber, *The Timurid Architecture of Iran and Turan* (Princeton, NJ, 1988), I, pp. 260–3 and II, plates 80–7, colour plate VI.
81. C. B. Asher, 'The Mausoleum of Sher Shāh Sūrī', *Artibus Asiae* 39, 3–4 (1977), pp. 273–98; see pp. 277–9 and pp. 287–9 for its Sultanate forebears.
82. G. D. Lowry, 'Humayun's tomb: form, function and meaning in early Mughal architecture', *Muqarnas* 4 (1987), pp. 133–48.
83. P. Brown, *Indian Architecture (Islamic Period)* (Bombay, 1956), pp. 99–100 and plates LXXV, LXXVII/1.
84. L. Golombek, 'From Tamerlane to the Taj Mahal', in Daneshvari, *Essays*, pp. 43–50 and figs 1–16; for its immediate Indian context, see R. Nath, *The Immortal Taj Mahal: the Evolution of the Tomb in Mughal Architecture* (Bombay, 1972).

INDEX

Note: illustrations are shown by page numbers in *italics*

ᶜArūḍī, Niẓāmī-yi, 32, 244
categories recommended by, 245–6
Four Discourses, 245–7
ᶜaṣabiyya, 192, 195–6
Ashᶜarism, 120, 125, 127, 133, 136, 146–9, 156, 230
Aşıkpaşazade, 87
Assassins, 65, 120, 230, 233
ᶜAtabat al-kataba, 161, 167
atabegs/atabegate, 1, 24, 63, 79–81, 161, 177, 193
of Ādharbayjān, 192, 195–6
authority, 1, 3, 18, 52, 137, 145, 152, 169, 230, 232, 235
caliphal, 118–19, 126, 150, 158, 192, 197, 228–9, 235–6
of emirs, 271
of Imams, 218–19, 222, 234
of *muḥtasib*, 157, 160, 163, 166, 174
of *raʾīs*, 196
sultanic, 28, 68, 74, 126, 150, 163, 186, 191–2, 230, 235
see also legitimacy
ᶜAwfī, 195
ᶜayyārūn, 126, 137, 150
Ayyubids, 6, 69, 71, 72, 120, 130, 154, 161, 164, 168–9, 259, 266

Baghdad, 2, 5, 15, 28, 54, 87, 129–30, 139
administrative district, 119–20
as caliphal capital *see* caliph/caliphate
intellectual productivity, 129
madrasas, 122–3, 124, 140–1, 144
non-Muslim communities, 128, 138, 165
Seljuq control, 117–18, 128–30
shared control, 125–7
Shrine College, 144
shrines in, 51, 135, 140–1, 143–4
Sufi/Sufism in, 129
urban development, 123–4
see also Iraq
baghy see rebellion
Bahrūz al-Ghiyāthī, 125–6
al-Bākharzī, 34
Balkh, 5, 102–5, 107–8, 110–12, 248, 251, 280
Barbahārī, 171
Barbarossa, Frederick, 259
Barkyāruq, 49, 55, 99, 100, 102–10, 113, 118, 132, 134, 136, 193, 230, 232
bathhouse, 165, 270–1
Bāṭinites, 230; *see also* Assassins
Baybars, 84
Bayezid I, Sultan, 88
Bayhaq, 101
Bayhaqī, 20, 245
Beddredin of Smavna, 89
al-Bīrūnī, 31
Böri Bars, 101–2, 105–7, 115
Bosworth, C. Edmund, 2, 3, 55, 100, 110, 113, 177
Browne, E. G., 247–8
building *see* nomads; Rum Seljuqs, urbanism
Bukhara, 15, 171, 183, 184
Bulliet, Richard W., 121, 133, 154, 199
al-Bundāri, 106–7, 140
Burids, 24, 187
Buyids, 28, 30, 40, 54, 65, 117–19, 129–30, 157, 165, 195, 204, 241, 252–3
and Abbasids, 118–19, 228–30
literature, 241–5, 251–2
muḥtasib, 158–9, 162–3, 164, 166–7
rival factions under, 127, 196
Shiᶜism, 65, 128, 143, 205, 214–15
Byzantines/Byzantium, 1, 4, 13, 23, 27, 44, 55, 66, 77, 87, 253, 256, 257, 269

Cahen, Claude, 1–2, 185, 259, 273
Cairo, 65, 176, 230, 303
Calder, Norman, 207
caliph/caliphate
administration (*dīwān*), 119–20
military power, 118–19, 120
and political/religious power, 228–30
and sultans, 118–20, 234–8
Sunni caliphs, 39, 40, 118–20, 150–2
see also Abbasids
Cenabi, 87
Cevdet Paşa, 91
Chabbi, Jacqueline, 147
Chaghrï Beg, 18, 19, 28, 49, 103, 110, 113, 183, 240
Chahār maqāla, 245–7
chancery, 119, 131, 138, 159, 161–2, 164, 167, 182, 245–7, 266, 268
Christians, 43, 66, 70–1, 128, 138, 214, 272
city building *see* nomads; Rum Seljuqs, urbanism
commanding right/forbidding wrong, 158, 163, 209–14; *see also ḥisba*; *muḥtasib*
Constantinople *see* Byzantines/Byzantium
Cook, Michael, 180, 211–12
court
artistic overview, 25–8

bureaucrats, 34
and Great Seljuqs, 23
and hunting, 34–5
men of letters, 31–4
nawba ceremony *see nawba*
Persian/Islamic background, 22, 35
poets, 32–3
rank, 25
Crone, Patricia, 229
crusaders, 6, 66–9, 73, 256, 259, 269

Dahistan, 278, 290
Damghan, 165, 291
Danishmendids, 68, 81, 82
dār al-Islām, 16, 66, 111, 121, 129
Dār al-Khilāfa, 119, 135, 141, 150
Dār al-Mamlaka, 124, 141, 151–2
Dār al-Sulṭāniyya, 54, 124
Dayā Khātūn, 285–6, 287, 288, 291
al-Dhahabī, 160, 161
Donohue, John, 159
Duqāq/Toqaq, 18, 40

elites, 2, 5, 6, 25, 31, 80, 124, 128–30, 133, 140–3, 146–8, 152–3, 159, 160–4, 183–97, 201, 256, 259–60, 272–3
emirs, 45, 50, 68, 92, 101, 106–11, 120, 124–6, 141, 192, 259–60, 261–3, 266, 269–70, 271–2

al-Farghānī, Mushaṭṭab b. Muḥammad, 51, 181
Fatḥnāma, 266, *267*, 268
Fatimids, 55, 65, 120, 128, 168–9, 173–4, 176, 178, 205, 221, 230, 234, 283
Feridun Beg, 88
fiefdoms *see iqṭā*ᶜ
Firdawsī, 80, 244, 246
Four Discourses, 245–7
Frye, Richard N., 243
*fuqahā*ʾ *see* jurists

al-Ghāzālī, Abū Ḥāmid, 24, 31, 50, 169–72, 228–38
anti-Ismaᶜili stance, 233–4
caliphs and sultans, 234–8
ethics, 232
historical background, 228–31
political contributions, 231
political thought, 232–6
religious thought, 236, 237
Ghaznavī, Khwāja Sadīd al-Dīn Muḥammad, 49
Ghaznavids, 16–19, 22, 24, 32, 75, 84, 143, 157, 244–5, 252–3, 280
Ghuzz, 14–15, 99, 103–4, 106, 110–13, 280–1; *see also* Oghuz
Gurgan, 15, 19

Ḥabashī b. Altūntāq, 47, 144
ḥājibs, 27, 52, 119–20, 127, 136
Hamadan, 23, 30, 49, 100, 102, 109, 186, 192, 214, 281, 307
al-Hamadhānī, 241–2, 243, 247–51
Ḥamdallāh Qazvīnī, 57, 84
al-Ḥamīdī, 181, 241, 247, 248; *see also Maqāmāt*
Ḥanafites/Ḥanafism, 51, 53, 57, 122–3, 129, 133–4, 138, 140, 144–6, 155, 163, 165, 180–1, 183–5, 189, 192, 196, 201–2, 220
madrasas, 122–3, 144, 145–6
Ḥanbalites/Ḥanbalism, 121–5, 127–9, 131, 133–4, 136, 138, 140, 145–50, 155, 168–9, 171, 175, 179–80, 196, 200
madrasas, 122–3
ḥarbiyyūn, 220, 223
al-Ḥarīrī, 247–51
Hārūn al-Rashīd, 22
Hashemites, 125, 127, 135, 137
Ḥawza, 206
Ḥayṣa Bayṣa, 33
al-Ḥillī, al-ᶜAllāma, 208, 219
ḥisba
changes, 157, 161, 162–3, 164–5
heresy, 168–9
interventionism/intrusiveness, 166–9, 172
Shiᶜi understanding, 208–14
see also muḥtasib; commanding right/forbidding wrong
Hogga, Mustafa, 237
Ḥudūd al-ᶜālam, 14, 15, 17
hunting, 4, 38, 125
and court, 25, 27, 34–5
and religious life, 45–8
Ḥusām al-Dīn Yūsuf, 261, 265–6, 268, 272
al-Ḥusaynī, 30, 81, 88, 101, 105

Ibn ᶜAbbād, 164, 166, 185, 243
Ibn Abī l-Majd, 220–1
Ibn al-ᶜAmīd, 242
Ibn ᶜAqīl, 129
Ibn al-Athīr
Ḍiyāᶜ al-Dīn, 164
ᶜIzz al-Dīn, 14, 18, 24, 54, 57, 60, 101, 106–7, 108, 137, 190, 196, 201–2, 206

Ibn Bābūya, 215
Ibn al-Barrāj, 217–18, 221–2
Ibn al-Bayāḍī, 140
Ibn Bībī, 73, 74, 81–2, 83, 87, 259, 260
Ibn al-Dajājī, 160, 175
Ibn Faḍlān, 15–17
Ibn Fāris, 243, 244
Ibn Funduq, 101, 112
Ibn al-Ḥabbāriyya, 33
Ibn al-Hajjāj, 158–9
Ibn Ḥamza, 209–14, 218, 220
Ibn Ḥanbal, 51, 60, 166, 229
Ibn Ḥassūl, 80
Ibn Idrīs, 207, 218, 222–3, 224
Ibn al-Jawzī
  Abū l-Faraj ᶜAbd al-Raḥmān, 129, 137–8, 140, 151–2, 154, 161, 168–70, 180, 190, 200, 206
  Muḥyī al-Dīn b. Muḥammad b. al-Jawzī, 161
  ᶜAbd al-Raḥmān b. Muḥyī al-Dīn b. al-Jawzī, 161
  see also Ṣibṭ b. al-Jawzī
Ibn Junayd al-Iskāfī, 217, 226
Ibn Khallikān, 33–4
Ibn Māza, 52, 171, 181
Ibn al-Muqaffaᶜ, 252
Ibn al-Qaṭṭān, 33
Ibn Yūnus, 169
Ibn Zuhra, 220, 224
ideology, 3, 4
  kingship ideology *see* Rum Seljuqs, kingship ideology
  see also propaganda
ignominious parade *see tashhīr*
Iḥyāᵓ ᶜulūm al-dīn, 169–70
Ikhwān al-Ṣafāᵓ, 169
Ildegüzids, 81
ᶜImād al-Dīn al-Iṣfahānī, 34, 195, 197
Imām Bāhir, mausoleum, 285, *285*
Imāmī, 51, 168, 207–24, 230–7; *see also* Shīᶜites/Shīᶜism
inshāᵓ see chancery
intertextuality, Arabic and Persian, 247, 252–3
iqṭāᶜ, 4, 45, 100, 109, 117, 181, 194, 259–60, 262
Iraq, 1, 3, 4, 23, 24, 32, 49, 54–5, 63, 65, 81, 110, 159, 165, 192, 281, 293–4; *see also* Baghdad
Isfahan, 23, 280, 293
  Khurasan families in, 183–6
  see also Khujandīs of Isfahan
isfahsālār, 260–2
Ismaᶜili/Ismaᶜilism, 40, 48, 50, 55, 101, 120, 165, 168, 184, 189–90, 194–6, 199, 228, 230–4, 237; *see also* Assassins; Bāṭinites
al-Iṣṭakhrī, 158

al-Jābrī, Muḥammad ᶜĀbid, 237
Jahān Pavlavān, 81
Jamāl al-Dīn al-Iṣfahānī, 193
Jand, 17–18, 19
Janssens, Jules, 236
Jarbādhaqānī, 195
Jews, 128, 138, 165, 214
jihād, 40, 42, 44, 67–8, 71, 73, 208, 214–18, 220–1
Jimrī, 83
judges, 51, 158, 160, 165, 171, 173, 183, 208
jurists, 53, 60, 122–3, 128, 134, 158–61, 160–2, 163, 169–72, 181, 183, 187–8, 190, 206, 216, 219, 222–4
Jūzjānī, 46

kalām, 133, 147, 169; *see also* theology
Karamanids, 83, 85–6, 89–91
al-Karkh, 124, 128, 134, 137, 150, 159, 175, 205–6
Kay Kāwūs I, 63–4, 69–71, 261, 265
Kay Kāwūs II, 83, 88, 89
Kay Khusraw I, 69, 71, 80, 82, 259
Kay Khusraw II, 82–3, 89
Kay Khusraw III, 83
Kay Qubādh I, 5, 63–4, 69–70, 71–3, 81–2, 87–8, 257, 269, 272
Kay Qubādh II, 87
al-Kaydarī, 220, 226
Kaykubādiyya palace, 88
Kennedy, Hugh, 31
khādims, 119, 125–6, 136; *see also mamlūks*
Khalaf b. Aḥmad, 195
khānqāh/ribāṭ/zāwiya, 45, 86, 121, 129, 139, 143, 147
Khāqānī, 195
Kharīdat al-qaṣr, 34, 195, 198
khāṣṣ see elites
al-Khaṭībī, 185
Khātūn bt. Malikshāh, 152
Khātūn al-Mustaẓhiriyya, 147
Khazars, 15, 16, 18–19
al-Khiraqī/al-Kharaqī, 165
Khudāy Naẓar Awliyā, mausoleum, 286–7, *287*

al-Khujandī
ᶜAbd al Laṭīf I, 195
ᶜAbd al Laṭīf II, 188–91, 195, 200
Abū Bakr Muḥammad I, 183–4, 185, 197; family, 188–9; pupils, 186, 187–8 *tables*; as scholar, 188, 190
Abū Bakr Muḥammad II, 186, 188, 189, 190, 194
Abū Bakr Muḥammad IV, 190, 192, 196
Abū l-Qāsim Masᶜūd, 184
Abū Saᶜd Aḥmad, 190
Masᶜūd, 195
ᶜUbayd Allāh, 193, 195
Khujandīs of Isfahan
competing factions and, 195–7
control of local elites, 183–4
cultural works, 195
emblematic status, 197–8
family tree, 191 *table*
forced collaboration, 191–3
knowledge, 186–9
as leading family, 182–3, 184–5
local influence, 193–7
main events, 189 *table*
networks, 195–6
origins, 183–6
power, 189–91
Ṣāᶜids, 196–7
urban polarisation, 196–7
wealth, 194–5
Khurasan, 5, 6, 9, 14, 16, 19, 24, 42, 43, 47, 49, 53, 56, 57, 69, 75, 81, 99–100, 119, 182, 241, 280, 281, 291
Arslān Arghūn, 101–2, 104, 110–15
families in Isfahan, 183–6, 190, 196–8
literature, 243, 248–9
relations with Baghdad, 119, 138, 147–8, 156
khuṭba, 66, 120, 119, 123; *see also* sermons
Khwarazm, 14–18, 39, 53, 81, 113, 114
Khwārazmī, Abū ᶜAbdallāh, 14
Khwarazmshahs, 39, 53, 81, 113, 177, 179, 196–7
al-Khwārizmi
Abū Bakr, 242–4
Naṣīr al-Dīn Maḥmūd, 52
Kiliç Arslan I, 66
Kiliç Arslan II, 66–70, 257
Kiliç Arslan IV, 83, 92
kingship ideology *see* Rum Seljuqs, kingship ideology
Kirman, 161, 167, 188
Kitāb al-Diryāq, 25, *26*, 27–8
Kitāb Tafḍīl al-atrāk, 80
Kiz Bibi mausoleum, Merv, *282*
Kiz Qalᶜa, Merv, *283*, *284*, 285, *286*
Klausner, Carla, 2, 121, 133
Kononov, A. N., 31
Konya, 66, 68–70, 84–6, 90–2, 95, 164, 257, 260, 268–9
*köshk*s, 283, 294
Kudherkin/Kül Erkin, 16
Kunya Urgench, 278, 280, 290
Kutalmiş b. Arslān Isrāᵓīl, 65–6

Laborde, Leon de, 268
Lambton, Ann K. S., 2, 125, 181, 234
Lapidus, Ira, 195
laylat al-waqūd, 151–2
legal schools *see madhhab*s
legitimacy, 79–92
in Anatolia, 63, 91–2
atabegate, 80–1
aura, 82–4
dubious claims, 82
dynastic prestige, 79–80
inherited, 79, 81–2
Karamanid, 89–91
kingship titles, 80
local loyalties, 84–5
longevity, 91–2
Ottoman, 79, 84, 86–91
persistance of claims, 86
political relevance, 83–4
prevelence of Saljūq name, 85–6
succession struggle *see* Arslān Arghūn
see also authority
Lesser Yināl, 16
Lewis, Bernard, 230
Leyizkus, 88
literature *see* Abbasids, literature; Buyids, literature; intertextuality, Arabic and Persian; Khurasan, literature; poets

*madhhab*s, 42, 52, 57, 122, 129, 139–40, 143–6, 148, 151, 158, 171, 181, 185, 188, 192, 196, 209, 218, 220, 223–4
madrasas, 39, 52, 55, 58, 69, 121–2, 133, 139–41, 161, 192, 230, 290, 298, 307
in Baghdad, 122–4, 128, 133–4, 140–6, 148–9, 151, 153, 154–6, 165, 169, 231
in Isfahan, 182–3, 186–90, 194–5, 199–200
see also Ḥawza

Mahdi, 207
Maḥmūd of Ghazna, 31, 37
Maḥmūd b. Malikshāh, 30–1, 33, 34–5, 99, 108, 109
Maḥmūd b. Muḥammad b. Malikshāh, 54, 124, 186
Maḥmūd b. Muḥammad Ṭapar, 47
Majd al-Mulk, 104
Makdisi, George, 2, 40, 121, 141
Malik-nāma, 17, 18
Malikshāh I, 5, 23, 24, 31, 32, 34, 65, 66, 85, 125, 192, 230, 257
  and Abbasids, 118–19
  and Baghdad, 124, 125, 131, 134, 146, 151
  piety, 43, 45–6, 49, 51, 55, 58, 181
  succession struggle, 99–100, 103, 104, 108, 184
Malikshāh III b. Maḥmūd b. Muḥammad, 48, 120
Mamluks, 83–4, 154, 174, 175, 176, 195, 259
*mamlūk*s, 5, 43, 46, 101, 109, 116, 136, 274, 275; *see also khādim*s
Manzikert, battle of, 23, 44, 54
Maqāmāt of al-Ḥamīdī, 241, 247–51
  author's intention, 248–9
  comparative analysis of trilogy, 249–50
  narrators, 250–1
  titles, 251
market inspector *see muḥtasib*
Marvazī, 14
Marw al-rudh, 104
Marwanids, 167
Mashhad-i Miṣriyān, 278
Masūd b. Maḥmūd of Ghazna, 18
Masūd b. Muḥammad b. Malikshāh, 32–3, 47–8, 118, 120, 126, 131, 134, 135, 186, 190, 193
Masᶜūd Bilāl, 126
Masᶜūd b. Tājir, 106–7
Maurozomes, Ionnes, 269, 272–3
mausoleum *see* tomb
al-Māwardī, 159, 170, 173, 179, 180, 229, 231, 235
Mayafariqin, 167
Mazandaran, 161, 167
Mehmed Beg b. Karaman, 83
Merv, 102, 103, 104–6, 111–13, 161
  Khujandīs from, 183
  Kiz Bibi mausoleum, *282*
  Kiz Qalᶜa, *283*, *284*, 285, *286*
  monuments, 278, *279*
  Shahriyar Arg palace, *296*
Mez, Adam, 159
Miḥna, 283
miḥna, 166
Mikāᵓīl b. Saljūq, 19, 40
minbar, 57, 66–7, 76, 190
mirrors for princes, 269; *see also Siyāsatnāma*
Modarresi, H., 206
Mongolia, 14–15
Mongols, 69, 72, 73, 81–7, 90, 92, 99, 111–13, 130, 182, 184, 189, 197, 278, 280, 290
mosques, 39, 41, 44, 52, 57, 69, 86, 90, 92, 104, 141, 142, 143, 145, 146, 148, 152, 251, 261, 270–1, 280–1, 288–91, 298, 303
  in Baghdad, 45, 122–4, 133, 135, 136, 141–3, 145–6, 148–50, 152, 165, 186, 206
  in Isfahan, 54, 65, 196
  of ᶜAlāᵓ al-Din Kay Qubādh, 66, 70, 76, 270
Muᵓayyid al-Mulk, 102, 104, 184
Mubāriz al-Dīn ᶜAbdallāh al-Mihrānī, 263
mudarris, 142
Muḥammad (the Prophet), 47, 229, 233, 245, 248, 269
Muḥammad. b. al-Dajājī, 160, 175
Muḥammad I Khujandī, 183, 185, 186, 188, 189, 195, 197
Muḥammad II Khujandī, 186, 188, 189, 190, 194
Muḥammad III Khujandī, 191
Muḥammad IV Khujandī, 186, 189, 190, 192, 196
Muḥammad I b. Malikshāh, 22, 30, 33, 51, 99, 124, 126, 133, 134, 136, 152, 184, 281
  and Isfahan, 186, 192, 193, 194
Muḥammad II b. Maḥmūd b. Muḥammad, 48
Muḥammad Shāh, 120
Muḥammad Ṭapar, 24, 46, 47, 51, 55, 66
Muḥammad b. Yaḥyā, 52
Muḥammad b. Zayd, mausoleum, *279*, 291, *292*, 294, 295
*muḥtasib*s
  appointment, 158–9
  coercive force, 127, 163–5
  fiqh definitions of role, 170–2
  heterodoxy, 149, 168–9
  ignominious parade, 165, 166, 168
  in Baghdad, 136, 160
  intrusiveness, 166–9
  public/private spheres, 169–72
  re-islamisation, 160–2

revitalisation of office, 159–60
see also *ḥisba*; commanding right/forbidding wrong
Muʿizzī, 32, 59
al-Mukhtārāt min al-rasāʾil, 182, 185, 195
Multān, 303
Müneccimbaşı, 86, 88, 102
al-Munqidh min al-ḍalāl, 232–3
Münşeat ü-Selatin, 88
Munshi, Naṣrullāh, 252
al-Muqaddasī, 241, 243
al-Muqtadī, 125, 135, 158, 165
al-Muqtafī, 120, 126, 136, 165, 192
Murad II, 87
Murad III, 88
Murghab, 103
al-Mustaḍīʿ, 68, 119, 120, 124, 135, 136, 168
al-Mustanjid, 120, 135, 136
al-Mustanṣir, 128
al-Mustarshid, 54, 118, 119, 124, 131, 135, 186
al-Mustaẓhir, 119, 135, 152, 165, 233, 234, 235
al-Mustaẓhirī, 232–6
al-Mutanabbī, 242
Myriokephalon, battle of, 68–9

nadīms, 32–3
Najaf, 34, 206, 214, 218, 223–4
Najm al-Dīn Yawāsh, 263, 274
naqībs, 125, 127, 135, 137
al-Nāṣir, 120
nawba, 28–31
colour system, 30–1, 35
disciplinary role, 30
drum ceremony, 28, 30–1
sources, 30
symbol of Muslim sovereignty, 28, 30
Neşri, 87
Nicaea/Iznik, 66
Nishapur, 52, 107, 112, 171, 183, 192, 195, 232, 280
seige, 101, 104
Nīshāpūrī, Ẓahīr al-Dīn, 30, 34, 48
Niẓām al-Mulk, 2, 24, 31, 32, 33, 34, 103, 148
assasination, 230
Baghdad residence, 124
control of local elites, 183–4, 194, 197
and *muḥtasib*, 163
piety of his sultan, 42–3
sons/grandsons in succession struggle, 101
and Sunnism, 51, 144, 149, 152, 231, 236, 237
see also viziers/vizierate
Nīẓāmī, 162
Niẓāmiyya madrasas, 169, 230
in Baghdad, 122, 140, 144, 148, 151, 192, 231
in Isfahan, 182, 195
nomads, 3, 99–111, 117, 280–1
Seljuq nomadic background, 14–15, 18, 22, 24, 28, 31, 35, 163
re-nomadisation, 111–13

Occultation, 207, 208
Oghuz, 13–18
chiefs, 16
cleanliness/sexual practices, 17
early beliefs, 15–16
harrying/plundering role, 16–17
migration, 15
Mongolian origin, 14–15
name, 13–14
nomadic presence, 14–15
rebellion, 80
urbanization, 17
see also Ghuzz
Oghuz-Khān, 87
Oghuz-nāma, 15
Öljeitü, tomb, 298
Oruç, 87
Osman, 87–9, 91
Ottoman legitimacy, 79, 84, 86–91

panegyrics, 32, 33, 162, 163, 195, 246
Paul, Jürgen, 181, 192
Peacock, Andrew, 2, 9, 111, 113
Pechenegs, 15
Persia
literature *see* intertextuality, Arabic and Persian
Perso-Islamic kingship, 64–5, 74
Seljuq period, 240–1
see also Iran
Perso-Islamic kingship, 64–5, 74
poets, 32–4, 81–2, 140, 148, 158–9, 161–3, 174, 190, 193, 195, 198, 241–6, 248–9, 252, 253–4, 262
Pritsak, O., 14
propaganda, 40, 56, 67–8; see also *ideology*
Pseudo-Galen, *Kitāb al-Diryāq* of, 25, *26*, 27–8
public/private spheres, 23, 31, 49, 53, 55, 127, 128, 139–41, 143–5, 148–53, 157, 166–72, 173, 213–14
Pullyblank, Edwin G., 31

Qāḍī Aḥmad, 85
qadīmī, 259
al-Qādir, 121, 138, 228–9
qāḍīs see judges
al-Qā°im, 28, 53, 55, 61, 119, 120, 135, 137, 138, 150
Qarakhanids, 19, 57, 99, 102, 104, 183
al-Qāshānī, 52
qaṣīda, 195
Qatwan, battle of, 53
Qubādābād palace, 271
Quhistan, 101
Qur°ān, 42, 57, 129, 151, 158, 194, 195, 243, 246, 248, 269, 271
al-Qushayrī, 148

Rabaṭ-i Malik, 283
Rahman, Fazlur, 232
ra°īs, 167, 181–2, 186, 188–92, 194–6, 199, 202
Rashīd al-Dīn, 34, 46, 48, 87
rationalism, 132, 145, 146, 149
re-nomadisation, 111–13
rebellion, 51, 65, 70, 74, 80, 85, 89, 90, 102–3, 110, 113, 189, 192, 280
  law of, 208–9, 214–24
religious life of the Seljuqs
  extent of devotions, 44–5
  and hunting, 45–6
  nature of sources, 41
  personal beliefs/practices, 41–8
  pious image, 39–41, 54–6
  public perception, 40–1
  and public policy, 53–6
  revisionist scholarship, 40, 54–5
  and Sunnism, 49–53
  topological actions, 43–4
  see also Shi°i; Sunni
ribāṭ see *khānqāh*
Ribāṭ-i Sharaf, 291
Richards, D. S., 106
riyāsa see *ra°īs*
Rum Seljuqs
  emergence, 82
  emirs, 259–60, 261–3, 266, 269–70, 271–2
  founding of, 65–6
  kingship ideology: °Ala° al-Dīn Kay Qubādh I, 69–70, 71–3; background, 63; collective sovereignty, 69; defence of Islam, 65–6, 68–9, 70–1, 73; epigraphic evidence, 64; Great Seljuq model, 64–6; honorific titles, 66–9; °Izz al-Dīn Kay Kāwūs I, 70–1; °Izz al-Dīn Kiliç Arslan II, 66–70; noble lineage, 72–3; Perso-Islamic kingship, 64–5, 74; purpose, 64; sources, 63–4
  map, *258*
  Mongol invasion, 72
  state centralisation, 257–60, 266, 268, 271–3
  urbanism: Alanya, 257, 270–1; Antalya, 257, 266–8, 269–70; background, 256–60; emirs, 259–60, 261–3, 266, 269–70, 271–2; epigraphic programme, 256; factors, 256–7; fortifications, 256–7; Konya, 257, 260, 268–9; labour, 257; patronage, 257; recycling principle, 256; Sinop, 257, 260–6, *262*, *264*, *265*; and state centralisation, 257–60, 266, 268, 271–3
Rūmī, 89

al-Ṣābi°, Hilāl, 28, 29, 247
Ṣābūr b. Ardashīr, 205
Sabzawar, 102, 107, 112
Sa°d al-Dawla Kawharā°īn, 125
sadhak, 151
al-Ṣafadī, 160, 161
Saffarids, 195
Safi, Omid, 2, 54, 141, 155
al-Ṣahrashtī, 218
Saljūq b. Duqāq/Toqaq, 17, 18–19, 40
Saljūq Shāhnāma, 90–1
Saljūqnāma, 39, 79, 81, 82, 85
Sallāmi, 14
Saltukids, 82
al-Sam°ānī, 190
Samanids, 14–15, 17–19, 22, 241, 268
  poets, 32
  Tomb of the Samanids, 286
Samarqand, 42, 152, 161, 183, 251, 303
Sanjar, 14, 30–1, 33, 41, 80, 81, 99, 107, 112–13, 115, 147, 161, 171, 181, 183, 240, 246–8, 280–1
  mausoleum, 291, *293*, 295, *297*, 298–300, *299*, *300*, *301*, 302–3, *302*
  piety, 46–7, 49–55, 171
Sarakhs, 104, 107, 112, 283, 291, 295, 298
al-Sarakhsī, 172
al-Sayyid al-Murtaḍā, 217, 218
Sebastos, 261
Selaniki, 90
Seljuq court *see* court
Seljuqs
  conversion to Islam, 17–19
  inauguration of Empire, 18, 19

Oghuz origins *see* Oghuz
origins, 17–19
rivalry with other families, 17, 19
sources, 23–4
Seljuq sultans, 2, 23–4, 30, 32–3, 35, 40–1, 56, 79, 117, 128, 229, 238
court *see* court
legitimacy *see* legitimacy
memory of the Seljuqs, 4, 15, 44, 158, 166
religion *see* religious life
'Sultan of East and West', 28
see also Rum Seljuqs, kingship ideology; sultans
sermons, 129, 147–8, 190, 200; *see also khuṭba*
Shāfiᶜites/Shāfiᶜism, 42–3, 52, 122–3, 129, 133–4, 138, 140, 145–6, 148, 156, 158–60, 165, 170, 174–5, 180–1, 182–3, 188, 190, 192, 196–7, 201–2, 230
madrasas, 140, 144, 183
treatment of heretics, 168–9, 170
Shāh Malik, 18, 19
al-Shahristānī, Jawād, 206–7
al-Shanfarā, 33
*shiḥna*s, 125–6
Shiᶜi/Shiᶜism/Shiᶜa, 43
in Baghdad, 128, 205
commanding right/forbidding wrong, 209–14
dominance, 55
fiqh, 208
Ḥawza, 206
intellectual activity, 206–7, 223–4
jurisprudence, 208, 224
law of rebellion, 214–24
powers, 120
Rum Seljuqs, 65
suppression, 205–6
Ṭūsī *see* al-Ṭūsī, Shaykh
see also Buyids; *ḥisba*
Shirwānī, 195
Shukrullāh, 86
shurṭa, 126–7, 137, 158, 164–5, 172, 178
Ṣibṭ Ibn al-Jawzī, 30, 48, 103, 144
Şikari, 89, 90
Sinop, 257, 260–6, *262*, *264*, *265*
Sinor, Denis, 31
Siyar al-mulūk (Buyid), 158, 164, 178
Siyar al-mulūk (Seljuq) *see Siyāsatnāma*
siyāsa, 163, 177, 229
siyāsa sharᶜiyya, 208, 229, 233
Siyāsatnāma, 24, 75, 161, 162, 164, 230, 236
slaves soldiers *see mamlūks*
Stewart, D., 223–4
sūbāshī, 260, 262, 263, 266
al-Subkī, 160, 161, 190
Sufi/Sufism, 39, 41, 44, 49–51, 60, 89, 129, 135, 169
in Baghdad, 129, 147, 149
al-Suhrawardī, Shihāb al-Dīn, 195
Sulaymān b. Kutalmış b. Arslān Isrāᵓīl, 66
Sulaymān b. Muḥammad b. Malikshāh, 47, 48
Sulṭāniya, 298, 303
sultans
and caliph/caliphate, 118–20
title, 80
see also Rum Seljuqs, kingship ideology; Seljuq sultans
Sunni/Sunnism
defence *see* al-Ghazālī
Ismaᶜili threat, 230
and religious life, 49–53
revival, 2, 4–5, 39, 40, 120–3, 128–9, 132, 139–53, 160, 230; factions, 147–50, 151; patronage, 140–4; people of the Sunna, 150–2, 153; public policy, 143; rulers' protection, 150–3; schools, 145–7; in Seljuq Baghdad, 118, 139–40, 152–3; traditionalists v. rationalists, 145, 149
and Seljuq sultans, 49–53
see also religious life; Shiᶜi/Shiᶜism
Sūzanī-yi Samarqandī, 161
Syria, 4, 23, 24, 34, 35, 65–6, 67, 71, 72–3, 80, 84, 152, 221

Tāj Mahal, 303
Talkhatān Bābā mosque, 288, *289*, *295*, *297*
Tārīkh-i guzīda, 39
Tarkān Khātūn, wife of Malikshāh, 99, 107–9
Terken Khātūn, wife of Sanjar, 112
Ṭarkhān, 16
tashhīr, 165, 166, 168, 178–9
tawqīᶜ/tawqīᶜāt, 55, 245, 263, 265, 271
Tekesh b. Alp Arslān, 51, 100, 102–5, 107–8, 110–11, 113–14
theology, 120, 127, 132, 146–9, 169, 208, 213–14, 216, 219, 228, 231–4; *see also kalām*
Tikrit, 103, 126, 175
Timurids, 81, 113, 278
Timurtaş, 85–6
Tirmidh, 102–3, 106–7, 110–11
tomb
of Abū Ḥanīfa, 51, 140, 144, 154

tomb (*cont.*)
of ᶜAlids, 51
of the Lesser Yināl, 16
of Muḥammad b. Zayd, *279*, 291, *292*, 294, 295
of Nūr-i Ṣūfī, 91
of Öljeitü, 298
of Rum Seljuqs, 86, 92, 95
of the Samanids, 286
of Sanjar, 291, *293*, 295, *297*, 298–300, *299*, *300*, *301*, 302–3, *302*
Topkapı Palace, 88
Toqaq *see* Duqāq
traditionalism, 2, 129, 138, 145, 147, 149, 153, 166, 224
Trebizond, 70–4, 260, 269
al-Ṭughrāʾī, 32–3
Ṭughril/Ṭoghrïl I, 18, 19, 22–3, 28, 80, 118
Baghdad buildings, 123–4
piety, 41–2, 47, 53–4, 55, 172
and Sunnism, 49, 120, 205–6
Ṭughril II b. Muḥammad Ṭapar, 47
Ṭughril III b. Arslān, 48, 120, 193
Tukharistan, 102, 107
Turkmenistan, monuments
background, 277
baked brick, 281–3
blind arches, 294
complex articulation, 283–8
distinguishing features, 294–5, 298–300, 302–3
distribution, 278, 280
geographical setting, 277–8
glazed tilework, 290–1
inscriptions, 290–1, 293
Iranian comparison, 288, 290–1, 293–303
mausolea, significance, 303
mosques/minarets/madrasas, absence, 290
political context, 280–1
structural features, 281–8
terracota/stucco ornamentation, 290, *291*, 293
Turkic, Western/Common, 13
al-Ṭūsī, Shaykh al-Ṭāʾifa
commanding right/forbidding wrong, 209–14
law of rebellion, 214–24
post-Ṭūsī scholars, 209
and Shᶜia decline, 206–8, 224
al-Ṭūsī, Shibāb al-Islām, 52
Tutush b. Alp Arslān, 100, 102–4, 107–9, 114

ᶜulamāʾ, 39–40, 44, 46–8, 51, 53, 55, 60–1, 121, 133–6, 139, 141–2, 166, 200, 229, 231, 233–4, 280
and Khujandīs, 182, 186, 190, 198, 202
and *muḥtasib*, 160–2, 167, 177
notables, 262
public/private conceptions, 169–70
ᶜUmar b. al-Khaṭṭāb, 163
Ünsi, 90, 91
urbanism *see* nomads; Rum Seljuqs, urbanism
Ürgüp, 92
Usāma b. Munqidh, 35
ustādār, 119
uṭāqbāshī, 270
Uyghur Khanate, 15

Vale, M. G. A., 23
Varqa va-Ghulshāh, 32
viziers/vizierate, 2, 30, 32–5, 42, 52, 54, 57, 61, 82–3, 86, 89, 102, 104, 119–20, 124–5, 132, 135, 137, 144, 148–50, 152, 155–6, 158–9, 164–5, 169, 174, 180, 184–6, 189–90, 199, 201, 205, 231, 242, 273; *see also* Niẓām al-Mulk

waqf, 122–3, 140–4, 146, 155, 186, 192, 194, 273
al-Warāwīnī, 195
Watt, William W., 230
Waṭwāṭ, 167–8
women,17, 25, *26*, 27, 46, 59, 159, 160, 162, 168, 186, 194, 218–19; *see also* Dayā Khātūn; Khātūn bt. Malikshāh; Khātūn al-Mustaẓhiriyya; Tarkān Khātūn; Terken Khātūn

Yabghu (title), 14, 16
Yāqūt, 205, 270
yaylaq-qishlaq pattern, 112
Yazd, 280, 290
Yazicizade Ali, 85–6, 87, 88

al-Zabīdī, 163
ẓāhir, 166, 167
Ẓahīr al-Dīn Fāryābi, 195
al-Zamakhsharī, 161–2, 171–2
Zangids, 120, 130, 186, 201, 266
Zarrīnkūb, A., 252
zāwiya see khānqā
Ziyarids, 247
Zoroastrians, 43, 185, 214
Zubdat al-nuṣra, 140

EU representative:
Easy Access System Europe
Mustamäe tee 50, 10621 Tallinn, Estonia
Gpsr.requests@easproject.com

www.ingramcontent.com/pod-product-compliance
Lightning Source LLC
Chambersburg PA
CBHW052148300426
44115CB00011B/1565